Few such intricate and complex his
and this unique piece is marked b
every setting of which they are a part. Though I would not ag......
with every woman documented in this volume, I would affirm the accuracy of this
extraordinary historian, Diana Severance. Not only does she reject any popular
revisionism, but she also approaches the stage of history with amazing perception
and sensitivity, pulling from the shadows some dedicated and gifted women who
have often been overlooked. This volume will be the centerpiece for our Women in
Church History course and is a book I recommend every woman read and study and
keep within reach for reference and inspiration! No woman should graduate from
Southwestern Baptist Theological Seminary without a copy in her personal library!

Dorothy Kelley Patterson
Professor of Theology in Women's Studies
Southwestern Baptist Theological Seminary
Fort Worth, Texas

'What women these Christians have!' exclaimed Libanius, the fourth century
teacher of rhetoric. His words are amply underscored and vividly illustrated in this
deeply researched and highly readable survey of the last 2,000 years – an appraisal
that Diana Severance invariably places against the enduring touchstone of Scripture.

Richard Bewes
OBE, Author and retired rector of All Souls Church
Langham Place, London

Feminine Threads is a must-read for men and women alike, but especially so for
young women who need to have a clear view of the contributions that women
before them have made to the Christian faith. Dr Severance has written
a volume that is both comprehensive and engaging. She wipes away the dust of
history to clear many false claims and popular misconceptions, leaving a clear
view of the inspiring efforts of women in the life of the church for the past
2,000 years. A much needed resource for the church at large!

Carolyn McCulley
Author of *Radical Womanhood: Feminine Faith in a Feminist World*
Arlington, Virginia

In *Feminine Threads* Diana Severance has given us an extraordinary and
valuable blend of biography, church history and biblical teaching on Christian
womanhood. Whilst running counter to the feminism of our own day, together
with its revisionist agenda, Dr Severance traces the remarkable story of the
role and influence of women in the life of the church from the time of Christ
to our present generation. Unafraid to include and evaluate the mixed and

occasionally confused contribution of some, she has provided us with a record packed with spiritual insights and one that is both timely and significant.

Faith Cook
Author
Derbyshire, England

Christian historians in the past have not always been as faithful in their calling as they could have been, for frequently they forgot one half of the story of God's Church, namely, the role of women in it. Diana Severance's study is therefore a welcome one, for with lively prose and scholarly care she has given us an excellent overview of the various ways in which Christian women have sought to live for Christ. A must read for all who are interested in the riches of Christian history.

Michael A. G. Haykin
Professor of Church History and Biblical Spirituality
Southern Baptist Theological Seminary
Louisville, Kentucky

I sat down to dip into this for half an hour and ended up reading it for three! It is a 'magnum opus' of heart-warming and inspirational testimonies. All the usual women of faith are here: Mary the mother of Jesus, Monica, Katie Luther, Susanna Wesley, Selina Hastings and Sarah Edwards, but so too are the less well known ones. I cried at the courage of Blandina, was rebuked by the single-mindedness of Leoba and challenged by the godliness of Margaret of Scotland. No-one reading this book can fail to be encouraged by the faith of these ordinary women who, in their own generation, humbly trusted the Word of God and lived to serve the Lord of whom it speaks. It left me wondering if there are any women in my own generation who trust and serve like this, and moved me to pray that there would be - and that, by the grace of God, I might be one of them.

Carrie Sandom
Author and Coordinator of Women's Ministry at *The Bible Talks*
Mayfair, London

This is a wonderful book about how God has used so many women in the history of the church to fulfill his purposes of grace and bring honor to the cause of Christ. Well researched and well written, this study of 'feminine threads' in Christian history makes for a tapestry of inspiration and instruction for all who love the Lord and his church — men and women alike.

Timothy George
Founding Dean of Beeson Divinity School
Samford University
Birmingham, Alabama

Feminine Threads

Women in the

Tapestry of Christian History

DIANA LYNN SEVERANCE

CHRISTIAN
FOCUS

Diana Lynn Severance (PhD, Rice University, Houston, Texas) is Director of the Dunham Bible Museum at Houston Baptist University and an historian with broad experience teaching in universities and seminaries. Her work has been published by Christianity Today, Inc., and Christian History Institute. Her books include *Against the Gates of Hell: The Life and Times of Henry T. Perry, a Christian Missionary in a Moslem World* and *A Cord of Three Strands: Three Centuries of Christian Love Letters.* Diana and her husband live in Texas.

Copyright © Diana Lynn Severance 2011

ISBN 978-1-84550-640-7

10 9 8 7 6 5 4 3 2 1

First published in 2011, reprinted 2012
by
Christian Focus Publications,
Geanies House, Fearn,
Ross-shire, IV20 1TW, Scotland
www.christianfocus.com

Cover design
by
Paul Lewis

Printed by
Bell and Bain, Glasgow

CONTENTS

Nineteenth-century author Elizabeth R. Charles wrote a fitting tribute to Christian women throughout the ages

'No cold gravestones are these memorials, but sun-pictures of our beloved ones who are withdrawn from our sight for a time, but whom we hope one day to see ... They are but leaves from the tree of life which is for the healing of the nations, always life and always healing, whether found in the chilliest zones of Christendom or in the most tangled wildernesses ... these, we must always remember, are no[t] ... portraits of an ... aristocratic caste of ... saints. They are specimens of the universal Christian life demanded of us all, lived by not a few; not perfect, ... but being perfected; not ... complete in any one; complete only in Him who is the Head and Life of all, and in His whole Body, which is the Church. Nor, thank God, are they records of a race and a life passed away. At this moment I could lead you into home after home around us now, blessed and hallowed by lives as Christ-like and humble and sweet.'

Elizabeth Rundle Charles. *Sketches of the Women of Christendom*. New York: Dodd, Mead & Co., 1880, pp. 333-4.

Preface

Christianity is a religion of history. Much of the Bible is an historical narrative of the outworking of God's redemptive plan in the lives and affairs of men. The dating system of the world today continues to be centered on an historical event – the birth of Jesus, the Christ, the Son of God. Every Christian has faith in not only the living Jesus Christ but also the historic person of Jesus and His sacrificial death on the cross as the Son of God. The birth of the Christian church continues the history recounted in the Jewish Scriptures – a continuity fully grasped and expounded by Peter at Pentecost, Stephen before his martyrdom, and Paul in his numerous sermons and writings. But the story does not end with the book of Acts. The history of God building His church and opening the hearts of men and women to the Gospel truths continues to our own day. As God continues to build His Church, His people can find examples, warnings, and encouragement as they examine the rich tapestry of Christian history, recognizing that

> The shadows as much as the sunlight, the agony as much as the ecstasy, are part of the divine purpose. In the tapestry of time, the hand of God weaves as many somber skeins as bright-hued silks. In our perceptions of history, we see only the reverse side of things; with all the muddle of loose strands, back-stitching and over-worked patterns. We see something of the design as it appears on the right side, but we never see it as it actually is; the clarity and beauty of the design as it appears face up are as yet denied to us.

> So the Christian both knows and yet does not know the meaning of history. On the one hand, he has particular insight into the nature of history because he knows the end of the story- and therefore he can gauge the true depth of the "thickness" of events. But at the same time he does not, and cannot know the full meaning of the story. [1]

---

1   John Briggs, "God, Time, and History," *Eerdmans' Handbook to the History of Christianity* (Tom Dowley, ed.). Grand Rapids, MI: Wm. B. Eerdmans Publishing Co., 1977, pp. 12-13.

11

This work examines the feminine threads in the tapestry of Christian history. Much of the material collected was first presented in "Women in Church History" courses I taught in various seminaries. The students and I were enthralled by the accounts of the numerous Christian women who had served their Lord and His Church in humility, faithfulness, and truth. We were also dismayed on two fronts. First, that feminist scholars had re-written the history of the early church to fit their particular agenda – blatently "reinventing," "re-imagining" and "reconstructing" (their terms!) a history which attacked the Church itself. Second, at the other end of the story, we were concerned about new ways of understanding "feminine" and "gender" being accepted by Christians, without their knowing the historic, often anti-Christian roots of these ideas. While primarily being a narrative history of women in the church, this work also aims to equip the reader to refute the distortions of women in Christian history which are often being made in academia and the wider culture. While a book about women, this is not a book for women only. The tracing of the feminine threads in the tapestry of Christian history will enrich the understanding of both men and women in Christ's work of building His Church.

In the past 30 years, women's history has become a major area of academic research and writing. This new discipline came into its own with the growth of social history, which has increasingly gained ground over the traditional approaches of political, military, diplomatic, and economic history. In addition, new stress on multiculturalism emphasized not only ethnic groups, but also women and homosexuals. These various self-proclaimed oppressed groups spawned a new history advocating their particular positions. Feminist historians often claimed they were specially qualified by their gender to speak with authority about women in history. Routinely they projected contemporary values on the past, and history in their hands often became propaganda.[2]

The new women's historians generally made several assumptions in their studies. They assumed that women throughout history had been routinely subordinated to men and that women's positions needed to improve. All inherited forms of authority were questioned, especially moral and religious authority. More often than not, feminists endorsed women's moral superiority to men who, they claimed, had been suppressing women for centuries. When dealing with religion, feminists usually asserted certain 'inalienable' women's rights. These usually included the right to ordination; the right to dismantle the 'sexist' language

---

2   This overview of the new women's history is heavily indebted to Elizabeth Fox-Genovese's analysis in the chapter 'Advocacy and the Writing of American Women's History' in *Religious Advocacy and American History* (ed. Bruce Kuklick and D.G. Hart). Grand Rapids, MI: Wm. B. Eerdmans, 1997, pp. 96-111.

of hymnals, prayer books, and the Bible; and the right to describe God in female terms. Elizabeth Fox-Genovese noted that to these feminists

> ...the very idea of a male God and His Son has emerged as the ultimate target. The supposed pretension that God is male brutally exposes the measure in which Christianity has always embodied a plot to discredit, devalue, and disempower women. No longer may any reasonable person expect women to worship a God who has not been cast in their image. And herein lies the ultimate revolution. According to the Bible, God made man in his own image. According to feminism, woman must make God in hers. That the faithful rather than God do the making reverses the central meaning of Christianity, thereby destroying Christianity.[3]

The methodology of the feminist writers has been very similar to that used by the Jesus Seminar and the 'new school' interpretation of the early Church. While repudiating the canonical Scriptures, they gravitated to writings of lesser authenticity and established a new canon of scriptures they found to be more congenial. Philip Jenkins noted that 'the willingness to claim such texts as part of a lost women's canon is troubling testimony to the ideological character of some modern interpretations of the hidden gospels.'[4] Behind this method was the belief that there was no 'true Truth,' as Francis Schaeffer would say, and that all these various writings were simply mythologies. By viewing the Bible as just another myth, the feminists could then select the Gnostic writings as myth more attractive and congenial to their postmodern souls. Viewing all ancient religious beliefs, including Biblical Christianity, as an assortment of mythologies, these scholars could then assert that none of the mythologies have a historical, evidentiary basis in fact. Indeed, the feminists found themselves back in the garden with Eve, questioning what God had said and deciding to choose what looked best to them, rather than listening to any authority or examining the historical truthfulness of competing interpretations. Media acceptance of feminist revisionist history and its presence in leading academic circles gave it an aura of authenticity which belied the evidence.

Feminist historians generally followed postmodern historical methods. Elisabeth Schüssler Fiorenza encouraged a 'hermeneutics of suspicion' in studying the early Church. In her influential *In Memory of Her: A Feminist Theological Reconstruction of Christian Origins*, she presumed that the writings from that period were patriarchal, demeaning to women, and did not describe the reality of conditions in the early Church. She contended that texts needed to be decoded to discover the hidden women's history. Texts, then, did not express the inherent meaning of the author. Rather, they were, at best, a collection of ambiguous words and

---

3   'Advocacy and the Writing of American Women's History,' p. 110.

4   Philip Jenkins. *Hidden Gospels*, p. 147.

phrases. In Dr. Fiorenza's view, the proper function of the modern reader was to give these words and phrases the meaning that the reader preferred in accordance with her agenda. Thus, the subjective interpretation by the modern reader was to take precedence over historical evidence or the intention of the author. Ancient texts were merely used to advance current opinions, and contemporary meanings were substituted for the original meaning of the text.

Karen J. Torjesen opened her book, *When Women Were Priests*, by saying she would unveil 'a hidden history of women's leadership, a history that has been suppressed by the selective memory of succeeding generations of male historians.'[5] Denying the truthfulness and integrity of the New Testament authors, Torjesen wrote that the conspiracy to suppress women's leadership began when Paul purposefully omitted any reference to Mary Magdalene's announcement of Jesus' resurrection.[6] She claimed that John, warning against 'Jezebel' in Revelation 2:20-23, was more concerned about opposing the women leaders in the Church than heresy.[7] Further, Torjesen consistently used sources from the second and third centuries as if they described conditions in the New Testament Church. None of the New Testament women discussed ever were elders, bishops, or pastor-teachers, yet Torjesen held them up as examples of feminine leadership in the early Church. Her bizarre concluding chapter called for a return to what she called the essential writings of Christianity – Goddess Worship:

> Knowing about our roots in the earth-centered religion of Old Europe, with its Mother goddess and its kin-centered culture, can augment our efforts to reclaim the non-violence and egalitarianism of the new order announced by Jesus... Christian churches need to return to their authentic heritage...and restore women to equal partnership in the leadership of the church.[8]

Such a claim could only be made by those who, against all evidence, had made the Gnostic writings the norm of the early Church. This approach may more accurately be described as 'propaganda' or 'advocacy' than history.

The history which follows is basically chronological, beginning with women in the Bible and concluding with Christian women in the twentieth century. Each chapter includes general background information important to understanding the historical era of the chapter. Within each chapter, stories of Christian women are grouped according to their most prominent roles during that period – wives, mothers, ascetics, queens, writers, educators,

---

5 Karen Jo Torjesen, *When Women Were Priests: Women's Leadership in the Early Church and the Scandal of Their Subordination in the Rise of Christianity*, New York: HarperSanFrancisco, 1993, p. 10.

6 *When Women Were Priests*, p. 35.

7 Ibid., p. 111.

8 Ibid., pp. 268-9.

reformers, evangelists, or philanthropists, etc. Wherever possible, the women are allowed to speak for themselves, from their letters, diaries, or published works. Often these words from centuries ago are as full of meaning and vitality as if spoken yesterday, testifying to a certain continuity of Christian women's experience through the ages. Footnotes direct the reader to the sources of specific quotes, and an extensive bibliography provides further references on women who might not be cited in the text. A growing number of digitized books and historical documents are available on the Internet and, where available, URLs connecting to sources for many of the Christian women are included.

Early chapters tell of Christian women as the Church spread throughout the Middle East, North Africa, and Europe. After accounts of women during the millennium of the Medieval Church, we turn to the stories of Christian women during the Reformation. For the period of the seventeenth through twentieth centuries, when the sources for information on Christian women expand dramatically, the focus is on Protestant Christian women in America and Britain.

Many Christian women, from queens to commoners, are recognized in secular histories for their achievements or influence without being acknowledged for the Christian faith undergirding their lives and works. These women as well as lesser-known Christians find their places in these pages. The choice of which Christian women to include depends in part on the sources which have survived. For the later periods, when the sources are more abundant, more selectivity was necessary. For example, there is a wealth of information on the lives and contributions of 19th and 20th-century women missionaries; space constraints limited the inclusion to a few of the most well known, though the bibliography points to sources for further study.

Christian women were integral to the life of the Church wherever Christianity spread, but what we know of their stories is limited by the sources that have survived. There is often more we would like to know about Christian women in various geographical places and times in history. Always there are the numerous 'common' people in the lower and middle classes whose stories frequently are unwritten and remain unknown. Yet, the history of women in Christian history does not need a revisionist makeover. We do not need to recreate an imagined narrative out of speculative evidence. Nor do we write histories – of commoners or of so-called elite – based on what we would have liked for them to have been. Neither do we seek to superimpose contemporary thought patterns and standards on earlier societies. Though at times the evidence might raise unanswered questions, or we might wish the facts to be different, the truth of the story of women in Christian history inspires, challenges and, above all, demonstrates the grace of God producing much fruit through Christian women throughout two millennia of the Church.

Tares Among the Wheat...
(A note to the reader)

This book does not follow the methodology of the feminists. Rather, it is a traditional, narrative history based upon reasonable consideration of the evidence. The Bible has been recognized throughout as the authoritative Word of God and the standard, or *canon,* of the Church. In its pages are the earliest accounts of Christian women as well as guidelines for the role of women in the Christian community. The Church through the ages must always be evaluated by the principles contained in the Scriptures. Through the centuries of history, as Christ has continued to build His Church, the visible Church has often included tares among the wheat, nominal Christians among the true, and false teaching alongside the truth of God. This mixture of wheat and tares is true of both women in the Church as well as attitudes towards women by the Church. The wheat (true Christians) might also have elements of spiritual blindness or sin which marred their lives. Just as the historical portions of the Bible includes people of dubious motives and actions as well as heroes of the faith, so Christian history includes admirable and questionable individuals. The reader is encouraged to discerningly use the truths of Scripture to evaluate the lives of the numerous women in *Feminine Threads.* The standards for Christian women and the Church should always be the Scriptures, not the practices of any individual or group, regardless of their influence or charisma.

The New Testament Era:
One in Christ Jesus

Galatians 3:28

A history of women in Christianity must begin with those women who were part of the earliest church – the women we find in the New Testament record. The role and position of women recorded in the Gospels and the rest of the New Testament provide the foundation for the study of women throughout the history of the Christian Church. The New Testament contains not only historical accounts of women in the early Church but also includes instruction as to the role and position of women in the Church.

Women were an integral part of Jesus' life and ministry as described in all four Gospels and were integral to the Church, which arose after His ascension. For example, Luke's two-volume work on the life of Jesus and the early Church, the books of Luke and Acts found in the New Testament, includes references to at least 67 women from a variety of ethnic backgrounds, social classes, and economic positions.

Jesus' Genealogy
Women, of course, had an important role in Jesus' ancestry and birth. Five women are especially named or mentioned in the genealogy of Jesus that opens the New Testament and Matthew's Gospel - Tamar, Rahab, Ruth, Bathsheba, and Mary.[1] Interestingly, the first three of these women were Gentiles or non-Jewish women, and three of the five were known for their immorality. Tamar was a Canaanite widow who played the part of a prostitute to seduce her father-in-law Judah, compelling him to protect her and provide her with children. Rahab had been a prostitute before she came to worship the God of Israel. Ruth was a Moabitess who also came to worship the God of Israel and married into Boaz's family in Bethlehem. Bathsheba was the wife of a Hittite and committed adultery with King David, later becoming the mother of Solomon, the greatest King of Israel. Whatever social, moral, or racial stigmas these women once faced, they

---

1   Matthew 1:3, 5, 6, 16

are part of Jesus' genealogical record. From positions of disgrace they were elevated to places of usefulness and honor.

Mary, the Mother of Jesus

Mary, the last of the women mentioned in Jesus' genealogy and the mother of Jesus, obviously is important to any account of the history of women in the Church. It is necessary, however, to distinguish the historical Mary of the Scripture from the legendary Mary of later centuries. Several things can be learned about this most important Christian woman by carefully reading the texts that refer to Mary in the Gospels. Mary is shown to be a woman of faith and obedience. When the angel made his announcement to Mary that she would conceive and bear a son, Mary believed this word from God and submitted to this promise. She knew that bearing a child was impossible via the normal means of conception; yet, God had spoken, and with God she could believe the impossible.[2] Mary was thoroughly acquainted with the Scriptures and humbly accepted the angel's announcement to her as the long-hoped-for fulfillment of centuries of prophecies of a coming Seed, a Messiah, who would bring blessing to all nations.[3] The very personal praise to God spoken by Mary when she met Elizabeth contained over twenty quotes or allusions to specific Scriptures:

My soul magnifies the Lord,
   and my spirit rejoices in God my Savior,
for he has looked on the humble estate of his servant,
   For behold, from now on all generations will call me blessed;
for he who is mighty has done great things for me,
   and holy is his name.
And his mercy is for those who fear him
   from generation to generation.
He has shown strength with his arm;
   he has scattered the proud in the thoughts of their hearts;
he has brought down the mighty from their thrones
   and exalted those of humble estate;
he has filled the hungry with good things,
   and the rich he has sent empty away.
He has helped his servant Israel,
   In remembrance of his mercy,
as he spoke to our fathers,
   to Abraham and to his offspring forever.[4]

---

2   Luke 1:26-38

3   Genesis 3:15; 12:1-3.

4   Luke 1:46-55. All quotations of Scripture are from the English Standard Version. Scriptures quoted or alluded to in Mary's Magnificat include 1 Samuel 2:1-10; Psalm 34:2; Habakkuk 3:18; Psalms 35:9, 138:6; 71:19; 126:2-3; 111:9; Gen. 17:7, 19; Exodus 20:6; 34:6,7; Psalms 103:17; 98:1; 118:15; Isaiah 40:10; Psalm 33:10; Isaiah 41:8; Psalms 98:3; 132:11.

In the ensuing events surrounding Jesus' birth, the Gospel writers showed Mary to be a woman of humility and faith in God's power, goodness, and the truth of His Word. Mary not only knew God's Word, but she meditated on the events brought into her life and how God might be working in them[5].

Before the angel had come to Mary with the announcement of the special child she would bear by the power of the Holy Spirit, Mary had been betrothed to Joseph. Joseph too was a man of faith who was able to accept God's revelation to him about Mary's child. He agreed to marry her, becoming the legal, though not the natural, father of the child he was told to name 'Jesus,' meaning 'Savior,' for He would 'save His people from their sins.'[6] After the birth of Jesus, Mary's firstborn, Mary and Joseph together had at least six other children – four boys and an unspecified number of daughters.[7] Perhaps Mary became consumed by the affairs of her growing family; perhaps the ordinariness of life caused her to no longer meditate on God's Word or His ways as much as she did when she was younger. At any rate, there are several scenes in the Gospel record that indicate Mary had difficulty understanding God's ways or trusting His direction as readily as she did at Jesus' birth. She still had to learn about God's timing and purposes. When Jesus was twelve years old, she was amazed to find Jesus discussing theology with the Jewish scholars in the temple. She did not understand Jesus' statement that He needed to be about His Father's business.[8] Had twelve years with the very human child Jesus dulled her awareness of His divine origin, nature, and purpose? Yet, eighteen years later, at the marriage feast in Cana, Jesus gently admonished His mother for rushing him into a public position before the time was right, saying, 'Woman, what does this have to do with me? My hour has not yet come.'[9].

The Gospels do not show Mary regularly following Jesus in His earthly ministry. Perhaps she was in Nazareth caring for her younger children. Joseph apparently had died, and Mary was living in a town that rejected Jesus' teaching and His claim to be the Messiah. The people of Nazareth even tried to throw Jesus off the cliff near the town.[10] Mary's other children followed the skepticism of the town and did not believe in Jesus during His years of ministry. Surrounded by skepticism and unbelief, Mary joined her children in trying to draw Jesus away from the crowds following Him, afraid people would think He was crazy because of His words and works. After all, hadn't John the Baptist lost his head

---

5   Luke 2:49-51

6   Matthew 1:21.

7   Matthew 13:55-56; Mark 6:3. I am extrapolating at least 2 sisters from the fact that these verses use the plural for sisters.

8   Luke 2:49-50

9   John 2:4

10   Luke 4:28-30

because of his forthright speech? Jesus implicitly rebuked His mother and His natural family for their lack of faith, claiming His true family consisted of those who believed in the Word of God and did it.[11]

Yet, Mary remained at the foot of the cross when all the disciples fled. The angel had told Joseph over thirty years before that Jesus was born to 'save the people from their sins.' At the cross Mary saw the fulfillment of the angel's word from God. In almost the last scene of Mary in Scripture, she is at the cross where her eldest son not only provided for her spiritual salvation, but provided for her physically by giving her into the care of the apostle John.[12]

After Jesus' resurrection, Jesus' half-brothers came to faith in Him as well. Mary and her sons were among those who gathered with the apostles in the Upper Room for prayer. Mary was obedient to her Son, as she had been obedient to God's earlier words to her through Gabriel, and remained in prayer with the other disciples in Jerusalem, awaiting the promised Holy Spirit, who had first come upon her in such a special way when she was yet a maid.[13]

In Scripture, Mary is last seen meeting in prayer with the disciples and other believers. In the fourth century, a legendary Mary began to receive adulations and devotion. Some extra-Biblical works, such as the second-century *Protevangelium of James*, elevated Mary's purity to the point of sinlessness. In these works, Mary was described as sinless from the time of her conception and ever a virgin, even after giving birth to Jesus.[14] Such fictitious accretions to accounts of Mary's life and person, however, should not obscure or devalue the historical Mary, part of the earliest Church in Jerusalem and the recipient of salvation from the Son to whom she had given birth. Though Mary's faith was sometimes clouded, she was a woman of simple faith and obedience, strong in Scripture.

Mary Magdalene – Fact and Fiction

After Mary, the mother of Jesus, the woman most frequently named in the Gospels was Mary Magdalene. She was one of six Marys among Jesus' female disciples, and she is mentioned twelve times in the Gospels. To distinguish her from the other Marys, she is called after the name of her native town – the fishing village of Magdala, on the western shore of the Sea of Galilee. At one time she was possessed of seven demons, but Jesus healed her (Mark 16:9). Mary became His faithful follower, joining the group of women who helped finance Jesus' ministry (Luke 8:1-3). She was in Jerusalem for the Last Passover and remained with Jesus' mother and other women at the crucifixion (Matt. 27:56; 28:1; Mark 15:40; Luke 23:55).

---

11   John 7:3-5; Luke 8:19-21; Mark 3:21, 31-35.

12   John 19:26.

13   Luke 1:35; Acts 1:4-5, 8, 14; 2:1.

14   Tim Perry. *Mary for Evangelicals*. Downers Grove, Illinois: IVP Academic, 2006. p. 128.

Mary was also with the women who came the following Sunday to properly prepare Jesus' body for burial, and she was the first to see the risen Lord. (John 20:1, 16-18). Her obedience to go and tell the disciples that Christ was risen gained her the title 'apostle to the apostles.'

The third-century writer Hippolytus identified Mary Magdalene with Mary of Bethany, Lazarus' sister, and with the sinner at Jesus' feet in Luke 7:37-50. In a series of powerful sermons preached in 591, Pope Gregory I combined the three women into one Mary Magdalene and also described her as a prostitute, causing many to equate her with the woman caught in adultery in John 8:1-11. The depiction of Mary Magdalene in art followed this blending and showed her as a weeping, penitent prostitute. The English word 'Maudlin', meaning weakly and sentimental, is derived from this picture of 'Magdalene.' Though the Western church blended the women in these Scriptural passages into one, the Greek Church always distinguished between Mary of Bethany, Mary Magdalene, and the sinner of Luke 7. In 1969, the Vatican also formally recognized the identities of the three as separate.

A second or third-century Gnostic writing called the *Gospel of Mary* depicted Mary as the recipient of secret knowledge from Jesus. The description of Mary's vision of the soul ascending through the various cosmic powers was typical of Gnostic thinking. Andrew and Peter confronted Mary, challenging her authority as a woman, but Levi intervened to substantiate her authority. Based on the *Gospel of Mary*, several feminist scholars claim that Mary Magdalene was an apostle, and indeed was the 'disciple whom Jesus loved.' Some have even claimed Mary wrote the fourth Gospel attributed to John. In their reconstruction of history, these scholars contend the early Church was really led by women, who later lost a gender struggle over control of the Church. Once the men gained authority, they supplanted such works as the *Gospel of Mary* with their own version of the gospel, which is what is found in the Bible. Such fanciful reconstructions ignore the evidence for the authenticity of the New Testament and are driven more by the personal agendas and creative imaginations of the writers than the evidence.

Jesus' Treatment of Women

Throughout Jesus' earthly ministry, women were among His followers, learning from His teachings and being healed and transformed by His miracles. As Jesus went through the cities and villages preaching the Kingdom of God, Luke wrote that 'the twelve were with Him, and certain women.' These women were described specifically as having been healed by Jesus either from evil spirits, such as Mary Magdalene out of whom Jesus cast demons, or from physical infirmities, such as Susanna and Johanna, the wife of Herod Antipas' steward. Many other unnamed women provided 'from their substance' to support Jesus' ministry.[15]

---

15   Luke 8:1-3.

While the Jewish rabbis of the day often had a demeaning view of women, refusing to speak to or even greet a woman, Jesus included women in His teaching and counted them among His friends. It was to a woman that Jesus first clearly revealed that He was the long-anticipated Messiah of Israel – and to a Samaritan, a woman of mixed Gentile and Jewish ancestry.[16] It was the offering of a poor widow that Jesus held up as an example and praised to His disciples.[17]

Jesus' friendship with Lazarus of Bethany embraced the friendship of his sisters Mary and Martha as well. Mary was always described as learning at Jesus' feet, as a disciple learning from a rabbi. Not only did Jesus praise her learning, but He rebuked her sister Martha for being consumed with work and not choosing to learn as Mary did. When Mary came and anointed Jesus' feet shortly before His death, Jesus commended her and said she was anointing Him for His burial. Of all Jesus' followers, she alone seems to have understood Jesus' words about His coming suffering and death.[18]

Many of Jesus' miracles recorded in the Gospels involved women, and undoubtedly there were other unrecorded women miraculously touched by Jesus. The miracles recorded included Jesus raising the son of the widow of Nain, healing the woman crippled for 18 years, healing Peter's mother-in-law, raising Jairus' daughter, healing the woman with an issue of blood, and healing the daughter of the Syrophoenician woman.[19]

Jesus' parables also included references to women – the ten wise and foolish virgins, the persistent widow appealing to the unjust judge, and the woman looking for a lost coin.[20] Though many of the Jewish leaders in Jesus' day allowed a man to divorce his wife almost at will, Jesus permitted divorce only in a case of sexual immorality. Jesus' limitation on the man's ability to divorce his wife protected women from being promiscuously cast away by their husbands.[21]

Throughout His ministry, Jesus' words and works demonstrated His respect and compassion for women. They were among His closest friends and supporters, and they remained with Jesus at the cross when most of the disciples fearfully fled for their own safety. After Jesus died, Joseph of Arimathea and Nicodemus hurriedly placed His body in the tomb, since the beginning of the Sabbath was near. The morning after the Sabbath,

---

16   John 4:26.

17   Mark 12:41-44.

18   John 11:5; Luke 10:38-42; Matthew 26:6-13.

19   Matthew 8:14; 9:18, 23; 9:20; 15:21; Luke 7:11; 13:11.

20   Luke 15: 8-10; 18:1-8; Matthew 25:1-13.

21   Matthew 19:1-9.

women were the first to return to the tomb to prepare Jesus' body for burial more properly. Their love and eagerness to serve Jesus even in death were rewarded by their being the first to learn of Jesus' resurrection and the first to see their risen Lord. Mary Magdalene; Salome, mother of James and John; Mary, the mother of James the less; Mary, Jesus' own mother; Joanna; and other unnamed women became the messengers of the resurrection to the disciples in Jerusalem.[22] That women would be entrusted with such an important message and responsibility reinforced Jesus' honor and respect for women.

Women in the earliest Church

After Jesus' ascension, Jesus' mother and undoubtedly other women remained in Jerusalem, often meeting with the disciples for prayer. Women were part of the foundation of the Church at Pentecost. In his Pentecostal sermon, Peter quoted the prophet Joel to describe what had happened, 'Your sons and your daughters shall prophesy … and on My maidservants I will pour out my Spirit in those days.'[23]

Women in Luke's Books

In his *The Gospel According to Luke*, Alfred Plummer (1907) described Luke's Gospel as 'the gospel of womanhood.' He calculated that one third of the material unique to Luke's Gospel dealt with women. Throughout his Gospel Luke paired male and female stories – Zechariah and Elizabeth, Mary and Joseph, Simeon and Anna, the healing of the demoniac and of Peter's mother, the healing of the centurion's servant and the widow's son, the healing of the woman with an issue of blood and Jairus' daughter. With his detailed, intimate records of Jesus' conception and birth (Luke:1–3), it seems probable that Luke personally interviewed Mary, Jesus' mother, when he was preparing material for his books.

In the book of *Acts*, Luke frequently included women in the accounts of the earliest Church and mentioned twelve women by name. These women were from the whole realm of ancient society and illustrated every class – homemakers, professional women, singles, married, sisters, mothers, mothers-in-law, Jews, Greeks, Romans, prophetesses, wealthy, queens, slaves, and teachers.

While at Pentecost Peter spoke of the Holy Spirit coming equally upon men and women, this spiritual equality included an equality of punishment for sin as well. When many in the infant Church began to donate their property or their wealth to help the Church in its ministry, Ananias and his wife Sapphira hypocritically claimed to have given all the proceeds from the sale of some property to the Church, though they really only gave a portion of the proceeds. Peter confronted Ananias about his lie, and the man fell dead at his feet. The same fate befell Sapphira, who had cooperated with her husband in the deception. The Scripture says 'great fear came upon all the

---

22   John 20:14; Mark 16:1-13; Matthew 28:1-10; Luke 24:1-11.

23   Acts 2:17-18; Joel 2:28-29.

Church and upon all who heard of these things.'[24] Men and women equally had to deal with the seriousness of sin in the Church.

Jews from all over the Roman Empire flocked to Jerusalem. Once there, in the city, they naturally clustered together in groups from their place of origin and background, whether North Africa, Asia Minor, Rome, or elsewhere. The Jews in Jerusalem had a program of supporting widows and the poor in Jerusalem. When any of the widows became a Christian, however, they were cut off from this support system. Naturally, the Christian community began to organize its own relief network to care for those in need. A problem arose within the Christian community when people from one group, the Hellenists or Greek-speaking Jews, complained against the native Hebrews that the Hellenist widows were not receiving their fair portion of the daily distribution. Perhaps the native Hebrew women were better known to the apostles and had even been among the followers of Jesus during His ministry. In any case, the whole administration of the widows' care became more than the apostles alone could handle, especially if they were to continue their appointed ministry of teaching the Word and prayer. Seven men from the Hellenist group were chosen to help in the distribution for the widows. Two of the seven men were Stephen, soon martyred for his faith, and Philip the evangelist, the same Philip who was later noted for having four virgin daughters who prophesied.[25] This added level of organization allowed the apostles to continue their ministry, while the Church grew and flourished.

Denied the use of the synagogues by the Jews, early Jerusalem Christians made the home of Mary, one of its wealthier women, a gathering place. Mary was the mother of John Mark and the aunt of Barnabas, Paul's companion on his first missionary journey. Many scholars speculate that Mary's home was also the location of the Upper Room where Jesus celebrated His last Passover meal with His disciples as well as the place where the apostles met for prayer in the days immediately following Jesus' ascension. Her home definitely was a place of meeting and prayer in the early Church and was the place to which Peter naturally went after the angel released him from prison.[26] The role of patroness of the Church and the grace of hospitality continued to be important for women in ensuing centuries.

Following Jesus' command to be witnesses of Him 'in Jerusalem, and in all Judea and Samaria, and to the ends of the earth,' the Church rapidly spread beyond Jerusalem, and women continued to have a part in the expansion. In the seacoast town of Joppa, Peter restored the beloved

24   Acts 5:1-11.

25   Acts 6:1-6; 21: 9.

26   Acts 12:12.

Tabitha, whose Greek name was Dorcas, to life and health. Tabitha was praised as a woman of 'good works and acts of charity,' who apparently used her sewing talents to minister to the widows and others in the community.[27] Perhaps she was even a leader in one of the early widows' associations of the Church.

When the apostle Paul began to take the gospel to the 'uttermost parts of the world,' women were among converts to Christ as well as fellow-laborers with Paul in the various churches. Two women at Lystra who early converted to faith in Christ were Lois and Eunice, a mother and daughter. These Jewish believers knew the Hebrew Scriptures and had taught them to their son and grandson, Timothy. Timothy became one of Paul's most faithful helpers and ministers of the gospel. At the very end of Paul's life, thinking of the genuine faith of Timothy, his mother, and grandmother brought joy to the aged apostle.[28]

When Paul, accompanied by Timothy, brought the message of Christ into Europe, a woman was the first to receive the gospel. Lydia was a successful Gentile businesswoman who worshipped the God of the Jews. Since there was no synagogue in the Greek town of Philippi, on the Sabbath day Paul found Lydia and a group of women who had met for prayer near the stream outside the city. Lydia was a dealer in purple cloth, a specialty of her native town of Thyatira. She became a convert to Paul's preaching of Jesus, along with others in her household, and received Christian baptism. Immediately she invited Paul and his companions to stay at her house. Like Mary's home in Jerusalem, Lydia's home became a place of meeting for the church in Philippi.[29]

As Paul took the message of the Christian gospel farther into Greece, leading Greek women as well as men in the towns of Thessalonica and Berea became Christian.[30] Though Jewish opposition followed Paul throughout his missionary journeys, a growing number of Gentiles, both women and men, were converted to faith in Christ.

Paul and Women in Christian Work

The vast majority of these early Christians are unnamed, but at the end of his letter to the Romans, Paul sent personal greetings to 28 people listed by name.[31] One third of those listed were women. A look at these women and what can be learned about them provide a glimpse of the position and role of women in the fledgling Church.

---

27   Acts 9:36.

28   Acts 13:13-14; 16:1; 2 Timothy 1:5.

29   Acts 16:15, 40.

30   Acts 17:4, 12.

31   Romans 16.

Heading the entire list was Phoebe, whom Paul described as 'our sister ... a servant of the Church at Cenchrea.' Paul encouraged the Roman Christians to 'welcome her in the Lord in a way worthy of the saints, and help her in whatever she may need from you, for she has been a patron of many and of myself also.' Cenchrea was a nearby port city of Corinth, where Paul wrote Romans. Phoebe was called a servant or *diakonos* of the Cenchrean Church. Scholars debate to what extent the term 'deacon' at this early date was an official office in the Church, but most probably the word is used in its most general sense of 'servant.' Phoebe, as all Christians are to be, was a servant of the Church. Whatever her official title, Phoebe had the responsibility to carry Paul's letter from Corinth to the Church at Rome. Apparently she was a single woman or widow, since no companions were mentioned with her. Most likely she was a businesswoman, as was Lydia. When Paul heard of her plans to travel to Rome, he used the opportunity to write a letter for her to take to the Roman Church, which he had not yet visited. When one thinks of the tremendous impact of Paul's letter to the Romans throughout Christian history, exemplified by the conversions of Augustine, Martin Luther, and John Wesley, through this part of Scripture, Phoebe's faithful transmittal of the letter to the Roman Church takes on added significance. Paul also described Phoebe as a 'patron' to many and to Paul himself, indicating Phoebe was a lady of some means. Very possibly the Cenchrean Church met in her house; most definitely Phoebe supported Paul in his ministry. Because of her service and help in the Church, Paul encouraged the Roman Christians to be hospitable to Phoebe.

Paul immediately followed his commendation of Phoebe with greetings to his fellow-workers Prisca and Aquilla. Priscilla (or Prisca, as Paul called her) was always mentioned in Scripture with her husband Aquilla; the couple worked as a team both in their business and in their Christian ministry. Aquilla was a Jew from the region of Pontus near the Black Sea. Some have speculated that Priscilla might have been a Gentile and possibly of a higher social status than her husband, though there is no real evidence to support such speculations. Priscilla and Aquilla first met Paul when he came to Corinth, where he joined them in their tent-making business. They had previously lived in Rome, until the Emperor Claudius expelled all the Jews from Rome in A.D. 49, for disturbances over the person of Christ. Apparently a growing number of Jews had become Christians, and this caused division and strife in the Jewish quarters of Rome. The disturbances came to the Emperor's attention, and he expelled all the Jews to keep the peace. Paul stayed with Priscilla and Aquilla in Corinth, and they followed him when he continued his missionary work at Ephesus. The couple supported Paul, at the risk of their own lives, when he faced stiff opposition in his trial at Corinth and when riots broke out in Ephesus. Some time after Paul left Ephesus, Priscilla and Aquilla were able to return to Rome. Wherever they went, the church seems to have met in their house. The pair personally mentored the eloquent Apollos, a preacher from Alexandria, and undoubtedly many others were guided in their Christian faith by this dedicated pair. In his last letter, Paul again sent greetings to this missionary team, who had returned to Ephesus.[32]

At the end of his Roman letter, Paul also greeted two other couples who were probably husband and wife – Philologus and Julia, and Andronicus and Junia. Paul described Andronicus and Junia as 'my kinsmen and my fellow prisoners. They are well known to the apostles, and they were in Christ before me.' Junia's name and Paul's description of her has been the cause of some scholarly controversy. Though many English translators translated the name as 'Junias,' which is masculine; most Greek texts and early Church sources have the name as 'Junia,' which is feminine. Some feminist scholars have contended that misogynistic scribes tried to remove the feminine from this text to avoid recognizing that there was a woman apostle in the early Church (This itself makes the rather chauvinistic assumption that all scribes were men, which was not the case at all.). The King James translation stated that Junias was 'of note among the apostles,' leading feminists to assert that the phrase 'among the apostles' indicated Junia was an apostle or held an apostolic position in the early Church. However, scholars who have made a detailed study of the vocabulary and grammar and compared them with contemporary usage have shown conclusively that the phrase is best translated 'well known to the apostles.'[33] Andronicus and Junia were Jews and Christians before Paul converted to Christ. Since they were well known to the apostles, they very likely lived in Jerusalem. Perhaps they had even been among those persecuted by Paul before his conversion. Paul did state that at some time he suffered persecution with them, and they were his 'fellow prisoners.'

Among the other women Paul greeted in Rome was Rufus' mother: 'Greet Rufus, chosen in the Lord, and his mother, who has been a mother to me as well.' Rufus was the son of Simon of Cyrene, who was forced by the Roman soldiers to help carry Jesus' cross. Rufus' mother would have been Simon's wife. Luke the historian recorded that men from Cyprus and Cyrene were the first to bring the gospel to Antioch. Were Simon and Rufus among these first missionaries? If so, possibly it was at Antioch that Rufus' mother had offered maternal care for Paul in his early Christian life.[34]

---

32 Acts 18:2, 18, 26; 1 Corinthians 16:19; 2 Timothy 4:19.

33 M.H. Burer and D.B. Wallace, 'Was Junia Really an Apostle? A Re-examination of Romans 16:7,' *New Testament Studies* 47 (2001): pp. 76-91.

34 Mark 15:21; Acts 11:20.

Paul also greeted other women in Rome who were his fellow-laborers in Christian work — Mary, Tryphena and Tryphosa (possibly twin sisters), and Nervius' sister. In other letters Paul greeted Nympha and the church that met in her house, and Philemon and his wife, Apphia, in whose house the church also met.[35] Two other women who had worked with Paul in Philippi were Euodia and Syntyche. These Philippian women might have been among those praying by the stream with Lydia when Paul first came to Philippi. They had worked with Paul in the Church when he was there, but some differences, which were bringing division to the Church, had arisen between them. Paul advised them to have the same humble mind as Jesus and to

> Rejoice in the Lord always. Again I will say, Rejoice! Let your reasonableness be known to everyone. The Lord is at hand! Do not be anxious about anything, but in everything, by prayer and supplication with thanksgiving, let your requests be made known to God. And the peace of God, which surpasses all understanding, will guard your hearts and your minds in Christ Jesus.[36]

Euodia and Syntyche's friction prompted Paul to write these words, which have challenged and encouraged many Christians in ensuing centuries.

Wherever the gospel of Christ was preached, women were among those drawn to its message. Paul recognized their contributions in many of his writings — calling them fellow-laborers in the gospel and gratefully acknowledging the help and support they had been to him in the work of the ministry. Some married women ministered with their husbands; others were single businesswomen. Wealthier women often opened their homes in hospitality to traveling Christians and for meetings of the Church. There was a spiritual equality in the Church, which Paul described: 'There is neither Jew nor Greek, there is neither slave nor free, there is neither male nor female, for you are all one in Christ Jesus.'[37]

Instructions to the Churches

There are several important New Testament passages of instruction that touch on women's roles and position in the Church and society. While it is not possible to examine all of these passages or the interpretive debates surrounding them in the present volume, it is important to have a basic understanding of these instructions as a reference point for the later history of women in the Church.

Paul kept informed of the spiritual growth and problems of the churches established throughout his missionary travels. When problems

---

35 Colossians 4:15; Philemon 2.

36 Philippians 4:4-7.

37 Galatians 3:28.

needed addressing or advice and encouragement needed to be given, he wrote a letter giving direction to the church. In almost all the churches, false teachers came in, attempting to undermine the purity of the gospel. Modern scholars often embrace these and later false teachers as examples of the diversity within the early Church. Paul (as well as Peter and John) saw their false teachings as heresies and threats to the truth revealed in Jesus Christ. Paul faithfully instructed the Church on how to deal with the false teachers and their teachings. He also instructed the Church in how to live Christianly in a Greco-Roman world whose values and culture were often antithetical to those of Christ. In addressing such wide-ranging issues, Paul on several occasions addressed the role and position of women in the Church –especially in letters to the Corinthian and Ephesian Churches.

Corinth was a cosmopolitan city of great wealth and diversity, famous for its debauchery and sexual immorality. It was not surprising that Paul was often concerned about the Corinthian Church's spiritual condition. His first letter to the Corinthians was full of advice on how to live as a Christian in a pagan society. In addressing questions of marriage, Paul advised Christians against changing whatever status they were currently in. If married, they should stay married; if single, stay single. Marriage was good, but Paul thought there was more freedom to serve Christ if unmarried, especially considering that the world was passing away. The idea that singleness could be an honorable option for women was revolutionary. Yet, logically, it made sense. Freedom to choose marriage or a single life devoted to Christ enhanced a woman's position individually, because marriage and family were no longer requirements for a woman's self-worth. All was relative to the ultimate goal of living a Christ-pleasing life. The world was passing away, and everything was less important than a life lived for Christ. Remaining single allowed one to be consumed by the things of Christ and not by the things of the world.[38]

Singleness was a gift from God as was marriage; and marriage was good, as was singleness. However, the immorality of the surrounding society must be avoided, and each husband and wife should be faithful to his or her spouse. Each should fulfill the marital duty to the other, thus preventing Satan from tempting them. Those married should not divorce; and if they did, they should not remarry. If an unbelieving spouse divorced, however, remarriage was permissible. If a spouse died, one was free to remarry, but Paul believed it would be better not to, if possible, and to be free to serve Christ wholeheartedly.

Paul had heard that the Corinthians were disorderly in their worship, and he discussed with them in detail what their conduct in worship should

---

38   1 Corinthians 7.

be – in the realms of dress, relationship between the sexes, the Lord's Table, food consumed, and the use of spiritual gifts. For all of these areas, Paul summarized the guiding principle: 'whether you eat or drink, or whatever you do, do all to the glory of God. Give no offense to the Jews, or to Greeks, or to the church of God, just as I try to please everyone in everything I do, not seeking my own advantage, but that of many, that they may be saved.'[39]

The behavior of the Christian was not to be offensive to the Jews or Greeks in the surrounding culture. Some women, however, were flaunting their freedom in Christ by throwing off the cultural norms. They were coming to the church meetings and praying and prophesying with their heads uncovered. In the Greco-Roman world of that day, only loose, immoral women went in public with their heads uncovered. By having their heads uncovered in worship, these Christian women were dressing like the prostitutes of Corinth, a shameful thing. By having their heads uncovered, like immoral women, they also showed their disrespect for their husbands.[40]

Paul repeatedly noted that the relationship between men and women was a relationship based upon God's created order. Man was created first, and then woman. Woman was created for the man, as man was created for God, therefore the woman was to be under the man's authority. Because of the order of creation the woman was also to keep silent in the churches. If she had a question, she should ask her husband at home. It was disgraceful for the woman to disrupt the church or to speak publicly and authoritatively in the church.[41] Paul recognized women shared in the spiritual gifts of the Church, and could pray and prophesy in church, yet the women were not to have authority over a man or to teach authoritatively.[42] This conclusion of Paul was clearly founded on the order of creation, not some culturally relative teaching.

In several of Paul's and Peter's letters to the churches, the apostles listed responsibilities of people in the household to each other – husband and wife, parent and child, slave and master.[43] Martin Luther later called these Biblical instructions on family life 'household tables' or Haustafel. The Romans recognized that the structure of society was rooted in the structure and stability of the family and had written 'household tables' to provide instruction for how the patriarch was properly to rule his family

---

39   1 Corinthians 10:31-33.

40   1 Corinthians 11:1-6.

41   1 Corinthians 14:33-40.

42   1 Corinthians 12: 28; Ephesians 2:20; 4:11; Acts 2:17-18; 21:9; 1 Corinthians 11:5.

43   Ephesians 5:21–6:9; Colossians 3:18–4:1; Titus 2:1-10; 1 Peter 2:18–3:7. Timothy G. Gombis, 'A Radical New Humanity: The Function of the Haustafel in Ephesians,' *Journal of the Evangelical Theological Society*. June 2005, vol. 48, Iss. 2, pp. 317-31.

and household. The Roman paterfamilias, or father of the family, was given supreme authority over his family and household.

The use of 'household tables' in letters to the churches has been interpreted a number of different ways by scholars. Some emphasize that under the household tables, women managed affairs within the house and the men dealt with affairs outside the house. Since the earliest church meetings were in houses, these scholars hold that women had the most authority in the earliest churches. When the Church moved from meeting inside houses to more public buildings, women lost their positions of authority over the Church, and the Church became more patriarchal. Though an interesting theory, this reconstructive history is driven by a feminist agenda for which there is little evidence. Others contend that since the early Church met in houses, the Church simply adopted the Roman household codes for its organizational pattern, and thus the Church's hierarchy became male-dominated. A variant of this view contends that the apostles' instructions to women in these passages simply borrowed from contemporary culture and negated the equality among the sexes in the earliest Church. They theorize that Paul (or later writers, since Paul's authorship of these epistles is frequently denied) reminded the Christians of what the cultural standards were and encouraged them to follow these standards so as not to bring reproach on the Church. Such interpretations are a disservice to Paul and Peter, and fail to recognize the degree to which Christianity transformed relationships as they were understood by the surrounding pagan society. The apostles did not accommodate their instruction to the culture, but enjoined Christians in their personal relations to live out their new life in Christ.

Paul told wives to 'submit to your own husbands as to the Lord;' Peter told them to accept their husband's authority. Husbands were told to 'love your wives and do not be harsh with them,' to 'love your wives just as Christ loved the church' and to 'live with your wives in an understanding way, showing honor to the woman'.[44] Nothing like these commands could be found in any Greco-Roman household management manuals. Paul and Peter were not just trying to maintain the social order. They were showing how Christians should live and ultimately transform the social order. The attitudes and behaviors of both husband and wife were to be molded by their relationship with Christ. The wife was to submit to her husband as if she were submitting to Christ Himself. The husband was to love his wife as Christ loved the Church. Both were to have attitudes of humility and service to the other. Though husband and wife had different positions or roles in the family, there was a spiritual equality as each lived life not for self but for and under Christ. The social structure of the Romans with

---

44   Ephesians 5:22-28; 1 Peter 3:1-2,7; Colossians 3:19.

the husband in authority was not overthrown, but it was transformed as both husband and wife became new creatures in Christ and lived under His Lordship. The model of the husband's proper use of his authority was Christ's loving, self-giving sacrifice. Though this was still patriarchy, it was a patriarchy transformed by new life in Christ. Nowhere in the Roman house codes was the husband told to show love or honor to his wife. Many feminists contend that the household codes of Ephesians 5, Colossians 3, and 1 Peter 3 mirrored the contemporary culture, were culturally defined, and are not for today's liberated woman. Such interpretations fail to grasp the truly revolutionary nature of the Christ-like authority of the husband and the Christ-like submission of the wife.

In the household table in Titus 2, Paul further elaborated on the proper behavior of men, women, children, slaves, the old, and the young. He prefaced his comments by noting that this instruction 'accords with sound doctrine.' The truth in Christ was a behavior-transforming faith. Older women, like the older men, were to

> be reverent in behavior, not slanderers or slaves to much wine. They are to teach what is good and so train the young women to love their husbands and children, to be self-controlled, pure, working at home, kind, and submissive to their own husbands, that the word of God may not be reviled.[45]

The behavior of the old and the young women was to be holy and pure so as not to discredit the truth of the gospel. Older women were to teach the younger how to love their children and love and be submissive to their husbands, 'working at home.' All Christians were to live 'self-controlled, upright, and godly lives in the present age.'[46] Such lives included differing responsibilities for the men and women in the Church. Christian behavior should always bring credit to the Savior, who sacrificed Himself to free His people from sin and lawlessness.

Paul's Last Words

The last writings from the apostle Paul in the New Testament were two letters to Timothy. Many scholars claim these books are pseudepigraphical and date them to the second century, decades after Paul's death.[47] They claim that women were treated negatively in these epistles and contend the restrictions placed on women in these books reflected a growing patriarchy

---

45   Titus 2:3-5.

46   Titus 2:12.

47   Pseudepigrapha are writings falsely claiming to be authored by Biblical characters. Several texts from the second through fourth centuries claim to have been written by one of the apostles, such as *The Gospel of Thomas*, or an early follower of Christ, such as *The Gospel of Mary*. Critics of the New Testament place Paul's Pastoral Epistles in this category.

in the Church, where the authority and equality women enjoyed in the earliest days of the Church were being stripped away – and the Church's centuries of repression of women thus began. However, the early Church accepted these letters as from Paul, though it rejected other books that falsely claimed to be Pauline. The vocabulary and style of the letters are compatible with the other Pauline writings. Though Paul was concerned about qualifications for Church leaders, his words do not require a highly organized hierarchy such as later developed in the Church. He only wrote of elders and deacons, offices which were found in the earliest churches.

Paul wrote these letters to his younger associate Timothy, whom Paul had sent to Ephesus to deal with some problems that had developed in the church there. The Ephesian Church had been founded by Paul; he had spent at least three years and much prayer in building up the church and its leadership. Though Paul had warned the Ephesian Church leaders some years before about the dangers of false teachers, false teachers had come to the church, corrupted its doctrine, and encouraged the Christians to an ungodly lifestyle.[48] Paul wrote Timothy to encourage, strengthen, and advise him on how to deal with these problems in the church.

The false teachers had persuaded many of the women to follow their teachings. Paul described the false teachers as 'the kind who creep into households and capture weak women burdened with sins and led astray by various passions, always learning and never able to arrive at knowledge of the truth… these men also oppose the truth – men corrupted in mind.'[49] Some of the women, especially the younger widows, had turned from the truth and followed Satan. Some were going from house to house as busybodies and gossips, living lives of idleness and sensuality.[50]

Paul began to instruct Timothy how to deal with these problems by describing the prayers and worship of the Church. The fact that he addressed only one sentence particularly to the men but seven to the women indicated that the women had some major problems that needed to be dealt with:

> I desire then that in every place, the men should pray, lifting holy hands without anger or quarreling, likewise also the women should adorn themselves in respectable apparel, with modesty and self-control, not with braided hair and gold or pearls or costly attire, but with what is proper for women who profess godliness – with good works.
>
> Let a woman learn quietly with all submissiveness. I do not permit a woman to teach or exercise authority over a man; rather, she is to remain quiet. For Adam was formed first, then Eve; and Adam was not

---

48   Acts 20:28-31.

49   2 Timothy 3:6-8.

50   1 Timothy 5:13-15.

> deceived, but the woman was deceived and became a transgressor. Yet
> she will be saved through childbearing, – if they continue in faith and
> love and holiness, with self-control.[51]

Apparently some women in Ephesus were dressing in such a way as to
flaunt their wealth and immodestly attract attention to themselves.
Remember, the women in Corinth also were misusing their freedom to
dress in rebellious ways. Paul counsels the Ephesian women that, rather
than adorn themselves outwardly with braided hair, pearls, and gold, they
should adorn themselves with attitudes of self-control and modesty. They
were not to dress sensually and flaunt their sexuality. If they professed
reverence for God, a godly fear, they should adorn themselves with
good works. Paul then stated that women were to learn or be discipled,
something not encouraged by the Judaism of that day. Yet, women were
to learn in a certain way – with submission. A woman was not to teach
or have authority over a man. Women and men were equal spiritually.
Salvation, learning the Word, and growth in Christ were equally available
to both women and men; but there was a difference in positions for
women and men. Women were not to have authority in the Church over
men; they were not authoritatively to teach doctrine in the Church. This
was not a culturally relative command; but again, as in 1 Corinthians, Paul
based his command for women's silence (limiting their teaching) on the
created order. Adam was created first, then Eve. The woman's position
of submission to the man was due to God's created design, not to any
relativistic cultural norm.

In much of his letter to Timothy, Paul dealt specifically with the nature
and character of the leadership of the Ephesian Church. He warned of
false teachers, and he reiterated the standards for true leadership of elders
and deacons. The attempts of women to assume positions of leadership
and authority was apparently one of the problems that had arisen in the
Church, and Paul commanded against such attempts. When Paul gave
Timothy specific instructions for the character and position of elders and
deacons in the Church, he treated them as male, 'the husband of one wife.'
In the New Testament, women were not shown to have had a position of
authority and leadership in the Church. There were no women apostles
or elders in the earliest Church. No women wrote any book of Scripture.

---

51   1 Timothy 2:8-15. This very important passage on the woman's role has been hotly debated
within and without scholarly circles. A summary of some of the differing interpretations can
be found in Douglas Moo, '1 Timothy 2:11-15: Meaning and Significance,' *Trinity Journal* 1
(1980), pp. 70-3, which was expanded into the chapter 'What Does It Mean Not to Teach or
Have Authority Over Men?' in *Recovering Biblical Manhood and Womanhood*. A detailed analysis of
grammatical, historical, spiritual, and social issues of interpretation can be found in *Women in
the Church* (ed. Andreas J. Köstenberger, Thomas R. Schreiner, and H. Scott Baldwin), Grand
Rapids, Michigan: Baker Books, 1995.

The false teachers in Ephesus encouraged the people to abstain from marriage, and refrain from certain foods.[52] Perhaps they also encouraged the women to be lovers of themselves, boastful, and arrogantly to assume authority in the Church – maintaining an outward form of religion but repudiating its power by not following the clear Scriptural commands and pattern for male leadership in the Church.[53] In the Garden, Eve ignored God's command as Adam had instructed her, was deceived by the serpent, and fell into sin. However, Paul wrote in his letter to Timothy that women could 'be saved in childbearing – if they continue in faith, love, and holiness with self-control.' Paul emphasized the childbearing, child-rearing function of women as

> a divinely intended and ongoing difference of function between men and women....The fact that God has ordained that women and only women bear children indicates that the differences in role between men and women are rooted in the created order...Salvation is not evidenced by childbirth alone. But the genuineness of salvation is indicated by a woman living a godly life and conforming to her God-ordained role.[54]

Many of the women at Ephesus, like Eve before them, had been deceived by the false teachers at Ephesus, who denigrated marriage, including the roles of wife and mother in marriage. Paul, as he had written to Titus, encouraged the women to continue in faith, love and holiness, recognizing the mothering, nurturing role of women.[55]

In the early Jerusalem Church, the care for widows had been a major issue. As the apostolic era came to an end, the provisions that needed to be made for the widows in the Church were again addressed. Paul spent some time instructing Timothy on the treatment of widows in the Church. Children should care for their widowed mothers if at all possible, repaying them for all they had given them. But a needy, godly widow without children to care for her should be cared for by the Church. She should be at least sixty years old and one who 'was the wife of one husband and has a reputation for good works: as one who has raised children, practiced hospitality, washed the feet of the saints, helped those in distress – as one who has exhibited all kinds of good works.'[56] Paul here described a woman's role in the Church – faithful wife, full of good works and hospitality, helping and serving others, raising children, involved in charity and helping others in need. A godly widow, whose husband and family were

---

52   1 Timothy 4:3.

53   2 Timothy 3:1-5.

54   *Women in the Church*, p. 151.

55   Titus 2:3-5.

56   1 Timothy 5:9-10.

gone, was devoted night and day to prayer, and set her hope in God. Paul specifically encouraged younger widows to remarry and raise children. Many had apparently taken vows not to remarry and then became sensual and broke those vows, living lives of idleness and uselessness. It was much better for them to marry again than to follow this path.

Many in the twenty-first century are offended by Paul's instructions concerning the place of women in the Church. Some say Paul is simply conforming to his culture by suppressing women and not giving them authority in the Church. This is hardly consistent with Paul's personal, working relationship with women and his earlier statements of the woman's spiritual equality and her godly submission to her husband. By grasping at authority and position for women in the Church, many fail to realize that in Christianity, the position of a humble servant – of washing the saints' feet as Jesus did – is the highest position. Jesus Himself addressed the issue of authority:

> You know that the rulers of the Gentiles lord it over them, and their great ones exercise authority over them. It shall not be so among you. But whoever would be great among you must be your servant, and whoever would be first among you must be your slave – even as the Son of Man came not to be served but to serve, and to give his life as a ransom for many.[57]

As Eve in the Garden focused on the fruit of the one tree she was forbidden to eat, so many who claim women should be priests and ordained ministers focus on the Scripture's prohibition of women assuming authority over men. In doing so they ignore or demean the numerous roles and positions of ministry for women in the New Testament, including ministries of prayer, mentoring other Christians, supporting the Church leaders, showing hospitality, fellow-laboring as missionaries, instructing other women, evangelizing and sharing the Word with others, teaching children, and helping those in need and distress. In these ministries of serving others, women in the earliest churches set a pattern and example followed by Christian women in ensuing centuries of the Church.

---

57   Matthew 20:25-28.

Christian Women in the Early Church:
A Good Testimony through Faith

Hebrews 11:39

By the time the last of Jesus' apostles had died, the Good News of salvation through Christ had spread throughout the Roman Empire and beyond. There were Christian house churches in all the major cities, including the capital city of Rome itself, and wealthy Christian women opened their homes for meeting places of the early Christians. Christianity was an unapproved, illegal religion in the Roman Empire; and persecution became a sporadic but persistent reality for Christians, with many women witnessing for their faith through martyrdom. Watching pagans also noticed the Christians honored marriage and children in a way distinct from others in society. A women's ministry developed from the first-century Church, with Christian widows helping others in the Church in a variety of ways.

Persecution and Martyrdom

For a time Christianity was seen as a Jewish sect, though the Jewish leaders persecuted Christians from the earliest days. Women were included in these earliest persecutions of the Church. When Paul, before his conversion, was persecuting and imprisoning the Christians, he was dragging off women as well as men.[1] Unlike Judaism, which had an established history and was a legal religion within the Roman Empire, Christianity had no separate legal status. Rome and its rulers were very tolerant and easily accepted new religions, especially those from the ancient East; but this new religion claiming to be the truth and teaching that the followers of other religions worshiped false gods was seen as a threat to the Empire. To say that Jesus was Lord rather than Caesar was treason against the Emperor, and Christians were sentenced to death for their faith.

Jesus had warned His followers that they would be brought before governors and rulers, both Jewish and Gentile, to testify of their faith. The disciple was not above his master. As Jesus had been persecuted, even to the point of death on the cross, so His followers could expect persecution

---

1   Acts 8:3; 9:2

– 'For whoever would save his life will lose it, but whoever loses his life for my sake will find it.'[2]

In the Scriptures, the word *marturion*, meaning 'witness,' was used not only to refer to those who were eye-witnesses of the life and resurrection of Christ but also to those who sealed their testimony with their execution.[3] From the earliest days of the Church, honor was given to those who gave their lives rather than betray their Lord. The death of Stephen, the first martyr, was covered at length in the book of Acts. History records that all of Jesus' apostles, except John, were martyred for their faith. Jesus' letter to the church at Smyrna in the book of Revelation spoke especially of the martyred Church. Many saw martyrdom as an imitation of Jesus' suffering and death. Martyrdom came to be seen as a struggle with the devil and demons and a pathway to enter heaven.

For the first three centuries of the Church, many Christians accepted death rather than renounce Jesus as their Lord. Christians were not encouraged to seek martyrdom, but in the second century Tertullian recognized that the 'blood of the martyrs is the seed of the Church.' In his Church history, the fourth-century historian Eusebius mentioned 120 men and 15 women as martyrs. From all other writings, we know about 950 names of Christian martyrs before A.D. 313, the date Christianity became a legal religion within the Empire. Of these 950 known martyrs, 170 were women. By their deaths, Christian martyrs caused the Greeks and Romans to notice Christianity. Christian women were among those whose martyrdoms 'contributed to the victory over paganism.'[4]

As in any court proceeding, official records were taken at the trials of the martyrs by the court stenographer.[5] Many writers in the early Church refer to these judicial court records. The records included the exact words of both the judge and the accused Christians at the trials. Christians obtained copies of these court records and added descriptions of the martyrs' deaths to make a complete record of the Christian's witness or martyrdom. Some judges later took measures to prevent the court records from being sold, duplicated or spread abroad. In A.D. 92, Clement of Rome ordered a compilation of the first Acts of the Martyrs. In 237, Bishop Anterus continued the work. He had copies of the Acts deposited in the fourteen churches in Rome, but

---

2   Matthew 16:25.

3   Acts 22:20; Revelation 2:13; 17:6

4   Everett Ferguson, 'Women in the Post-Apostolic Church,' *Essays on Women in Earliest Christianity* (ed. Carroll D. Osbourn). Joplin, Missouri: College Press Publication Co., 1993, p. 501.

5   There was a syllabic shorthand used in the ancient world which died out during the Middle Ages. The shorthand was used for keeping records of court proceedings, and was also the way many of the sermons of the Church Fathers were preserved. Origen had seven stenographers working at one time and girls assisting as copyists. Debates of church councils also were taken down by the stenographers.

was prosecuted and executed by the pagan Pontifex Maximus for his zeal. Other Roman bishops continued the practice of collecting martyrdom accounts. The 56 folios of Acts of the Saints ultimately were compiled in the eighteenth century in France. Accretions were added over time, but a root of history can be found in these accounts.[6]

Among the early martyrs whose history has come down to us was Blandina, a slave girl from Gaul, in what is modern France. Christians from Asia Minor had first brought the gospel to the region, and contact between the Christians of Asia Minor and of Gaul continued. A letter from the Christians of Lyons to Christians in Asia Minor provides the details of the martyrdom of Blandina and her companions.

In 177, in the cities of Lyons and Vienne, the townspeople became increasingly hostile to the Christians there. Christians were attacked, stoned, and robbed by mobs, and prevented from appearing in the markets, baths, or anywhere in public. Some of the Christians' servants were seized. Under torture, the servants falsely accused the Christians of cannibalism and incest. The authorities brought some of the Christians into the forum for questioning, and some recanted under pressure. Others were imprisoned and tortured. Among the latter was the Bishop Pothius, Deacon Sanctus, Attalus, a recent convert Maturus, and the slave Blandina. Bishop Pothius, who was over 90 years old, was severely beaten and then released; he died shortly after. The others were tortured in various ways and finally sent to the arena to be tormented before the people.

Blandina was the last of the group to suffer in the arena. Though she was a slave, her witness was the most bold, showing, as the account of her martyrdom stated, that Christ uses the weak and obscure to bring great glory to Himself. Her tormentors had to admit they could not break her. They were

> astonished at her endurance, as her entire body was mangled and broken; and they testified that one of these forms of torture was sufficient to destroy life, not to speak of so many and so great sufferings. But the blessed woman, like a noble athlete, renewed her strength in her confession; and her comfort and recreation and relief from the pain of her sufferings was in exclaiming, 'I am a Christian, and there is nothing vile done by us....'[7]

After being tormented herself and watching others suffer cruel deaths, Blandina was suspended on a stake in the arena and left to be devoured by wild beasts. However, when the beasts did not come near her, she was taken down and cast into prison. An observer described her as 'small and

6   A full text database of the Acta Sanctorum can be found at http://acta.chadwyck.co.uk/.

7   The letter describing the martyrdom of Blandina and the other martyrs from Lyons can be found in Eusebius. *Church History,* V, 1-3. This can be read online at the Christian Classics Ethereal Library: http://www.ccel.org/ccel/schaff/npnf201.iii.x.ii.html.

weak and despised yet clothed with Christ the mighty and conquering Athlete.' Her courage in overcoming the adversary many times was a source of inspiration to the other prisoners.

On the last day of the contest, Blandina was brought out with Ponticus, a fifteen-year-old boy. Every day the two had watched the sufferings of the others and had refused to swear by the idols, infuriating the crowd even more. Finally, Blandina, 'having, as a noble mother, encouraged her children and sent them before her, victorious to the King, endured herself all their conflicts and hastened after them, glad and rejoicing in her departure as if called to a marriage supper, rather than cast to wild beasts.' Blandina was scourged, thrown to wild animals, and placed on a red-hot iron seat so that her flesh was burned. Finally, she was placed in a net and thrown before a bull. The animal tossed her about, 'but feeling none of the things which were happening to her, on account of her hope … her communion with Christ,' she also died. And the heathen themselves observed 'that never among them had a woman endured so many and such terrible tortures.' The bodies of the martyrs were exposed for six days, then burned to ashes and thrown into the Rhone River so that no trace of them would remain on the earth. By such efforts the persecutors thought the hoped-for resurrection of the Christians would be impossible.

A quarter of a century after the martyrdom of the slave Blandina, a young woman of some social standing suffered for her faith in North Africa. The first writing we have by a Christian woman is Vibia Perpetua's account of her imprisonment before being martyred in Carthage in 203.[8] In 202, Emperor Septimius Severus issued a decree forbidding conversion to Judaism and Christianity. In Carthage, five young catechumens still being instructed in the Christian faith were arrested – Saturninus and Secundulus, the servants Revocatus and Felicity, and Vibia Perpetua, in her early twenties. Saturus, a fellow-Christian who was not originally arrested with the five, surrendered to the authorities so that he could share the captivity of his brothers and sisters in the faith. For a time the catechumens were under a kind of house arrest; but when they were baptized, completing their conversion to Christianity, they were moved to prison.

Where was Perpetua's Husband?

Why Perpetua's husband is not mentioned in the account of her imprisonment and martyrdom has been a subject of debate. Some speculate he was a pagan and it was he who reported Perpetua and the other converts to the authorities. Others think he had died. Still others postulate that Saturus, the most mature of the imprisoned Christians, had turned himself in to join his wife Perpetua in prison.

---

8   Links to a variety of translations of Perpetua's work as well as further information on her can be found online at http://home.infionline.net/~ddisse/perpetua.html.

Perpetua was a respectable, well-educated, twenty-one-year-old woman who was married and had an infant son. She was loved by her parents and two brothers. She wrote an account of her imprisonment and the struggles she had with her family to maintain her Christian convictions. Perpetua's mother and brothers were Christians, but her father pled with her to renounce her Christianity and spare herself and her infant son. He begged her to consider how the rest of the family would suffer if she were condemned. The Proconsul sympathized with the father and also urged Perpetua to reconsider her commitment to her Christian faith. Perpetua firmly replied that 'I am a Christian' and that she could not

---

Was Perpetua a Montanist?

Montanus was the leader of a movement that arose in Asia Minor in the second century. Montanus fell into ecstatic states and claimed to be the voice of the Holy Spirit. He was joined by Prisca and Maximilla, two women who left their husbands and also began prophesying. The Montanists developed a rigorous morality and ascetic lifestyle. Distrusting the clergy, they put forward alternative leaders for the Church, including women. The North African apologist Tertullian became a Montanist for a time, and the Montanist teaching became strong in Carthage and the surrounding area.

There is substantial evidence that Perpetua was influenced by the Montanists, if not actually a member of that group. Her reliance on personal revelation and visions as the leading of the Holy Spirit was an important aspect of Montanism. The superior honor given to the martyrs over the clergy in her visions was also a Montanist belief.

The Montanists' chief error was their reliance on ecstatic prophecies more than the authority of Scripture. Some used the fact that women were important leaders in this unorthodox sect as evidence that women were easily deceived and an argument against women assuming leadership positions in the Church.

---

be called by anything other than that name. She observed that just as a pot cannot be anything other than a pot, so a Christian cannot be anything but a Christian. When Perpetua was placed in the dungeon, she became quite despondent and depressed by the absolute darkness. As her faith strengthened, however, she wrote that the dungeon became like a palace to her. She gave her baby into the care of her relatives. Other Christians (not imprisoned because they were not recent converts) came and ministered to those in prison, paying the guards so that Perpetua and her companions could have more time in the lighted courtyards.

When Perpetua was taken before the Procurator Hilarianus, her father appeared in court with her infant son and pled with her to change her mind and renounce her Christian conversion. Hilarianus encouraged Perpetua to sacrifice to the pagan gods for the well-being of the Emperors and had her father beaten with rods when she refused (as paterfamilias, the father was responsible for all the affairs in his own household, including his daughter's sacrifice to the emperor). Perpetua was deeply saddened to see her father so treated, but she steadfastly maintained her faith in Christ. Hilarianus had no choice but to condemn her to the wild beasts. Besides, he needed a certain number of criminals for the games celebrating the birthday of Geta, Emperor Septimius Severus' son and heir.

Perpetua showed spunk in the way she responded to her treatment. When the Christians were not given enough food, she asked her keepers, 'If we are to be sacrificed, shouldn't we be fattened up?' She refused to wear the clothes of the pagan gods going into the arena; she wanted liberty to serve Christ.

Perpetua wrote graphic descriptions of three visions she had while in prison. Her emphasis on visions and personal revelation have led some scholars to conclude that Perpetua was part of the Montanists, a sect that was gaining strength in North Africa. The visions themselves provide insight into Perpetua's understanding of Scripture and her theological perspective.[9]

In the first vision, Perpetua climbed to heaven on a narrow golden ladder with swords and hooks on the side and a large dragon at the bottom. The image itself recalled the ladder Jacob saw ascending to heaven with angels going and coming on it (Gen. 28:12). The narrowness of the ladder reflected Jesus' words that 'the gate is narrow, and the way is hard that leads to life, and those who find it are few' (Matt. 7:14). The Roman government used fear of the sword and death to deter Christians from the narrow way. The dragon at the foot of the ladder was certainly 'the dragon, the serpent of old, who is the Devil and Satan' (Rev. 12:9, NKJV). As she ascended the ladder, Perpetua stepped on the head of the dragon, reminiscent of God's promise to Eve in the garden that her seed would bruise the serpent's head (Gen. 3:15).[10] Jesus Himself had told His disciples, 'Behold, I have given you authority to tread on serpents and scorpions, and over all the power of the enemy' (Luke 10:19). In martyrdom, Perpetua would be ascending the ladder to heaven and reaching the garden at the top, mirroring the Garden of Eden of Genesis 2 and the tree of life of Revelation 22. In her vision, Perpetua met in the garden a tall grey-haired man, resembling the Ancient of Days of Daniel 7:9. There also was a Shepherd, symbol of the Lord throughout both the Old and New Testaments, and thousands of white-robed attendants, the martyrs who had come out of the great tribulation (Rev. 7:9-14).

A second vision concerned Perpetua praying for her dead brother Dinocrates, who had died of face cancer when seven years old. Dinocrates

---

9   Rex D. Butler. *The New Prophecy & 'New Visions': Evidence of Montanism in the Passion of Perpetua and Felicitas*. Catholic University of America Press, 2006.

10   Also see Romans 16:20.

was thirsty and in a gloomy place, but through Perpetua's prayers was healed and brought into a bright light and was drinking from a refreshing pool. This vision implied a belief in praying for souls in a kind of purgatory.

The day before her battle with the wild beasts in the arena, Perpetua had a third vision, in which she was ushered into the arena by deacon Pompanius dressed in white. She was amazed when she was confronted with a horrible Egyptian rather than the expected wild beasts. She suddenly became a man and struck the Egyptian's face with her heels and trod on his face so that he rolled in the dust (as a serpent would – Gen. 3:14). She realized then that she would be fighting the devil, not beasts, and that her victory was assured.

Perpetua's writings gave a woman's perspective on her suffering and of the suffering of the slave Felicity imprisoned and martyred with her. Her account was full of emotion and contained many references to childbearing, nursing and family relations. Her visions and her comments upon them conveyed several theological beliefs. Perpetua's God was a sovereign God who ultimately was in control of human events. Death was not an accident, but a call from God. The martyr's adversary was a very personal devil, seen in the images of the dragon, the Egyptian, and wild animals. The early Christians viewed their salvation as a cosmic salvation, a deliverance from the demonic forces that controlled the whole world. Christ won the victory over death and Satan at the cross. The inner presence of Christ was very real to Perpetua. It was only Christ's strength and power through her that enabled her to endure. Since eternal life was the destiny of the martyr, the day of martyrdom was a time of joy and entrance into life eternal.

Perpetua and Felicity

Though there were several Carthaginian Christians martyred together, the martyrdom is always remembered by the names of the two women in the group – Perpetua and Felicity. By the fourth century, a basilica in Carthage was dedicated to the memory of Perpetua and Felicity, and in the reign of Constantine, the date of their martyrdom was added to the calendar of the church of Rome. Perpetua's own story was read yearly in the North African church, and in at least one sermon Augustine sternly warned the people not to think the account itself was canonical Scripture.

Augustine preached several sermons on Perpetua and Felicity's memory as he celebrated the feast day of the Carthaginian martyrs. Three of the sermons have survived the years. Augustine often played upon the names of the martyred women as he preached. He told that these women were able to achieve such victories because of an inner strength, 'a male virtue struggled on behalf of perpetual felicity.' He asked, 'How did Perpetua become perpetually blessed…? …What made Felicity fit for such infinite felicity, but her not being terrified by momentary infelicity?' He encouraged women: 'let them fix their minds on Perpetua, fix them on Felicity, and so take hold of perpetual felicity.'

God's vengeance and judgment was certain upon His enemies, but the martyrs did not take the judgment of their opponents into their own hands. Though persecuted by Rome, they never attacked or criticized Rome. Perpetua's martyrdom, her witness (for, as we saw above, the Greek word 'martyr' meant 'witness'), was a renunciation of her entire world – her motherhood, her family, and her social position – for a primary identification with Christ Himself, whatever the cost. Maintaining truth was more important than torture and physical pain – it was the Truth to which Perpetua was a witness. The paradox was that Christians were sacrificed to maintain the authority and social order of Rome. Yet, their humility under torture actually subverted that order and caused the Church to grow.

Others, of course, added the descriptions of Perpetua's and her companions' deaths and their last moments in the arena.. As Perpetua walked into the arena and passed Hilarianus, her last words to him were as if the judge himself were on trial, 'Thou judgest us, but God will judge thee.' Perpetua and Felicity were tossed about by a mad heifer and finally killed by having their throats cut.

Perpetua's story was a story of transformation. A 21-year-old woman from a wealthy family, with a new husband and a one-year-old child, gave up her life. She had power to defeat sin, death, and the devil as God worked through her. How can this be? Perpetua would answer now as then, 'I am a Christian.'

The account of Blandina's and Perpetua's suffering and death, as well as those of their companions, revealed the attitude of the early Church to martyrdom itself. Though persecuted, beaten and tortured, God gave the martyrs strength. The view developed that Christ suffered in them and overcame the adversary, the devil, through their deaths. The martyrs were in the arena as athletes for Christ in a spiritual conflict. They also were the Bride of Christ and looked forward to the Marriage Supper of the Lamb at the end of their conflict. Such themes were found in the many other martyrdom stories of women during the period. Since women were viewed as weaker, the acts of strength of female martyrs were more remarkable, giving them a stature equal to and often higher than that of male martyrs. Although excessive devotion to martyrs eventually led to the cult of the saints, many Christians both now and in earlier centuries have been encouraged by the stories of the earliest martyrs.

Influence of Christianity on Roman Society

Though the early Christians are often depicted as from the poor and lower classes, there were Christians from the higher social strata as well. From his prison in Rome, Paul wrote the Philippians that 'all the saints salute you, chiefly they that are of Caesar's household.' (Phil. 4:22 KJV). Those Christians 'of Caesar's household' might have been slaves, but there were also some Christians, or people with Christian sympathies, among the Roman aristocracy from the earliest days of the Christian Church.

There is some evidence that there were Christian women among the ruling class, even before Paul's arrival in Rome. According to the Roman historian Tacitus, Pomponia Graecina, wife of Aulus Plautius, the first Roman conqueror of Britain, was accused of a 'foreign superstition' and handed over to her husband for trial.[11] Plautius heard his wife's case in front of her relatives and found her innocent. Many historians believe the 'foreign superstition' Tacitus referred to was the Christian faith. Was Plautius protecting his wife from punishment by his declaration of her innocence? Tacitus further stated that Pomponia 'lived a life of unbroken melancholy' and wore only mourning clothes after the murder of her dear friend Julia, Drusus' daughter. Though moving in the aristocratic (and often murderous and maniacal) circles of Claudius' and Nero's Rome, Pomponia remained somewhat apart from that life. Several Christians from the Pomponius family are buried in the Roman catacombs of St. Callistus. Were these the descendants of this early Christian Roman lady from the reign of Claudius? The Pomponius family members are found in the crypt of Lucina. Some have speculated that Lucina was the baptismal name of Pomponia and that she herself donated the land for the cemetery. All of this is tantalizing, though not conclusive, evidence of Pomponia's Christian faith. It was enough, however, for Pomponia to become an important Christian character in Henryk Sienkiewicz's well-researched historical novel *Quo Vadis*.

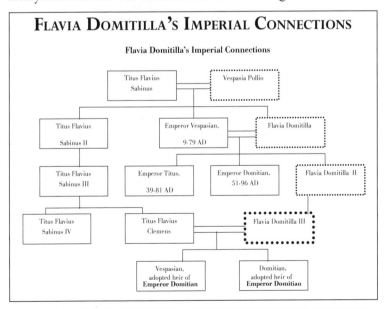

FLAVIA DOMITILLA'S IMPERIAL CONNECTIONS

Flavia Domitilla's Imperial Connections

Titus Flavius Sabinus — Vespasia Pollio

Titus Flavius Sabinus II | Emperor Vespasian, 9-79 AD | Flavia Domitilla

Titus Flavius Sabinus III | Emperor Titus, 39-81 AD | Emperor Domitian, 51-96 AD | Flavia Domitilla II

Titus Flavius Sabinus IV | Titus Flavius Clemens | Flavia Domitilla III

Vespasian, adopted heir of **Emperor Domitian** | Domitian, adopted heir of **Emperor Domitian**

11   Tacitus, *Annals*, XIII, xxxii.

The ancient historians Suetonius and Dio Cassius provide some evidence for the Christian faith of another Roman matron, Flavia Domitilla.[12] Flavia, who lived at the end of the first century, was the granddaughter of the Emperor Vespasian and the third Flavia Domitilla in her family. She had married Titus Flavius Clemens, a great-nephew of Emperor Vespasian and a colleague of Emperor Domitian in the consulship. Flavia and Clemens' two sons were adopted by Domitian as his successors to the throne. Flavia Domitilla was thus centered at the pinnacle of Roman power with important connections to the Emperors themselves. However, Clemens was executed within a year of his assuming the consulship, and Flavia was banished to the island of Pandataria in the Tyrrhenian Sea. Her crime? She was accused of 'atheism' and practicing Jewish rites and customs. Christianity was at that time still closely associated with the Jewish faith, and the fact that Christians worshiped an invisible God rather than idols often led them to be accused of atheism. Other accounts indicate Flavia's niece (daughter?), also named Flavia Domitilla, was banished to the island of Pontia. What happened to the sons is not known, since Domitian was soon assassinated and his successor was appointed by the Roman Senate.

Substantiation for the Christian faith of Flavia Domitilla and possibly her husband Titus Flavius Clemens can be found in a church and a cemetery in Rome. The Church of St. Clement (San Clemente), on the Coelian Hill, was among the earliest churches in Rome. A church was built on the site in the fourth century, as soon as Christianity was no longer an illegal religion. Located in the heart of Imperial Rome only a few steps from the Colosseum, the fourth-century church was constructed on top of a large house that had been built after the Neronian fires destroyed much of Rome. An ancient inscription beneath the church's altar states that 'Flavius Clemens, martyr, is in joyfulness buried here.'[13] The evidence suggests that the house of Flavius Clemens and his wife Flavia Domitilla was one of the early house churches in Rome. One can only imagine the prayers and sermons which might have been heard in this home – and how Flavia's young boys, adopted heirs to the imperial throne, might have been brought up in the Christian faith. The Catacombs of Domitilla, near the Appian Way in Rome, contain the monuments and tombs of many

---

12   Suetonius, *Vita Domitiani*; Dio Cassius, *Roman History*, lxvii.4; See also Eusebius, *History of the Church*. III : 18.

13   Though lacking an inscription, the remains of St. Ignatius are also in this church. Ignatius was one of the disciples of the apostle John, Bishop of Antioch, and by legend the little child Jesus chose to teach about the children coming unto him. Ignatius was brought to Rome and martyred in the Colosseum about A.D. 107.

early Christian martyrs. Inscriptions in the catacombs indicate they are on land donated by Flavia Domitilla.

Flavia and her husband suffered under Emperor Domitian, under whom John the apostle was sent to the Island of Patmos. By the time of the death of the apostle John, the last of the apostles, the gospel of Jesus Christ had been preached throughout the Roman world and even as far as India, if ancient stories of the ministry of the apostle Thomas are to be believed. Where the gospel was preached, lives were transformed, and Christians gained a new citizenship. The second-century *Epistle to Diognetus* best described these new Christians:

> For the Christians are distinguished from other men neither by country, nor language, nor the customs which they observe. For they neither inhabit cities of their own, nor employ a peculiar form of speech, nor lead a life which is marked out by any singularity. The course of conduct which they follow has not been devised by any speculation or deliberation of inquisitive men; nor do they, like some, proclaim themselves the advocates of any merely human doctrines. But, inhabiting Greek as well as barbarian cities, according as the lot of each of them has determined, and following the customs of the natives in respect to clothing, food, and the rest of their ordinary conduct, they display to us their wonderful and confessedly striking method of life. They dwell in their own countries, but simply as sojourners. As citizens, they share in all things with others, and yet endure all things as if foreigners. Every foreign land is to them as their native country, and every land of their birth as a land of strangers. They marry, as do all [others]; they beget children; but they do not destroy their offspring [lit. 'cast away fetuses']. They have a common table, but not a common bed. They are in the flesh, but they do not live after the flesh. They pass their days on earth, but they are citizens of heaven. They obey the prescribed laws, and at the same time surpass the laws by their lives. They love all men and are persecuted by all. They are unknown and condemned; they are put to death, and restored to life. They are poor, yet make many rich; they are in lack of all things, and yet abound in all; they are dishonoured, and yet in their very dishonour are glorified. They are evil spoken of, and yet are justified; they are reviled, and bless; they are insulted, and repay the insult with honour; they do good, yet are punished as evil doers. When punished they rejoice as if quickened into life; they are assailed by Jews as foreigners, and are persecuted by the Greeks; yet those who hate them are unable to assign any reason for their hatred. To sum up all in one word – what the soul is in the body, that are Christians in the world…[14]

---

14 *Epistle from Mathetes to Diognetus*, v-vi. *Ante-Nicene Fathers*, vol. 1, online at http://www.ccel. org/fathers2/ANF-01/anf01-08.html.

SOME WOMEN MARTYRS FROM THE EARLY CHURCH

Felicitas	c. 162	Roman lady who brought up her seven sons in the Christian faith. She was seized and called on to give up Christ to spare her family; but she remained faithful to Christ. Her sons too refused to sacrifice to the Emperor. They all were executed – Felicitas and her sons Januarius, Felix, Philippus, Sylvanus, Alexander, Vitalis, and Martialis.
Blandina	177	Female slave martyred at Lyons. Though the weakest of the martyrs that day, she showed the most courage. She was thrown to the wild beasts and finally gored to death by a bull.
Donata	c. 180	One of 12 Christians from the African town of Scilita who were martyred at Carthage. When called upon to sacrifice, she replied, 'We render to Caesar as Caesar, but worship and prayers to God alone.'
Caecilia	c. 180	Referred to in many martyrs' lists, but information on her is sketchy. She was a Roman Christian whose martyrdom is surrounded by many legends and has been used by many artists and writers (including Chaucer). Considered the patron saint of music. There is a Church of St. Caecilia in Rome on grounds which might have been her family's property.
Potamiaena	Late 2nd cent.	Martyr in Alexandria during the Severan persecution. Tortured and had burning pitch poured over her from head to feet.
Felicity and Perpetua	202-203	Famous martyrs from Carthage. Perpetua's account of their imprisonment is the first writing extant by a Christian woman.
Caritas, Faith, Hope, and Wisdom	?	The date of their martyrdom is unclear, but the virgin sisters of Faith, Hope, and Charity and their mother Wisdom seem to have been real martyrs. The four are buried in St. Caecilia's Church
Apollonia	248	Martyr in Alexandria in her old age. She was beaten, her teeth were knocked out, and then she was brought to be burned outside the city. She threw herself into the fire to hasten her death.

Dionysia	251	Mother martyred at Alexandria
Agatha	251	Quintius, governor of Sicily, fell in love with Agatha. When she refused him, he became resentful, especially when he learned she was a Christian. He ordered her scourged, burnt with a red-hot iron, and torn with sharp hooks. She also was laid naked on live coals mingled with glass. She died in prison.
Prisca	275	Roman convert to Christianity who was tortured and beheaded for refusing to abjure Christianity and sacrifice to idols.
Statonice	c. 300	Martyr at Cyzicum in Mysia with Seleucus her husband at the quinquennalia of Galerius during Diocletian's persecution. Converted when she saw a large number of Christians tortured, and she converted her husband. Her father became her accuser when he could not win her back to paganism. She and her husband were beheaded and buried together, and Emperor Constantine built a church over their tomb.
Agnes	303	12-13-year-old virgin who died under the Diocletian persecution. She rejected her suitors, saying she had consecrated herself to a heavenly spouse. Suitors accused her of being a Christian, thinking this would change her mind. She was beheaded, and Emperor Constantine built a church in Rome in her honor.
Anastasia	c. 303	Christian martyr in Rome under Diocletian. Father was a pagan but mother was a Christian who instructed Anastasia in the faith. After her mother died, she married a Roman knight, Publius Patricius, who obtained a rich patrimony. When he discovered his wife was a Christian, he treated her harshly and spent her wealth. When he died, Anastasia spent her fortune on the poor and imprisoned. She and three female servants were arrested and told to sacrifice to idols. When they refused, the three servants were put to death, and Anastasia was burnt alive.
Lucy	305	Born at Syracuse. She devoted herself to religion and refused to marry. She gave her fortune to the poor to try to prevent a suitor's advances. The young man was enraged and reported her Christianity to judge Paschasius. She was then executed.

Catherine	310	Well-educated, noble virgin of Alexandria who converted to Christianity. Emperor Maximinus ordered her to dispute with 50 heathen philosophers. When they were reduced to silence and converted to Christianity, she was then martyred. The Emperor ordered her crushed between wheels of iron, with sharp blades. The wheels broke, so she was beheaded – at the age of 18. Catholic legend holds her corpse was transported to Mt. Sinai by angels – hence St. Catherine's monastery there.

Distinctive Christian Attitudes to Marriage and the Family

The *Epistle to Diognetus* summarized the Christians' noticeably different attitudes and practices from other citizens of the Roman world, including their treatment of women and attitude to marriage. Marriage was honored, and both men and women were expected to be faithful to their spouse. Children from the marriage were also respected and honored. Though abortion and infanticide were accepted practices in the pagan world, Christians valued life, even if the life was that of a baby girl.[15]

Men outnumbered women in the Greco-Roman world, but women seem to have outnumbered men in the early Church. Women, especially in the upper classes, were attracted to Christianity. This was so much the case that the pagan Celsus criticized Christianity as a religion only for slaves, women and children. Celsus said Christianity had a corrupting influence on women, but this might be because they began to think and act differently from the accepted standards of paganism.[16]

The disapproval of infanticide was one area of Christian disagreement with the prevalent social standards. It was rare for a Roman family to have more than one girl in the family; unwanted girls were just left to die. An example of this can be seen from a letter of a man named Hilarion to his pregnant wife, Alis:

> Know that I am still in Alexandria. And do not worry if they all come back and I remain in Alexandria. I ask and beg you to take good care of our baby son, and as soon as I receive payment I shall send it up to you. If you are delivered of a child [before I come home], if it is a boy keep it, if a girl discard it. You have sent me word, 'don't forget me'. How can I forget you? I beg you not to worry.[17]

---

15   Rodney Stark, *The Rise of Christianity.* HarperSanFrancisco, 1997, pp. 95-128.

16   *Contra Celsum*, 3.44, online at http://www.ccel.org/fathers2/ANF-04/anf04-57.html#P8471_2133330 .

17   *Rise of Christianity*, pp. 97-8.

Second-century apologist Minucius Felix criticized the pagan world's embrace of abortion and infanticide:

> And I see that you at one time expose your begotten children to wild beasts and to birds; at another, that you crush them when strangled with a miserable kind of death. There are some women [among you] who, by drinking medical preparations, extinguish the source of the future man in their very bowels, and thus commit a parricide before they bring forth. And these things assuredly come down from your gods. For Saturn did not expose his children, but devoured them. With reason were infants sacrificed to him in some parts of Africa.[18]

Minucius Felix himself was from North Africa and was familiar with the child sacrifices which had been a part of the religious rituals there since the Phoenicians had imported the practice centuries before. That Christians did not condone infanticide, even female infanticide, would have demonstrated to the watching world that women had value, dignity, and respect within the Christian community. Abortion was a high cause of death among women, and the Christian disapproval of the practice would have saved many women from a painful end.

The Christians' more favorable view of women was also evident in their condemnation of divorce, marital infidelity, and polygamy. Pagans were part of a male-dominated culture which held marriage in low esteem. Christians, however, sanctified marriage and condemned promiscuity in both men and women. This gave Christian women a greater marital security than their pagan counterparts enjoyed. Christians stressed the obligations of husbands toward their wives as well as those of wives toward their husbands.

In the pagan society, women were frequently forced into marriage at a very young age, whereas Christian women often married at an older age and had more choice about their marriage. In the Christian community, virginity was recognized as a viable choice, and a woman or man could choose not to marry. Widowhood was also highly respected among Christians, in contrast to pagan and even Jewish society. Many Christian leaders, however, established standards beyond those of Scripture and discouraged second marriages so that the remainder of the widow's life could be devoted to prayer and service to God.[19]

Christianity thus offered women freedoms unavailable elsewhere, and women were often the first to convert to Christianity in a region. Though women might not have positions of leadership within the Church, their influence was strong. Since there were fewer men than women in

18   Minucius Felix, *Octavius*, xxx, online at http://www.ccel.org/fathers2/ANF-04/anf04-34.htm#P5530_808394.

19   Compare with 1 Timothy 5:11, 14.

EARLY CHURCH FATHERS ON CHRISTIAN MARRIAGE

Polycarp *(To the Philippians 4:2-3)*

Teach your wives to walk in the faith given to them, in love, and in purity, to be altogether truly affectionate to their own husbands, to love all others equally in all chastity, and to bring up their children in the discipline of the fear of God.

Clement of Alexandria *(Miscellanies 4:19, 20)*

It is possible for man and woman equally to share in perfection...The wise woman then would first choose to persuade her husband to be a partner with her in the things that lead to true happiness. If that should be impossible, alone she should be diligent in virtue, being obedient to her husband so as to do nothing against his will except in regard to those things that are considered to make a difference to virtue and salvation ... Marriage then that is fulfilled according to reason is sanctified, if the union is subjected to God...The truly happy marriage must be judged by neither wealth nor beauty but by virtue.

Tertullian *(To His Wife 2.8)*

How can I paint the happiness of a marriage which the church ratifies, the oblation celebration of communion confirms, the benediction seals, angels announce, the Father declares valid? Even upon earth, indeed, sons do not marry without the consent of their fathers. What a marriage is that between two believers! They have one hope, one desire, one way of life, the same religion. They are brother and sister, both fellow servants, not divided in flesh or in spirit – truly 'two in one flesh,' for where is one flesh there is also one spirit. They pray together; they prostrate themselves together; they carry out fasts together. They instruct one another and exhort one another. Side by side they are present in the church of God and at the banquet of God; they are side by side in difficulties and in consolations. Neither ever hides things from the other; neither avoids the other; neither is a grief to the other. Freely the sick are visited and the poor are sustained. Without anxiety, misgiving, or hindrance from the other, they give alms, attend the sacrifices [of the church], perform their daily duties [of piety]. They are not secretive about making the sign of the cross; they are not fearful in greetings; they are not silent in giving benedictions. They sing psalms and hymns one to the other; they challenge each other as to who better sings to God. When Christ sees and hears such things, he rejoices. He gives them his peace. Where two are together in his name, there is he, and where he is, there the evil one cannot come.

the Church, and more men than women in the surrounding culture, Christian women frequently married unbelieving husbands and became the instruments of their conversion to Christianity. Historian Peter Brown called women the 'gateway' into pagan families. As wives, servants, and nurses of unbelievers, they were able to share the gospel and convert others to the Christian faith. By the fourth century, many upper-class families in Rome were Christian, with the husband often coming to faith through the witness of his Christian wife.

Tertullian and some others, however, attacked the mixed marriages that had become popular among the upper-class Christians. He noted that the activities of Christian fasts, vigils, visiting the poor, going to evening love feasts, exchanging the kiss of peace, and showing hospitality could all seem suspicious to an unbelieving spouse. Then too, the pagan husband would want his wife to participate in the pagan rituals and practices.

Pope Callistus in the third century upset many when he ruled that Christian women could live in 'just concubinage,' being in a permanent relationship with a man without entering into marriage legally. Possibly Callistus was trying to deal with the problem of there not being enough eligible Christian men in the upper classes, yet upper-class Christian women could lose their property and privileges of wealth if they legally married below their ranks. Earlier, Hippolytus had accepted into the full fellowship of the Church a slave woman who was in faithful concubinage to one man and reared her own children. Slaves were not allowed to marry under Roman civil law, but the Church created an ecclesiastical law of marriage which in effect elevated the position of the slave woman, recognizing her faithful concubinage as marriage.[20]

Early church leaders continued to look to the apostolic writings of the New Testament for their understanding of the position of women in the family, society, and the church. Ignatius and Polycarp, both disciples of the apostle John, echoed the New Testament writings. Ignatius encouraged the Philadelphian wives to 'be subject to your husbands in the fear of God' and husbands to 'love your wives as fellow-servants of God, as your body, as partner of your life, and your co-adjutors in the procreation of children.' Marriage was honorable, as was virginity, if Christ was always before you. Ignatius, like Paul and John, had to contend with early Gnostics who held that the flesh was evil, marriage was polluting, and certain foods were abominable. Ignatius plainly said that the one who teaches such things 'has the apostate dragon dwelling within him.'[21] Everett Ferguson concluded that 'Women as wives and mothers gave the Christian home the strength that made it such a powerful influence in the spread of Christianity in the Roman world.'[22]

---

20   Hippolytus. *Apostolic Tradition*, xvi.24. Charles Ryrie. *The Role of Women in the Church*. Chicago: Moody Press, 1970, p. 129.

21   Ignatius, *Letter to Philadelphia*, available online at http://www.ccel.org/ccel/schaff/anf01.v.vi.vi.html.

22   'Women in the Post-Apostolic Church,' p. 486.

Women's Ministry – Widows and Deaconesses

Both Ignatius and Polycarp reiterated Paul's advice concerning widows. Widows should not be 'wanderers about, nor fond of dainties, nor gadders from house to house,' but they should be praying continually and avoiding slandering tongues full of falsehood and every kind of evil. Polycarp even called the widows the 'altar of God,' for through their sacrifice of prayer God was worshipped, honored, and served.[23]

Christianity was unique in valuing widows. Nothing in Judaism or paganism paralleled Christianity's exaltation of widowhood. Under Emperor Augustus, a law was passed which penalized widows if they did not remarry after two years. The Church, however, took care of widows, and remarriage was not encouraged. Christians considered it a duty to support widows and orphans, and historians recognize that the Church helped alleviate poverty in antiquity by this support. In 253, the Roman Bishop Cornelius noted that the Roman church supported 1500 widows and poor persons. Later, in the fourth century, the church at Antioch supported 3000 widows and virgins. Christianity took away the shame of widowhood. By elevating the widows to a life of prayer and contemplation, widowhood became noble. Widows were seen as intercessors who prayed specifically for those whose names were given to them by the bishops. The third- century *Didascalia Apostolorum* described these Christian widows:

> … a widow who wishes to please God sits at home and meditates upon the Lord day and night, and without ceasing at all times offers intercession and prays with purity before the Lord. And she receives whatever she asks, because her whole mind is set upon this. Her prayer suffers no hindrance from any thing, and thus her quietness and tranquility and modesty are acceptable before God, and whatever she asks of God, she receives …[24]

However, widows were not simply cared for by the Church; they were also important to the functioning of the Church. They were given the responsibility of nursing the sick, caring for the poor, dispensing the alms of the Church, and evangelizing pagan women. The age and character requirements the apostle Paul had given for widows supported by and working within the Church, including that they remain unmarried, became the foundation for an order of widows within the early Church.[25]

Though the Church's general treatment of widows was commendable and virtuous, some in the Church apparently were taking advantage of the

23   *Epistle of Polycarp*, 4, available online at http://www.ccel.org/ccel/schaff/anf01.iv.ii.iv.html .

24   *Didascalia Apostolorum* , chs. 14-15, quoted in Jean La Porte, *The Role of Women in Early Christianity*, p. 63.

25   1 Timothy 5:5-10. Some later church rules lowered the age requirement for the rank of widows to age 50 rather than Paul's requirement of age 60.

widows. In 370 Emperor Valentinian I addressed a ruling to the Bishop of Rome that male clerics and unmarried ascetics should not loiter around the houses of women and widows trying to get bequests for the Church, to the detriment of the widows' families and relatives. The temporal wealth of the Church had apparently greatly increased from such bequests.

The organizational structure of the Church developed and changed over time and over different geographical areas. These developments and changes can be gleaned from the varied writings and inscriptions from the early Church and are not always as clear as one might like. However, by the second century, widows were listed as having a position in the Church along with bishops, presbyters, and deacons. 'Deaconess' as a position in the Church seems to have developed from the order of widows and performed the same services as the widows. In time, however, the person(s) who held this position were unmarried, took vows of chastity, and came to be over the widows. The third-century *Didascalia* gave a specific ritual for the consecration of widows and deaconesses. A principal work of the deaconesses was to help prepare women for baptism. This included instruction as well as helping in the baptism of women, which in the early Church was by immersion. They also instructed women at marriages. In the early Church, men and women separated during the worship meetings of the Church. In this setting, deaconesses helped the presbyter distribute communion to the women, both in church and to those who were sick at home. In all their work, whether teaching, conducting rituals of the Church or distributing charity, the deaconesses worked primarily with other women and under the authority of the presbyter.

As the Church became more structured, the widows were placed under the authority of the deaconesses; and by the end of the fourth century, widows as a special position in the Church seems to have been abandoned. The order of deaconesses remained for several more centuries, especially in the Eastern Church. In the sixth century, the church staff of St. Sophia in Constantinople included 60 priests, one hundred deacons, forty deaconesses and ninety sub-deacons. By the eleventh century, however, the position of deaconess had virtually disappeared.

The evidence for deaconesses as a special part of the Church's organization is indisputable, and in various areas there were ordination services for the deaconesses as well as for the deacons and clergy. The deaconesses' responsibilities, however, were always seen as primarily teaching and working among the women, not as being preparatory to the priesthood or as sharing in any of the priestly functions. Especially in the area of baptisms, deaconesses were important in helping the women in their preparations when it was inappropriate for a man to be alone with a woman. If there were women priests, as some feminists maintain, a special office of women to teach and work with women catechumens would not have been necessary.

The third-century *Didascalia Apostolorum* gave detailed regulations and instructions on the widows and deaconesses. The women were specifically told that their realm of ministry was distinct from that of the deacons and priests, who were to be male. When Jesus sent out the twelve to instruct the people, there were no women among them. If women were to be the main teachers in the Church, Jesus would have appointed some women as his apostles and ministers. If women were to administer baptism, Jesus would have been baptized by Mary, not John. The *Didascalia* advised women not to imperil themselves by acting outside of the law of the gospel. Historian Everett Ferguson concluded that in the mainstream circles of the early Church, 'the same situation prevailed as that reflected in the New Testament documents; a very full involvement of women in every aspect of the Church's life except speaking in the public liturgical assemblies and serving as elders/bishops.'[26]

Some feminist scholars maintain that the patriarchal forces of the Church restricted the role of women, but there is little evidence to support this argument. The decline in the position of deaconesses in the Church was not dictated by a male-dominated priestly hierarchy; other historical forces were at work. Once the Church became institutionalized after Constantine and babies were born into 'Christendom,' adult baptisms at conversion declined and infant baptism became the norm. The need for women to teach women and help women during the rite of baptism, one of the prime functions of the deaconesses, was diminished. The growth of cloistered, monastic societies at the same time diverted those women with a Christian calling to no longer serve in an open society but within the cloistered walls. The development of monasticism as a competing authority was an important change which was not in any way under the influence of patriarchy.

Virgins and a Growing Asceticism

The deaconesses in the early Church were most often either widows or unmarried women. Christianity's value of unmarried women was as unique as was its value of widows. Christians were the first to recognize that unmarried women could be worthy of honor, dignity, and respect. In view of Christ's expected soon return, Paul had counseled those who were single in the Corinthian Church to remain unmarried so they would have more freedom to serve the Lord.[27] The four prophesying daughters of Philip the evangelist possibly remained virgins for such greater Christian service.[28]

By the end of the first century, a popular order of virgins had arisen in the Church. These virgins dedicated themselves to a single life of service to

---

26   Everett Ferguson, *Early Christians Speak*, Abilene Christian University Press, 1999, p. 235.

27   1 Corinthians 7:26, 40.

28   Acts 21:9.

Christ and His Church. They lived at home but put themselves under the bishops to help the Church in whatever ways were needful. Like the widows, virgins sought a life of prayer and contemplation as well as service. Though most of the women in the early Church were married, more was written about the single, contemplative life of the virgins than about married life. Perhaps some chose the single life because of the fewer number of Christian men than women. Others chose a life of virginity in revulsion to the extreme lustfulness of the surrounding sex-crazed pagan society. Most of the dedicated virgins were from upper-class families who had independent wealth.

Though the apostle Paul had taught that both marriage and celibacy were honorable and one could live an honorable Christian life in either condition, some began to elevate virginity and an ascetic life as more noble than married life. Paul had warned against such tendencies in his last letters to Timothy. The apostle specifically warned that false teachers, inspired by deceiving spirits and demonic doctrines, would forbid marriage and require abstinence from certain foods which God had made to be received with thanksgiving.[29] Rather than teach the sound doctrines of the Scripture, false teachers turned ears away from the truth and taught according to their own desires.[30] Despite these apostolic warnings, an asceticism and dualism came into the Church, which adopted some of the beliefs of pagan philosophy and Gnosticism. Leaders arose who, borrowing from Greek philosophy, taught that matter and the body were evil and that denying the body was a virtue leading to a purer life of the spirit. That Jesus Himself was celibate was taken by many as an example and encouragement to celibacy. Virgins and ascetics claimed to live a higher level of Christian life than those caught up in the mundane affairs of marriage, family, and business. An emphasis on celibacy became a distinguishing feature of a higher Christian life. The more perfect Christian was thought to be the one who lived removed from the world and its passions.

Of course, the virgins and celibates had to deal with pride and personal conceit, which easily accompanied such an assumed lofty spiritual position. Many of the early Church fathers who wrote on virginity (and they nearly all did) wrote that virginity was more a matter of the soul than the body. Hoping for a higher reward in heaven, all earthly desires were renounced as the virgins struggled with the flesh to achieve the sexless, angelic state of eternity.

Vows of virginity were first mentioned by Tertullian early in the third century, but Cyprian (c. 200-258) said that a marriage contract taken after a vow was legal. Penalities for breaking a vow of virginity were soon implemented, however. The Council of Elvira in Spain (306) imposed

---

29   1 Timothy 4:3.

30   2 Timothy 3:12-17; 4:3-5.

a lifelong excommunication for breaking a vow of virginity. Since the virgin had taken a vow as the Bride of Christ, the Council of Ancyra (314) considered those who married after taking such a vow guilty of bigamy. By the end of the fourth century, taking a vow of virginity had become a special ceremony before a priest, who bestowed a veil and a special robe upon the female virgin. Male ascetics of that time, however, made no public vow and did not wear any special clothing.

A popular piece of fiction elevating the female virgin was the second-century *Acts of Paul and Thecla*.[31] Manuscripts of the story have been found in several languages, including Greek, Coptic, Ethiopic, and Armenian. The Syrian and Armenian Churches included the *Acts of Paul and Thecla* in their early Biblical canons. Though there apparently was a real person named Thecla who had a great impact on southeastern Asia Minor, the *Acts of Paul and Thecla* was early recognized as fiction. Tertullian stated the work was a forgery and that he knew the pastor-author who wrote it. According to the story, Thecla was a virgin of Iconium who converted to Christianity after listening to the apostle Paul. She was engaged but broke off her impending marriage so she could follow the apostle. Paul, however, was banished from the town for the disturbance he caused, and Thecla was sentenced to be burned at the stake. Divine intervention miraculously prevented her martyrdom, and Thecla was able to follow Paul. She cut her hair, baptized herself, dressed like a man, and took up life as a wandering evangelist. At one point along her journey she was thrown to wild beasts and again miraculously delivered, through the kindness of a lioness. After following Paul for a time, the Apostle commissioned Thecla to teach and return to Iconium.

A cult developed around Thecla, and women especially went on pilgrimages to Seleucia, the place of Thecla's birth, and several places in Egypt where St. Thecla was venerated. Archaeologists have found items at these various pilgrimage sites, such as flasks with Thecla's name and image on them, from the fifth and sixth centuries. Because of her fictional story, however, Thecla was removed from the Roman Catholic calendar of saints at Vatican II (1962-65).

Though fiction, Thecla's story held up virginity as superior to marriage. The persecution Thecla endured at various points in the story paralleled the martyrdom that real Christian women endured as they stood firm in their faith. Tertullian, for one, was most displeased with the Thecla story for the way it supported the right of women to teach and baptize. Many modern feminists rely heavily on Thecla's fictional story as 'evidence' of the leadership roles they contend women had in the early Church. They assert this is one remnant of evidence, most of which was destroyed by patriarchal Church leaders, of women's position of leadership in the early

---

31   Online at http://www.ccel.org/fathers2/ANF-08/anf08-89.htm#P7548_2309231.

Church. The story is also valued for the earliest physical description of the apostle Paul, 'of a low stature, bald (or shaved) on the head, crooked thighs, handsome legs, hollow-eyed; had a crooked nose; full of grace; for sometimes he appeared as a man, sometimes he had the countenance of an angel.' Whatever grain of truth might be in this description of the apostle is not known any more than what kernel of history might be contained in the story of Thecla herself.

Gnosticism and Feminist History

The *Acts of Paul and Thecla* is one of several post-apostolic writings that have become favored by recent historians as alternative accounts of conditions in the early Church. Some assert that these alternative writings were actually contenders for becoming the Scripture of the Church but were disallowed by later patriarchal Church rulers. Works such as the *Gospel of Thomas, Gospel of Phillip, Pistis Sophia, The Thunder Perfect Mind*, and *Gospel of Mary*, despite being named after various apostles or their contemporaries, were all written in the second century or later, well beyond the apostolic period when the Scriptures were written.

Feminist activists either totally deny the Bible's authority or seek to re-interpret the Bible in accordance with their feminist presuppositions. One argument they have chosen is to say the Bible is not the authority for the Christian because the Gnostic writings preceded the Bible and thus speak of the earliest days of the Church. One problem with this is that the Gnostic documents all date to a century or more *after* the apostolic period. Gnostic ideas, however, are very congenial to the postmodern mind, and some scholars continue to contend that the Gnostics represent the original, true Christian teaching.[32]

Gnosticisim comes from the Greek word gnosis, meaning 'knowledge.' The Gnostics purported to have a hidden, secret knowledge available only to those initiated into Gnosticism. The Gnostics were syncretists who blended ideas from philosophy, ancient mystery religions, and Christianity. They claimed to have a hidden wisdom unavailable to most. There was much variety in Gnostic writing and thought, making it difficult to describe Gnostic beliefs coherently. Generally, however, Gnostics were dualists, believing that matter, which included everything in the world, was evil and

---

32   Philip Jenkins. *Hidden Gospels: How the Search for Jesus Lost Its Way* (Oxford University Press, 2001) is an excellent analysis of the use of the Gnostic gospels by those who wish to denigrate Christian origins. Other recent works which ably refute the claims of the new history of the early church based on these alternative Scriptures include Richard Bauckham, *Jesus and the Eyewitnesses: The Gospels as Eyewitness Testimony* (Grand Rapids: MI: Wm. B. Eerdmans, 2006); Darrel Bock, *The Missing Gospels* (Nelson Books, 2006); Craig Evans, *Fabricating Jesus* (Downers Grove, IL: InterVarsity Press, 2006); N.T. Wright, *Jesus and the Gospel of Judas: Have We Missed the Truth About Christianity?* (Baker Books, 2006).

that spirit was good. It followed that the God who created the heavens and earth according to Genesis 1 created an evil, material world (even though He pronounced it very good).[33] The Gnostics believed in reincarnation of the soul to different successive levels of being as it progressed on its spiritual journey. The real human being was androgynous, both male and female, and devoid of sexuality. Believing that matter was evil, Gnostics believed that Jesus' incarnation, His taking on human flesh, was evil and that Christ's sacrifice for sin was a monstrous invention. The Gnostics claimed they were the Christians who first accepted Christ in the fullest, spiritual sense.

To many Gnostics, Sophia or Wisdom was the female manifestation of God, 'a breath of the power of God and a pure emanation of the glory of the Almighty.'[34] Some Gnostic writings spoke of women prophets and leaders, and Mary Magdalene was often denominated a leading disciple, with the suggestion that she even shared a sexual intimacy with Jesus. Leading feminists, including Karen Torjesen and Karen King, have used the Gnostic *Gospel of Mary* as evidence that women were leaders and priests in the early Church but were suppressed by the male apostles, led by Peter. Mary Magdalene has become the chief of the apostles for modern feminists, who contend that the *Gospel of Mary* was one of the books excluded from the Bible because of the suppression of the male hierarchy of the Church. Such a reconstruction ignores the facts of history. The *Gospel of Mary* was written at least 100 years after the writing of the Biblical Gospel of John, too late even to be considered for inclusion in the Christian Bible. The Mary depicted in the Gospel is a character of fiction, with no historical roots. She has as much historical validity as a character in a novel, which is exactly what occurred in the novel, *The Da Vinci Code*. Unfortunately, many will ignore the facts of history and accept a novel as truth because it comfortably fits with their own predilections.

Gnostic writings are not new as historical sources, but have been emphasized today in current social and ecclesiastical debates. They are being used to radically reconstruct religious belief and practice by postmodern academics, feminists, and media, so that their agenda has become accepted as truth throughout much of the popular culture today. Philip Jenkins well summarized the interpretive issues by saying that the willingness to claim the Gnostic writings as a lost 'women's canon' of Scripture 'is troubling testimony to the ideological character of some modern interpretations of the hidden gospels.'

While the Gnostic writings have become favorite sources for contemporary feminist historians, interestingly, feminists of earlier centuries favored them as well. The idea that the Gnostics were the real Christians of

---

33   Genesis 1:31.

34   *Wisdom of Solomon* 7:25-26, as quoted in *Hidden Gospels*, p. 130.

the early Church was commonplace among earlier women occult writers such as Madame Blavatsky, Annie Besant, and Anna Kingsford. In 1909, theosophist and occultist Frances Swiney wrote in *The Esoteric Teachings of the Gnostics* that the Gnostics were chiefly supported by emancipated women of the Roman Empire, 'early pioneers of the liberation movement of their sex, dialectical daughters questioning the truth and authority of received opinions, earnest intellectual women.'[35] She saw Gnostics as predecessors of the suffragettes of her day and maintained that the Gnostics accepted the life of Christ, not his death, as key to their doctrine. Swiney wrote that the Gnostics were subjected to the bloodiest of persecutions by the orthodox priests in order to suppress women: 'The Gnostics kept true to the original pristine faith in the Femininity of the Holy Spirit. A truth universally suppressed in the fourth century AD by the male priesthood of the Christian church.' She contended that this exclusion of women from the faith and its Scriptures was the cause of 'the persecution, degradation and maltreatment of womanhood' through following centuries.[36]

Scholar Elaine Pagels studied the ancient texts found at Nag Hammadi, Egypt, forty years after Swiney wrote, yet the thesis in Pagels' award-winning *The Gnostic Gospels* (1979) was similar to that of the earlier feminist. Pagels wrote that the patriarchal establishment condemned Gnosticism because it gave too much authority to women and other members of society who did not normally exercise authority. Under this perspective, social position rather than truth determined orthodoxy. Pagels accepted the basic thesis of Walter Bauer's *Orthodoxy and Heresy in Earliest Christianity*, first published in German in 1934 and translated into English in 1971. Bauer's thesis was that in earliest Christianity, orthodoxy and heresy did not stand in relation to one another as primary to secondary, but that in many regions heresy was the original manifestation of Christianity. This thesis, however, does not stand up to an examination of the evidence. Examining the *earliest* Christian documents clearly indicates a set of core beliefs, which were orthodox teaching. Diversion from such teachings has always clearly been seen as heresy.[37]

Pagels found two different attitudes towards the female in orthodox Christian and Gnostic groups. The Gnostics described the deity using both masculine and feminine terms, while the orthodox used only masculine terms. She contended that Gnostic exegesis of Creation focused on Genesis 1, male and female, whereas orthodox analysis emphasized Genesis 2, placing the woman secondary. This claim ignored the extensive commentaries on Genesis 1 by the Church Fathers. Yet, from this mistaken evaluation, Pagels

---

35   Frances Swiney, *The Esoteric Teachings of the Gnostics*, (London: Yellon, Williams and Co., Ltd., 1909) as quoted in *Hidden Gospels*, p. 128. However, there is no evidence that the Gnostics ever endured the bloodiest of persecutions, either before or after the fourth century.

36   *Esoteric Teachings of the Gnostics, 5*, p. 40.

37   *Missing Gospels*, pp. 49-55.

held that the orthodox 'subordinated' women while the Gnostics elevated women and gave them positions of equality. From these premises, she reached a flawed conclusion: In Gnostic societies women were equal with men; in orthodox societies they were subordinated. As with many of the feminist reconstructions of history, the evidence linking women's authorities with heretical communities failed to be substantial enough to make the case. However, Pagels and many today continue to find the Gnostics very relevant because they sought truth within the individual rather than in a rigid historical truth, such as orthodox Christians found in Scripture.

Were Women Priests ?

An extensive amount has been written in recent decades about the position of women within the organization of the early Church. This is usually put by the question 'Were women priests?' The question itself is an anachronistic question for the early Church. The Jewish priesthood, with its extensive rules, ceremonies, and sacrifices, was not continued in the early Church. When the veil in the temple was torn at Christ's crucifixion, the way was open for all to approach God freely, without the intermediary of a priest. As the writer of the book of Hebrews emphasized, the old priesthood was done away with the old covenant. Jesus Christ Himself was the High Priest who opened the way to God's throne. Because of Christ's atoning death on the cross, there was no longer needed a sacrifice for sin. Every Christian, male and female, was now a priest who could freely offer sacrifices of praise and thanksgiving and who could through prayer boldly approach God's throne of grace. Early Church writers such as Justin Martyr and Irenaeus, and even later writers such as Origen and Augustine, speak of the priesthood of all believers as a distinct mark of Christianity's superiority to other religions. In time, however, the Lord's Supper came to be seen as the Christian offering and a Christian priest (presbuteros) became the mediator between the congregation and God. Old Testament as well as pagan concepts of priesthood were absorbed into the Church, so that the priesthood of the later medieval Church differs from that of the earliest Church.

Too often the hierarchical Roman priesthood is anachronistically read into the early Church. The clergy/laity distinction was not nearly as distinct as it later became in the Church hierarchy, especially under the later sacramental system. For a woman to be ordained a deaconess did not mean she had started up the ladder to become a priest, as such ordination might mean in later centuries. Ordination simply was a way to set apart a person for service or ministry; it did not carry a sacramental meaning until later Church history and did not mean that women were the leaders of the church or were the main spokespersons or preachers for the congregation.

Feminist historians endeavor to reconstruct the historical evidence to show that women held leadership positions in the earliest Church but in time were suppressed by patriarchal authorities. However, the circumstantial evidence put forth to support the claim that women priests served in the early Church is not persuasive, and the conclusions of the feminist historians are undermined by logical and factual flaws.

The evidence put forward for women priests may be grouped into four categories, listed below along with reasons to question the legitimacy of the feminist conclusions:

1. **Examples of women priests in Montanist and Gnostic groups.** However, no woman serving as priest in such groups can be documented until the second century. There is no logical reason why such later heretical groups, who clearly rejected the authority of the Scriptures, can be assumed to have been the models and patterns for the early Christian women.

2. **Inscriptions, especially sarcophagus and tomb inscriptions, call some women 'priestesses' or 'bishopesses.'** Celibacy is not a requirement in the Eastern Church and was not a mandatory requirement for even the Roman Catholic priesthood until 1123 in the Western Church. When a priest married, it was common to give his wife the honorary title of priestess, or presbuterae. This remains true in the Greek Orthodox Church today. The use of the title in itself is insufficient evidence to indicate a 'priestess' who functions as the counterpart of the male priest. While there are a few inscriptional and documentary references to presbuterae or female priests, there is not enough context for these references to build a case for any significant number of women clergy in the early Church. Some of the presbutera clearly refer to the wives of priests; others refer to Montanists or sects of Gnostic groups, who tottered between the outer periphery of Christianity and false doctrine.*

3. **Documents instructing women not to serve as priests or deaconesses.** This is an argument based on inference. The assumption here is that such documents would never have been written if women were not already serving as priests. One letter frequently cited is that by Pope Gelasius (492-96) discouraging women participating at the altar in matters that belong to men. Yet, this letter says nothing about ordination or the women actually being priests. That women might have been ordained as priestesses in some regions, however, is not evidence that this ever was the norm. More likely, it indicates the Church in a region compromising with the practice of competing heretical groups rather than following the Scriptures' guidelines for Church organization.

4. **Ancient art has pictures of women serving as priests.** All the artwork put forward as showing women priests or bishops can just as easily be interpreted in other ways. A woman pictured in the catacombs as raising her hands in prayer is no positive indication that she was a priest, but simply a woman in prayer. Most frequently cited is a mosaic of the basilica in Rome for Sts. Prudentiana and Praxedis, which includes a woman labeled as 'Theodora Episcopa,' interpreted by feminist revisionist historians as 'Bishopess Theodora.' Of all the Church offices for which there is ample documentation, certainly the Bishop of Rome tops the list, yet there is no documentation of a Bishopess Theodora. Revisionists might argue that the patriarchal rulers destroyed all the documents. If so, would they have left

intact a large mosaic in a Roman Church in plain view for all to see? Much more plausible is the explanation given in the Church itself – Theodora was given the honorary title of 'Episcopa' because she was the mother of Pope Paschal I, the Bishop of Rome who built the Church of Sts. Prudentiana and Praxedis.

There is no evidence to show that women were priests or leaders in the earliest Church and were denied such leadership at a later time as the patriarchal forces asserted their power. Those who assert such must, as they themselves say, 're-imagine' and 'reconstruct' history, reading their own predilections into the early Church rather than letting the historical evidence speak for itself.

---

*   Kevin Madigan and Carolyn Osiek, *Ordained Women in the Early Church: A Documentary History*, Baltimore & London: Johns Hopkins University Press, 2005, 8-9, 163.

3

Christian Women in Late Antiquity:
Reverent in Behavior

Titus 2:3

The fourth century began with one of the most cruel and barbarous Christian persecutions in the history of the Roman Empire. The Church had prospered during much of Emperor Diocletian's twenty-year reign from 284 to 305. Though Christianity was still illegal, there was little persecution, and a number of church buildings were beginning to appear. Christians held positions of importance within the army and the government, and Diocletian was tolerant toward Christianity and other religions. Diocletian realized that the Empire had outgrown its government structure and implemented a series of reforms to better administer the Empire. He divided the Empire into East and West. Each part of the Empire was ruled by an 'Augustus' and a subordinate 'Caesar.' Galerius was the Caesar subordinate to Diocletian, who was the Augustus in the Eastern Empire.

Galerius' mother, a pagan priestess, urged her son to suppress the growing Christian religion. With Galerius' prodding, Diocletian issued an edict in 303 to 'tear down the churches to the foundations and to destroy the Sacred Scriptures by fire.' The edict also commanded that those in government or the army who were Christians would be demoted unless they denounced their faith. Further edicts were issued in 303-304. The first ordered the imprisonment of bishops, presbyters, and deacons. The second required that all clergy who would not sacrifice to the Emperor be tortured. The third extended the same imprisonment and torture to the laity. The edicts were enforced with all their cruelty. The entire population of one town was killed because it was Christian. Diocletian abdicated in 305, but when Galerius became Augustus, he continued the persecution for seven more years, until his own death.

During the continued struggle over imperial power, Galerius' son-in-law, Maxentius, tried to assume the position of sole Emperor over both the eastern and western portions of the Empire. Maxentius consolidated his power in Italy and North Africa while Constantine, who succeeded his father as Caesar in the West in 306, was defending the Empire against the Germans on the northern border. Constantine moved south to defeat Maxentius' imperial claims. Along the way Constantine had a vision of a cross of light with the Greek words *en touto niké,* meaning 'in this sign conquer.' Because of this vision, Constantine was convinced that through the sign of the cross he would win over the armies of Maxentius, even though Maxentius' army heavily outnumbered his. Constantine had all the soldiers place a cross on their shields. In October 312, as Constantine and his army crossed the Tiber near the Milvian Bridge outside of Rome, they successfully defeated Maxentius' army. In February the next year, 313, Constantine and Licinius, whom Galerius had appointed Caesar of the West, jointly issued the Edict of Milan, which for the first time gave Christianity legal status within the Empire. By the Edict of Milan, Christianity was no longer an illegal religion. Constantine later became full Emperor in his own right and took an imperial interest in the Christian Church.

The new position of Christianity within the Empire affected women in a number of ways. Constantine implemented legal protections for women and marriage. Women could now travel freely within the Empire for Christian purposes, and pilgrimages to Jerusalem and Biblical sites began. The ascetic life, a life separated from the things of the world, became more highly valued. There are rich sources documenting these changes and providing insights to the personal lives of Christian women during this period.

Legal Changes Concerning Women

Though Christianity was no longer persecuted by the State, the alliance and even blending of the State and the Church weakened the Church's spiritual power and moral authority. The Edict of Milan (313) gave Christianity legal status within the Empire, but not until the Theodosian Decrees of the 390s was Christianity established as the official religion. Pagan Greco-Roman civic rites were abolished and no longer state-supported, but paganism persisted in the beliefs of many. All too often the Church and its leaders became pawns of imperial political intrigue, and the Church itself adopted some pagan ideas and practices as its own. Though nominally Christian, the lives and manner of rule of Constantine and many of the emperors who followed him failed to manifest a life transformed by the resurrected Christ.

Beyond dispute, however, is the fact that Constantine and emperors after him did try to implement laws that reflected Christian morality. Church historian Philip Schaff called Constantine the turning point for enacting Christian justice. Crucifixion was abolished as a punishment; gladiatorial games and cruel rites were prohibited; infanticide was discouraged; the emancipation of slaves, benevolence to the poor, and clemency to prisoners were all encouraged.

Many of the changes in Roman law had direct effects on women. In 321, Constantine granted women the same right as men to control their respective properties, except in landed estates. The law respected their modesty and prohibited their being summoned to appear in person before a public tribunal. From Constantine on, the rape of consecrated virgins and widows was punishable by death. Constantine abolished penalties against celibacy and childlessness, which had been in f[orce] He also made legal the Old Testament proh[ibition] degrees of consanguinity. Marriage was protect[ed] forbidding concubinage, and punishing adulter[y] was under the jurisdiction of the civil authoritie[s] did marriage become a rite of the Church). mothers certain guardianship rights previously

Society continued to be patriarchally o[rganized] influence women received greater legal pr[otection] the most influential women in the early c[hurch] found in the fourth and fifth centuries, cent[uries] historians assert the patriarchal Church beg[an] removing them from positions of leadership. Many women of wealth and substance used their positions to minister to others and advance the cause of Christ. They labored in the sphere in which God had called them and made a difference in their world.

Early Pilgrims to the Holy Land: Empress Helena and Egeria

Constantine's mother, Helena (c. 250-330), was the first Christian empress-mother in history. Little is known about her personal life, not even where she was born, but Helena left her mark on the Christian Church. She was of humble birth; one source said she was the daughter of an innkeeper.

Old King Cole's Daughter?

Nothing is known about Queen Helena's youth, but later tradition had her born in Britain and the daughter of the King of Britain, Cole of Colchester. The legend, made popular by Geoffrey of Monmouth in the twelfth century, was that King Cole made an alliance with Constantius to avoid further war between the Britons and Romans. Constantius then married King Cole's daughter Helena. A remote source of the legend might have been the 5th-century historian Sozomen's statement that Constantine converted to Christianity in Britain. Otherwise, there is no evidence that Helena was from Britain — or old King Cole's daughter!

Constantius, a young officer in the army, apparently took Helena as his concubine. Marriage was out of the question since Constantius' family, related on his mother's side to the Emperor Claudius, was of a higher social position than was Helena's. Some sources said that Constantius married Helena after their son Constantine was born. Such arrangements were not unusual in Roman times.

Neither was it unusual when, after twenty years of marriage (or concubinage), Constantius divorced Helena when he was chosen Caesar in 292. Remember, she was of a lower social class than he. The Augustus Maximian required the divorce for political reasons – so that Constantius could marry his stepdaughter Theodora.

Did Helena Discover the True Cross?

Helena's pilgrimage to the Holy Land is associated in legend with her discovery of the wood of the cross of Christ. Is there evidence to support this discovery? The evidence (decades after Helena and often conflicting) may be summarized in chronological order as follows:

- Eusebius, c. 338, in writing of Helena's pilgrimage does not mention the wood of the cross.

- Cyril of Jerusalem, c. 346, in a sermon states that the wood of the cross is 'visible among us still today,' but doesn't mention Helena.

- Chrysostom, 387, speaks of the wood of the true cross, but not Helena.

- Sulpicius Severus, c. 395, was the first to say that Helena discovered the place of Christ's passion and three crosses. The true cross was identified from among the three by the wood's alleged capacity to miraculously restore life when the wood was placed on a dead body.

- Ambrose, 395, said Helena was inspired by the Spirit to seek the true cross and was able to identify it by the inscription on it. He said two of the nails were used by the Emperor – one to fix his crown and the other as a bit for his horse's bridle.

- Rufinus, c. 400, said that Helena's journey was inspired by God and the place of Christ's Passion was miraculously revealed. The three crosses were found jumbled, with the title separate. The true cross was identified through the healing of a sick lady.

- Paulinus of Nola, c. 403, wrote that Helena discovered the place of the Passion by testimony of Jews and Christians in the city. Though pieces were taken from the cross, it continued to be preserved.

- Jerome, c. 406, mentioned one nail from the cross being in the Emperor's crown and another in the bridle. He said images of Jove and Venus stood on the site of Jesus' crucifixion until the time of Constantine.

- Socrates, c. 430, said Helena was told in a night vision to go to Jerusalem. Following the vision, she found the site of the Passion, though with difficulty.

Years later, when Constantine succeeded his father as Caesar in 306, he apparently brought his mother to court. Coins were struck with a female head on one side and a laurel crown on the other with the inscription, 'most noble lady Helena.' Though later stories ascribe Constantine's Christian conversion to Helena's influence, the Church historian Eusebius wrote that Helena became a Christian through Constantine's influence.

Under circumstances not at all clear, in 326 Constantine had his son Crispus as well as his wife Fausta put to death. Helena bitterly complained about these events. Possibly she convinced Constantine of his sin, and he sent his mother on her famous pilgrimage as some penance for his wrongdoing. Whatever the exact cause, when she was nearly 80 years old, Helena made a pilgrimage to the Holy Land to give thanks to God for His mercies to her family.

Constantine had begun a large building program establishing churches on sacred sites throughout the Empire. He had located the debris-covered place of Jesus' burial in Jerusalem, which had been converted into a shrine to pagan gods. Constantine ordered the area cleared and purified, and in 326 began building the Church of the Holy Sepulchre. Constantine gave his mother seemingly unlimited supplies of money for her pilgrimage, and she freely spent it on charity for the poor and bonuses for the soldiers along the way. She freed prisoners and political exiles and gave lavish offerings to the churches she attended. She dedicated the Church of the Nativity in Bethlehem. On the Mt. of Olives she dedicated a Church of the Ascension and erected a statue of Christ. Helena's reverent, charitable visitation of sites connected with the life of Jesus became an example of pilgrimage that has been followed through the centuries. As many queens after her, she used her royal position to further the cause of Christ.

In 381, fifty-six years after Helena made her pilgrimage to the Holy Land, a Spanish lady named Egeria began her three-year journey from Spain to the Holy Land. Little is known about Egeria herself. She apparently was a lady of some wealth and leisure to be able to make such a journey. Some think she was a nun writing to her fellow nuns back in Spain. At the time of her travels, the Emperor was Theodosius the Great, who was from Spain. Possibly Egeria had some connections with Spanish people at the court in Constantinople. Theodosius' wife and niece, Aelia Flacilla and Serena, were staunch Christians who would have shared Egeria's interests.

Though the beginning and ending of Egeria's journal have not survived, the middle portion is rich with descriptions of her travels and experiences from Mt. Sinai through her long stay in Jerusalem.[1] Egeria's purpose was to visit places where Biblical events occurred and to deepen her understanding of the Scriptures. Everywhere she went she found religious leaders and local guides who showed her the sites, and then she read the Scriptures focusing on those sites. Always she was eager to see the places

---

1   Society for the Promotion of Christian Knowledge's 1919 edition of *The Pilgrimage of Etheria* [sic] can be found at http://www.ccel.org/m/mcclure/etheria/etheria.htm.

as they were from the Scripture's viewpoint. She climbed to the top of Mt. Sinai where the glory of God had shown. Monks showed her where they thought the golden calf had stood, as well as the burning bush – whose roots they claimed were still there! Egeria visited Mt. Nebo, where Moses died, and Haran, where she was shown what purported to be Job's tomb and Abraham's house. Sometimes Roman soldiers provided escorts for her travels, and monks and religious leaders provided hospitality.

The most interesting portion of Egeria's journal is her detailed account of the worship practices of the Jerusalem Christians. There were six churches in Jerusalem associated with events in the life of Christ. Daily and weekly services at each church focused on the event particular for each site, but an annual series of celebrations also developed in accord with the liturgical year. Egeria described in detail the celebration of Holy Week – the Scriptures read, the vigils, the fasts, the processions. On Friday, the 'wood of the cross' was brought out, and pilgrims filed by the wood for hours. The three-hour service at noon was most meaningful, as Scripture was read the entire time and hymns sung, and the people were shown that everything prophesied about Jesus' suffering and death had been fulfilled. All were moved to tears to hear of the Lord's suffering for them. Egeria found a greater emphasis on the preaching of Scripture in Jerusalem than she found at home. People were always learning about the Bible. People coming to Jerusalem from elsewhere learned about the Scriptures connected with the various feasts of the Church and took this understanding of the Christian year back to their home churches. At a time when few people had a copy of the Scriptures for themselves, the liturgy and practices of the Church in Jerusalem increased the people's understanding of the Scriptures and their faith.

Egeria's descriptions are so detailed and accurate that archaeologists have used her journal in planning their work. For example, she wrote that St. Peter's house near the synagogue in Capernaum was made into a church, just as archaeologists are now able to show. Behind everything Egeria did was a spiritual purpose – to verify and confirm her faith in the truth of Scripture through contact with the physical places in which the Bible had recorded God had particularly worked. She sought to meet and pray with those in the region who best exemplified the Christian life.

A Praying Mother and her Son

Probably the one person from the early centuries of the Church who influenced later Church history more than any other was Augustine (354-430), who became Bishop of Hippo in North Africa. Augustine himself, however, recognized that to a great degree his Christian faith was an answer to the prayers of his mother Monica. Most of what is known about Monica is found in Augustine's *Confessions*. There Augustine described

Monica as God's servant, 'who brought me to birth both in her body, so that I was brought into the light of time, and in her heart, so that I was born into the light of eternity.'[2]

Monica was born into a Christian family about 333. There were several sisters in the family, and Monica was cared for by an old maidservant who had cared for her father when he was a child. This servant was noted for her Christian and moral character and cared for all the daughters in the family. She was more important than their mother in the instruction and training she provided. She had a 'holy severity in administering correction,' restraining the young girls' appetites with her authority. In the days before sophisticated water purification, diluted wine was a common drink. However, the servant did not allow the girls to drink except at mealtimes so that they would not develop a taste for wine. Despite the servant's efforts, however, Monica developed a weakness for wine. Whenever she was sent to bring wine from the cask, she would drink a little. This began just for the mischief of it. The older servant didn't see Monica do this, but a servant girl did and taunted Monica. These taunts brought healing to Monica and kept her from this practice. In her childhood home, Monica learned modesty, sobriety, and obedience to her parents.

Monica married Patricius, who was not a Christian. He was not tremendously wealthy but had a few acres and servants and was on the town council in the North African town of Thagaste. Patricius could be both kind and quick-tempered, and, acceptable to the mores of the day, often unfaithful to Monica. Monica truly lived a life patterned on 1 Peter 3:1-2, 'wives be subject to your own husbands, so that even if some do not obey the word, they may be won without a word by the conduct of their wives when they see your respectful and pure conduct.' As Augustine later wrote, Monica spoke of Christ to Patricius 'through her virtues' by which Christ had made her beautiful. She never quarreled with Patricius about his infidelities, hoping that once he converted to Christianity he would become chaste. She never opposed him when he was angry but waited until he calmed down to explain her actions, if they had caused the offense. Patricius could not help but respect and love her.

Monica was a peacemaker who often reconciled quarreling people, never revealing information to another unless it would help them. When Monica first married, her mother-in-law was hostile to her, largely because of gossip spread by the maidservants. Yet Monica's consistent respectfulness won over her mother-in-law, and she denounced the gossipy maidservants to Patricius.

---

2   Augustine. *Confessions*, Book IX.

Monica also counseled other wives about their marriages. She told them, only partly in jest, that the brutality of their husbands was due in part to their own sharp tongues. The marriage contract was binding and made wives servants of their husbands; women should not stand up in rebellion to their husbands because of this contract. The women were astounded. They knew Patricius could be a violent man, but he never beat or harmed Monica in any way. Women who followed Monica's advice were grateful. Those who did not and stood up to their husbands were often maltreated by them.

Monica was a servant of servants, caring for all as if they were her children. She cared for her parents and her family with Christian devotion. She brought up three children – Augustine, his brother Navigius, and a sister traditionally named Perpetua – and endured travail as they wandered astray. Yet, before her death, all were bound together in the community of Christ. Patricius converted to Christianity before his death, was baptized, and led a life befitting a Christian thereafter. When Patricius died Augustine was 16, and starting to become wayward. Patricius' salvation encouraged Monica just at the time Augustine's rebelliousness began.

Patricius never prevented Monica's Christian instruction of the children. Augustine recounted that as children he and his siblings were instructed in the Christian faith as catechumen 'about the humility of our Lord God, coming down to our pride.' When he was a small boy, Augustine was deathly ill with a fever and begged for baptism, which instruction in the Christian faith had well prepared him for. He became better, however, and Monica deferred the baptism, thinking he might as a youth commit sin that the waters of baptism would need to wash away. Since it was commonly thought that the waters of baptism washed away sin and that major sins committed after baptism would have no means of remission, the practice had developed of delaying baptism as long as possible.

Patricius was little concerned about the morality of his children, so it was Monica who warned the youthful Augustine about the sins of fornication and adultery. Augustine scorned her advice. However, even though Monica was aware of her son's emerging sexuality, she took no measures to try to restrain this by seeking marriage for him. Both Monica and Patricius shared worldly ambitions for Augustine, and they looked forward to the day he could marry into wealth and assume a public role in the world. No austere restrictions were placed on Augustine's behavior, but he was encouraged to seek a literary education in rhetoric so that he could advance to the law courts.

Augustine began seeking meaning and purpose in life more in secular education than in Christian teaching. For a time he became a Manichean. Manichaeism was a dualistic, syncretistic, philosophical religion from

Persia, which was similar to Gnosticism in its emphasis on intellectual knowledge. Monica recognized that Augustine was spiritually 'in the grip of death' by his adherence to this false faith. She refused to let her son live in the house any more, so repulsed was she by the error of the Manicheans. About that time, however, she had a dream encouraging her to allow Augustine to eat at her table. The vision was of her weeping for Augustine's perdition, and a young man appearing asked her the cause of her weeping. The young man told her to observe that where she was, Augustine was also. When Monica told Augustine about the vision, he tried to twist the vision to say she would join him in the Manichean belief. She responded, 'No, the vision was, you will be where I am!' Monica's quick reply affected Augustine more than the dream itself had. Monica took comfort in this dream that predicted the joy of Augustine's ultimate salvation, though he continued to wander in unbelief for nine more years.

Monica went to the bishop and asked him to talk to Augustine about the Manichean errors, but the bishop refused. He assured Monica that though Augustine was still unready to learn and was caught up with the novelties of his heresy, yet 'it cannot be that the son of these tears shall perish.'

Augustine decided to go to Rome to further his career, but Monica tearfully begged him not to. She was fearful that in the decadence and corruption of Rome he would be forever lost to the gospel. Augustine deceived Monica and slipped away to Rome without her knowing. Monica's prayers that Augustine not go to Rome were not answered, but the deepest longings of her heart were answered. That Augustine did not die when fearfully ill in Rome was undoubtedly due to Monica's faithful prayers, and it was in Italy that Augustine finally became a Christian.

Monica later followed Augustine to Milan. She found her son depressed at not being able to find the truth, but no longer a Manichean. In Milan Monica attended Ambrose's church and grew under his ministry. In North Africa she had been accustomed to bring bread, wine, and cakes to offer to the memorials of the saints, but Ambrose banned such pagan customs, and Monica accepted this without dispute. Ambrose appreciated Monica's religious fervor and praised her to Augustine.

Finally, when Augustine was 30 years old, Monica found a wealthy wife for her son. A wealthy wife was necessary to help pay for the many expenses for public donations and buildings expected of a man of position in that society. The girl chosen was about 10 at the time, so Augustine had to wait two more years to marry, twelve being the legal age for marriage. Possibly the girl was from a Christian family, since Monica was involved in the choosing. Monica hoped that once married, Augustine would then become a Christian. Augustine had been faithfully living with a concubine for many years and had a son, Adeodatus, by her. The concubine, whom Augustine never named, apparently was of a social class beneath him and was sent away when Augustine's marriage was arranged. Young Adeodatus had been raised a Christian, so his mother was probably a Christian. She was torn by grief when she had to return to Africa, leaving her son with Augustine, and she vowed never to marry.

When Augustine did come to faith in Christ, he was baptized by Ambrose in the church where Monica had often prayed for his soul. Her grief turned to joy. With her son's salvation, she felt she was no longer needed on earth. When Augustine, Monica, and their group decided to return to Africa, they stopped at the Italian port of Ostia. Augustine and Monica conversed together about eternity, recalling that 'eye has not seen, nor ear heard, neither have entered into the heart of man, the things which God hath prepared for them that love Him' (1 Cor. 2:9, KJV). They shared a vision of the Eternal, climbing step by step beyond the corporeal senses so that this world and its delights became worthless. Monica shortly after became ill of a fever and died before sailing. She was 56, and Augustine was 33.

At a time of growing asceticism in the Church, Monica was the example of a godly wife, who sought the good of her spouse in God's way. She was a chaste, humble widow who was liberal in almsgiving, avoided vain and gossipy chatter, and sought God in Scripture and unceasing prayer. Though as a mother she was marred by a lack of firm discipline and by having worldly ambitions for her son, she continues to be an example of a mother whose heart for God and unceasing prayers for her children were constant. She lived to see her son become a Christian. She could not know the deep influence her son would have on Christians in his own day and for centuries to come.

Christian Women and the Ascetic Life

There had been those who chose an ascetic life since the earliest days of the Church, but monasticism itself, the idea of total separation from the world, did not develop until the second half of the third century. Implicit in the development of monasticism was the idea that the material world and the flesh were evil and that moral perfection could be obtained through separation from the world and all the normal associations with the world. Historically, such an isolated life was first begun by St. Anthony when he left his life of wealth and ease and went to live in the Egyptian desert. Colonies of hermits developed in the desert soon after. Athanasius wrote a life of Anthony which spread the hermitic and monastic idea far beyond the borders of Egypt.

Numerous sisters or daughters of Church leaders, as well as some wealthy Christian women, established monasteries for women during this period. Ambrose's sister headed a monastery of women in Rome.

Constantine's daughter established a community of virgins of St. Agnes in Rome. Constantine himself founded convents of women in Jerusalem so that every church had its convent. Melania the Elder and Younger from Rome as well as empress Eudoxia from Constantinople also established monasteries for women in Jerusalem. Augustine's sister headed a monastery of women in Hippo, in North Africa. Benedict of Nursa's sister Scholastica headed a monastery of women.

In 423 Augustine wrote a letter to the nuns at the monastery at Hippo, of which his sister was prioress before her death, rebuking them for their turbulent behavior, showing dissatisfaction with his sister's successor. He concluded his letter laying out rules for the monastery. These rules were among the earliest monastic rules written. Centuries later, Benedict adapted them for his rule at Monte Cassino. Augustine wrote that foundational to the monastery should be the spirit of oneness of all in the community with each other and with God. Those who entered the monastery with worldly goods should cheerfully have them become common property. All in the monastery were to be equal, but the pride lurking behind such equality must be avoided. Those who had much and gave all to the poor and yet were proud of their good works had undone those very good works by their pride. The monastery became hurtful to the poor if those who were once impoverished now lifted up their heads with pride because they now associated with the rich.

The nuns were to be regular in their prayers at the appointed hours and times. The oratory, or place of prayer, was to be used only for prayer and for no other purpose, so that those wishing to pray at unscheduled times might use it freely. As far as health permitted, fasting and abstinence from meat and drink should be followed. At the mealtime, there should be no talking but only listening to the reading: '... let not your mouths alone be exercised in receiving food, let your ears be also occupied in receiving the word of God.' Those who were weak or delicate because of their early training should be treated out of consideration for their infirmity, without others thinking they, too, should receive such treatment.

Clothes should be inconspicuous; behavior rather than clothes should be designed to please others. The hair should be totally covered, neither disheveled nor adorned. When going out, the nuns were told they should always go together. The prioress, not the individual nun, should choose who went out together. When going abroad, eye contact might briefly be made with a man, but the eyes were never to become fixed with a man. Wanton eyes should be avoided, for wanton eyes led to wanton hearts, even if no physical contact was made. If any was observed making such eye contact with a man, for the healing of her own soul, she should be rebuked by her sisters.

All clothes were to be held in a common store place, as was done with the food. If a gift of clothes was brought for a particular nun from her family, this, too, should be placed in the common storeroom. If anyone concealed a gift privately, she was guilty of theft. Clothes should be washed only when approved by the prioress, 'lest the indulgence of undue solicitude about spotless raiment produce inward stains upon your souls.' Baths should be taken not more than once a month, unless an illness required otherwise, and not fewer than three should go to the bath at any one time.

Quarrels should be unknown, and if they occurred, repentance and forgiveness should be swift. There should be a spiritual love among all in the community. The prioress was as a mother of the community and should be obeyed. She must see that all the rules were observed. Augustine concluded his letter with the following hope:

> The Lord grant that you may yield loving submission to all these rules, as persons enamoured of spiritual beauty, and diffusing a sweet savour of Christ by means of a good conversation, not as bondwomen under the law, but as established in freedom under grace. That you may, however, examine yourselves by this treatise as by a mirror, and may not through forgetfulness neglect anything, let it be read over by you once a week...[3]

The emphasis on the virtue of the ascetic life which became so strong in the fourth century continued throughout the ensuing Middle Ages. Women (or men) who lived married lives and reared children were not considered as holy and virtuous as those who chose an ascetic life. Not until the Reformation was the virtue of family life and motherhood recovered for the Church. One historian summarized the skewed exaltation of virginity as follows:

> ...it must be acknowledged that the Nicene and post-Nicene Fathers spent their strength in advocating and glorifying an unnatural virginity – a pitiable substitute for a higher social morality and purer morals for the ordinary individual. Without a first-hand acquaintance with those ancient writers, it is impossible to conceive to what a degree the idea of celibacy was exalted in their teachings. It overshadowed everything else. It overturned every establishment of reason. It vitiated all the pure springs of life. It proceeded on the assumption that everything that is natural is monstrously evil.[4]

---

3   Augustine, Letter CCII, *Nicene and Post-Nicene Fathers of the Christian Church*, Grand Rapids: Wm. B. Eerdmans, 1988 reprint, pp. 563-8. Online at http://www.ccel.org/ccel/schaff/npnf101. vii.1.CCXI.html.

4   Rev. Alfred Brittain and Mitchell Carroll. *Women of Early Christianity*. New York: Gordon Press, 1976 reprint of 1907 edition, p. 113.

Celibacy, submission, and poverty were thought to be the cures for lust, pride, and avarice. True holiness by and through God's grace was replaced by a salvation of personal endeavor, and the spiritual sphere was all-important, to the neglect and denial of the physical and material. Ascetics were elevated to a super-spiritual status above the common Christians who were married and had families.

Aristocratic Christian Roman Women

Extensive information remains about the activities and lives of wealthy Christian women of the fourth century. Many of these women corresponded with Christian leaders of the day, and the letters of Jerome, Chrysostom, Augustine, Basil, and others to these women have survived. Unfortunately, few of the letters of the women survive. Reading the letters to these women is like listening to one half of a telephone conversation – we can learn much, but there is more we would like to hear from the other side! Nevertheless, the correspondence reveals women with a rich spiritual life active in scholarly and philanthropic activities and supporting Christian ministries and ministers throughout the Roman Empire. Ironically, though a few of the Church fathers' polemical writings have scathing remarks about women's intelligence and discernment, the same fathers, in their personal dealings with the women, credited them with keen intelligence and spiritual acumen.

By the fourth century, there were families whose members had been Christians for several generations. Among these was the family of Macrina the Younger (c. 327-379). Macrina was named after her grandmother, Macrina the Elder. Macrina the Elder had married into a wealthy family of Pontus and was dearly remembered by many for a generation after her death in 340. She and her husband had suffered persecution for their Christian faith during the Diocletian persecutions and had taken refuge in the forests of Pontus for a considerable time. Her granddaughter, Macrina the Younger, was a very beautiful woman, as well as intelligent and learned. She had memorized the psalms and the ethical portions of Solomon's writings as a child. The oldest of 10 children, Macrina helped her mother Emmelia administer the family's large estate and care for the other nine children after her father's death. At age 12 she was betrothed to a jurist of a distinguished family. When her fiancé died, she refused to marry anyone else, though she had many suitors, and chose to devote herself to Christian life and ministry. She claimed that betrothal to her fiancé was equivalent to marriage, therefore she would not remarry. She said her beloved was on a far journey, and it would be wrong to take a husband while he was traveling far; she would rejoin her husband in heaven. Macrina's younger brother Peter became Bishop of Sebaste. Her more famous brother Basil became Bishop of Caesarea, while her brother

Gregory was a leading theologian. Both Basil and Gregory were defenders of Nicene theology.

Macrina's brother Gregory wrote the *Life of Macrina*, as well as a dialogue with her, *On the Soul and the Resurrection*. How much of what Gregory recorded were Macrina's actual words and how much were Gregory's own theological musings cannot be determined at this date. However, because of the closeness of Macrina to her famous brothers and her high level of education, her own theological perspectives and passions were undoubtedly to some degree reflected in the dialogue and Gregory's biography of her. Gregory presented his sister as a philosopher and wondered whether he should even call her a woman, since she had intellectually advanced far beyond the level that men thought women could attain. He recalled Macrina's influence on his brother Basil, after he returned to Asia Minor from his schooling in Athens:

> Macrina took him over and lured him so quickly to the goal of philosophy that he withdrew from the worldly show and began to look down upon acclaim through oratory and went over to this life full of labor for one's own hand to perform, providing for himself, through his complete poverty, a mode of living that would, without impediment, lead to virtue.[5]

Basil and Macrina established separate monasteries for men and women near their home. Macrina's was the first monastery for women established in the East, and wealthy women of Pontus and Cappadocia were attracted to the sisterhood there. Macrina also established a hospital, where she ministered to the physical as well as the spiritual health of the people.

Gregory recorded that Macrina in her last hours encouraged him. Recalling the prayers of their parents for him, she challenged him in his Christian work: 'Churches summon you as an ally and director. Do you not see the grace of God in all this?... Do you fail to recognize the cause of such great blessings, that it is your parents' prayers that are lifting you up so high, that you have little or no equipment within yourself for your success?' Gregory wrote that Macrina 'seemed to be hurrying toward Him whom she desired, that she might speedily be loosed from the chains of the body.' He recorded her dying prayer as follows:

> Thou, O Lord, has freed us from the fear of death. Thou has made the end of this life the beginning to us of true life. Thou for a season dost rest our bodies in sleep and wake them again. Thou givest our earth, which Thou hast fashioned with Thy hands, the earth to keep in safety. One day Thou will take again what Thou hast given, transfiguring with

5   *Life of Macrina*, ch. 6, as quoted in Philip Rousseau, '"Learned Women" and the Development of a Christian Culture in Late Antiquity,' *Symbolae Osloenses*, vol. 70, 1995, pp. 116-47. Also see http://www.ccel.org/ccel/pearse/morefathers/files/gregory_macrina_1_life.htm.

immortality and gracing our mortal remains. Thou hast saved us from the curse and from sin, having become both for our sake.

Thou hast shown us the way of resurrection, having broken the gates of hell, and how to overcome him who had the power of death – the Devil. Thou hast given a sign to those that fear Thee in the symbol of the Holy Cross, to destroy the adversary and save our life. O God eternal to whom I have been attached from my mother's womb, whom my soul has loved with all its strength, to whom I have dedicated both my flesh and my soul from my youth up until now – do Thou give me an angel of light to conduct me to the place of refreshment, where is the water of rest, in the bosom of the holy father.

Thou didst break the flaming sword and didst restore to Paradise the man that was crucified with Thee and implored Thy mercy. Remember me, too, in Thy kingdom, because I, too, was crucified with Thee, having nailed my flesh to the cross for fear of Thee. And of Thy judgments have I been afraid. Let not the terrible chasm separate me from Thy elect. Nor let the slanderer stand against me in the way; nor let my sin be found before Thine eyes, if in anything I have sinned in word or deed or thought, or been led astray by the weakness of our nature.

O Thou who hast power on earth to forgive sins, forgive me, that I may be refreshed and may be found before Thee when I put off my body, without defilement on my soul. But may my soul be received unto Thy Hands spotless and undefiled, as an offering before Thee.[6]

In the western part of the Empire, a group of wealthy women in Rome were also devoting themselves to an ascetic or monastic life. When Athanasius came to Rome as an exile in 340, he brought news of Anthony of Egypt, who had disposed of all his possessions and gone to live an isolated, ascetic life in the Egyptian desert. One of the people deeply influenced by Athanasius' accounts of Anthony was Marcella (325-410). Marcella, then a teenager, was from a wealthy and ancient Roman family; but as soon as she heard of Anthony, she longed for the ascetic life.

Marcella married as her parents arranged; but when her husband died a few months after the wedding, she refused to remarry, even to a very wealthy suitor. She lived with her mother in their palatial Aventine palace, but in the utmost simplicity. When the Biblical scholar Jerome came to Rome in 382, Marcella sought him out to learn as much of the Bible from him as possible. She began a ladies' Bible study in her home, and her house became a center for Bible study, prayer and psalm singing.

Marcella had a seemingly insatiable hunger for the Scriptures and exhausted Jerome with her numerous questions. When Jerome left Rome, Marcella continued to send him letters full of her questions about Scriptures and details of Hebrew exegesis. Over fifteen of Jerome's replies

---

6   As quoted in Edith Deen's *Great Women of the Christian Faith*. A Barbour Book, 1959, pp. 13-14.
      Also available online at http://www.tertullian.org/fathers/gregory_macrina_1_life.htm.

to her questions remain.[7] They cover topics such as the ten names given God in the Hebrew Scriptures; an explanation of the untranslated Hebrew words *Alleluia, Amen, Maranatha* and *Selah*; an explanation of the ephod and teraphim; how Jerome collated the Greek and Hebrew Old Testament when making his Latin translation; and what was the 'sin against the Holy Ghost.' Marcella's knowledge of Scripture astonished Jerome, and in her thirst for knowledge she pressed Jerome to teach her more. At one point Jerome wrote her in protest.

Even when Jerome was in Rome, people and priests came to Marcella to consult her about the meaning of Scripture. She had scribes copying the Scripture, and her home became the local Bible society, the place where people could obtain copies of the Scripture. When Origen's *On First Principles* was first translated into Latin, Marcella pointed out heretical passages to the Pope, who then condemned it. In 410, when Marcella was 85, Alaric the Goth sacked Rome. The Goths came to her home, demanding gold, but she said she had none and showed them her poor clothes. Thinking she was concealing her wealth from them, they whipped her severely. Marcella died a few days later.

Marcella's influence on other women of the Roman aristocracy was great. It was Marcella who led Paula (347-404), the influential patroness of Jerome, to Christianity. Paula's ancestry itself was legendary. Her husband was of the Julian family and related to Aeneas, the Trojan hero who became a founder of Rome. Her parents were related to the Scipios, Gracchi, and Agamemnon himself. Paula was married when she was seventeen and had four daughters and a son. When her husband died, she was overwhelmed with grief. Marcella, her neighbor, urged her to consider Christianity. This gave purpose to Paula's life again. Like Marcella, Paula began to live simply and give her wealth to charity. Two of Paula's daughters died shortly after Paula's commitment to the ascetic life. The eldest daughter, Bresilla, was quite a beauty and delighted in nice things. Her husband died seven months after her marriage, and Bresilla became very ill. She was converted during that illness, and Jerome began counseling her in the ascetic life. Bresilla tried to live as an ascetic, but weakened further and died. Paula was very distraught at her daughter's death and fainted at Bresilla's funeral.

Jerome was heavily criticized for his closeness with Paula and the way he guided her and Bresilla in asceticism. The Roman clergy investigated, and though they could find no misconduct, advised Jerome to leave Rome. The clergy were undoubtedly also jealous of Jerome's growing influence in Rome and the belief of some that Jerome should become Pope. Previously Jerome and Paula had talked of going to Jerusalem together, but after the

---

7   Letters 23-9, 32, 34, 37-38, 41-4, 46, 59.

clerical investigation, they decided to go separately. Jerome left first, and then Paula followed at a slower pace. She took her daughter Eustochium with her but left her young son in Rome. Jerome said the abandonment of her children was against nature, but was in keeping with Jesus' words in Mark 10:29-30.

When a teenager, Eustochium had decided to remain a virgin and live an ascetic life, and Jerome wrote her a long letter of encouragement with detailed advice about asceticism.[8] Eustochium was perfectly suited to join her mother in the monastic life in the East. In their travels east, Paula and Eustochium visited the places associated with Christian history, especially concerning Christian women, beginning with a stop at the tomb of Flavia Domitilla. In Palestine, they visited Caesarea, associated with Philip's daughters (Acts 21:8-9); Joppa, where Peter raised Dorcas (Acts 9:36-41); the home of Mary and Martha in Bethany (Luke 10:38-42); the well where Jesus spoke with the Samaritan woman (John 4:7-30); and, of course, the places associated with the life of Jesus. At various sites, Paula experienced ecstatic visions. At the tomb of Christ, she rolled about on the floor in an ecstatic frenzy and licked the stone where Jesus' body had lain. For a woman who had denied all normal physical needs, Paula evidently still felt the need of a connection with the material, physical world touched by the physical, historical Christ. Paula and her daughter Eustochium finally joined Jerome in Bethlehem.

Paula's wealth was immense; she even owned entire towns. After her conversion she began spending her fortune (and that of her children) on charity. She founded and headed three convents in Palestine as well as a monastery headed by Jerome. She also established a church and a hospice to shelter pilgrims, orphans, the sick, poor, and elderly.

While helping and reaching out to others, Paula continued to live an ascetic life, denying herself the luxuries with which she was born, and even priding herself that in her denial of the flesh she never bathed! (Hopefully she meant she never attended the Roman baths, not that she never washed). Jerome held up Paula as an example of how the wealthy patrician lady could be remade into a lady of grace. He praised her submissive and silent spirit which accepted the authority of men (namely his!).

The scholarly study of Scripture was Paula's major interest. She knew Greek and learned Hebrew so that she could sing the psalms in the original Hebrew. Paula was the main sponsor of Jerome's work, and he heavily relied on her financially. In Bethlehem Jerome was working on his translation of the Bible into common or vulgar Latin (hence the name the 'Vulgate' translation) instigated by

---

8   Letter XXII is probably the most famous of Jerome's letters, full of Scripture references and detailed advice on the motives and methods of the monastic and ascetic life. Online at http://www.ccel.org/fathers2/NPNF2-06/Npnf2-06-03.htm#P583_110510.

Pope Damasus in 382. Paula paid for Jerome's rare manuscripts and books for his Biblical studies. A major task in Paula's convents was the copying of manuscripts. Indeed, that monasteries should become the center for manuscript copying as they were in the Middle Ages was a practice actually begun by Paula. Jerome dedicated several of his translations and commentaries to Paula and her daughter Eustochium, noting,

> There are people who take offense at seeing your names at the beginning of my works. These people do not know that while Barak trembled, Deborah saved Israel; that Esther delivered from supreme peril the children of God. I passed over in silence Anna and Elizabeth and all other holy women of the Gospel, but humble starts compared with the luminary, Mary. Is it not to women that our Lord appeared after His resurrection? Yes, and the men could then blush for not having sought what the women had found.[9]

Jerome believed that education, especially education in the Scriptures, was important for women. Paula's daughter-in-law wrote Jerome asking him for advice on how to raise her daughter, Paula's namesake, and Jerome

---

A Virgin at the Center of Controversy

Demetrias was from the Anician family, one of the wealthiest families of ancient Rome. Her father died just before Alaric attacked Rome in 410. As Alaric approached Rome, the family fled to their property in Africa, watching Rome burn as they set sail.

At the age of fourteen Demetrias decided to take a vow of virginity, and her entire family and the churches in Rome supported her decision. Demetrias' grandmother Proba wrote letters to the Church leaders Pelagius, Jerome, and possibly Augustine for advice to Demetrias as she took this important step. Jerome's letter was very similar to the letter he wrote to Eustochium many years before, urging the practices of prayer, fasting, obedience and constant industry as well as study of the Scriptures. Pelagius wrote a long letter to Demetrias giving guidelines on the importance of choosing a moral life without sin, and stressing that a moral life was a choice the innately good person could make. He held out the possibility of sinless perfection for the Christian after baptism. Augustine wrote a letter to Demetrias' mother warning her of those who deny the grace of God and teach that virtue lies within man's nature apart from God's grace. The correspondence surrounding Demetrias revealed the key points at issue in the Pelagian-Augustinian controversy over the nature of man's will and the necessity for God's grace.*

---

* Information on the letters surrounding Demetrias may be found in Andrew S. Jacobs, 'Writing Demetrias: Ascetic Logic in Ancient Christianity', *Church History*, Vol. 69, No. 4 (Dec. 2000), pp.719-48. The letters themselves are Augustine, Letters 150, 188; Jerome, Letter 130; and Pelagius, 'Letter to Demetrias.'

---

9   *Preface to Commentary on Sophonius* as quoted in H.J. Mozans, *Woman in Science*, New York and London: D. Appleton & Co., 1913, p. 34.

Jerome - on raising children

wrote an extensive letter outlining a program for little Paula's education. Jerome recommended that the little girl should hear and speak only what related to the fear of God. She should not sing worldly songs, but only the Psalms. She should be kept away from lustful boys and worldly maidservants. Among her first toys should be tiny boxwood or ivory letters to play with. As she grew older, she should be given a stylus and wax to begin writing the letters herself. Prizes should be given to her as she mastered spelling different words. She should always be praised in her learning so as to encourage excitement in intellectual achievements. Early she should be taught Greek and Latin. Her treasures should not be silks or gems but manuscripts of the Holy Scriptures, judged not by their binding or calligraphy, but by the 'correctness and accurate punctuation.' Little Paula should daily be encouraged to share with others the 'flowers that she has culled from the Scriptures.' She should not go out in public without her parents; she was to be protected as a flower. Finally, Jerome urged little Paula to be sent east to be with her grandmother and aunt, since Rome was very corrupt.[10] When little Paula grew up, she did indeed go east and succeeded Paula and Eustochium as head of the convents in Bethlehem.

Paula the elder was greatly revered throughout the region of Palestine, and her burial in Bethlehem was attended by poor and great alike. Six bishops took her body to the tomb, choirs of virgins sang for three days prior to the funeral, and the poor came to show the clothes they had received from her.

Other wealthy Roman women adopted the ascetic life as well, among them Melania the Elder (341-410) and her granddaughter Melania the Younger (385-439). A brief summary of Melania the Elder's life provides a window into the connectedness of the Roman Empire and the Christians within the Empire. Melania was born in Spain, married at 14, and moved with her husband to Rome. By the time she was 22, her husband and two sons had died, and she was a widow with one son remaining. Melania then became a Christian and joined the ascetics in the desert near Alexandria, Egypt. She also went to Jerusalem and founded a monastery there. When she returned to Rome in 404 to see her son, she stopped in North Africa to visit Augustine of Hippo.

Melania the Elder was an inspiration to Olympias (c. 368-408), a wealthy young widow in Constantinople. Olympias was born into a pagan family of high rank in the Empire. Her father Seleucus died when Olympias was a young girl, and her uncle Procopius became her guardian. He was a devout Christian and a friend of Gregory Nazianzen, theologian and in-

---

10   Jerome Letter 107, 'To Laeta.' Online at http://www.ccel.org/ccel/schaff/npnf206.v.CVII. html.

structor of Jerome. Olympias was very beautiful and heir to a great fortune. In 384 she married Nebridius, a young man of high rank and irreproachable character. When Nebridius died about two years later, Olympias took this as a sign she should not be married again.

Emperor Theodosius wanted to marry her to a kinsman of his, but she refused, so Theodosius had her property confiscated until she was thirty. Olympias maintained her position and sarcastically wrote the Emperor thanking him for relieving her of a heavy burden. She said he could not have bestowed a greater blessing upon her unless he had distributed her wealth to the churches and the poor. Theodosius relented and cancelled the confiscation!

Olympias was an austere ascetic who renounced the luxury of the bath, wore coarse clothing, and restricted her food and sleep. She devoted her wealth and time to her Christian faith, ministering to the sick and poor and

Pulcheria and Eudoxia

Pulcheria (399-453) was the only woman to rule the Roman Empire in her own right. After Pulcheria's father, Emperor Arcadius, died in 408, the eastern Empire was ruled by regents for several years until 414, when at the age of fifteen Pulcheria was declared empress by the Senate and took over the regency for her brother Theodosius, who was two years her junior. When Theodosius gained his majority, Pulcheria continued as joint ruler with him for ten years. Theodosius preferred working on manuscripts while his sister ruled. Pulcheria, who was very well educated and a committed Christian, was an excellent administrator. She arranged for Theodosius to marry an Athenian girl named Eudoxia. Pulcheria had persuaded Eudoxia to convert to Christianity and helped educate her in the faith. Under Pulcheria's influence, Eudoxia composed poetical paraphrases of Scripture, including the five books of Moses, Joshua, Judges, and Ruth, as well as the prophecies of Daniel and Zechariah.

When Theodosius died in 450, Pulcheria became sole ruler. Thinking it improper for a woman to rule in her own name, Pulcheria took a distinguished general, Marcian, as her husband. Though formally married, she maintained the vow of virginity she had taken decades earlier.

Pulcheria built numerous churches and established hospitals and homes for pilgrims. She defended orthodox Christianity against the heresy of Nestorius, then Patriarch of Constantinople, and in 451 was invited to attend the Council of Chalcedon, which drew up the statement concerning the nature of Christ – 'One Christ…in two natures, without confusion, without change, without division, without separation.'

donating lavishly to the Church in Greece, Asia Minor, and Syria. When she was thirty she was made a deaconess in the Church. Whether she was chosen at such a young age (the requirement was age 60) because of her spirituality or her immense wealth is not stated in the early documents. John Chrysostom, Archbishop of Constantinople, reminded her that her wealth was a trust committed to her by God and that she needed to be wise in its administration and beware of indiscriminate distribution of her wealth. Some of the avaricious bishops in the Empire resented this advice! Olympias helped care for Chrysostom's physical wants, supplying him with food and making certain he didn't strain himself too much by his fasting. When Chrysostom was exiled from Constantinople through the political intrigue of others, Olympias was accused of starting a fire that broke out and destroyed the Cathedral and Senate house. Though placed under much pressure, Olympias could not be frightened into falsely confessing her guilt, and her fortitude encouraged Chrysostom in his exile. The letters he wrote to Olympias during this time show a strong spiritual companionship between the two.

Melania the Elder's only surviving son was the wealthy Roman Senator Publicola. His only daughter, Melania the Younger, was promised against her will in marriage to Pinian, another wealthy Roman, when she was only 13. Melania struck a bargain with Pinian – she would produce two children for him, and then they would be free from sex and live together in chastity. She did bear two sons, but they then died. Nevertheless, Pinian supported Melania in her desire for chastity and devotion to Christian work. They liquidated much of their property and used the money to establish monasteries in Antioch, Palestine, and other areas. Melania freed 8000 of her slaves who wished to be freed and allowed her brother to take the others for three coins. She sold all of her property in Spain, Aquitania, Taraconia and Gaul, only keeping her property in Sicily, Campania, and Africa to help provide for her monasteries. Just before the Visigothic invasions during which their Roman home was burned, Pinian, Melania, and her mother left for North Africa. There they spent time with Augustine before going on pilgrimage to Egypt, Syria, and Jerusalem, where they met Jerome. After Pinian's death, Melania built a monastery for men and a chapel in his honor in Jerusalem. She traveled often to Constantinople, and became friends with Eudoxia, the wife of Emperor Theodosius. Melania's biographer wrote that 'The blessed woman read the Old and New Testaments three or four times a year. She copied them herself and furnished copies to the saints by her own hands.'

Mariolatry[11]

Throughout the second century, interest in Mary, the mother of Jesus, was primarily Christological, emphasizing the reality of the incarnation (as opposed to Docetism, which said that Jesus was not really human). Mary was a human mother of a real human baby, Jesus. In the second century also, a parallelism between Eve and Mary developed. In his *Dialogue with*

11   A detailed history and assessment of the development of the Church's treatment of Mary can be found in Tim Perry's *Mary for Evangelicals* (IVP, 2006) and Jaroslav Pelikan's *Mary through the Centuries* (Yale University Press, 1998).

Trypho, Justin Martyr said 'Christ became man by the virgin in order that the disobedience that proceeded from the serpent might receive its destruction in the same manner in which it derived its origin.' As sin came through Eve and her disobedience, so salvation came through Mary's obedience and bearing of Jesus. Irenaeus said that as the human race fell into bondage of death by means of a virgin, so was the race rescued by a virgin who gave birth to the Savior. In the third century, Tertullian wrote that as the virgin Eve listened to the serpent and produced death, so the virgin Mary listened to Gabriel and God sent His Word. The parallel that Paul had developed between the first and last Adam (Rom. 5:12-21) was expanded to a parallel between Eve and Mary.

In the second century, several popular apocryphal writings embellished the story of Mary's background and childhood. Most popular of these fictional works was the *Protevangelium of James*, purporting to be written by the stepbrother of Jesus. The *Protevangelium* told of Joachim and Anna, who had Mary as a miracle baby in their old age. From the time she was three, Mary lived in the temple and was even fed food by angels. At the time of her puberty the widowed Joseph was chosen to be her guardian and protector. Mary was described as a sinless, perpetual virgin. Her delivery of Jesus was painless and preserved her virginity. The brothers and sisters of Jesus described in the Gospels were really the children of Joseph by his first marriage. Such apocryphal stories often became accepted into popular belief and were expanded upon in later writings. However, though there were numerous references to Mary's virginity in the writings of the Church fathers, all of them referred to a time before Jesus' birth. Only in the apocryphal writings is the perpetual virginity of Mary espoused.[12]

As the nature of Jesus and the relation between His human and divine natures was debated, Mary's role also came under consideration. The Council of Ephesus in 431 proclaimed that Mary's proper title was *Theotokos,* the 'Bearer of God.' This emphasized that the person Mary bore was fully God and fully man. Monophysites later used *Theotokos* in a heretical way, denying Jesus' humanity. Orthodox Christians then began to use the term 'mother of God' for Mary, which in turn tended to encourage a focus on her spiritual motherhood. Nestorians (who were condemned at the Council of Ephesus) thought calling Mary '*Theotokos*' was a relapse to heathen mythology and worship of the Mother Goddess, if not blasphemy against the immutability of God.

---

12   Stephen Benko, 'Second Century References to the Mother of Jesus,' in *Women in Early Christianity* (ed. David M. Scholer). New York & London: Garland Publishing Co., 1993.

The idea of Mary's perpetual virginity began to be emphasized with the development of monasticism.[13] Joseph was seen as a protector and only nominally a husband, while the brothers of Jesus were seen as Joseph's by an earlier marriage or as cousins. Alexandrian theologians Proclus and Cyril of Alexandria gave Mary such titles as 'crown of virginity,' 'indestructible temple of God,' 'dwelling place of the Holy Trinity,' 'paradise of the Second Adam,' 'Bridge from God to man,' and the 'Loom of the Incarnation.' In the West, Ambrose and Augustine presented Mary's virginity, sinlessness, and Christian perfection as a type of the Church. Ambrose said, 'The role of the church, like that of Mary, is to conceive by the Spirit and to bring new children into the world.'

By the fourth century, the perception of Mary had gone far beyond the Biblical record. Apocryphal literature included stories about Mary's assumption into heaven. Originally, these stories concerned just the soul, but then the assumption was thought of as being physical as well. As historian Philip Schaff noted, the mother of the Lord had become the Mother of God, the handmaid of the Lord became the Queen of Heaven, Mary highly favored became the dispenser of favors, Mary as blessed among women became the intercessor of women, and the redeemed daughter of fallen Adam became a sinlessly holy co-redeemer. The veneration of Mary became the worship of Mary, which flowered during the Middle Ages. Schaff noted that 'the entire silence of history respecting the worship of the Virgin down to the end of the fourth century proves clearly that it was foreign to the original spirit of Christianity, and belongs among the many innovations of the post-Nicene age.'[14]

By the beginning of the fifth century, the worship of saints with Mary at their head was in full bloom. Many of the practices adopted by the Church were simply pervasive polytheism in Christian forms. Numerous churches and altars were dedicated to Mary. Emperor Justinian I in a law implored Mary's intercession with God for the restoration of the Roman Empire. In 608, Pope Boniface I turned the Pantheon in Rome into the Church of Mary and the Martyrs. Popular belief added to the Scriptures' description of Mary and ascribed to her sinless conception, a sinless birth, resurrection and ascension to heaven, and sharing all power in heaven and earth. The Catholic Church, however, did not accept the doctrine of the immaculate conception (Mary herself being conceived and born without sin) as an article of faith until 1854. Mary's bodily assumption into heaven became dogma in 1950. In 1964, following Vatican II, Mary was given the title 'Mother of the Church.' These nineteenth and twentieth-century

13   The perpetual virginity of Mary was even later accepted by some Protestants, such as Martin Luther. Luther felt it irreconcilable with the dignity of Christ for any other to share Mary's womb.

14   Philip Schaff, *History of the Christian Church*, Vol. 3, p. 423.

changes in the Roman Church's doctrines concerning Mary were acceptance of popular beliefs and superstitions, which dated from the late patristic period, but certainly had no basis in Scripture.

The worship of Mary is a principal separator between Greco-Roman Catholicism and Protestantism. Philip Schaff again noted that worship of Mary, 'is one of the strongest expressions of the fundamental Romish error of unduly exalting the human factors or instruments of redemption, and obstructing or rendering needless the immediate access of believers to Christ, by thrusting in subordinate mediators.'[15]

Christian Marriage

The abundance of data from late antiquity on wealthy, ascetic Christian women contrasts sharply with the limited information about ordinary wives and mothers who made up the majority of the women in the Church. The story of Monica gives us a glimpse of a wife and mother living Christianly in those days. Emmelia, daughter of Macrina the Elder and mother of Macrina the Younger, as well as Bishops Basil, Gregory, and Peter, enjoyed a Christian marriage, which produced a prominent group of leaders in the fourth-century Church. Gregory of Nazianzen paid Emmelia this tribute:

Christian family

> The union of [Basil's] parents, cemented as it was by a community of virtue, no less than by cohabitation, was notable for many reasons, especially for generosity to the poor, for hospitality, for purity of soul as the result of self-discipline…[I]n my opinion, however, their greatest claim to distinction is the excellence of their children. For the attainment of distinction by one or two of their offspring might be ascribed to their nature; but when all are eminent, the honor is clearly due to those who brought them up. This is proved by the blessed role of priests and virgins, and of those who, when married, have allowed nothing in their union to hinder them from attaining an equal repute…. [After describing Emmelia's husband, Basil the elder, Gregory continues:] Who has not known Emmelia, whose name [meaning harmoniousness, gracefulness] was a forecast of what she became, or else whose life was an exemplification of her name? For she had a right to the name which implies gracefulness, and occupied, to speak concisely, the same place among women, as her husband among men.[16]

Godly mother

Anthusa, mother of John Chrysostom, provides another glimpse of a Christian mother and her influence. Anthusa was married to Secundus, a man of great influence and commander of the cavalry forces of the Eastern Roman Empire. However, when Anthusa was 20, Secundus

15   *History of the Christian Church*, Vol. 3, p. 411.

16   *Oration* 43.9-10, quoted in 'Women in the Post-Apostolic Church,' pp. 495-6.

died, leaving her with an infant son and a young daughter. Anthusa never remarried, but as a single mother devoted herself to raising and educating her children. Her son John, later known as John Chrysostom (John the Golden-tongued), studied with Libanius, a leading pagan orator, and practiced law for a time. Though noted for his brilliant court speeches, Chrysostom disapproved of the fraud and avarice he found among the businessmen of Antioch. From his youth, Anthusa especially taught John to love the Bible, and it was due to her guidance that he studied theology and became an eloquent preacher and expositor of the Scripture. In later years, when Archbishop of Constantinople, Chrysostom looked back on the early Biblical training he received from his mother and recognized her importance to his spiritual development. Simply from his contact with Anthusa, Libanius, Chrysostom's early teacher, exclaimed, 'What wonderful women these Christians have!'

Though a great advocate of the ascetic life, Chrysostom preached to all kinds of people, most of whom were not ascetics. He expounded the Scriptures and encouraged his hearers to apply the words of Scripture to their lives. Even today his sermons are profitably read. Chrysostom's sermon on Ephesians 5:22-24 is an example of the Christian ideal of marriage placed before the people.[17] Chrysostom held:

> ... there is nothing which so welds our life together as the love of man and wife. For this many will lay aside even their arms [weapons], for this they will give up life itself. And Paul would never without a reason and without an object have spent so much pains on this subject, as when he says here, 'Wives, be in subjection unto your own husbands, as unto the Lord.' And why so? Because when they are in harmony, the children are well brought up, and the domestics are in good order, neighbors and friends and relations enjoy the fragrance. But if it be otherwise, all is turned upside down, and thrown into confusion.

Chrysostom, following Paul in Ephesians 5, explained the woman's submission and the man's authority in the family, using the relationship of the head and the body. The head gives direction, but the head is nothing without the body. The husband is head of the wife as Christ is head of the Church, but both husband and wife are, as part of the Church, subject to Christ Himself. Though Chrysostom developed the wife's responsibility to submit to the authority of her husband, he spent even more time explicating the command for husbands to love their wives as Christ does the Church. To the husband, he said, 'Wouldest thou have thy wife obedient

---

17   Homily XX on Ephesians, available online at http://www.ccel.org/fathers2/NPNF1-13/ npnf1-13-27.htm#P1356_727848 . For a more in-depth look at Chrysostom's teaching on women, see David C. Ford, *Women and Men in the Early Church: The Full Views of St. John Chrysostom* (South Canaan, Pennsylvania: St. Tikhon's Seminary Press, 1996).

unto thee, as the Church is to Christ? Take then thyself the same provident care for her, as Christ takes for the Church, even if it is necessary to give your life for her.'

A wife should be sought for her beauty of soul, for 'affectionateness, modest-mindedness, gentleness,' not for her outward beauty or wealth. The wife should not demand equality with the head, her husband. God placed 'the one in subjection and the other in authority that there may be peace, for where there is equal authority there can never be peace; neither where a house is a democracy, nor where all are rulers; but the ruling power must of necessity be one.' Chrysostom said the household should be regulated as a little church; everything should be done for the sake of the Lord. In such a home there is no teasing or dissension, but harmony and oneness in the Lord.

But how can the wife endure poverty and hardship? A wife should not berate her husband if she does not have all the wealth and riches she desires. If she complains, the husband should not respond with angry words and blows, but should exhort and admonish his wife concerning the true meaning of wealth and riches. The husband was to instruct and lead his wife in true godliness:

> If she be instructed in the true riches, in the heavenly philosophy, she will make no complaints like these. Let him teach her then, that poverty is no evil. Let him teach her, not by what he says only, but also by what he does. Let him teach her to despise glory…let him, from that very evening on which he first receives her into the bridal chamber, teach her temperance, gentleness, and how to live, casting down the love of money at once from the outset and from the very threshold.

The husband should treat his wife with affection. From the specific examples he gave, it is easy to imagine marital situations Chrysostom encountered in his pastoral work. Chrysostom encouraged the husband to say something like:

> 'I was taught well and truly that money is no real possession, but a most despicable thing, a thing which moreover belongs as well to thieves, and to harlots, and to grave-robbers. So I gave up these things, and went on till I fell in with the excellence of thy soul, which I value above gold. For a young damsel who is discreet and ingenuous, and whose heart is set on piety, is worth the whole world. For these reasons then, I courted thee, and I love thee, and prefer thee to my own soul. For the present life is nothing. And I pray, and beseech, and do all I can, that we may be counted worthy so to live this present life, as that we may be able also there in the world to come to be united to one another in perfect security. For our time here is brief and fleeting. But if we shall be counted worthy by having pleased God to so exchange this life for that one, then shall we ever be both with Christ and with each other, with more abundant pleasure. I value thy affection above

all things, and nothing is so bitter or so painful to me, as ever to be at variance with thee…'

Show her too that you set a high value on her company, and that you are more desirous to be at home for her sake, than in the market-place. And esteem her before all your friends, and above the children that are born of her, and let these very children be beloved by thee for her sake. If she does any good act, praise and admire it; if any foolish one, and such as girls may chance to do [remember, 12 was the marriageable age], advise her and remind her. Condemn out and out all riches and extravagance, and gently point out the ornament that there is in neatness and in modesty; and be continually teaching her the things that are profitable.

Let your prayers be common. Let each go to Church; and let the husband ask his wife at home, and she again ask her husband, the account of the things which were said and read there … Teach her that there is nothing in life that is to be feared, save only offending against God. If any marry thus, with these views, he will be but little inferior to monks; the married but little below the unmarried.

Though Chrysostom, as most of the Church leaders during this period, valued celibacy and an ascetic life above marriage, Chrysostom considered those who denied the goodness and value of marriage as heretics.

Chrysostom further advised that the words 'mine and thine' should be banished from the wife's (and husband's) soul. If she claimed something as 'mine,' the husband should allow this and say, 'why everything is thine and I am thine.' If, as Paul says, the husband has not power over his own body but the wife does, then she has power over all his possessions as well. Never call the wife simply by her name, 'but with terms of endearment, with honor, with much love. Honor her, and she will not need honor from others, if she enjoys that which comes from thee.'

Chrysostom's exposition of Ephesians 5 maintained the distinctive roles of husband and wife in marriage, and made it clear that the woman was to be respected and honored. With her husband the wife shared a oneness with Christ which would last forever. Chrysostom concluded his sermon by noting that:

If thus we regulate ourselves, and attentively study the Scriptures, in most things we shall derive instruction from them. And thus shall be able to please God, and to pass through the whole of the present life virtuously, and to attain those blessings which are promised to those that love Him, of which God grant that we may all be counted worthy, through the grace and loving-kindness of our Lord Jesus Christ, with Whom, together with the Holy Ghost, be unto the Father, glory, power, and honor, now, and ever, through all ages. Amen.

Christian Women in the Early Middle Ages:
Vessels of Gold and Silver

2 Timothy 2:20

At its height, the Roman Empire stretched from the British Isles to the Tigris and Euphrates Rivers and from the Rhine and Danube Rivers to the Sahara Desert of North Africa. The ease of communication and travel as well as the peace and order provided by the Roman army and government were important catalysts in the spread of Christianity. Though at first frequently a persecuted religion, Christianity rapidly spread throughout the Empire and in the fourth century became the Empire's official religion.

About the time of Christ, tribes from Scandinavia began migrating southward into what is now Poland and along the Vistula River. Known as the Goths, these tribes displaced the Vandals, who had settled the area after having left Scandinavia in the second century B.C. These migrating Vandals and Goths began placing pressure on the northern boundaries of the Roman Empire. In 267 the Visigoths sacked Athens, but they were persuaded to move back north of the Danube River and become allies with the Roman forces protecting the Empire's borders. By the third century, the Goths split into two groups – the eastern Ostrogoths and the western Visigoths. The Vandals and then the Visigoths moved into what is modern France and down the Iberian Peninsula. Through trade contacts, the Gothic tribes became increasingly Romanized, and many adopted the Arian tradition that denied Jesus as the Son of God as equal with God.

The pressure of these tribes on the borders of the Empire increased further in the fifth century with the expansion of the Asiatic Huns' empire, from the steppes of central Asia to Germany and from the Black to the Baltic Seas. About the time Rome began to withdraw its troops from Britain to protect its home territory in Italy from barbaric invasions, the Angles, Saxons and Jutes invaded Britain. The Ostrogoths controlled much of the Balkans. In 410 the Visigoth Alaric successfully captured Rome, though later he withdrew. Four decades later, in 455, the Vandals sacked Rome and then moved into North Africa, replacing Roman rule which had brought much prosperity to the region. In 476, Rome fell to the German Odoacer. Though the eastern Roman Empire endured for another millennium, the western Roman Empire had come to an end. The Ostrogoths controlled Italy with the Lombards and the Burgundians to the north. The Franks expanded into the area of France, and the Visigoths ruled Spain.

In his address to the Athenians on Mars Hill, the apostle Paul had spoken of such vast movements of people and the readjustment of boundaries when he told that God

> made from one man every nation of mankind to live on all the face of the earth, having determined allotted periods and the boundaries of their dwelling place, that they should seek God, in the hope that they might feel their way toward him and find him. Yet he is actually not far from each one of us…(Acts 17:26-27).

For the next 500 years, the history of the Germanic peoples who had moved into regions of the former Roman Empire would in large part include the story of their Christianization. Women played an important role in the evangelization process and the maturation of the Church in these regions. Queens of the Germanic tribes, often the first among their people to believe the gospel, were instrumental in leading their husbands and their people into the Christian faith. Women often oversaw monastic establishments, important in educating the nobility of both sexes. Women wrote creative dramas and didactic material to help others grow in the Christian faith. With the turn of the millennium, however, changes were implemented which restricted Christian women in their service within the Christian community.

Christian Queens of the Barbarian Tribes

The history of the conversion of the various barbarian tribes from paganism to Christianity repeatedly included a story with four key elements. First, the Christian queen was important in bringing the gospel and the witness of Christianity to the pagan court. Second, the power of the Christian God was seen in His giving victory in battle when the pagan gods were impotent. Third, the king was reluctant to leave the idols for the Christian God and was unsure if his people would follow him in the faith. Finally, the king was baptized, along with his family and many of his followers. Several letters remain from various Popes who corresponded with Christian queens encouraging them in their duty to bring their kingly husbands to the Christian faith. The Popes quoted 1 Corinthians 7:14, 'the unbelieving husband is made holy because of his wife,' to encourage the Christian queen in leading her heathen husband to Christ. Since the king was the leader of the nation, it was natural for the king to think that when converted to

Christianity, his people would follow him in the faith. By the ninth century, the coronation rituals in France specifically said the queen's role was 'to summon barbarian peoples to acknowledgement of the Truth.'[1]

One of the most famous of the Christian queens of the Germanic tribes was Clothilda (474-545), daughter of Chilperic, King of the Burgundians at Lyons, and his wife Caretena. As in the days of David and Solomon, royal marriages were used to seal alliances among the various tribes or kingdoms. Clovis, King of the Franks, sought to marry Clothilda, not simply for her beauty and person, but also to expand his Frankish kingdom by an alliance with the Burgundians.[2] When Clothilda married Clovis, however, she was seeking an expansion of the kingdom of Christ more than an earthly kingdom. She maintained the Christian faith she had been taught by her mother and sought to persuade her husband to embrace the Christian truth as well. Gregory of Tours later recorded that Clothilda told Clovis:

> The gods you venerate are nothing, as they are unable to provide for the needs of others. They are idols made of wood, stone, or metal... They are magicians, their power does not have a divine origin. The God who must be worshipped is he whose Word brought out of nothing the heavens, the earth, the sea, and all they contain... It is by his will that the fields produce their harvests, the trees, their fruits, the grapevines, their grapes. It is by his hand that the human race was created. Thanks to his liberality, all creation has been set to serve man, is submitted to him and showers him with its blessings.[3]

Clovis, however, continued to trust in his gods and discounted that the Christian God should be numbered among the gods at all.

Clothilda bore Clovis a son, who was named Ingomir at his baptism. When the infant died shortly thereafter, Clovis claimed the infant's death proved the impotence of Clothilda's God. Clovis was angry with Clothilda and claimed that if Ingomir had been dedicated to his gods, he would have survived. Clothilda replied, 'I thank Almighty God, Creator of all things, who has deigned to honor my unworthiness by opening his kingdom to this child to whom I gave birth. My soul is not touched by pain, for I know that, taken from the world in the innocence of his baptism, my son is being nourished by the contemplation of God.' When another son was born, Clothilda named him Chlodomer at baptism. When he too became ill, the King assured his wife that he would die also since he had been

---

1   Richard Fletcher. *The Barbarian Conversion from Paganism to Christianity*. New York: Henry Holt & Co., 1997, pp. 104,123.

2   Clovis' name is variously spelled Chlodowech, Chlodovech, Chlodovic, Chlodovicus, and Chlodwig! Interestingly, in French this is the origin of the name 'Louis,' popular for later French kings; in German it is the basis for the name 'Ludwig.'

3   Gregory of Tours. *History of the Franks*, II. p. 29.

baptized in the name of Christ. Clothilda prayed, and the child became well. Clothilda continued to urge Clovis to recognize the Christian God, but he refused. However, when Clovis found himself on the losing side of a fierce battle against the Alemanni, he raised his eyes to heaven and called on Christ for help. The Alemanni fled, and Clovis' forces won the battle. Clovis returned to Clothilda and told her how Christ had won the battle for him. Clovis gladly began to receive instruction in the Christian faith from Remi, bishop of Rheims. Clovis doubted, however, that it would be possible to draw his people away from the worship of their gods. When Clovis approached his people to urge them to forsake their idols and worship the Creator of heaven and earth, the people themselves said, 'O pious king, we reject our mortal gods, and we are ready to follow the immortal God whom Remi preaches.' Clovis and his sisters as well as 3000 of Clovis' followers were baptized.

Through the influence of Queen Clothilda, the Franks became at least nominally Christian, though history would show this national conversion did not mean that all truly accepted the Christian faith or way of life. Clothilda bore Clovis five children – Ingomir, who died in infancy; one daughter, also named Clothilda, and three other sons – Clodomir, Childebert, and Clotaire. Clovis died in 511, but Clothilda's thirty-four years of widowhood were not peaceful. The lives of her sons were not in any way marked by a Christian spirit. Clodomir killed his cousin Sigismund, King of Burgundy, and his whole family. Sigismund's brother then killed Clodomir. When Clothilda adopted Clodomir's three sons to raise them as her own, her other two sons, not wanting to share their inheritance with their brother's offspring, killed two of the boys; the youngest escaped and became a monk.

Needless to say, Clothilda was devastated by this family feuding. She withdrew from Paris to Tours, where she lived a life of prayer and devotion, but she could not escape her family trials. Her daughter Clothilda II was cruelly mistreated by the Visigothic King Amalaric. Clothilda II's brother Childebert defeated and killed Amalaric in battle, but Clothilda II herself died shortly after from her hardships. As if she had not had enough grief, Clothilda's two surviving sons, Childebert and Clotaire, began quarreling, and serious war seemed imminent. Clothilda spent all night in prayer at the tomb of St. Martin of Tours, tearfully imploring that war would not break out. A terrible storm that caused the two armies to disperse then arose, an answer to the poor Queen's prayer.

Bertha, Clothilda's great-granddaughter through her son Clotaire, was influential in taking the gospel to the Anglo-Saxons in England. The Anglo-Saxon King Ethelbert had increased the size of his kingdom to the point that he could make an alliance with the Franks, the most powerful state in Europe at the time. To secure the alliance, Ethelbert married Bertha, daughter of the Frankish King. Part of the marriage agreement was that Bertha would be able to continue to live and worship as a Christian in the pagan Anglo-Saxon court. Bertha took her chaplain, Liuhard, with her to Canterbury, capital of Ethelbert's kingdom. In the town they repaired an old, unused Christian chapel, which remained from the time of Roman rule, for use by the Frankish Christians.

Bertha's aunt Brunhilda, the Visigothic princess who had married Sigebert, grandson of Clovis and Bertha's uncle, was raised an Arian but accepted Christianity on her marriage to Sigebert. Several letters from Pope Gregory the Great to Brunhilda and other Frankish leaders, in which he encourages the Franks' help in the Christian mission to the English, survive. Pope Gregory the Great praised Brunhilda for her support of the mission and said she had done more for the English mission than anyone except God.

Though the story is often told of Pope Gregory the Great sending Augustine as a Christian missionary to England in 597, after he saw some Angle (English) slaves in the market with faces he described as like angels, Pope Gregory's letters indicate the English requested Christian missionaries be sent. Undoubtedly, this request came because of Bertha's influence at the English court. No records of Bertha's words, deeds or thoughts remain of her life as a Christian among pagans. Yet, there is a testimony of her faith in the Christian witness she was to her husband, leading to Ethelbert's positive acceptance of Augustine as a Christian missionary to the English. Bertha had replanted the seeds of Christianity in England, preparing the way for Augustine's later fruitful mission.

CHRISTIAN QUEENS OF INFLUENCE AMONG THE FRANKS AND ANGLO-SAXONS

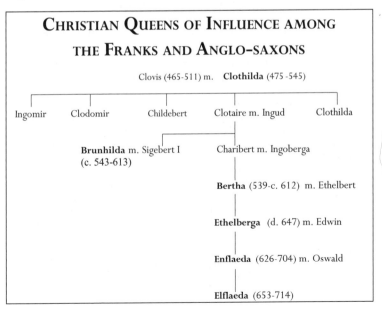

Clovis (465-511) m. **Clothilda** (475-545)

Ingomir — Clodomir — Childebert — Clotaire m. Ingud — Clothilda

Brunhilda m. Sigebert I (c. 543-613)

Charibert m. Ingoberga

Bertha (539-c. 612) m. Ethelbert

Ethelberga (d. 647) m. Edwin

Enflaeda (626-704) m. Oswald

Elflaeda (653-714)

Ethelbert and many of the leaders in the kingdom were baptized as Christians by Augustine in Canterbury. In 601, Pope Gregory the Great wrote a letter to Bertha praising her, saying that as God:

> kindled the hearts of the Romans towards the Christian faith by means of the ever memorable Helena, mother of the most pious emperor Constantine, so we trust that His mercy is working through your earnestness, O glorious one, upon the English race. And indeed it was your duty this long time past, by the excellence of your prudence, like a true Christian, to have predisposed the mind of our illustrious son, your consort, to follow the faith which you cherish, for the salvation of his kingdom and of his soul.

Ethelberga, daughter of Bertha and Ethelbert, followed in the family tradition and in 625 married the pagan King Edwin of Northumbria. As with her mother before, Ethelberga and her retinue were allowed to continue their Christian faith. Ethelberga brought with her the monk Paulinus, who had been part of Augustine's mission. Boniface, Bishop of Rome, sent Ethelberga a letter encouraging her in her Christian duty of bringing her husband and the people of her kingdom to the Christian faith. Boniface rejoiced in Ethelberga's conversion and that she excelled in the performance of pious works. He praised her that:

> you likewise carefully refrain from the worship of idols and the deceits of temples and auguries, and having changed your devotion, are so wholly taken up with the love of your Redeemer, as never to cease lending your assistance for the propagation of the Christian faith.

Boniface was sad to hear, however, that her illustrious husband still worshipped idols. He exhorted Ethelberga to 'not defer to do that which, both in season and out of season, is required of us,' so that her husband might also be added to the number of Christians:

> to the end that you may thereby enjoy the rights of marriage in the bond of a holy and unblemished union. For it is written, 'They two shall be in one flesh.' How can it be said, that there is unity between you, if he continues a stranger to the brightness of your faith, by the interposition of dark and detestable error?
>   Wherefore, applying yourself continually to prayer, do not cease to beg of the Divine Mercy the benefit of his illumination; to the end, that those whom the union of carnal affection has made in a manner but one body, may, after death, continue in perpetual union, by the bond of faith. Persist, therefore, illustrious daughter, and to the utmost of your power endeavour to soften the hardness of his heart by insinuating the Divine precepts; making him sensible how noble the mystery is which you have received by believing…Inflame the coldness of his heart by the knowledge of the Holy Ghost, that by the abolition of the cold and pernicious worship of paganism, the heat of Divine faith may enlighten

his understanding through your frequent exhortations; that the testimony of the holy Scripture may appear the more conspicuous, fulfilled by you, 'The unbelieving husband shall be saved by the believing wife.'

Boniface encouraged Ethelberga with frequent prayers and asked her to inform him when her husband was converted. Boniface also sent Ethelberga a 'silver looking-glass, and a gilt ivory comb, which we entreat your glory will receive with the same kind affection as it is known to be sent by us.'[4]

On Easter 627, King Edwin, together with his young son by Ethelberga and others in the royal retinue at York, was baptized. Among those baptized by Paulinus in Northumbria was Hilda, who later became the founder and abbess of the famous double abbey at Whitby. Though Christianity had a beginning in Northumbria through Queen Ethelberga's witness, the King of Mercia soon invaded Northumbria, and King Edwin was killed at the Battle of Hatfield in 633. Queen Ethelberga, her children, and her chaplain Paulinus managed to escape back to Canterbury. Ethelberga's brother, now the king there, gave her a ruined Roman villa in nearby Lyming, where Ethelberga established the first nunnery in England.

Enflaeda, Ethelberga's daughter, broke the family pattern by marrying a Christian king - Oswald, King of Bernicia and Deira, near Northumbria. Enflaeda used her position for the advance of Christianity. After her husband's death while on pilgrimage to Rome, she became a nun at Whitby, succeeding Hilda as abbess at the monastery. She was the last in a line of royal Frankish women who used their royal position to spread Christianity among the people.

The Abbesses Rule[5]

Among those baptized at York with King Edwin during Easter of 627 was Hilda, the King's great-niece. Hilda was born in 614, seventeen years after Augustine came to England. Her father was poisoned when Hilda was just a toddler; Hilda and her sister Hereswith were raised by Queen Ethelberga at the Northumbrian court. Queen Ethelberga and her chaplain Paulinus undoubtedly taught the young girls the truths of the Christian faith during their childhood so that as teenagers they joined their King and guardian in Christian baptism. When Hereswith married the prince of East Anglia, Hilda seems to have accompanied her to her new home. When she was thirty-three, Hilda planned to join another sister who was a nun in Gaul; but Aidan, Irish founder of the monastery at Lindisfarne and missionary

---

4   Letter in Bede's *Ecclesiastical History of the English Nation*, Book 2: xi.

5   An extensive amount of work has recently been done on women in monastic institutions during the medieval period. 'Monastic Matrix' is a valuable website from which to access this material, and can be found at: http://monasticmatrix.usc.edu/dematrice/history.php.

to Northumbria, asked Hilda to start a small monastery in Northumbria. Hilda served as abbess in two small monasteries before she established what would become one of the most famous monasteries in England – the double monastery at Whitby.

Double monasteries, where both men and women lived in adjoining houses, sharing a common church and being ruled by one superior, were often found in the East. Basil and his sister Macrina had established adjoining monasteries for both men and women. In the double monasteries, the church separated the buildings of the men and the women, and sometimes a high wall divided the church to keep the men and women separated there as well. Columba and the Irish also established double monasteries, which were most often ruled by an abbess or Mother Superior. A woman with such authority was seen as exercising her maternal function. Because the abbess was the administrative head of the affairs of the monastery, she was also a kind of feudal lord with influence in the wider community. Ruling over vast territories, she held temporal as well as spiritual power. Abbesses met with local councils and synods, and at least four sat in the Saxon Parliament as peers.

Hilda herself was from the royal family, and most of those who entered the monastic life were from noble families. The monastery was a teaching center, and many sons and daughters of kings and nobles were trained there. The Venerable Bede, the chief source of information about Hilda, wrote of Hilda's Whitby:

> After the example of the primitive Church, no one there was rich, no one was needy, for everything was held in common, and nothing was considered to be anyone's personal property. So great was her prudence that not only ordinary folk, but kings and princes used to come and ask her advice in their difficulties and take it. Those under her direction were required to make a thorough study of the Scriptures and occupy themselves in good works, to such good effect that many were found fitted for Holy Orders and the service of God's altar. Five men from this monastery later became bishops.[6]

However, Hilda was not only interested in those of noble lineage. Bede recounted the story of Caedmon, an uneducated herdsman on the monastic lands who couldn't sing and always left a gathering when the harp was being passed around and coming near to him. One night, however, he had a dream in which a person asked him to sing a song. Caedmon replied that he could not sing, and that was the reason he left the entertainment. The person then gave Caedmon a song to sing about the creation:

6   Venerable Bede. *Ecclesiastical History of the English Nation*. Book 2 xxiii, 'Of the Life and Death of the Abbess Hilda,' available at 'The Medieval Sourcebook', http://www.fordham.edu/halsall/basis/bede-book4.html.

Praise we the Fashioner now of Heaven's fabric,
The majesty of his might and his mind's wisdom,
work of the world warden, worker of all wonders,
How the Lord of Glory everlasting,
Wrought first for the race of men
Heaven as a rooftree,
Then made the Middle Earth to be their mansion.[7]

When Caedmon's dream was told to Hilda, she brought him into the Abbey and began teaching him Scriptures. Caedmon began to compose poems about Genesis and the Exodus, and Christ's life and His teachings. Caedmon's poems were the earliest poems known in the English language, though what survives today are only revisions into other languages.

In 664, Whitby hosted the important Synod that settled the disputes between the Celtic and Roman Churches over church practices such as the date of Easter and priest's tonsures. Hilda and some of her nuns attended the Synod. Though Hilda herself had followed the Celtic practices, she accepted the decision of the Synod and followed the Roman ways thereafter. Hilda died at Whitby in 680. Enflaeda, daughter of the Queen Ethelberga who had raised Hilda as a child, succeeded Hilda as Abbess.

The English monasteries and nunneries were centers of education and scholarship and played an important role in spreading Christianity among the still-heathen tribes of Europe. The leader in the missionary activity among the German tribes was Winfrid (c.680-754), a native of England and a man of noble descent. From his earliest years, Winfrid felt called to a religious life and finally persuaded his father to allow him to enter a monastery, where he came to excel in learning as well as preaching. Winfrid was intent on bringing the gospel to the Anglo-Saxons in Germany, and in 716 he set out on his mission. Whether Winfrid took the name 'Boniface' at the time of his ordination or some time later is not known. Traveling throughout Germany, Boniface found the German peoples still living a heathen life and worshiping idols, with some Christianity mixed in. To show the heathen how powerless their gods were, Boniface cut down the oak sacred to the chief god, Thor. The people were amazed that thunder and lightning did not come and destroy Boniface, and many converted to Christianity. As the Christian gospel spread among the people, Boniface built churches and monasteries to establish Christianity more firmly in the region. He wrote to the English monasteries and asked for both men and women to come to Germany and help in the work. Walburga and Leoba, both relatives of Boniface, were the most famous of the nuns sent to work among the Germans.

7   Bede, *Ecclesiastical History*, Book 4 xxiv.

Leoba (700-779) was born to older parents who had despaired of ever having children. When Leoba's mother became pregnant, she dedicated the child in her womb to God. Leoba was taught the Scripture from her infancy and later was brought to be educated in the monastery. Her biographer, Rudolf of Fulda, wrote that Leoba

> had no interests other than the monastery and the pursuit of sacred knowledge. She took no pleasure in aimless jests and wasted no time on girlish romances, but, fired by the love of Christ, fixed her mind always on reading or hearing the Word of God. Whatever she heard or read she committed to memory, and put all that she learned into practice...She prayed continually, knowing that in the Epistles the faithful are counseled to pray without ceasing. When she was not praying she worked with her hands at whatever was commanded her, for she had learned that he who will not work should not eat. However, she spent more time in reading and listening to Sacred Scripture than she gave to manual labour.[8]

Leoba was well read in the Church Fathers and in the Scriptures.

When Leoba went to Germany, Boniface placed her as abbess over the nuns at the monastery at Bischofsheim in the diocese of Mainz. There she trained many nuns who went on to become abbesses throughout Germany. Her reputation for learning and godly living spread far and wide, and she often was summoned to the Frankish court, where she was highly respected by King Pepin and his successor, Charlemagne. Because of her wisdom and knowledge of Scripture, the princes and nobles of both the Church and state discussed spiritual matters with her. Charlemagne's queen Hiltigard would have liked Leoba to remain at court to help her in her own spiritual growth, but 'Leoba detested the life at court like poison.'

Even before Boniface had requested that Leoba and others come to Germany and help with the Christian evangelization and teaching, his letters to monasteries in England were filled with requests for books to be sent to him. Women as well as men were involved in the production of books – the scribal activity of copying manuscripts, the work of illumination, and the binding of books, as well as the preservation of them in the monastic libraries. Charlemagne's sister Gisla and his daughter Rotrud both retired to the monastery at Chelles, where they spent their time in scholarly pursuits. The eminent scholar Alcuin asked them to critique his commentary on the Gospel of John while he was still writing it, and they encouraged him to complete the work. The nunneries of the early Middle Ages were places of influence and scholarship where women not only educated the children of nobility, both male and female, but studied, copied, and preserved the Scriptures and other manuscripts.

8   C.H. Talbot, *The Anglo-Saxon Missionaries in Germany, Being the Lives of SS. Willibrord, Boniface, Leoba, and Lebuin together with the Hodoepericon of St. Willibald and a selection from the correspondence of St. Boniface,* (London and New York: Sheed and Ward, 1954) as found at the Medieval Sourcebook, http://www.fordham.edu/halsall/basis/leoba.html.

Christian Women Writers for Their Families and the Court

Few compositions written by women have survived from the Middle Ages. One of the earliest and most fascinating is also one of the oldest treatises on education, the *Manual for My Son* written by Dhuoda in the mid-ninth century.[9] Dhuoda's work provides the 21st-century reader with a rare look into the thoughts and passions of a ninth-century Christian woman and mother who lived outside of the nunneries and inner court circles. Dhuoda came from a noble, possibly imperial, family. On June 29, 824, she married Bernard of Septimania in the imperial palace of Aachen. Bernard's father was a first cousin of Charlemagne. In 826, Dhuoda's son William was born, and in 841 her second son was born. The times were tumultuous, as the empire of Charlemagne's son Louis was falling apart. Louis' four sons, Charles the Bald, Louis the German, Pepin of Aquitaine, and Lothair, were at war. Dhuoda's husband pledged allegiance to Charles the Bald. As a pledge of his good faith, Bernard sent his 14-year-old son William to Charles' court. Bernard took his infant son, only a few months old and not even christened yet, to Aquitaine under his own care, leaving Dhuoda alone on the family lands in Uzès. Under these circumstances Dhuoda wrote her *Manual* to her son William. Since she was unable to give advice, guidance, and protection to her son in person, Dhuoda wrote the manual as a kind of mirror, which William could have when Dhuoda herself was gone. Though others could teach William many lessons, none could teach in the same way as his mother, 'with the heart burning within, as I with mine, my firstborn one.'

Kassia: Early Woman Hymnwriter

Kassia was born in Constantinople in the early ninth century. Her father had a position at the imperial court, and Kassia was educated in the Greek classics as well as the Scriptures. When Theophilus became Emperor, as the story goes, in choosing a bride, he used the ancient custom of a beauty line-up. Kassia was among the six maidens chosen for the honor and was reputed to be the most beautiful and becoming. When the Emperor came to her, he tested her and said, 'From woman flowed corruption,' alluding to Eve's role in the Fall. Kassia boldly replied, 'But also from woman sprung forth what is superior,' referring to the birth of Jesus. The Emperor didn't like that Kassia's wit had bested him, and chose another for his bride.

Kassia founded a monastery in Constantinople in 843 and composed music and liturgical verses for the services of the monastery. Twenty-three of her hymns still remain in use as part of the Orthodox liturgical cycle. The most famous, 'The Fallen Woman,' based on the anointing of Jesus' feet from Luke 7:36-50, is sung during Holy Week:

---

9   Dorothy Disse's online resource *Other Women's Voices: Translations of Women's Writings before 1700* contains the writings of several Christian women writers before 1700, including Dhuoda's: http://home.infionline.net/~ddisse/dhuoda.html.

> O Lord, the woman who had fallen into many sins,
> perceiving Thy divinity,
> took upon herself the duty of a myrrh-bearer;
> with lamentation she bringeth Thee myrrh oils
> before Thine entombment,
> 'Woe unto me,' she said,
> 'for night is become for me a frenzy of licentiousness,
> a gloomy and moonless love of sin.
> Receive the fountains of my tears,
> O Thou Who dost gather into clouds the water of the sea.
> Incline unto the sighings of my heart,
> O Thou who didst bow the heavens by Thine
> ineffable kenosis [self-emptying]
> I shall kiss Thine immaculate feet,
> and wipe them again with the tresses of my head,
> those feet at whose sound Eve hid
> herself for fear when she heard Thee walking
> in Paradise in the afternoon.
> The multitude of my sins
> and the abyss of Thy judgments, who can search them out, O my Saviour of souls?
> Do not disdain me, Thy handmaiden, O Thou
> Whose mercy is measureless.*

---

*   Hagiography of Saint Kassiani, http://www.antiochian.org/sites/antiochian.org/files/sacred_music/MGF_0192a.HolyWeek.Kassiani.pdf .

Dhuoda's writing was personal, meditative, and full of passion and introspection; she sought to guide her son into a life that would honor God, his human father, and the court at which he served. Her *Manual* is a rare example from the Middle Ages that discusses how to live the Christian life in the world rather than moving into a monastery or cloister. Dhuoda began her writing with a prayer to God:

> You centre that enclose the whirling firmament,
> Folding ocean and fields within your hand,
>
> To you I commend William, my son – at your command
> May well-being be lavished on him in all ways.
>
> In all his course, all his moments and hours,
> May he love you, his maker, most of all.
>
> May he deserve to climb the highest peak,
> Swift-footed, happy, with those who are yours.
>
> May his perceptions always be alert,
> Open, to you; may he live blissfully for ever;
>
> When he's hurt, let him never burst into anger

Or wander away, severed from your friends;

May he jubilate joyously, through a glad course of life,
Radiant in virtue, may he reach the heights...

May your generous grace penetrate him,
With peace and security of body and mind,

In which he may flourish in the world, and have children,
Holding what's here so as not to lose what's there...

Let him be generous and prudent, loyal and brave,
Let him never abandon moderation.

He will never have one like me to tell him this,
I who, though unworthy, am also his mother,

I who always, at all moments and all hours,
Am asking you with all my strength: have mercy on him[10]

In her prologue, Dhuoda wrote;

> I, Dhuoda, though frail in sex, living unworthily among worthy women,
> am nonetheless your mother, my son William: to you the words of my
> handbook are directed now. For, just as playing at dice seems for a time
> most comely and apt to the young, amid other worldly accomplishments,
> or again, as some women are wont to gaze in mirrors, to remove their
> blemishes and reveal their glowing skin, concerned to please their
> husbands here and now – in the same way I want you, when you're
> weighed down by hosts of worldly and temporal activities, to read this
> little book I have sent you, often, in memory of me; don't neglect it –
> use it as if it were a matter of mirrors or of games at dice.
>   Even if, more and more, you acquire books, many volumes, may
> it still please you to read frequently this little work of mine – may you
> have the strength to grasp it profitably, with the help of almighty God.
> You will find in it, in epitome, whatever you choose to get to know;
> you will also find there a mirror in which, beyond a doubt, you can
> examine the condition of your soul, so that you can not only please the
> world, but please him in every way who fashioned you out of clay. So
> it is altogether necessary for you, my son William, to show yourself, in
> both ventures, as one who can be of service to the world and at the same
> time can always, through every action, give delight to God.[11]

Dhuoda began her *Manual* with a chapter on the love and sublimity of
God and then wrote of the Trinity, faith, hope and charity, and the nature
of prayer and the sign of the cross. Dhuoda wrote that the love of God
should take precedence over everything else in life, including filial and
feudal reverence. Dhuoda's words were filled with practical advice her son

---

10   As quoted in Peter Dronke, *Women Writers of the Middle Ages: A Critical Study of Texts from Perpetua
      to Marguerite Porete* (Cambridge University Press, 1984), p. 42.

11   *Women Writers*, pp. 40-1.

could use throughout his life. She included a chapter on vices and virtue, and a detailed examination of the trials of life – false riches, persecutions, temptations, sickness, and danger. She emphasized that whatever trials came, God could be glorified throughout. Dhuoda described for William fifteen stages to perfection or maturity, followed by a section discussing the double birth (bodily and spiritual) and double death (temporal and eternal):

> According to the sayings of scholars, two births can be seen in each man, a fleshly birth and a spiritual birth, and spiritual birth is more noble than fleshly birth. These two births correspond to two deaths, the first is suffered by every human being, and the second one may be avoided altogether. 'He who conquers shall not be hurt by the second death.'

Throughout, Dhuoda included Biblical principles, people, and allusions in her instruction. When young, both Samuel and Daniel were able to judge old men; she trusted William would follow their example. She held up Jonathan as a symbol of faithfulness while Absalom was a symbol of rebellion. Jacob's son Joseph was set forth as a model of Christian manliness: 'Beautiful in his looks, more beautiful in his mind ... very handsome and an enjoyer of the world, he was always acceptable to God and man in everything.'[12] Her work was full of Scripture references. She encouraged her son to show deference to both great and small, for God Himself took a servant's form (Phil. 2:7). God casts down the mighty and raises the lowly (Luke 1:52) and is no respecter of persons (Acts 10:34). Christians should remember that the strong should be helpers of the weak (2 Cor. 8:14). Writing in Latin, Dhuoda also included references to many classical authors. Publishers of a recent edition of her work listed her quotations from various sources, and they fill eight two-columned pages.[13] Her writing was also filled with her own poems, many of which were in acrostics and often contained riddles.

Dhuoda gave her son instruction in the importance of prayer and advised him particularly to pray for the clergy and kings, for his feudal lord, his father, the souls of his ancestors (who had furnished William with the wealth he would inherit), his godfather, and the souls of those who were unworthy (presumably this included the enemies of William and his father Bernard). All personal prayer was based on the psalms, and Dhuoda showed how reading the psalms could bring comfort and light in every circumstance of life. Dhuoda included a sample prayer William could say 'wherever the opportunity presents itself':

---

12 *Women Writers*, p. 44.

13 Pierre Riché. *Dhuoda: Manuel pour mon fils.* (Paris, 1976), pp. 375-85.

> Mercy-giving and Merciful, Just and Pious, Clement and True, have pity on Your creation, whom You created and redeemed with Your blood; have pity on me, and grant that I may walk in Your paths and Your justice; give me memory and sense that I may understand, believe, love, fear, praise and thank You and be perfect in every good work through proper faith and goodwill, O Lord, my God. Amen...[14]

Dhuoda included a curious chapter on numerology, which some have speculated was based in part on writings of Boethius. Numbers one and three recalled the Holy Trinity and brought about the three virtues of faith, hope, and charity, whose practice required a triple effort, 'Search with your thought, ask with your knock, find with your works.' She noted that there were seven gifts of the Spirit, seven days of the week, seven ages of the world, and seven consecrated lamps giving light in the Holy of Holies. Throughout the work, such as in the excerpt above about the two deaths and two births, Dhuoda used numerology in developing her thoughts.

Dhuoda concluded her *Manual* with her last words to William:

> Have frequent recourse to this little book. Always be, noble child, strong and brave in Christ! ...Here ends, thanks be to God, the Manual of William, according to the word of the Gospel: 'It is finished.'[15]

The passion of a mother's heart and of a heart full of devotion to God shone throughout Dhuoda's charming work. There are hints in the work that she was not in the best of health when she wrote, and it is not known how long she lived thereafter. Did she live to see the violent deaths that came to her husband and son? Bernard was on the losing side of the tumultuous fighting among Charlemagne's descendants. He was accused of treason for supporting Pepin of Aquitaine against Charles the Bald and put to death in Toulouse in 844. William, the son for whom Dhuoda wrote the *Manual*, was also beheaded for treason in 849. Dhuoda's younger son, Bernard, seems to have had a long career. In 910 his son, William the Pious, founded the abbey of Cluny, which worked for religious reform in the Church.

Like Dhuoda, Hrotsvit (c. 935-1000) synthesized the secular and Christian in her writings.[16] Hrotsvit lived at the Benedictine Abbey of Gandersheim, which had been founded in 852 by members of the Saxon aristocracy. Like many of the abbeys of the day, Gandersheim's residents were drawn mostly from the nobility. The abbess at the time of Hrotsvit was Gerberga, a niece of Emperor

---

14   Excerpt found in Amy Oden, *In Her Words* (Nashville: Abingdon Press, 1994), p. 96.

15   *In Her Words*, p. 98.

16   Background information and some of Hrotsvit's writings can be found in *Other Women's Voices: Translations of Women's Writings before 1700,* http://home.infionline.net/~ddisse/hrotsvit.html.

Otto I. Hrotsvit herself was probably of noble descent and was educated at Gandersheim from childhood. Hrotsvit was a canoness, which meant that she never did renounce the secular world. Though she lived in the abbey, she was not cloistered. She could keep her property, retain her servants, and remain a member of her family. There are indications in her writings that she was familiar with Emperor Otto's court, and her plays were very likely read dramatically there.

Founded by Emperor Otto's great-grandfather, Gandersheim was a royal abbey responsible directly to the Emper-

A Garden of Delight

Herrad von Landsberg was abbess (1167-95) of the convent of St. Odile in Hohenbourg. As abbess she wrote an encyclopedia of learning for the women in her convent which she called *Hortus Deliciarum* or the 'Garden of Delights.' Consisting of 300 parchment folio-size leaves, the manuscript was a selection of writings from Scripture, ancient writers and early Church fathers through the most recent scholarship of Anselm, Bernard of Clairvaux, and Peter Lombard. The manual also contained 344 illustrations, 130 of which were brightly illuminated. Manuscripts with such extensive illustrations were unusual at the time.

Herrad wrote, 'Like a bee inspired by God, I collected from the diverse flowers of sacred scripture and philosophic writings this book, which is called the *Hortus Deliciarum*, and I brought it together to the praise and honor of Christ and the church and for the sake of your love as if into a single sweet honeycomb. Therefore, in this very book, you ought diligently to seek pleasing food and to refresh your exhausted soul with its honeyed dewdrops...'

The original manuscript of *Hortus Deliciarum* was destroyed by fire at Strasbourg's library in 1870. Before its destruction, however, copious notes and line-drawing illustrations had been made by 19th-century scholars. The episode reminds us of the transitory nature of handwritten works, when there might be only one copy available, before the fifteenth-century invention of the printing press made books more accessible.*

* *Other Women's Voices*, http://home.infionline.net/~ddisse/herrad.html.

or, not the Church. This gave the abbey a great amount of independence. In 947, Otto freed the abbey from royal rule and allowed the abbess to have a seat in the Imperial Diet, coin money, maintain an army, and hold her own law court. The abbey itself was a place of education and culture where noble women were schooled in the liberal arts and read classical literature, as well as Scripture and the lives of the saints. Emperor Otto encouraged the building up not only of the court libraries but also of the libraries of the abbeys. Hrotsvit thus had access to the best scholarly works.

Hrotsvit's writings included many different forms – eight legends, six plays in classical form, two epics, and a short poem, all written in Latin. Adapting the style of the Latin author Terence, Hrotsvit was the first Christian writer to write plays. Her plays are as delightful today as they were a millennium ago when first written and continue to be published in German, French, English, Hungarian, Italian, and Dutch. Her sources and subjects covered a wide range, from early Christian apocrypha through tenth-century Spain. A key theme of Hrotsvit's work was the conflict between paganism and Christianity. In several of her works, Christian martyrs are shown to have truly triumphed in their defeat of Satan and their victory in Christ. Hrotsvit's plays included the earliest record of a man making a pact with the devil, the forerunner of the *Faust* story. Hrotsvit obviously delighted in portraying scenes in which pagan Roman authority could not stand against the power of Christ, especially when shown through the courage and wisdom of young virgins. These were writings that would be appreciated and enjoyed in the abbey, as well as at Otto's court. Hrotsvit explained her reason for writing as follows:

> I do not deny that by the gift of the Creator's grace I am able to grasp certain concepts of the arts because I am a creature capable of learning, but I also know that through my own powers, I know nothing. I also know that God gave me a sharp mind...and that thus, the Giver of my talent all the more justly be praised through me, the more limited the female intellect is believed to be. This alone was my intention in writing, my only thought; this alone was the reason why my work was wrought.[17]

In the preface to her plays, Hrotsvit wrote that she preached 'Christ's glory and strength as it works through His saints to the extent He grants me the ability to do so.'

Changes of the New Millennium

The centuries opening the second millennium saw a number of important changes within the Church as well as secular society. The Church was rife with corruption – positions in the Church were bought and sold, civil authorities appointed Church officials, and immorality was widespread among the clergy. Reform movements began both within the Church and the monastic orders. The monastery at Cluny (established by Dhuoda's grandson) began a movement for monastic reform, which spread throughout the West when one of its own, Hildebrand, became Pope Gregory VII. The Gregorian reforms sought to free the Church and the clergy from secular control, making the Church totally independent from the state, and sought to bring moral reform to the Church.

One of the changes that directly affected women was the Roman Church's requirement of celibacy for priests (a requirement not accepted

---

17   As quoted in Brenda Johnson, 'Hrotsvit of Gandersheim: Tenth Century Poet and Playwright,' Mount Saint Agnes Theological Center for Women, 2001, at http://www.mountsaintagnes. org/Resources/ResearchPapers/Detail.aspx?id=636. Some of Hrotsvit's plays and writings can be found at www.fordham.edu/halsall/basis/roswitha-toc.html.

by the Eastern Church). Though asceticism and celibacy had been valued since the early Church, celibacy did not become a universal requirement for the priesthood of the Roman Church until the twelfth century. The Second Lateran Council in 1139 articulated and promulgated the first universal law of clerical celibacy. The implementation of clerical celibacy was socially disruptive and took centuries to implement. With the Second Lateran Council, priests were required to divorce their wives, and their children became illegitimate. Their wives and children often became serfs or slaves of the Church. Many wives preferred to commit suicide than to live in serfdom. There was strong opposition from the clergy as well. They noted that priests in the Old Testament could marry. In addition, they contended that priests were not angels and should not be forced to deny their very natures. However, clerics were required to abstain from sex before serving the Eucharist, and since the Eucharist was celebrated every day, permanent abstinence was required.

Sex almost became synonymous with impurity. Women were demonized and vilified to make marriage less attractive to the clergy. Peter Damian, speaking against clerical marriage, clearly saw women as the enemy:

> I speak to you, o charmers of the clergy, appetizing flesh of the devil, that castaway from paradise, poison of the minds, death of souls, companions of the very stuff of sin, the cause of your ruin. You, I say, I exhort you women of the ancient enemy, you bitches, sows, screech-owls, night-owls, blood-suckers, she-wolves – come now, hear me, harlots, prostitutes, with your lascivious kisses, you wallowing places for fat pigs, couches for unclean spirits.[18]

Such a denigrating attitude to women was far removed from the New Testament attitude in which male and female were equal in Christ. Yet, Peter Damian's attitude did have some roots in Church history. As the early Church was influenced by Greek philosophy and the Scripture began to be interpreted allegorically, 'woman' became identified with the flesh and all that would debase and bring 'man,' the spiritual, into sin. Since the flesh was considered evil, sex itself, even within marriage, could be defiling. The monks in the Egyptian desert had often visualized temptation in the form of a lustful woman. Though some of the writings of the early Church fathers, including those of Augustine and especially of Jerome, contained anti-feminine outbursts, in their personal relations with women, they showed respect for women. Many of the letters the various fathers wrote to women reflected respect and appreciation for the spiritual and even intellectual attainments of women, which seemed at variance with the disparagement of women found elsewhere in their writings.

18   As quoted in Anne Llewellyn Barstow, *Married Priests and the Reforming Papacy: The Eleventh Century Debates,* (The Edwin Mellen Press, 1982), p. 60.

At the same time that clerical celibacy began to be strictly enforced, the cloistering of nuns for moral purposes was increasingly required. Pope Boniface VIII issued the first decree for the universal enclosure of women in religious orders in 1298. Conventual clothing became mandatory, and the activities of the nuns were restricted; women were losing their place of service in the Church. Though clerical marriage might have declined under the new regulations, clerical concubinage continued to flourish, which, of course, demeaned both the women and the priests.

With the abolition of lay investiture,[19] the power of the Church hierarchy itself increased. A growing gap developed between clergy and laity, with the laity being viewed as second-class Christians. Power and obedience became more important than love and example. The power the clergy possessed was in part connected with the growing sacramental system. Under the doctrine of transubstantiation, the priest at mass had the cultic power to transform the bread and wine into the substance of the body and blood of Christ. The sacrament of penance gave the priest localized control over the parish through the confessional. The sacramental authority of the priests brought about a declining influence of the convents. Since the priest could celebrate the Eucharist, pray masses for the dead, and grant absolution for sins, the priest had more power than the nuns. More funding went to the monasteries and Church establishments, and the basic equality that had existed between the male and female monasteries was destroyed. Most monks were ordained to the priesthood, destroying the lay monasticism which had promoted the equality of men and women.

Material changes of the period undoubtedly affected the lives of those common women about whom so little is known. Simple developments often had important effects on the lives of women. During this time the chimney stack was developed. No longer would the smoke from the fire permeate the home before finding its way through a hole in the roof. With the knowledge of currents and pressure, the orientation of prevailing winds according to the local geography, and the proper placement of conduits and pipes, the chimney greatly improved the home's fireplace. The hearth became the meeting and working place for the home. Mills replaced the grindstone for the grinding of grain, reducing woman's work. Window glass and glass mirrors improved the homes of a growing middle class. The development of hard soap enhanced cleanliness. Buttons added design and utility to clothing. Though these physical changes affecting the lives of ordinary women can be documented, little documentation remains of their spiritual lives.

The growing towns competed with each other to see which could build the tallest and grandest cathedral. Universities grew out of the

---

19   Lay investiture was the appointment of priests and ecclesiastical officers by the civil rulers.

cathedral schools, but education at the growing universities was restricted
to clerics, and the quality of education that had once been available for
women in nunneries declined. The schoolmen of the medieval universities
used dialectical reasoning in attempting to reconcile Christian theology
and ancient classical philosophy. Aristotle's teaching that women were
intellectually and morally inferior to men influenced the scholastics, who
often expressed disdain for women and their abilities. Such disdain is
evident in the behavior of Abelard (1079-1142). Abelard was among the
most famous of the early scholastics. His scholarship and skill in debate led
him to establish his own school by the age of 21. Though a brilliant scholar,
Abelard is probably best remembered today for his immorality and sordid
affair with Heloise, a woman twenty years younger than he.[20] The disdain
for women found in Abelard and other scholastics of the period was a
result of scholastic reasoning supplanting the truth and power of Scripture.

The monastic ideal of living apart from the world and spending time
in constant prayer, psalm singing, and Bible study became less attractive
to women in the opening centuries of the new millennium. The freedom
and autonomy of the early medieval nunneries were replaced by a stricter
clerical control and administration. The female monasteries were no
longer places of intellectual stimulation and study, and the universities
denied scholarly pursuits to women as well. At the same time, in the late
Middle Ages, women developed new forms of spiritual expression, and
female mystics became prominent.

20   Ruth A. Tucker, 'Heloise and Abelard's Tumultuous Affair,' *Christian History (Women in the Medieval Church Issue)*, Issue 30 (Vol. X, No. 2), pp. 28-30. The letters of Abelard and Heloise can be found at www.sacred-texts.com/chr/aah/index.htm. See also *Other Women's Voices*, http://home.infionline.net/~ddisse/heloise.html.

Christian Women in the Late Middle Ages: *Well Reported for Good Works*

1 Timothy 5:10

The Late Middle Ages was the age of great cathedral building, the founding of universities, and scholastic learning. These and other epochal developments marked a metamorphosis from medieval to modern times. Political, social, and ecclesiastical changes included the rise of nation states, growth in trade, the expansion of urban centers with a rising middle class, campaigns against heresy, the emergence of mendicant (begging) religious orders, the cult of the Virgin Mary, political struggles of the papacy, and a new emphasis on the humanity of Christ. Many historians have noted a change in the expressions of piety around the thirteenth century, responding to these numerous changes in both society and the Church. It is not surprising, then, to find medieval women expressing their piety in new forms. The number of female saints canonized by the Church doubled during this period. These female saints were from a broader spectrum of society than previously and included lay women as well as cloistered females.

Women's position in the Church during this period differed in many respects from the early Church and the period of the barbarian conversions. The powerful abbesses and the double monasteries of the early period were no more. The quasi-clerical role of women in the nunneries, where women preached to women under them and even administered communion, existed no longer. As the Christian celebration of communion developed into the ceremony of the consecration of the Eucharist, the priesthood gained in power and authority. The role of priest became primarily to officiate at the ceremony allegedly transforming the bread and wine into Christ's body and blood. As more priests were needed to perform repeatedly and routinely the ritual celebration of the mass at cathedrals and chapels throughout Europe, the number of priests available for the spiritual oversight of women's convents declined, and the creation of new nunneries was restricted. The older convents originally established for the nobility did not expand to embrace the growing number of women from middle-class artisan and merchant families. New avenues for female religious life consequently developed, and some Christian women formed new organizations for Christian service beyond the convent. Women seeking personal religious experiences were at the center of the new mysticism arising in the Church. At the same time, a craze of witchcraft-hunting based more on skewed philosophical reasonings than on Scripture was a witness to the denigration of women found among some Church leaders and scholastics during this period

Reformers and Para-Church Groups

Throughout the centuries, traditions and accretions have attached themselves to the Church, often diluting and distracting the Church's clear gospel message and focus on Christ. Always, men and women have arisen to call the Church to return to the narrow way of Christ. In an age of growing wealth and prosperity for the Church, Francis of Assisi (1182-1226) renounced his wealthy inheritance and took a vow of poverty. Rather than retreat behind monastic walls, Francis and his followers sought to follow the via apostolica and became itinerants, preaching and caring for the poor and the sick among the common people. In 1210, Francis' rule gained approval from Pope Innocent II. Two years later Clare Scefi, a wealthy young woman of Assisi, heard a sermon Francis preached and saw the vanity of earthly things.[1] Only sixteen and expected to enter into a well-matched marriage, Clare instead put on sackcloth and went out to care for the poor. In 1212, Francis built a little cloister for Clare and her sister Agnes near the Church of St. Damian. Her mother and younger sister soon followed her there, to be joined by other women from the nobility. In 1215, Clare established the order of Poor Clares, which was closely associated with the Franciscans and also was devoted to the ideal of poverty.

The rule of the Poor Clares, drawn up in 1246, stressed poverty, fasting, and abstinence. The rule prohibited both individual women and the nunnery from holding any property. Clare never left the cloister, yet maintained a close spiritual bond with Francis. Her life of simple devotion not only influenced Francis but many others as well. The Poor Clares spread beyond Assisi to other towns in Italy, as well as to England, France, Germany, and Bohemia. For the last twenty-eight years of her life, Clare was unable to walk, probably due to severe austerities in her early days. When Agnes, daughter of the King of Bohemia and niece of the King of Hungary, joined the Order of Clares, Clare wrote her, 'Since our bodies are not of brass and our strength is not that of stone, but instead we are

---

1   *Other Women's Voices*, http://home.infionline.net/~ddisse/clare.html.

weak and subject to infirmities, I implore you vehemently in the Lord to refrain from exceeding rigors of abstinence [e.g. fasting] which I know you practice.'[2]

While the Poor Clares lived a cloistered life, others sought to help the poor without totally removing themselves from the world. In Belgium a religious movement arose among women which spread to France, Germany, and beyond. Due to the effects of wars, crusades, and feuds, the female population greatly outnumbered males. Many of the women who desired a life dedicated to God remained in their own homes and community while dedicating themselves to the service of others. Living a simple life, they became involved in education and cared for the sick, the orphaned, and lepers. They did not take vows or relinquish their property, but they ministered in their own communities in the name of Christ. Called Beguines, a name of uncertain derivation, women also sought to live life in the simple manner of the early apostles. In time, however, formal institutional patterns were established. Several European cities today have the remains of beguinages, districts where the Beguines lived and carried out their varied activities.

The personal religion provided by mysticism flourished among the Beguines. Many of the Beguines became particularly devoted to the Eucharist and desired the mystical union of the soul with God. Hadewijch of Brabant (c. 1200), in her book of visions, described in erotic terms the oneness with Christ brought through the Eucharist:

> ...looking like a Human Being and a Man, wonderful, and beautiful, and with glorious face, he came to me as humbly as anyone who wholly belongs to another. Then he gave himself to me in the shape of the Sacrament, in its outward form, as the custom is; and then he gave me to drink from the chalice, in form and taste, as the custom is. After that he came himself to me, took me entirely in his arms, and pressed me to him; and all my members felt his in full felicity, in accordance with the desire of my heart and my humanity. So I was outwardly satisfied and fully transported...I saw him completely come to nought and so fade and all at once dissolve that I could no longer recognize or perceive him outside me, and I could no longer distinguish him within me. Then it was to me as if we were one without difference.... After that I remained in a passing away in my Beloved, so that I wholly melted away in him and nothing any longer remained to me of myself, and I was changed and taken up in the spirit...[3]

While the Scriptures described the Church as the Bride of Christ, Hadewijch and many of the women mystics saw themselves as personally

---

2   Quoted in *Great Women of the Christian Faith*, p. 41.

3   Quoted in *In Her Words*, p. 116.

and individually the spiritual Bride of Christ. Hadewijch and many of her fellow-Beguines wrote in the vernacular rather than the Latin of the educated elite. This was a movement which reached the middle-class women of the towns.

The Helfta Convent

The Helfta Convent, near Eisleben in Saxony, was an outstanding convent for women. Helfta was both an intellectual and spiritual center, and under abbess Gertrude of Hackeborn (1251-92) was a center of mysticism as well. The convent took in orphans and young girls for schooling. Three women of Helfta wrote spiritual works which influenced later mysticism or continue as part of Roman Catholic devotion today: Gertrude the Great (1256-c.1302), Mechthild of Hackeborn (1240-98), and Mechthild of Magdeburg (c.1210-c.1283). Mechthild of Magdeburg left her life as a Beguine and spent her last years at Helfta. Many in the convent were skilled craftswomen, especially at making books, and the convent's choir was renowned.*

---

* *Other Women's Voices,* http://home.infionline.net/~ddisse/gertrud.html.

Mechthild of Magdeburg (c. 1210-1280), another Beguine, collected the mystical visions and reflections she had received since she was twelve in *The Flowing Light of the Godhead.*[4] Mechthild saw God in everything and taught that the true home of the soul was in God alone. She taught that not only did the soul long for God, but that God needed and longed for man's soul. Her writings were translated into Latin, and some think they influenced Dante's depiction of Paradise. While Mechthild's work continued to have influence, the work of a later Beguine, Marguerite Porete (d. 1310), caused charges of heresy to be brought against her. In *The Mirror of Simple Souls*, Marguerite wrote that the soul could be so absorbed in a complete union with God that it no longer had a separate existence.[5] Marguerite's work was condemned as heretical, and when she continued to distribute it and support its claims, she was condemned as a relapsed heretic and burned at the stake in Paris in 1310.

　　Though at first accepted by the Roman Church, the Beguines later fell out of favor. The Church had no control over these uncloistered women free from the regulations of vows of obedience. Their industriousness and work, especially in textiles, threatened the economic privileges of the cloth industry guilds, which were developing in the towns of the time. There was, too, always the suspicion that women were more prone to heresy; their spiritual ideas needed better oversight than the loosely organized Beguines provided.

4　　*Other Women's Voices,* http://home.infionline.net/~ddisse/mechthil.html.

5　　*Other Women's Voices,* http://home.infionline.net/~ddisse/porete.html.

In the fourteenth century, the English scholar John Wycliffe (c. 1329-1384) encouraged the reformation of the Church by a return to the Scriptures. He confronted the hierarchical structure of the Roman Church as well as the Church's wealth and large land holdings. He also opposed transubstantiation, claiming Christ was spiritually, not physically, present in what was still the bread and wine of the Eucharist. Most importantly, Wycliffe taught that the Scriptures, the Word of God, should be available to the people. He encouraged, if he did not actually participate in, the first translation of the complete Bible into English.

Followers of Wycliffe's ideas became known as Lollards. In the fourteenth and fifteenth centuries, Lollard lay preachers travelled throughout England and Scotland teaching the Bible, and a loose network of Lollard supporters developed. The sparse evidence indicates that whenever women were a part of Lollardy, they most often were acting with their husbands in attending the meetings. Lollardy was a family, not a monastic, affair. In Bristol, for example, Christiana and William More, members of the governing class of the city, shared interests in the Lollard cause. They even supported a Lollard chaplain in their home for a time. When Christiana became a widow in 1412, she continued to manage her husband's estate and provided patronage to the Lollards. In 1414 she was among eight 'heretics' brought before the Bishop. She was probably spared execution because of her social position.

There is evidence that some women learned to read specifically so that they could read the Lollard literature, and several Lollard women are known to have been active in book distribution. Copies of the Scriptures themselves were scarce, and women learned long Scripture passages, which they could recite in meetings. Some married couples are known to have worked together as missionaries among the people, spreading the truth of the Scriptures. There are also records of daughters continuing the missionary work of their Lollard fathers, learning Scripture passages to recite at meetings.[6] The clerical authorities, however, were horrified that the Scriptures were being opened to the inferior understanding of women.

Ruling Saints

As in earlier periods, during the Middle Ages Christian queens continued to use their influence and patronage to further the cause of Christ. By her godly manner of life, Margaret of Scotland (1045-1092) shaped the court of Scotland along a more Christian path. Margaret, daughter of the exiled English Prince Edward Atheling of the Royal House of Wessex, was born at the court of St. Stephen, King of Hungary. Her mother Agatha was the niece of the Holy Roman Emperor, Henry III. Prince Edward and his

---

6   Claire Cross, 'Great Reasoners in Scriptures: The Activities of Women Lollards, 1380-1530,' Derek Baker, ed. *Medieval Women* (Oxford: Basil Blackwell, 1978), 359-79.

family returned to England under King Edward the Confessor. However, after England's defeat at the Battle of Hastings in 1066 and the death of her husband, Prince Edward, Agatha was returning to Hungary with her children when her ship was driven up the Firth of Forth to Dunfermline, where the family was warmly received by Malcolm III, King of Scotland. Malcolm was the son of Duncan I, who had been killed by Macbeth. Malcolm lived in exile until he himself defeated and killed Macbeth in 1057 and succeeded to the throne. When Agatha and her family arrived in Scotland, Malcolm's wife had died, and he offered to marry Margaret, then about 23.

Margaret was leaning to becoming a nun, but she found a position of Christian service in her marriage to Malcolm. Early chroniclers wrote:

> And this Edgar's sister Margaret, King Malcolm united to himself in wedlock with the consent of her kindred; a woman noble in her royal descent, but much more noble in her prudence and religion. By her zeal and industry the king himself lay aside his barbarity of manner and became more honourable and more refined.[7]

Malcolm was a virtual barbarian who relished savage attacks on the English. He could neither read nor write. Yet, as the Anglo-Saxon Chronicle stated, Margaret 'was to increase God's praise in the land and to direct the king from the erring path and to bend him to a better way, and his people with him, and to suppress the evil customs which the people did formerly use …'[8] Margaret seemed to be a wife who followed the apostle Peter's advice, to let the example of her life, even more than her words, be the means of bringing her husband to Christ[9].

Turgot, Bishop of St. Andrews, wrote that Malcolm

> could not but perceive from her conduct that Christ dwelt within her; nay, more, he readily obeyed her wishes and prudent counsels in all things. Whatever she refused, he refused also; whatever pleased her, he also loved for the love of her. Hence it was that, although he could not read, he would turn over and examine books which she used either for her devotions or her study; and whenever he heard her say that she was fonder of one of them than the others, this one he too used to look at with special affection, kissing it and often taking it in his hands. Sometimes he sent for a worker in precious metals, whom he commanded to ornament the volume with gold and gems, and when the work was finished, the King himself used to carry the volume to the Queen as a kind of proof of his devotion.[10]

7   Quoted in Lavinia Byrne, *The Life and Wisdom of Margaret of Scotland*, (New York: Alba House, 1998), p. 17

8   Byrne, *Margaret of Scotland*, p. 18.

9   1 Peter 3:1-6.

10   Turgot. *The Life of St. Margaret, Queen of Scotland* (trans. William Forbes-Leith, S.J.).Edinburgh: David Douglas, 1896, 2.13; available at http://mw.mcmaster.ca/scriptorium/margaret.html.

One such book was probably Margaret's book of the Four Gospels, now in the Bodleian Library at Oxford. In 1887, the librarian at a parish library in a small English villa offered a shabby brown volume for sale. It was a medieval octavo volume, which he sent to Sotheby's. The Bodleian Library bought it for £6. The writing on vellum was from the eleventh century. A 23-line poem inside the cover told the story that the book belonged to Margaret of Scotland. The book was beautifully bound with precious stones and gilt figures of the four Evangelists. All capital letters were radiant with gold. A person carrying it once let the book slip out unawares and it fell into a stream. The book was found open at the bottom of the river, but when it was brought up, it was virtually uninjured. After the book was so amazingly preserved, the Queen valued the book more than she had before.[11]

In her roles as wife, mother, and queen, Margaret was able to let the light of the gospel of Christ shine throughout Scotland. She created a comfortable and elegant home for her family, developed economic trade for the nation, and established charities and spiritual havens for the poor and suffering. The Chronicler Freeman wrote:

> There was no need for Margaret to bring a new religion into Scotland, but she gave a new life to the religion she found existing there, and she made changes in various points where the traditions of the Scottish Church still differed from the received practice of Western Christendom ... No royal marriage was ever more important in its results for both of the countries concerned. It was through Margaret that the old kingly blood of England passed into the veins of the descendants of the Conqueror; it was in her daughter [Matilda, who married England's Henry I, fourth son of William the Conqueror], the heiress of her virtues, that the green tree began to return to its place....[12]

The *Douay Chronicle* recorded that

> ... her palace, her furniture, offices, maids of honour, table and all that appeared externally, were indeed suitable to the state and dignity of a Queen, but her secret life was such as became a true servant of God.[13]

Turgot even noted that Margaret encouraged the wearing of the plaid cloth which has come to characterize the dress of Scotland:

> It was due to her that the merchants who came by land and sea from various countries brought with them for sale different kinds of precious wares which until then were unknown in Scotland. And it was at her instigation that the natives of Scotland purchased from these traders clothing of various colours, with ornaments to wear, so that from this period, through her suggestion, new costumes of different fashions

---

11 *Life of St. Margaret*, III. p. 33

12 *Margaret of Scotland*, p. 18.

13 Ibid., p. 19.

were adopted, the elegance of which made the wearers appear like a race of new beings.[14]

Margaret's first action upon becoming queen was to add a chapel, apse, and tower to the Church of the Holy Trinity at Dunfermline. Heavily influenced by and in close touch with Lanfranc, Archbishop of Canterbury, she convened Church councils and worked to get the Scottish or Culdee Church to follow the Roman rites and customs. She encouraged the 40-day fast during Lent, regular communion and observance of the Lord's Supper, a standardized liturgy, and Sunday as the Lord's Day. Margaret also led a life of personal devotion, rising early and spending much time in prayer and the reading of the Psalms, as well as caring for the orphans and needy. Margaret had six sons and daughters. Her sons secured two hundred years of peace for Scotland, an unbroken line of seven kings. Her daughter Matilda became Queen of England as the wife of King Henry I.

Two centuries after Margaret, Elizabeth of Hungary (1207-1231) also used her queenly position and wealth to show Christ's love to her people. Elizabeth was the daughter of King Andrew II and Queen Gertrude of Hungary. When she was only four years old, she was betrothed to Ludwig, son of the Landgrave of Thuringia, and she went to live with her in-laws at the Wartburg Castle (later made famous as the place where Martin Luther translated the Bible into German). When she was seven, Elizabeth's mother was murdered in a political assassination. Even as a child, Elizabeth prayed for the murderers. Her mother had a strong Christian faith, and two aunts and an uncle were leaders in the Church. One aunt founded a convent for lepers, another was an abbess, and the uncle was Bishop of Bamberg.

Elizabeth married in 1221, when she was 14. Having grown up together in the castle, Elizabeth and Ludwig always called each other 'Sister' and 'Brother.' Ludwig lived up to his motto of 'Piety, Chastity, and Justice,' and opened his home to help nuns, monks, and those in need. Elizabeth was stirred by the poverty and message of St. Francis and used her wealth to help others. When the kingdom suffered a famine in 1226, Elizabeth fed the people from her own stores and distributed firewood to the weak. She sold her jewels and her silver cradle and gave the proceeds to those in need. Ludwig appreciated Elizabeth's work and was thankful she had kept so many in his kingdom from starvation: 'Let her do good and give to God whatever she will, so long as she leaves me Wartburg and Nurnberg. Alms will never ruin us.'[15]

Though they had five castles, Elizabeth considered her four children her greatest treasures and heritage of the Lord. One child was born after

---

14   Ibid., p. 20.

15   As quoted in *Great Women of the Christian Faith*, p. 46.

Ludwig died in 1227 from a fever while on a crusade. At Ludwig's death Elizabeth prayed:

> I give Thee thanks, O Lord, that Thou hast been pleased to grant Thy handmaid the great desire I had to behold the remains of my beloved, and in Thy compassion to comfort my afflicted soul. I do not repine that he was offered up by himself and by me for the relief of Thy Holy Land, although with all my heart I love him. Thou knowest, O God, that I would set his presence, - most delightful to me – before all the joys and enchantments of this world, had Thy graciousness yielded him to me. But now I lay at Thy disposal him and me, as Thou wilt. Nay, though I could call him back at the cost of the smallest hair of my head, I would not call him back against Thy will.[16]

After Ludwig's death, his brother disapproved of Elizabeth's works of charity and threw her out of the castle. Ludwig's fellow Crusaders successfully demanded that Elizabeth be reinstated to her position. With her dowry money Elizabeth established a hospital. Below the Wartburg Castle she built a leprosarium, and she operated the first orphanage in Eastern Europe. Elizabeth was never idle and was often at her spinning wheel, where she spent time in prayer while she worked.

In 1231, Elizabeth died at the age of twenty-four. Though her life was brief, she had totally devoted it to the service of Christ. The poor, the blind, the lepers, and the lame attended her funeral. When she was declared a saint four years later, two hundred thousand people gathered at her grave in Marburg to honor her.

Saints or Witches?

Mysticism was an alternative to the scholasticism of the schools and theology of the monasteries – an alternative especially available to women. Mysticism may be defined as a human mind's effort to merge indescribable thoughts with transitory feelings in an effort to seek joyful communion or oneness with God. Grounded on two such variables – vague thoughts and feelings – mysticism is not capable of more precise definition. Mystics sought to find the sacred in their own lives, going beyond the creeds, dogmas, and ideas of the faith in an effort to actually experience God. Christian mystics very often used the same mystic meditative and contemplative techniques found in other religions, but used the symbolism and words of Christianity, such as the Crucifixion, Resurrection, Father, Son, and Holy Spirit. By means of a series of mystical exercises, the mystic sought to progress through various stages towards the highest level of mysticism: unity with God, the 'true peace of the soul.' The soul was prepared for mystic union with God through

---

16   Ibid., p. 48.

self-sacrifice, self-chastisement, and extreme asceticism (today, many of these 'holy women' would be recognized as anorexic).[17] In some ways, the mystics partook of Gnostic teaching and practices; secret and subjective knowledge and experience became more important than the Word of God. The death, burial, and resurrection of Christ were not so much historical, redemptive facts as symbols of the 'inner Christ' in the heart. For the mystic, the soul's experience of oneness with Christ replaced obedience to Christ's commandments. Since this 'experience of oneness' was entirely subjective, it was difficult to challenge, verify, or transmit to another.

Hildegard of Bingen (1098-1179) is among the medieval mystics who have enjoyed growing popularity in recent years, beginning especially with the 900th anniversary of her birth in 1998.[18] Hildegard was the daughter of a knight and his pious wife. Since Hildegard was their tenth child, they offered her as a tithe to God. At the age of eight she was taken to live with Jutta von Sponheim, an anchorite or religious hermit. Jutta lived in a cell adjoining the church at Disibodenberg, near Mainz, Germany, where she could daily hear mass. Hildegard was locked into the cell with Jutta and her servant (Jutta was a noblewoman, and as such could have a servant, even if she was an anchorite). As other women joined her, Jutta became abbess over her community.

With Jutta, Hildegard learned the psalms in Latin and how to sing the monastic hours. From Hildegard's later writings, obviously her education under Jutta was broad and included Biblical commentaries, monastic works, liturgical texts, writings from the fathers, and medical and rabbinical treatises. Hildegard was also tutored by Volmar, a monk and librarian at the nearby monastery. Volmar became Hildegard's spiritual director and lifelong secretary. When Jutta died, Hildegard, at the age of 38, was elected her successor. Hildegard later moved the nuns to Bingen.

From early childhood, Hildegard had visions and occasionally prophesied the future. Not until she was a teenager did she realize that other people were not seeing the same things she saw. She later described these early visions:

> From my early childhood, before my bones, nerves and veins were fully strengthened, I have always seen this vision in my soul, even to the present time when I am more than seventy years old. In this vision my soul, as God would have it, rises up high into the vault of heaven and into the changing sky and spreads itself out among different peoples,

---

17 Caroline Walker Bynum's *Holy Feast and Holy Fast: The Religious Significance of Food to Medieval Women* (University of California Press, 1987) is the groundbreaking treatment of the ascetic practices of medieval women mystics.

18 *Other Women's Voices*, http://home.infionline.net/~ddisse/hildegar.html.

although they are far away from me in distant lands and places...I do not hear them with my outward ears, nor do I perceive them by the thoughts of my own heart or by any combination of my five senses, but in my soul alone, while my outward eyes are open. So I have never fallen prey to ecstasy in the visions, but I see them wide awake, day and night. And I am constantly fettered by sickness, and often in the grip of pain so intense that it threatens to kill me, but God has sustained me until now.

The light which I see thus is not spatial, but it is far, far brighter than a cloud which carries the sun. I can measure neither height nor length, nor breadth in it, and I call it 'the reflection of the living Light.' And as the sun, the moon, and the stars appear in water, so writings, sermons, virtues, and certain human actions take form for me and gleam within it....what I write is what I see and hear in the vision. I compose no other words than those I hear...And the words in this vision are not like words uttered by the mouth of man, but like a shimmering flame, or a cloud floating in a clear sky. Moreover, I can no more recognize the form of this light than I can gaze directly on the sphere of the sun. Sometimes – but not often – I see within this light another light, which I call 'the living Light.' And I cannot describe when and how I see it, but while I see it all sorrow and anguish leave me...And when I see and hear things in this vision, my soul drinks them in as from a fountain, which yet remains full and unexhausted. At no time is my soul deprived of that light which I call the reflection of the living Light, and I see it as if I were gazing at a starless sky in a shining cloud. In it I see the things of which I frequently speak, and I answer my correspondents from the radiance of this living Light.[19]

In 1917, Charles Singer, a historian of science, diagnosed Hildegard with 'scintillating scotoma,' a form of migraine accompanied by visions of flashing light and circles of light within light. Some have also found evidence that Hildegard suffered from migraines in the coloring and design of the pictures she made illustrating her visions.

Hildegard did not speak of her visions of light until she was 42, when she received what she thought was a divine call to share her visions. As she described the event in the prologue to the *Scivias*, the work recording her visions:

It happened in the year 1141 of the Incarnation of God's Son Jesus Christ, when I was forty-two years and seven months old, that the heavens were opened and a fiery light of great brilliance came and suffused my whole brain and set my whole heart and breast afire like a flame – yet not burning but warming, as the sun warms an object on which it sheds its rays. And suddenly I came to understand the meaning of the book of Psalms, the Gospel, and the other canonical books of both the Old and New Testaments – ...in a marvelous way, I had sensed the power and

---

19   Hildegard of Bingen, *Epistle* 2, translated by Barbara Newman, 'Hildegard of Bingen: Visions and Validation,' *Church History*, Vol. 54, No. 2 (June 1985), 164-5. Selections from Hildegard's works are available at *Other Women's Voices*, http://home.infionline.net/~ddisse/hildegar.html.

> mystery of secret, wonderful visions in myself from girlhood, from the
> age of five, even to the present time.[20]

Hildegard considered her visions almost as inspired as Scripture. She
professed a direct experience of God and claimed to speak the word of
God as a prophetess. Since she was in direct communication with God, she
did not need the mediation of anyone in her approach to God.

Hildegard's visions were the basis of her authority as a teacher, for
Hildegard did not remain cloistered with her fellow-nuns. She traveled
and preached throughout southern Germany and into Switzerland and
as far as Paris, where the faculty at the new University of Paris approved
her works. Her surviving works include letters to Popes, bishops, nuns,
and nobility, often attacking corruptions in the Church and society and
warning the contemporary leaders of impending judgment on iniquity.

Hildegard is astonishing for the sheer range of her interests and
accomplishments. As one of her biographers noted, 'she would have been
extraordinary in any age.'[21] For her visions and her preaching Hildegard
received the full support of the Church hierarchy. Volmar first brought
Hildegard's visionary experiences to the attention of the Church authorities,
who gave Hildegard permission to keep records of her visions. Bernard of
Clairvaux endorsed her visions. At the Council of Trier in 1147, the Pope
saw an early version of Hildegard's *Scivias*, dealing with the content of
Hildegard's visions, and approved her writings – making Hildegard the first
woman permitted by the Pope to write a theological book. In describing her
visions in the *Scivias*, she extensively used allegory and parable to present
Church doctrines. Like several visionaries after her, Hildegard claimed to
have the spirit of prophecy and to speak the words the Holy Spirit had given
to her. In deference to these claims, she was permitted to speak publicly to
mixed audiences of both clergy and laity, even though a woman.

In recounting her visions, Hildegard also included drawings that
depicted what she had seen. In her drawings, Hildegard represented the
cosmic egg,[22] Sophia as the Wisdom of God, and employed the mandala to
bring unity between the soul and the cosmic order.[23] Hildegard's creation-
centered theology was very close to pantheism and has been embraced by

20   As translated by Newman, 'Visions and Validation,' p. 166.

21   Barabara Newman, ed. *Voice of the Living Light: Hildegard of Bingen and Her World*. Berkeley:
      University of California Press, 1998, p. 1.

22   The 'cosmic egg' is a creation myth found in many cultures, in which the world system comes
      into being by 'hatching' from the egg.

23   A *mandala* is a schematic depiction of a harmonious universe, usually consisting of concentric
      squares or circles, in each of which is an image of God or a symbol of deity, e.g., a cross.
      Kaleidoscopic in appearance, mandalas are commonly found in Oriental art.

New Age supporters as they return to the goddess religions of the pagan past.

Seventy-two of Hildegard's liturgical chants survive, along with their musical notations. These became amazingly popular when performed and recorded in the 1990s. Hildegard wrote a musical morality play about the battle for the Soul between the Virtues and the Devil. Though the Soul at first listened to the Virtues, it turned aside to follow the Devil. Learning that following the Devil only brought misery, however, the Soul returned to the Virtues. Hildegard wrote nine books, including a commentary on the Gospels and the Athanasian Creed and *De Operatione Dei*, a work on ethics. She was the first known woman to write extensively on medicine and natural science.

Bernard of Clairvaux (1090-1153), who encouraged Hildegard in her prophecies, greatly influenced the direction of the mysticism of the late Middle Ages. Bernard was a strong opponent of Scholasticism and was the prosecutor at Abelard's heresy trial. He worked tirelessly for the peace of the Church and the healing of the schism that had led to the simultaneous existence of two Popes. Bernard encouraged the veneration of the Virgin Mary and a more personal, rather than simply liturgical, devotion. His sermons on the Song of Solomon fostered a mysticism expressed in the most erotic imagery, with the Christian soul as the Bride ravished by Christ's love. This religious mysticism was much more prominent among women than among men, and the thirteenth and fourteenth centuries were especially replete with renowned female mystics.

The mystic Julian of Norwich (1343-1413) was an anchoress who lived a much more solitary life than Hildegard.[24] A contemporary of John Wycliffe and Geoffrey Chaucer, Julian lived in a cell built on the wall of the Church of St. Julian in Norwich. She had a window through which she could daily hear mass and receive communion, and another window through which she could speak to those in the outside world. In this cloistered setting, Julian spent her days in prayer, meditation, and the worship of God. She prayed specifically for three things: a bodily sight of Christ's passion so she could share in His suffering as His mother had; illness that would purge through suffering all love for worldly things; and three wounds – a sorrow for sin, suffering with Christ, and a longing for God. When she was 30 years old, she became ill for five days, so ill that the last rites were called for. When the priest lifted the crucifix at the foot of the bed, the light focused on the face of Christ and all Julian's pain left. The following day Julian received sixteen revelations or 'showings' of God's love, including visions of the Passion. Twenty years later, in 1393,

---

24   *Other Women's Voices*, http://home.infionline.net/~ddisse/julian.html.

Julian wrote down her visions and the continued inward teachings she had received on them.

Julian's *Reflections on Divine Love* was the first spiritual book written by an Englishwoman. That Julian wrote in English, as did her contemporaries Chaucer and Wycliffe (at least the Wycliffite Bible was in English, though Wycliffe himself wrote many scholarly treatises in Latin), was some indication of the growing importance of the vernacular languages at this time. Julian's writings were not well known in her day, however. Only four manuscripts of her book are known to exist. In 1902, Julian's *Reflections on Divine Love* was printed for the first time and soon became widely popular.

In an age which emphasized God's judgment for sin, Julian focused on God's love and compassion through Jesus Christ. She also minimized human sinfulness. In a story of a Lord and his Servant, Julian related that a Servant was rushing to do his Lord's bidding when he fell into a gully and was badly hurt. The Lord lovingly looked upon the Servant and rejoiced at the great rest and glory he would bring the Servant by his grace. Julian interpreted this parable in relation to the fall of Adam. In doing so, she suggested that the fall of Adam was simply an accident and not the result of disobedience or deliberate wrongdoing. Even after he fell, the Servant still wanted to do the Lord's will. The Lord was never angry with the Servant, but only looked upon him with love. So, God looks upon fallen man with love, not anger. The condemnation and judgment that resulted from the fall, of which Paul wrote in Romans 5:15-17, were not part of Julian's perspective. She believed that 'in every soul that shall be saved there is a godly will that never assented to sin, nor ever shall. This will is so good that it can never will any evil. But always and forever it wills good, and does good, in the sight of God.'[25] For Julian, as for Thomas Aquinas, original sin was considered merely the absence of the higher gifts of grace; sin was not the guilty transgression of God's law. In grace, God merely filled in what was missing in our human nature, which nature in itself was good. Sin had no substance and was only known by the pain it caused. Adam's sin was the worst harm that had ever been done, and since Christ's atonement brought more good than Adam's sin did harm, then Christ will bring good out of all lesser evils too. This was the foundation of Julian's most oft-quoted phrase, 'All shall be well, and all shall be well, and all manner of things shall be well.'

Contradicting Paul's clear statements in Romans 6, Julian said that sin will be a glory, not a shame to man; the mark of sin will become honor. There was no anger in God; God pities man but does not blame him for sin. Many of these statements by Julian would have been considered unorthodox and heretical in the fourteenth century. Perhaps that was the reason Julian's

---

25 *Showings of Reflections of Divine Love*, Ch. 52, as quoted in Sheila Upjohn, *Why Julian Now?: A Voyage of Discovery* (Grand Rapids, Michigan: William B. Eerdmans Publishing Co.), 1997, p. 35.

Revelations were not well known in her day and were only quietly passed around among friends. That she became revered after her work was published in the early twentieth century was in part due to the decline in importance of doctrine among many Christians at that time.

Julian lived during the difficult days of the Hundred Years War, and she was six years old when the Black Death first entered England. Outbreaks of the plague continued throughout her lifetime. It is understandable that in a world of such disruption and tragedy Julian turned to God's love as solace for her soul. Julian's spiritual lesson from a hazelnut in one of her visions demonstrated this focus on God's love:

> And then he showed me a little thing, the size of a hazelnut, in the palm of my hand, and it was as round as a ball. I looked at it with my mind's eye and I thought: 'What can this be?' And the answer came 'It is all that is made.' I marveled that it could last, for I thought it might suddenly have crumbled to nothing, it was so small. And the answer came into my mind: 'It lasts and ever shall, because God loves it.' And so all things have being through the love of God.[26]

Thus, Julian not only understood the greatness of God but also the importance of His love in sustaining all He had made.

Some have speculated, with some plausibility, that Julian was married and lost at least one child and possibly her husband to the Black Plague (or to the Hundred Years War). Julian's understanding of maternal feelings seems to come from her own experiences. As Christ died on the cross, He bore people into new life, just as a woman might die in childbirth, bringing new life as well. Julian not only spoke of God using maternal images, but repeatedly called God 'Mother':

> I contemplated the work of all the blessed Trinity. In which contemplation I saw and understood these three properties: the property of the fatherhood, the property of the motherhood, and the property of the lordship in one God. In one almighty Father we have our protection and our bliss, ... and in the second person, in knowledge and wisdom we have our perfection, as regards our sensuality, our restoration and our salvation, for he is our Mother, brother, and saviour and in our good Lord the Holy Spirit we have our reward and our gift for our living and our labour...the high might of the Trinity is our Father, and the deep wisdom of the Trinity is our Mother, and the great love of the Trinity is our Lord,...And furthermore I saw that the second person, who is our Mother, substantially the same beloved person, has now become our mother sensually, because we are double by God's creating, that is to say substantial and sensual...And so our Mother is working on us in various ways, in whom our parts are kept undivided; for in our Mother Christ we profit and increase, and in mercy he reforms and restores us, and by

---

26   As quoted in *Why Julian Now?*, p. 131. Julian's writings can be found at 'Julian of Norwich ~ her "Showing" and its Contents,' http://www.umilta.net/julian.html.

the power of his Passion, his death, and his Resurrection he unites us to our substance.[27]

Many feminists in the Church today have embraced the descriptions Julian gave of loving God as our Mother. Julian's extensive development of the theme of God as Mother, however, reflected her own times and feelings more than the truth of Scripture. Julian, along with most during the Middle Ages, primarily interpreted Scripture allegorically, a hermeneutic espoused by Philo and Origen. Allegorical interpretations easily allowed flights of personal fancy or experience to be superimposed on the Scripture. Anyone who reads the Gospels' historical presentation of the person and work of Christ on earth would not call Christ 'Mother' as Julian did. In Julian's writings, the historical Christ of Scripture who walked the earth, ascended and is seated at the right hand of the Father was replaced by a Christ of her visions, conforming to her own need for love, consolation, approval, and assurance.

Doctors of the Church

Catherine of Siena is one of three women 'Doctors of the Church.' In the Roman Catholic Church, there are 33 'Doctors of the Church,' who benefited the entire Church, were eminent in doctrine, had lived a holy life, and who had been proclaimed by the Pope as a 'Doctor.' In 1970, Catherine of Siena and Teresa of Ávila (1515-1582), a Spanish Catholic mystic, were both proclaimed Doctors of the Church. In 1997, Teresa of Lisieux (1873-1897) was also declared a Doctor of the Church.

While Julian lived a reclusive life, her contemporary, Catherine of Siena (1347-1380), influenced leaders in both Church and state.[28] Catherine was the 24th of 25 children of a Sienese dyer; her twin sister died at birth. When Catherine was a year old, a plague swept through Italy, killing 30,000 people in Siena alone. A very sensitive child, Catherine always felt she survived for some purpose. She had her first vision when she was six; she saw in the sky above the church Christ the King seated on a throne surrounded by Peter, Paul, and John. Catherine lived near a Dominican monastery, and she believed St. Dominic appeared to her in a dream urging her to enter his order. Catherine's mother wanted her to marry and opposed Catherine's decision to become a Dominican. When she was twelve, Catherine cut off her long blonde hair to avoid attracting suitors. Three years later she had smallpox, which destroyed her beauty, and Catherine's mother relented her opposition to Catherine becoming a Dominican tertiary or lay member.

---

27   *Reflections of Divine Love*, Ch. 58, from *In Her Words*, pp. 183-4.

28   *Other Women's Voices*, http://home.infionline.net/~ddisse/siena.html.

Wanting to be alone with God, Catherine was given a small room in the basement of her father's shop, where she lived for three years and practiced extreme asceticism. She ate only uncooked herbs with oil, fruit and bread. She scourged herself three times a day – once for herself, once for the living, and once for the dead. When she was 19, Catherine envisioned Christ coming to her in spiritual marriage and placing a ring upon her finger, which she alone could see. Catherine's union with Christ was intense; she felt as if she had a close association with both Christ and His mother. She drank blood from Christ's side and milk from Mary's breast. Her hagiographer claimed she lived for years on nothing but the Eucharistic bread.

Catherine of Siena's works, including her numerous letters and her *Dialogue*, are among the classic writings in the Italian vernacular, along with the letters of Petrarch and Dante's *Divine Comedy*. Catherine continues to be known for her *Dialogue*, which was taken down by her secretaries while Catherine was in an ecstatic state.[29] In the dialogue between God and the soul, which was, of course, Catherine herself, the discussions cover the knowledge of God and oneself, divine

---

Bridget of Sweden (1303-1373)

Bridget, the mother of eight, was widowed after she and her husband returned from a pilgrimage to Spain. From one of the wealthiest families in Sweden, Bridget devoted her wealth and life totally to religion. Her personal revelations were published and read throughout the Middle Ages, and she founded the religious order of Briggitines, directed particularly to learning. The order had both male and female monasteries, which shared a chapel. While in Rome seeking approval for her new religious order, Bridget worked with Catherine of Siena to return the papacy to Rome from Avignon. When she was seventy, she accompanied a son and daughter to the Holy Land; she died on the return trip. In 1999 Pope John Paul II chose St. Bridget as the patron saint of Europe.*

Other Women's Voices, http://home.infionline.net/~ddisse/birgitta.html.

---

providence, obedience, the mystical body of the Church, and true holiness. God's Son, Jesus Christ, was shown as the bridge from heaven to earth, by which God joined Himself to humanity. The bridge had three stairs. The first were the feet, symbolizing the affections. The affections lifted the feet off the earth and the soul was stripped of sin. At the second stair, the soul saw the heart of the Son and knew how greatly it was loved. The third stair was at the mouth of the Son, where the soul tasted peace. God's Son was the only bridge between heaven and earth, and by him 'divinity is kneaded into the clay of your

---

29   Catherine of Siena. *Dialogue of Catherine of Siena* (trans. Algar Thorold), available at http://www.ccel.org/ccel/catherine/dialog.html.

humanity like one bread.'[30] Catherine's *Dialogue* concluded with a paean of rapturous praise of the eternal Father for His mercy and immeasurable love:

> To you, eternal Father, everything is possible. Though you created us without our help, it is not your will to save us without our help. So I beg you to force their wills and dispose them to want what they do not want. I ask this of your infinite mercy. You created us out of nothing. So, now that we exist, be merciful and remake the vessels you created and formed in your image and likeness; re-form them to grace in the mercy and blood of your Son.

After the vision of her spiritual marriage, Catherine left her isolation and again lived in her family's main house. She began to live a life of service to others – visiting prisons and caring for the sick and poor. When the Black Death came to Siena in 1374 and hundreds died daily, Catherine devoted herself to nursing the sick without fear or revulsion. Concerned about political and ecclesiastical corruption, Catherine wrote letters and began visiting political leaders to bring about peace between feuding Italian cities and the papacy. She urged Pope Gregory XI to abandon his dependency on the French court, leave Avignon and return to Rome. She challenged the Pope to act like a man, and at last he did return to Rome under Catherine's persuasion. Catherine criticized the power of the papal legates, the vices of the monasteries, the luxuries of the Church who took offerings from the poor, and the decline of personal piety among the clergy. She looked forward to a thoroughgoing reformation of the Church:

> The bride, now all deformed and clothed in rags, will then gleam with beauty and jewels, and be crowned with the diadem of all virtues. All believing nations will rejoice to have excellent shepherds, and the unbelieving world, attracted by her glory, will be converted unto her.[31]

Pope Urban VI personally sought Catherine's advice, and she went to Rome at his bidding, working for the unity of the Church. Broken in health by her extreme ascetic practices, Catherine suffered her last illness and died in Rome at the age of 33.

Because of her desire to reform the Church, some have seen Catherine as a forerunner of the sixteenth-century Reformation. Yet, as historian Philip Schaff noted, Catherine

> moved within the limits of the medieval Church. She placed piety back of penitential exercises in love and prayer and patience, but she never passed beyond the ascetic and conventual conception of the Christian life into the open air of liberty through faith. She had ...the spirit of

---

30   *Dialogue*, ch. 26.

31   As quoted in Philip Schaff, *History of the Christian Church*, vol. VI, pp. 203-4.

fiery self-sacrifice for the well-being of her people and the regeneration of Christendom, but she did not see beyond the tradition of the past....[32]

Fifty years after Catherine's death, another young mystic showed courage equal to Catherine's in the political field. Joan of Arc (1412-1431) was born in 1412 at Domrémy in northeast France, the youngest of four children. Her family was a pious one – one of her brothers was a parish priest, as was an uncle. The Hundred Years War between England and France was in its 75th year when Joan was born. The English and their Burgundian allies controlled France north of the Loire, and seemingly in time they would likely occupy the entire land. King Henry VI of England and Isabella, the Queen Mother of France, had both disinherited the heir to the French throne, Dauphin Charles.

When she was about thirteen, Joan began hearing voices allegedly from the archangel Michael and the martyred saints Margaret and Catherine. Joan also claimed she heard God's voice speaking to her. These voices directed her to go to the aid of the French forces and tell them that the siege of Orléans would be broken, the English defeated, and the Dauphin crowned King of France within the year. She persisted in attempting to reach the French leaders and finally gained an audience with the Dauphin. When she claimed to be God's messenger to him, he was unimpressed. He had Joan examined by Church officials, who questioned her for three weeks and scoffed at her visions and voices. Joan finally was led to the army, and it was agreed that she would be allowed to lead an expedition to Orléans. Joan cut her hair, donned the shining armor given to her by the Dauphin, and mounted her horse to go into battle. Priests chanting psalms and hymns led the march before her. Before the battle Joan addressed the army and encouraged the soldiers to renounce their sins and receive the sacrament. The soldiers had renewed confidence and courage and followed Joan into battle. After victory at Orléans, Joan led the French army into four other battles and accompanied the Dauphin to Reims, where he was crowned King Charles VII of France. A later attack on Paris failed, however, and Joan was wounded by an arrow in the thigh. The Burgundians captured her and sold her to the English. Despite all she had done to rally the French forces and establish him on his throne, King Charles VII did nothing to try to rescue Joan.

Joan was tried in Rouen before thirty theologians and priests on twelve counts as a heretic and a witch. The chief count was that Joan claimed to be directly responsible to God rather than to the Church. The court records, which still remain, show that Joan answered her accusers with an innocent simplicity.[33] She was reluctant to speak of her visions and voices, but claimed

---

32   Schaff, *History of the Christian Church*, Vol. VI, p. 204.

33   An English translation of minutes from Joan's trial can be found at www.fordham.edu/halsall/basis/joanofarc-trial.html.

she was simply following God's instructions in her actions. She obviously had little understanding of the worldly ways of the court or the Church of her day. Found guilty by the court, at the age of 19, Joan of Arc was burned and her ashes thrown into the River Seine. Her last words were, 'Jesus, Jesus.' A quarter of a century later, Charles VII ordered a retrial at which Joan was found innocent. In 1920, Joan of Arc was canonized as a patron saint of France.

The fluctuating position of Joan of Arc — whether witch or saint

---

Christine de Pizan's *City of Ladies*

Christine de Pizan (c. 1363-c. 1431) was the first European woman to make a career as a writer. Though born in Italy, Christine was raised in France, where her father was astrologer and physician to Charles V. She married in her teens and had three children, but when her husband died she supported herself through her writing. Her most famous work, *The City of Ladies*, defended women against Jean de Meun's satirical attacks in *Roman de la Rose*. Though feminists have often claimed Christine as one of their own, her work actually espoused Christian values contrary to the feminist agenda. Christine praised women who were chaste, humble, faithful, and obedient to authority — whether of their husbands, the Church, or the government. Though women might not be called to a heroic public life, Christine wrote that women could be higher in the things of the spirit by following the Christian virtues.*

---

*Other Women's Voices, http://home.infionline.net/~ddisse/christin.html.

— reflected somewhat the tensions in the spirituality of the Church itself during this period. During the twelfth and thirteenth centuries, female mystics were heralded as important purifiers of the Church, focusing attention on individual spirituality more than hierarchical, liturgical processes. The fire of the mystics balanced somewhat the aridity of scholastic debate. Jesus had told the Samaritan woman (John 4) that worship was to be in spirit and in truth. Throughout the history of the Church the pendulum has often swung between one and the other. Exclusive focus on the truth at times produced an intellectual dryness that quenched the spirit. Exclusive focus on the spirit apart from the truth of Scripture led to heresy. By the fifteenth century, both the spirit and truth became clouded by personal preference and tradition, and the witch-hunting hysteria began. Without reliance on the clear light of Scripture, the Church often found it difficult to distinguish between a saint and a witch:

> By 1500, indeed, the model of the female saint, expressed both in popular veneration and in official canonizations, was in many ways the mirror-image of a witch. Each was thought to be possessed, whether by God or by Satan; each seemed able to read the minds and hearts of others with uncanny shrewdness; each was suspected of flying through the air, whether in saintly levitation or bilocation, or in a witches'

Sabbath. Moreover, each bore mysterious wounds, whether stigmata or the marks of incubi, on her body.[34]

Women visionaries claimed to speak for God because of the direct revelation they claimed to receive from Him. Julian of Norwich's explanation of the necessity of her sharing her visions with others is similar to what is found in the works of Hildegard, Catherine, and other visionaries:

> But God forbid that you should say or understand that I am a teacher, for I do not mean that, and I never meant that; for I am a woman, ignorant, feeble, and frail. But I know well, this that I say, for I have it from the revelation of He who is sovereign teacher....Because I am a woman should I therefore believe that I should not tell you of the goodness of God, since I saw at this same time that it is His will that it be known?[35]

Because women were thought to be innately prone to heresy, women mystics were required to live in obedience to a male spiritual director who checked the orthodoxy of their visions and their use of Scripture. The spiritual director often served as an amanuensis recording the woman's revelations, which she sometimes dictated while in an ecstatic state. The accounts of many of these women visionaries have come down to us through the writings of the men who were their spiritual directors and confessors. To what degree these lives were embellished to suit the perspective of the male authors has been the subject of some scholarly debate.

What is not debatable is that in the fourteenth and fifteenth centuries, women increasingly came under suspicion for heresy. Jean Gerson, chancellor of the University of Paris (and leader at the Council of Constance, which condemned John Wycliffe and John Huss), wrote a treatise on *The Examination of Doctrine* in which he emphasized that

> Every teaching of women, especially that expressed in solemn word or writing, is to be held suspect, unless it has been diligently examined, and much more than the teaching of men....Why? Because women are too easily seduced, because they are too obstinately seducers, because it is not fitting that they should be knowers of divine wisdom.[36]

Two generations later, Dominican inquisitors Heinrich Kramer and Jacob Springer wrote *Malleus Maleficarum,* or *The Witches' Hammer,* a detailed inquisitorial handbook on the detection, prosecution, and punishment of witches. The work overflowed with the most derisive estimates of women, even erroneously deriving *feminine* from *fides minus,* meaning 'less faith.'

---

34   *Holy Feast and Holy Fast,* p. 23.

35   As quoted in Lesley Smith and Jane H.M. Taylor, eds., *Women, the Book, and the Godly,* selected proceedings of the St. Hilda Conference 1993, Vol. 1, p. 65n.

36   *Women, the Book, and the Godly,* p. 64.

Kramer and Springer claimed that weeping, spinning and deceiving were women's nature. Having been formed from Adam's rib, women were by nature crooked. This crookedness made them natural allies of demons, and the authors thanked God that they themselves were men, not women. *Malleus Maleficarum* included a historical survey of every evil woman found in classical, patristic, and scholastic authors – from Helen of Troy to Jezebel to Cleopatra. Following Thomas Aquinas, the authors contended that sin itself was perpetuated in the human race through the marriage bed. Contorted use of history, Scripture, philosophy, and theological speculation, all coupled with a truly misogynist mindset, produced a most contemptible picture of all women, including those who might not be found guilty of witchcraft. Not until the Reformation again viewed women from the clear light of Scripture would the dignity of women be restored, equal with men in being made in God's image and saved by the cross of Christ.

Women in the Early Protestant Reformation:
Loving their Husbands and Children

Titus 2:4

The sixteenth-century Reformation shaped anew the structure and theology of the Church in Europe; even the way society was organized changed. Nowhere did the Reformation produce greater societal change than in the position of women.

In some ways, the Reformation was related to the Renaissance that had begun in the fourteenth century. Both used works from antiquity as sources for their thoughts and ideas. Just as the Renaissance sought inspiration from ancient Greek and Roman classics, so the Reformation looked to the ancient Hebrew and Greek Scriptures. The Reformers looked to the Bible, rather than to the tradition and hierarchy of the Roman Church, as the source of truth.

Though a monk, Martin Luther (1483-1546), a leader of the Reformation, had not even seen a Bible before he was twenty. All he knew were the portions of the Gospels and epistles used in the service of the Roman Catholic mass. When Luther discovered a Bible in the library at the Augustinian monastery at Erfurt, he began reading it with increasing wonder. His preceptor told him, 'Ah, brother Martin. Why trouble yourself with the Bible? Rather read the ancient doctors who have collected for you all its marrow and honey. The Bible itself is the cause of all our troubles.'[1] However, Luther was drawn even more to the Scriptures.

Luther was terrified of God. He knew that in his own unworthiness and sinfulness he had no place in God's righteous presence. All his penitent acts did not elevate him to a position worthy to stand before God. One day Luther read in Romans 1:17 that in the gospel, 'the righteousness of God is revealed from faith to faith; as it is written, "The just shall live by faith."' Luther began to realize that he could acquire Christ's righteousness through faith, not by any

---

1   From Luther's *Table Talk* as quoted in Samuel Smiles, *The Huguenots*, (London: John Murray, 1868), 13.

works of his own. 'Justification by faith alone' became a rallying cry for Martin Luther and for the Reformation of the Church.

Martin Luther on Women

'...the woman appears to be a somewhat different being from the man, having different members and a much weaker nature. Although Eve was a most extraordinary creature – similar to Adam so far as the image of God is concerned, that is, in justice, wisdom, and happiness – she was nevertheless a woman. For as the sun is more excellent than the moon (although the moon, too, is a very excellent body), so the woman, although she was a most beautiful work of God, nevertheless was not the equal of the male in glory and prestige....the woman was created by a unique counsel of God in order to show that this sex, too, is suited for the kind of life which Adam was expecting and that this sex was to be useful for procreation. Hence it follows that if the woman had not been deceived by the serpent and had not sinned, she would have been the equal of Adam in all respects. For the punishment, that she is now subjected to the man, was imposed on her after sin and because of sin...Eve was not like the woman of today; her state was far better and more excellent, and she was in no respect inferior to Adam, whether you count the qualities of the body or those of the mind.'*

'Imagine what it would be like without this sex. The home, cities, economic life, and government would virtually disappear. Men can't do without women. Even if it were possible for men to beget and bear children, they still couldn't do without women.'**

---

*Lectures in Genesis, 1535, quoted in Luther on Women, pp. 25-6.
** As quoted in Zophy, 'We Must Have the Dear Ladies...', p. 149.

The conviction that salvation came only through faith in Christ alone and by His grace alone was based on the Bible's teachings, but was contrary to the Roman Church's teaching on indulgences and purgatory. In 1517, Luther published 95 Theses against the teaching on indulgences and other practices of the Church contrary to the Scriptures. This marked the beginning of the Protestant Reformation, in which the authority of the Scriptures replaced the authority of the Pope and medieval traditions. Justification by faith alone led to a de-emphasis on external rituals and an increased focus on the inner spiritual life. Preaching, even by lay preachers, became more important. The priesthood of every believer replaced monasticism as the ideal of holiness. Each person's calling was considered a divine service. Among those now known as Protestants, the seven sacraments were re-evaluated, and baptism and the Eucharist were recognized as the only two sacraments; marriage became a civil ordinance.[2] The family came to be seen as a household of faith. Martin Luther's own marriage and family became an example to others.

The pattern of family life established by Luther and other Reformers contrasted with the supreme value placed on celibacy and virginity in the medieval period. Marriage itself was seen as designed by God and a tool for the sanctification of Christians. With the increased availability of the printed Scriptures, a growing number of women became literate and wise in the Scriptures. Many willingly suffered death for their faith when persecution arose again.

Martin and Katie Luther: The Protestant Parsonage

When he was a monk, Martin Luther held that celibacy enabled the highest form of spiritual life; marriage was disparaged as partaking of the fleshly world. This medieval attitude that the flesh was evil, sex was fleshly, and women were seductive was a result of incorporating Platonic and Manichean ideas into Christian teaching. The 11th-century imposition of celibacy on the priesthood under the Gregorian reform further disparaged women and marriage itself. The introduction of Aristotle in Scholastic thinking abetted the disparagement. In nature, Aristotle saw men as spiritual and women as material. These ideas were all part of Luther's training as a young boy and as a monk. Even after his conversion Luther could voice a denigrating attitude towards women. However, he did change, and he did come to recognize the equality of Christian men and women in the Church as well as the importance of marriage as an institution. In his early *Address to the German Nobility* (1520), Luther encouraged the end of clerical celibacy and noted that marriage could be a restraint on sexual temptation and immorality. In this work he also encouraged education for girls as well as boys, a novel idea at the time.

Though some of the clergy began to marry while Luther was under edict and hidden in the Wartburg castle, marriage was not in Luther's thoughts.[3] Luther was not personally averse to marriage; but since he daily expected to die as a heretic, he didn't see marriage in his future. Katharina von Bora changed that.[4]

When Katharina was barely six, after her mother's death and her father's remarriage, she was placed in the Marienthron convent in Nimbschen. Katharina was of aristocratic background, and the convent was considered

---

2   The seven sacraments under the Roman Church are baptism, confirmation, penance, communion (Eucharist), matrimony, holy orders, and extreme unction (or the last rites).

3   After Luther's trial at Worms, Germany, Emperor Charles V issued an edict calling for Luther's arrest. Luther had already been excommunicated by Pope Leo X in 1521.

4   See Concordia Historical Institute's online exhibit, 'My Lord Katie: Katharina von Bora Luther' http://chi.lcms.org/katie/.

a place of prestige, protection, and education. At sixteen, Katharina was consecrated as a nun in a rite in which the Church recognized her as the Virgin Bride of Christ.

Katharina was eighteen when Martin Luther published his *95 Theses*, and news of the Reformation and its teachings soon reached the convent. Some of the nuns were especially interested in Luther's attack on monasticism as not based on God's commandments or the Word of God. The nuns' families would not help them leave the convent, however, so they secretly wrote a letter to Luther asking for his help. The letter was delivered by Leonard Koppe, a merchant and respected citizen of Turgau who delivered herring and supplies to the convent. He may have also brought Luther's writings hidden among his goods during earlier visits to the convent. Luther was able to arrange with Koppe for the nuns' escape. On Easter 1523, 11 nuns were hidden in the merchant's wagon so that they could escape the convent (The tale that they actually hid in empty herring barrels appears 'fishy' and does not seem to be based in fact!). Katharina, then 24, was among those who escaped. Luther later wrote the merchant: 'You have liberated these poor souls from the prison of human tyranny at just the right time – Easter, when Christ liberated the prison that held His own.'[5] Within two years the nuns were placed with relatives, in various homes for work, or married to suitable husbands – except for Katharina. Katharina was almost engaged to a former Wittenberg student from Nürnberg; but his parents disapproved, and he married a rich wife. Another man, a doctor in theology, offered her marriage, but Katie refused, saying she would only marry Luther. Katie saw Luther as a liberator and someone she could trust. Luther was hesitant to marry, yet finally decided to marry Katie; he was 42 and she was 26. Luther thought the marriage would 'please his father, rile the pope, cause the angels to laugh and the devils to weep.'[6]

Martin and Katie Luther were married June 13, 1525, in the presence of four friends. They celebrated a nuptial feast with their parents and many others two weeks later. On their invitation they stated

Luther on Marriage

'Were all the leaves in the woods of Torgau each given a voice, they would still be too few to sing the praises of marriage and condemn the wickedness of celibacy.'

'The dearest life is to live with a godly, willing, obedient wife in peace and unity. Union of the flesh does nothing. There must also be union of manners and mind.'*

---

* From *Table Talk* as quoted in *Great Women of the Christian Faith*, p. 96.

---

5   As quoted in Rudolf and Marilynn Markwald, *Katharina von Bora*, (St. Louis, MO: Concordia Publishing House), 2002, p. 50.

6   *Katharina von Bora*, p. 70.

that marriage was an act of confession and obedience to God's act of creation. Luther later wrote to a friend, 'There is a lot to get used to in the first year of marriage. You wake up in the morning and find a pair of pigtails on the pillow which were not there before.'[7]

Luther's opponents reacted violently to his marriage. Satirical poems and dramas with lusty monks and wanton nuns featured Luther and Katharina as main characters. Catholic tracts and pamphlets held up to ridicule the marriage of a heretical ex-monk and an ex-nun. Johann Hasenberg, Vice Chancellor of the University of Leipzig, wrote a letter to Luther criticizing his marriage and calling him the 'Most insane and libidinous of apostates.' His associate Joachim von der Heyden wrote to Katie rebuking her: 'Woe unto you poor, misled woman…you left the cloister in lay clothes like a dancing girl…'. The bishop of Ghent, William Lindanus, castigated Luther's marriage as well: 'Thou vile Venus with thy crafty boy Cupid has puffed up poor Luther with over fierce a fire, with over great … a long lasting lecherous lust.' Woodcut cartoons also ridiculed the marriage.[8] In spite of opposition and ridicule, the marriage of Martin Luther and Katie von Bora became an exemplar of Christian marriage.

Luther had been given the Augustinian monastery, the old Black Cloister, as a home, and it was there Katie moved upon her marriage. Katie cleaned up the monastery and brought order to Luther's daily life. After a year of marriage Luther wrote a friend, 'My Katie is in all things so obliging and pleasing to me that I would not exchange my poverty for the riches of Croesus.'[9]

The Black Cloister was a large establishment which not only was the Luthers' home, but also became a kind of hotel and boarding house for students and visiting scholars. Though she did have help, Katie oversaw the whole and was a gardener, fisher, fruit grower, brewer, horse breeder, cook, bee-keeper, and vintner – besides caring for Luther's health and depressions and being a mother to their six children and the four orphans they took in. Luther

---

Luther's Prayer for His Family

'Dear heavenly Father, because You in Your name and in the honor of Your office have ordained and want to name and honor me as father, grant me grace and bless me so that I may govern and nourish my dear wife, children, and servants in a godly and Christian manner. Give me the wisdom and strength to govern and raise them well, and give them a good heart and the will to follow your teaching and to be obedient. Amen.'*

---

* *Luther on Women*, p. 204.

---

7   As quoted in Dolina MacCuish, *Luther and his Katie*, (Christian Focus Publications, 1999), p. 69.

8   Jeanette C. Smith, 'Katharina von Bora Through Five Centuries: A Historiography,' *Sixteenth Century Journal*, vol. 30, No. 3 (Autumn, 1999), pp. 754-5.

9   As quoted in Schaff, *History of the Christian Church*, Vol. VII, p. 460.

continued as Katie's spiritual guide, encouraging her ongoing Biblical studies. He promised her 50 Gulden if she would read the Bible in a year. He also encouraged her to memorize Scriptures, especially the Psalms. Katie's encouragement and support were important to Luther's ongoing work of the Reformation. She was his secretary, publishing agent, advisor, and doctor. Her management of the finances and household helped free Luther's mind for his writing, teaching, and ministry. Together Katie and Martin elevated both marriage and motherhood as natural reflections of God's creation. Luther, who had based his life and faith on the authenticity and authority of the Bible, wrote a friend, 'Next to God's Word, there is no more precious treasure than holy matrimony. God's highest gift on earth is a pious, cheerful, God-fearing, home-keeping wife, with whom you may live peacefully, to whom you may entrust your goods and body and life.'[10]

Katie and Martin were married twenty years, and their family life of mutual help and support for each other in the Lord became a model for Christian marriage as well as for pastoral marriage. In 1546, Martin Luther died suddenly while away from home. In his will he left all his estate and the care of his children in Katie's hands. It was extraordinary in Luther's day to leave all to a wife in this manner, and Luther stated three reasons for his actions:

> first, my Catherine has always been a gentle, pious and faithful wife to me, has loved me dearly and by the grace of God has given me and brought up five children still living: second, she will have to settle any debts outstanding at the time of my death: third, and most important, it is my wish that the children be dependent on her, not she upon the children, that they honour her and be submissive to her as God has commanded. I consider, moreover, that the mother will be the best guardian of her children and that she will not abuse this confidence I place in her but will always be a good mother to her children whom she loves tenderly, and will conscientiously share everything with them.[11]

Katie was full of grief at Martin's sudden death, and wrote her sister-in-law:

> ..in truth so painful has been my grief that I cannot express to any my heart-suffering. I don't really know what I think or feel. I can neither eat or drink nor can I sleep. If I had had an earldom or a kingdom I would not have felt their loss so deeply as now when our dear Lord has taken from me, and not from me only but from the whole world, this dear and well-loved man. When I think about it I can, for sorrow and weeping (as God well knows) neither speak nor write.'[12]

Psalm 31 became Katie's comfort; she had memorized the psalm years before.

---

10   As quoted in *History of the Christian Church*, Vol. VIII, 461. This translation modernized the spelling of 'Katherina' to 'Catherine'.

11   As quoted in *Luther and his Katie*, pp. 119-20.

12   As quoted in *Luther and his Katie*, p. 121.

In spite of Martin's provision for Katie in his will, the years following his death were difficult. The year of Luther's death, Emperor Charles V waged the Schmalkaldic War against the Protestants, and armies moved on Wittenberg. Katie and her children were forced to flee. When she returned, her property was destroyed, her gardens ruined, her cattle gone, and new taxes had been imposed. Katie again took in student boarders and borrowed money to rebuild. A few years later, the bubonic plague came to Wittenberg, and Katie again fled. During the journey, the horses pulling the wagon became frightened; and when Katie tried to stop the horses, she fell into a ditch of water. She developed bronchial trouble, never recovered, and died in 1552. In her last days, she prayed as follows:

> Lord, my Saviour, Thou standest at the door and wouldst enter in. O come, Thou beloved guest, for I desire to depart and be with Thee. Let my children be committed to Thy mercy. Lord, look down in mercy upon Thy Church. May the pure doctrine which God has sent through my husband be handed down unadulterated to posterity. Dear Lord, I thank Thee for all the trials, through which Thou didst lead me, and by which Thou didst prepare me to behold Thy Glory. Thou hast never forsaken nor forgotten me. Thou hast evermore caused Thy face to shine upon me, when I called upon Thee. Behold, now I grasp Thy hand and say, as Jacob of old: Lord I will not let Thee go, unless Thou bless me. I will cling to Thee forevermore.[13]

A New Ideal: Marriages of the Reformers

Historian Philip Schaff summarized the great change in Christian ideals exemplified in Martin and Katie's marriage as well as those of other Reformers:

> The medieval ideal of piety is the flight from the evil world: the modern ideal is the transformation of the world. The model saint of the Roman Church is the monk separated from the enjoyments and duties of society, and anticipating the angelic life in heaven where men neither marry nor are given in marriage: the model saint of the Evangelical Church is the free Christian and useful citizen, who shows his piety in the performance of social and domestic duties, and aims at the sanctification of the ordinances of nature. The former tries to conquer the world by running away from its temptations – though after all he cannot escape the flesh, the world, and the Devil in his own heart: the latter tries to conquer the world by converting it. The one abstains from the wedding feast: the other attends it, and changes the water into wine. The one flees from woman as a tempter: the other takes her to his heart, and reflects in the marriage relation the holy union of Christ with his Church. The one aims to secure chastity by abstinences: the other proves it within the family. The one renounces all earthly possessions: the other uses

---

13   As quoted in *Great Women of the Christian Faith*, p. 98.

them for the good of his fellow-men. The one looks for happiness in heaven: the other is happy already on earth by making others happy. The daily duties and trials of domestic and social life are a better school of moral discipline than monkish celibacy and poverty. Female virtues and graces are necessary to supplement and round out the character of man. Exceptions there are, but they prove the rule…the Reformers burst the chains of papal tyranny, and furnished the practical proof that it is possible to harmonize the highest and holiest calling with the duties of husband and father. Though falling short of modern Protestant ideas of the dignity and rights of woman, they made her the rightful companion of the Christian pastor and among those companions may be found many of the purest, most refined, and most useful women on earth. The social standing of woman is a true test of Christian civilization.[14]

The ascetic standard of spirituality which had prevailed since late antiquity was replaced by one which transformed society's living and working patterns. The roles of wife and mother were elevated as worthy spiritual vocations, in keeping with God's original created order. Since most women through the ages have been wives and mothers, the Reformers' emphasis on family life has been seen as liberating for women and as placing important value on their most frequent roles. More recently, however, feminist historians have interpreted the Reformers' position as restricting women. Since celibacy and singleness were no longer esteemed as they were in the medieval period, some contend the Reformers limited women's choices by confining them to the domestic sphere. Such historians ask, was it truly elevating to women to confine them to the home as wives and mothers subservient to their husbands' authority? The Reformers' wives themselves did not seem to have had such objections. They fully embraced their spiritual equality with their husbands as well as male leadership in the home. The family and marriage, not the convent or monastery, were the main areas where faith and obedience to Christ were lived. In marriage, men and women could enjoy love and companionship, as well as produce children in the Lord. For the Reformers, there was both a spiritual equality of men and women as well as a patriarchal headship in marriage.

The religious differences brought on by the Reformation often led to persecution, and the persecuted sought refuge in other states where their faith was permitted. The refugee problem intensified in Switzerland as times of warfare broke out between the Catholic and Protestant cantons. Often pastors' wives took the lead in caring for the refugees. One such caring woman was Anna Adlischwyler Bullinger (1504?-1564), wife of Heinrich Bullinger, pastor of the Cathedral Church at Zurich. Like Katie Luther, Anna had been a nun before hearing the teachings of the Reformation. When she

---

14   *History of the Christian Church*, Vol. VII, pp. 477-8.

and many of the other nuns heard the Scriptures clearly explained, they realized that convent life was not something required in Scripture for a spiritual life. Many left the convent, but Anna remained to care for her ailing mother who was boarding there. One day the convent's chaplain brought Heinrich Bullinger to the convent, where he met and talked with Anna. Heinrich later wrote Anna a fourteen-page letter proposing marriage! In it he praised marriage as an opportunity 'to exercise all virtue, faith, love, compassion, hope, patience, moderation, discipline, and all godliness in Christ.' He further wrote that

> You alone are the only one I have fixed upon. God alone knows whether you are meant for me and my choice rests on your manner of speaking and conduct. I have come to imagine you as a woman of breeding in whom the fear of God dwells and with whom I would like to live in love and in suffering and in everything God wills.[15]

Bullinger further commended himself as not an ordained priest, a drunkard or gambler. He concluded that

> The sum of it all is, that the greatest, surest treasure that you will find in me, is fear of God, piety, fidelity, and love, which with joy I will show you, and labor, earnestness and industry, which will not be wanting in temporal things. Concerning high nobility and many thousand gulden, I can say nothing to you. But I know that what is necessary to us, will not be wanting. For Paul says, 'We brought nothing into the world, and we will take nothing out.' Therefore, if we have clothing and food it is enough.[16]

Anna accepted Bullinger's proposal within weeks, though her ailing mother opposed the marriage. Anna waited two years for her mother's death before marrying Bullinger. Heinrich wrote Anna a little book to help prepare her for her wifely role – *Concerning Female Training, and How a Daughter Should Guide Her Conduct and Life*. When the Bullingers married in 1529, Heinrich wrote Anna a poem:

> You are my solace, my joy and refuge,
> haven to my heart,
> worshipped alone, loved alone,
> for I am yours, solely yours.[17]

Heinrich Bullinger's strong appreciation for marriage and family interestingly came from his parents – Heinrich Bullinger and Anna

---

15   Patrik Miller, 'Bullinger – Family Man,' *Annex*, 2004, p. 7.

16   As quoted in 'Anna Bullinger,' *Leben*, (January-March 2007, 15), excerpted from Rev. J.I. Good's *Famous Women of the Reformed Church*.

17   'Bullinger – Family Man,' p. 7.

Wiederkehr. The elder Heinrich was a priest who faithfully lived with Anna as his wife, though they could not legally marry since the Church forbade priests marrying. As common-law wife of the dean of the church, Anna Wiederkehr raised five sons, hosted dignitaries, and cared for the poor and sick of the town of Bremgarten. The legal wife of her son Heinrich filled similar roles.

In 1531, Heinrich the younger was chosen pastor of the cathedral Church of Zurich, succeeding the Reformer Ulrich Zwingli who had been killed at the battle of Cappel a few months earlier. The conflict between Swiss Catholic and Protestant forces which had recently fought at Cappel produced a stream of refugees and grieving people. Among these were Ulrich Zwingli's widow and children. After speaking out against monasticism and the requirement of clerical celibacy for some years, Zwingli had been the first of the Reformers to marry. In her new role as pastor's wife, Anna Zwingli became known as the 'apostolic Dorcas' for her care of the persecuted who fled to Zurich. In 1531, however, she found herself among the bereaved. Her husband, leader of the Reformation in Zurich and chaplain to the Protestant forces at the battle of Cappel, was killed early in the battle. Also killed in the battle were Anna's oldest son Gerold, her brother, and her brother-in-law. A son-in-law died shortly after from his battle wounds. The Bullingers cared for Anna Zwingli as their own mother until her death seven years later.

Anna Bullinger not only cared for the many refugees, but had eleven children and supported her husband's important ministry as pastor of Zurich's largest church. The Bullingers' marriage and family centered on their unshakeable faith in Christ. Their life together demonstrated the Christian family ideal of the Reformation. Anna Bullinger died of the plague in 1564. Heinrich died eleven years later.

The Reformers realized that a life of marriage and family was more in keeping with God's created order and the Bible than an ascetic life of enforced celibacy. Friends of John Calvin, the great Reformer of Geneva, urged him to marry and suggested a number of eligible women. Calvin wrote his friends:

> Remember what I expect from one who is to be my companion for life. I do not belong to the class of loving fools, who, when once smitten with a fine figure, are ready to expend their affection even on the faults of her whom they have fallen in love with. The only kind of beauty which can win my soul, is a woman who is gentle, pure, modest, economical, patient, and who is likely to interest herself about my health.[18]

---

18   As quoted in *Great Women of the Christian Faith*, p. 322.

Calvin found such a woman in Idelette de Bure (1509?-1549), a member of his congregation in Strasbourg.

Idelette and her husband John Stoudeur were Anabaptists who fled to Strasbourg from the persecution in the Low Countries. When Calvin was exiled from Geneva and went to Strasbourg in 1539, the Stoudeurs were in Calvin's church and came to accept his Scriptural teaching. In the spring of 1540, John Stoudeur suddenly died of plague, leaving Idelette with three young children. Calvin recognized in Idelette the gentle, modest Christian woman he had been looking for in a wife; Idelette undoubtedly saw in Calvin a good father for her children. The two were married in Strasbourg following a large ceremony, with representatives of several Swiss and French towns attending.

The earliest months of their marriage were marked by extended illnesses on both sides and a long separation as Calvin attended a major imperial conference on Protestants and Catholics. When Calvin accepted a call back to Geneva the following year, the Geneva Council sent a two-horse carriage to bring Idelette, the children, and their family possessions to Geneva. The Geneva Council also helped furnish their new house at Number 11 Rue de Chanoines, which Idelette easily made into a home. Behind the house was land where Idelette planted a vegetable garden, herbs, and fragrant flowers. John enjoyed showing Idelette's garden to visitors.

Idelette brought calm and stability to John Calvin's world, and his friends noticed the improvement in his temper. Through the times of turmoil in Geneva's political and religious strife, Idelette cared for Calvin's health and comforted and encouraged him, and fervently prayed for peace and safety for her husband. All five of the children Idelettte bore Calvin died in infancy; critics said this was God's punishment upon Calvin for his beliefs. Idelette, probably suffering from tuberculosis, grew increasingly weak and ailing. As she lay dying, Calvin tried to comfort her and said he would continue to care for her children. Idelette said she had already entrusted them to God. Calvin said that did not relieve him of his responsibility to them. Idelette replied, 'I know that you would not neglect that which you know has been entrusted to God.' Calvin later wrote that on the day of her death, Idelette

> suddenly cried out in such a way that all could see her spirit had risen far above this world. These were her words, 'O glorious resurrection! O God of Abraham and of all of our fathers, the believers of all the ages have trusted on Thee and none of them have hoped in vain. And now I fix my hope on Thee.'

Idelette died with peace on her face. John was grief-stricken. He wrote a friend:

John Knox and Women

John Knox was leader of the Reformation in Scotland. His dealings with the queens of Scotland were often fractious.

Knox fled to Europe when **Mary Tudor** became queen in 1553. When Protestant persecutions and martyrdoms increased under her reign, he encouraged people to pray for her death, for a Jehu to rise up and slay that Jezebel and her followers.

When **Mary of Guise** first reigned as regent in Scotland, she seemed sympathetic to the Reformation and suppressed a heresy trial against Knox. However, when Knox wrote her a letter encouraging her to follow the Reformation, she treated it as a joke and allowed the bishops to hold a mock trial and burn Knox in effigy. Knox later wrote that the regent's crown on her was as fitting as 'a saddle upon the back of an unruly cow.' Knox then wrote *The First Blast of the Trumpet against the Monstrous Regiment of Women*, calling for rebellion against female rulers, especially Mary Tudor. Knox wrote that women were not meant to govern but to be subject to men. Knox's timing was not good, for Mary soon died and **Elizabeth I** became queen of England. Knox would not support her position, though she was Protestant.

Knox clashed most strongly with **Mary Queen of Scots** when she took the throne of Scotland. Knox had five stormy interviews with the Catholic queen, the last during his trial for treason (at which he was acquitted).

Yet, Knox's dealings with women other than queens were much more amicable. **Elizabeth Bowes** was a patron and supporter of Knox, and Knox patiently answered her numerous questions on Biblical interpretation and theology. Knox married Elizabeth's daughter **Marjory.** Marjory died five years after her marriage, and some years later Knox married **Margaret Stewart**. Their descendants continued as leaders of the church in Scotland for several generations. **Anne Locke**, wife of a London merchant, followed Knox's advice during the persecution under Queen Mary and fled to Geneva. When she returned to England and he to Scotland, she continued to support Knox's ministry. Anne also translated Calvin's sermons into English. She shared Knox's views on the proper position of women and wrote, 'Everyone in his calling is bound to do somewhat to the furtherance of the holy building, but because great things by reason of my sex I may not do, and that which I may I ought to do, I have according to my duty brought my poor basket of stones to the strengthening of the walls of that Jerusalem whereof (by grace) we are all both citizens and members.'*

* As quoted in Robert Healey, 'Knox's Curious Attitude Toward Women,' *Christian History*, Issue 46 (Vol. XIV, no. 2), p. 38.

You know how ... soft my heart is. If I did not have strong self-control I would not have been able to stand this long. My grief is very heavy. My best life's companion has been taken from me. Whenever I faced serious difficulties she was ever ready to share with me, not only banishment and poverty, but even death itself.[19]

19   Quotes cited in William J. Petersen, 'Idelette: John Calvin's Search for the Right Wife,' *Christian History*, Vol. V, No. 4, p. 15.

Anabaptist Women

Throughout much of history there has been a close alliance between religion and the state. The Egyptian Pharaohs were not only heads of state, but were considered sons of the sun god Ra. The Roman Caesars not only ruled an empire, but were regarded as gods who deserved offerings. When the Emperor Constantine endorsed Christianity, he began the practice of using the powers of the state to enforce Christian belief and practice. The fourth-century Church leader Augustine misused Jesus' words in the Parable of the Great Supper (Luke 14:23) to advocate compelling people by force to enter Christ's kingdom. Though Jesus Himself proclaimed His Kingdom was 'not of this world,' Augustine approved the use of government power to coerce faith, thereby encouraging Christians to actively engage in persecution. During the Reformation era, each province generally followed the religion of its ruler. The government allied with the dominant faith used its power to persecute the minority faith, sometimes resorting to open warfare to enforce what each considered the true Christian faith. This shared belief that government should use its power to suppress a rival faith led Protestants and Catholics to share another belief – that the Anabaptists were a danger both to religion and society.

The Anabaptists, forerunners of the Mennonites and Amish, believed that their loyalty was to Christ alone and that they had no need to pledge loyalty or follow the dictates of a worldly state or government. They also believed that baptism was a rite to be administered after conversion, not to infants. Their very name, 'Anabaptists,' meaning 're-baptizers,' reflected the practice of baptizing believers, even if they had been christened as infants. Catholic as well as Reformed leaders saw this as an attack on the foundation and unity of Christendom. They also saw the Anabaptists as a threat to society and government as well as the Church. These Anabaptists were often persecuted by Catholics and Protestants alike. Many Anabaptists were executed by drowning, as a perverse punishment for their rebaptism.

In 1660, the *Martyr's Mirror* was published, memorializing the godly lives and glorious deaths of 930 Anabaptist martyrs from 1524-1660.[20] One half of the martyrs memorialized were women. From the records of their trials and letters which have survived, much can be learned about these Anabaptist women. Some boldly debated with theologians, displaying a strong understanding of Scripture and doctrine. In addition to their roles as wives and mothers, Anabaptist women hosted prayer meetings, held sewing circles where the Bible was also studied, took care of the poor, and housed itinerant ministers. Some took unofficial leadership roles when men were not available. Elisabeth Dirks learned Latin in a convent, studied the Latin Bible, and became a respected teacher before she was

---

20   Available online at http://www.homecomers.org/mirror/contents.htm.

executed by drowning on March 27, 1549. Lijksen Dirks exchanged letters of mutual encouragement with her husband Jeronimus Sogeanz when they were in separate prisons in Antwerp in 1551. Jeronimus wrote to his wife: 'And though they tell you to attend to your sewing, this does not hinder us, for Christ has called us all, and commanded us to search the Scriptures, since they testify of him.' Husband and wife were both later tortured and killed.

Some of the songs written by Anabaptist women martyrs have survived. The following was written by Annelein of Freiburg, who was drowned and then burned for her faith in 1529:

Everlasting Father in heaven,
I call on you so ardently,
Do not let me turn from you.
Keep me in your truth
Until my final end.

O God, guard my heart and mouth,
Lord watch over me at all times.
Let nothing separate me from you.
Be it affliction, anxiety, or need.
Keep me pure in joy.

My everlasting Lord and Father,
Show and teach me,
Poor unworthy child that I am,
That I heed your path and way.
In this lies my desire.

To walk through your power into death,
Through sorrow, torture, fear, and want.
Sustain me in this,
O God, so that I nevermore
Be separated from your love.

Many travel along this road.
The cup of suffering lies there,
And also many untrue teachings
Which try to turn us away
From Christ our Lord.

To you I raise up my soul, Lord.
I depend on you in misfortune.
Do not let me come to harm,
That my enemy not stand over me
On this earth...

I do not doubt God's power.
His judgments all are true
He will not abandon anyone
Who stands firm in the faith,

And stays on the true paths.

Be comforted you Christians and rejoice,
Through Jesus Christ forevermore,
Who gives us love and faith.
God comforts us through his holy word,
On that we should rely.

I entrust myself to God and his church.
May he be my protector today.
For the sake of his name.
May this come to pass, Father mine,
Through Jesus Christ, Amen.[21]

Not all suffered martyrdom, however. Margarette Pruess, daughter of a Strasbourg printer, survived three husband-printers and became known for publishing Anabaptist works. The first Protestant woman writer, Argula von Grumbach (1492-1568), had Anabaptist sympathies.[22] Because of her knowledge of Scripture and conviction of the truth, she stood against university leaders, city council, and nobles.

Born Argula von Stauff into a privileged family in Bavaria, Argula was taught to read early. When she was ten, her father gave her a beautiful German Bible. Franciscan preachers discouraged her from reading it, saying it would confuse her if she tried to understand it. However, when Argula joined the court of Queen Kunigunde, sister of Emperor Maximillian, she found a great interest in spiritual affairs at court. Argula began reading the Bible in earnest. John von Staupitz, the mentor of Martin Luther, spoke frequently at court. He taught that Christ's merits, not ours, bring salvation, and he criticized many of the superstitions of the day. In 1509, when she was seventeen, both of Argula's parents died of the plague. Seven years later, her guardian, Uncle Jerome, was executed for favoring the losing side in the struggle for Bavarian succession. In 1516, Argula married Friedrich von Grumbach, with whom she had four children. Though her husband remained a Catholic, Argula adopted the belief of justification by faith in Christ alone. She corresponded with Luther and other leaders of the Reformation and educated her children in Protestant schools.

In March 1522, the Bavarian court at Münich issued a mandate against the reception of Lutheran ideas. A teacher who had been to Wittenberg and was full of reforming ideas was arrested at the University of Ingelstadt and confined to a monastery. Argula was outraged and sent a long letter to the rector and the University, challenging them to show any errors

---

21   "Song of Annelein of Freiburg, who was drowned and then burned in 1529," *Women of Christianity*, http://www.womenofchristianity.com/?p=2281 , accessed June 2, 2011 .

22   *Other Women's Voices*, http://home.infionline.net/~ddisse/grumbach.html.

in the teacher's views. Though a woman, she said she had to speak out because the men were remaining silent. She wrote as a 'member of the Church of Christ against which the gates of hell shall not prevail...' Argula marshaled strong arguments for the necessity of speaking against the University's actions: Ezekiel 33 said that if you see your brother sin, you should reprove him; Jesus said whoever confessed Him before men, him He would confess before His Father (Matt. 10:32); Christ and the apostles did not imprison, burn or banish anyone. In her letter, Argula cited over eighty Scriptures. The Reformer Osiander encouraged Argula to have her letter printed, and within two months the letter went through fourteen printed editions. While the Ingelstadt theologians called Argula a silly bag, a wretched daughter of Eve, a female desperado, an arrogant devil, and a shameless whore, the Reformers supported her. Balthesar Hubmaier called her a pious woman, a Christian woman, and someone who knew the Divine Word better than the clergy. He compared her with Deborah and Hulda in the Old Testament and the daughters of Philip in the New.

Argula believed that the Scriptures prohibited a woman from speaking openly in the churches, but she could speak in her own home, on the streets, and through her pamphlets. As Argula wrote,

> God did indeed order me to spin wool and keep house, but let the university faculty not forget that God also called me to hear his word!... and I remain obedient to God and to my husband, and my soul could be no more dear to me than that.[23]

Argula's husband lost his government position because of her outspokenness, yet Argula in good conscience could not keep silent. She was not the only Christian woman of that day who made her voice heard through the printed word.

Women Writers

Martin Bucer, an early Protestant Reformer, was a Dominican monk in Germany when he began studying the Bible. He also studied the writings of Erasmus, Aquinas, and Luther. He met Luther in 1518 and corresponded with him in ensuing years.

> The true and entire purpose of marriage is that the spouses serve one another in all love and fidelity, that the woman be the aid and the flesh of the man and the man the head and savior of the woman.
> — Martin Bucer
>
> Quoted in Jane Dempsey Douglass. *Women, Freedom and Calvin*, p. 86.

23   As quoted in Paul A. Russell, *Lay Theology in the Reformation: Popular Pamphleteers in Southwest Germany 1521-1525*, (Cambridge University Press, 1986), p. 199.

The Dominicans, suspecting Bucer of evangelical views, made accusations against him to Rome, and he left the monastery. In 1522 he became a pastor in Landstuhl and took the bold step of marrying the ex-nun Elizabeth Silberstein. Bucer was one of the first priests to break his vow of celibacy and marry. Under persecution, he and his new wife fled to Strasbourg in 1523.

In Strasbourg Bucer officiated at the marriage of seven priests, who were soon excommunicated by the Church. Among them was the forty-year-old Matthew Zell, the first Protestant preacher in Strasbourg. Zell married Katherine Schütz (1497/98-1562), who was twenty years his junior. Katherine bore two children who died in infancy and then had no more children. Critics said her childlessness was punishment for her sin in marrying a priest. Katherine, however, was devoted to her husband, writing that they were 'of one mind and of one soul...What bound us together was not silver and gold. Both of us possessed a higher thing, Christ was the mark before our eyes.' She wanted only to be a helpmate to her husband, a 'little piece of the rib of the sainted Master Zell.' [24]

In 1524, she wrote and published a letter to the bishop answering the charges which were made against clerical marriage. She argued that clerical celibacy was a profit-making practice for the Church and not based on any Biblical principles. Priests paid money to the bishops for remission of their sins with whores. If clerics married, the Church feared property would be passed to their children rather than to the Church. Reflecting on Joel 2:28, 'I will pour forth my spirit upon all flesh, and your sons and your daughters will prophesy,' Katherine told the bishop, 'I do not pretend to be John the Baptist rebuking the Pharisees; I do not claim to be Nathan, upbraiding David. I aspire only to be Balaam's ass, castigating his master.' [25]

Though Katherine had a sharp tongue, she had courage, a keen wit and a wide knowledge of Scripture. She also had a kind and caring heart and worked tirelessly for the good of others. In 1524, 150 men in one night fled the town of Kenzingen to Strasbourg, leading their evangelical pastor out of town to protect him from the Hapsburg forces coming for his arrest. Eighty of the men found refuge in the Zell home, and Katherine fed 50-60 there for several weeks. She was unwearied in caring for the refugees. The Hapsburg forces, however, came against Kenzingen while the men were gone, and many of the women remained without their husbands for some time. Katherine published a letter 'To the Suffering Women of Kenzingen Parish.' In it she gave examples of heroic women of the past and encouraged the women in the sufficiency of God's Word

24   James I. Good. *Women of the Reformed Church*. Sunday School Board of the Reformed Church in the United States, 1901, pp. 46-7.

25   Roland Bainton. *Women of the Reformation in Germany and Italy*. Minneapolis, 1971, 55. cf. Numbers pp. 22-24.

and the promise of salvation. Until their husbands returned, she exhorted the ladies to continue the work required of every Christian. Katherine concluded by quoting the beatitudes, giving comfort to those persecuted for righteousness (Matthew 5:1-10).

Katherine also wrote an introduction to a Bohemian Brethren hymnbook (1535) and authored a book of meditations on selected Psalms and the Lord's Prayer (1558). The latter was written for a magistrate who became leprous and had to live outside the city. Additionally, Katherine's writing included extensive correspondence with other leaders of the Reformation throughout Europe. She defended the Schwenckfelders and Anabaptists as fellow-Christians and spoke out against their persecution. Katherine's tireless, unremitting works of charity and caring for others added power to her words.

Marie Dentière (c. 1495-1561) was a contemporary of Katherine Zell in Geneva and a woman remarkable enough for her name to be included on the Reformation Monument in Geneva as a precursor of the Reformation, along with Peter Valdes, John Wycliffe, and John Huss.[26] Marie Dentière became abbess of the Augustinian convent of Tournai in Flanders in 1517, the year Martin Luther published his *95 Theses*. Luther's ideas quickly spread to Flanders, and around 1524, Marie converted to the belief that salvation came by faith in Christ, not works in the Church. Forced from the convent and abandoned by her family, Marie fled to Strasbourg. There she met and married a former priest, Simon Robert. When Robert died in 1533, Marie married Antoine Froment, a Reformer in Geneva. Antoine at the time was a teacher and a merchant, though later he became a pastor. Marie helped Antoine in the shop while also caring for her three children.

Geneva had been disputing with its ruler, the Duke of Savoy, since the 1520s, with many of the city's merchants wanting to ally themselves with the Protestant Swiss city-states. Armed conflict often broke out within the city as well as with outside armies. In 1535, the male citizens voted to accept Reform. Marie, as a former nun, went to the Franciscan monastery at Geneva to try to persuade the nuns to accept the truths of salvation by grace alone. She gave her personal testimony, stating, 'I spent a long time in the darkness of hypocrisy but God alone showed me my condition and led me to the true light of truth.'[27] Marie was unsuccessful in convincing the nuns, however, and they went into exile at Annecy.

The following year, Marie anonymously published the first Protestant history of the Genevan Reformation — *The War and Deliverance of the City*

---

26   *Other Women's Voices*, http://home.infionline.net/~ddisse/dentiere.html.

27   Rev. Dr. Isabelle Graesslé, 'Reformation Sunday,' *Reformed World*, Vol. 53, No. 1 (March 2003), of the World Alliance of Reformed Churches, accessed at http://www.warc.ch/24gc/rw031/14.html.

of Geneva. This small book described the victory of the gospel over the tyranny of the Pope and the Duke of Savoy. Her history was not merely a chronicle of contemporary events but a theological reflection upon them. She wrote to convince the Genevans of God's purpose for their city. Soon after, John Calvin arrived and worked with William Farel to establish the government of the city based on the Bible.

When Farel and Calvin were expelled from Geneva in 1538, apparently Marguerite of Navarre, a sympathizer with the Reformers, wanted to know details about the banishment. Marie published a letter to Marguerite. In it she defended Calvin and Farel and reminded Marguerite that good and faithful servants of God, including Jesus Christ Himself, had been rejected and condemned by false teachers and heretics. She noted that throughout the land there were dissensions, divisions, warfare, and riotings among those who called themselves Christians. Marie's letter to Marguerite is important as a letter from a woman to a woman. Although women were not permitted to preach publicly or in church, they could write and admonish one another in love. Marie wrote Marguerite

> to give courage to other women detained in captivity, so that they might not fear being expelled from their homelands, away from their relatives, and friends, as I was, for the word of God. And principally for the poor little women, wanting to know and understand the truth, who do not know what path, what way to take, in order that from now on they be not internally tormented and afflicted, but rather that they be joyful, consoled, and be led to follow the truth, which is the Gospel of Jesus Christ.[28]

Marie included with her letter a 'Defense of Women,' explaining women's right to read and interpret Scriptures. She provided Biblical examples of women emboldened by God's truth: Moses' mother who disobeyed Pharaoh's law and saved her son; the woman at the well who told the people of Samaria about Jesus; and the women at the empty tomb who were the first to preach the good news of Jesus' resurrection. She concluded:

> ...if God has given grace to some good women, revealing to them by his holy scriptures something holy and good, should they hesitate to write, speak, and declare it to one another because of the defamers of truth? Ah, it would be too bold to try to stop them, and it would be too foolish for us to hide the talent that God has given us. God will give us the grace to persevere to the end.[29]

---

28   Marie Dentière (Mary B. McKinley, trans.). *Epistle to Marguerite de Navarre and Preface to a Sermon by John Calvin,* (University of Chicago Press, 2004), p. 53.

29   *Epistle to Marguerite de Navarre,* p. 56.

Marie believed women had freedom to evangelize and bring the gospel to the poor and rich, and she spoke openly in the streets and even in the taverns about the gospel.

Huguenot Women

Marie's correspondent, Marguerite, Queen of Navarre (1492-1549), was sister to King Francis I of France and was able to use her position to protect the persecuted of the Reformed faith.[30] Though Marguerite lived amidst the corruption and immorality of the French court, she had a hunger for truth and righteousness. She learned of Biblical truth from Jacques Lefevre D'Etaples, the 'Pioneer Spirit of the Reformation.' Lefevre's preaching called for a return to the Christianity of Christ and the apostles and pointed out the need for Church reform several years before Luther's *95 Theses*. Lefevre became Marguerite's spiritual advisor.

Marguerite was very close to her brother, King Francis I, who once said, 'My sister Margaret is the only woman I ever knew who had every virtue and every grace without any admixture of vice.'[31] Yet Marguerite recognized herself as a sinner in need of God's saving grace. In 1533, Marguerite published *The Mirror of the Sinful Soul*, a cycle of poems based on Psalm 42 and David's words from Psalm 51, 'Create in me a clean heart, O Lord.' Included were the poems, 'Primacy of Scripture,' 'Justification by Faith,' and the 'Doctrine of Election.' The Sorbonne condemned the work because it made no mention of purgatory or the intercession of the saints in salvation. King Francis was infuriated, banished some of the clergy, and had the condemnation removed. Marguerite also wrote *Heptameron*, a collection of tales to be read over a week. The humorous stories of human frailty showed that one could not rely on one's own strength but in all circumstances should look to God for strength. Marguerite was a patroness of literature in addition to being a writer herself. Her valet de chambre, or personal secretary, was Clement Marot, a French hymn writer and a translator of the Psalms sung in France for the last four centuries.

At seventeen Marguerite was married to Charles, Duke of Alençon. On his death, Marguerite and Henry II of Navarre entered an arranged political marriage. Marguerite continued to worship in her private apartments, where Lefevre and other Protestant Reformers preached. Marguerite's husband did not share her faith, and Marguerite looked more firmly to the Lord for her strength. She put her prayer into poetry:

> Would that the day were come, O Lord,
> So much desired by me,

---

30 *Other Women's Voices*, http://home.infionline.net/~ddisse/navarre.html.

31 *Women of the Reformed Church*, p. 60.

When by the cords of heavenly love
I shall be drawn to Thee,
United in eternal life
The husband Thou and I the wife.

That wedding day, O Lord,
My heart so longs to see,
That neither fame nor wealth nor rank
Can give to me;
To me the world no more
Can yield delight;
Unless Thou, Lord, be with me here,
Lo! All is dark as night. [32]

One day, angered by her religious meetings, Marguerite's husband burst into her chambers and struck her on the face. Marguerite reported the incident to her brother, the King of France, who readied an army to bring against the King of Navarre. This frightened Henry, who begged Marguerite's forgiveness and promised to investigate the truth of the Reformation teachings. Soon, Henry had a change of heart and was also involved in Bible studies around the dinner table and protecting Protestant refugees from persecution. Though Marguerite sympathized and favored the Protestants, she remained within the Catholic Church until her death.

Marguerite's life and works were a testimony to her faith. She cared for the poor, protected the suffering and persecuted, sponsored faithful preaching of the Scriptures, and worked tirelessly for others. With her husband she improved agriculture and commerce in Navarre, encouraged cloth manufacture, fostered education, and opened an orphanage and numerous hospitals. As she lay dying, she said, 'God, I am well assured, will carry forward the work He has permitted me to commence, and my place will be more than filled by my daughter, who has the energy and moral courage, in which I fear I have been deficient.'

Marguerite's daughter, Jeanne d'Albert (1528-1572) did indeed show the strength of courage her mother foresaw in her. Though a woman of position, influence and wealth, whose son was next in line to the throne of France, Jeanne always placed higher value on truth and things of the spirit than those of the world. When she became Queen of Navarre in 1555, Jeanne proclaimed Calvinism the religion of Navarre. She protected the French Protestants or Huguenots, and established a college of theology. Her chaplains translated the New Testament into the dialect of the Basques of Lower Navarre, giving these people the Bible in their own language for the first time. Catherine de Medici, queen-regent of France, advised Jeanne to conceal her Protestantism and at least make an outward show of

---

32   Ibid., p. 66.

Catholicism, but Jeanne replied, 'If I, at this very moment, held my son, and all the kingdoms of the world together, in my grasp, I would hurl them to the bottom of the sea, rather than peril the salvation of my soul.'[33]

Jeanne was firm in her convictions of the errors of the Catholic Church, stating boldly:

> The Church has not maintained her pristine innocence and vigor – her purity and holiness of doctrines and practice. The Church has exchanged the spiritual for the carnal. Her roses are become thistles. Her charity is nothing but chilling vanity. Her priests and bishops, who should be like Timothy, chaste, sober, humble, hospitable, watching night and day to cherish the holy fire which glows in the bosom of every true priest of God, have defiled themselves.[34]

In removing the images from the churches, she sought to imitate King Joash of Judah who, upon removing Baal worship and repairing the temple, proclaimed, 'I have not undertaken to start a new religion, but only to build up the ruins of our ancient faith …[35]'

Catherine de Medici, called a Jezebel by some, plotted against Jeanne and the Huguenots. Jeanne's husband, Antoine de Bourbon, was also a regent of the French King and often had to be away in Paris. There, Catherine worked to win Antoine back to the Catholic faith and separate him from Jeanne. When Jeanne visited Paris, Antoine tried to force her to renounce her Protestantism, but Jeanne realized she was surrounded by danger and managed to escape Paris. As Jeanne returned to Navarre, a Huguenot army protected her from Catherine's assassination plots. In 1563, Pope Pius IV cited Jeanne to appear before the Inquisition and to forfeit her territories for herself and her children, but the French King Charles IX protected her and annulled the Pope's bull.

Though Jeanne's husband supported the Catholics in the French Wars of Religion, which broke out in 1562, Jeanne and her son Henry supported the Protestants. In an effort to bring about peace between the warring parties, a marriage was arranged between Jeanne's son, the Protestant Henry of Navarre, and the Catholic Margaret of Valois, daughter of Catherine de Medici and the sister of the King of France. Jeanne was very concerned about the prospects of this marriage and told her son,

> My son, if you ever had need to supplicate the Almighty, it is now in this our extremity. I, for my part, pray to him incessantly to aid us in this negotiation, so that this marriage may not be accomplished in wrath but granted as a merciful blessing to augment His glory and our

---

33   As quoted in *Great Women of the Christian Faith*, p. 86.

34   Ibid., p. 87.

35   Ibid.

repose...I pray God that for your salvation and His glory, He may give you all needful things.[36]

As the wedding approached, Jeanne went to Paris and was dismayed by the excesses and immorality of the French court. She wrote her son to escape Paris and its corruption as soon as the wedding was over:

> Your betrothed is beautiful, very circumspect and graceful, but brought up in the worst company that ever existed (for I do not see a single one who is not infected by it)...I would not for anything have you come here [Paris] to live. This is why I desire you to marry and to withdraw yourself and your wife from this corruption which (bad as I supposed it to be) I find still worse than I thought. If you were here, you could not escape contamination without great grace from God.[37]

Jeanne suddenly became ill and died in Paris just weeks before the wedding. There was speculation she was poisoned by Catherine de Medici.

The wedding itself brought crowds to Paris. With so many Huguenots brought together for the festivities, excitement in the city was high. Catherine, ever the power behind the French throne, plotted the assassination of the Protestant leader de Coligny. When the assassination attempt only wounded de Coligny, Catherine instigated the massacre of all the Protestants in the city and surrounding areas. Known as the St. Bartholomew's Day Massacre, between 40,000 and 100,000 Protestants were killed in the next few days. Henry of Navarre escaped with his life only by pretending to accept the Catholic faith for a time.

In 1589, Jeanne's son Henry became King of France. To keep peace and assure his kingship, he formally accepted the Catholic faith. His sympathies with the Protestant cause continued, however, and in 1598 he issued the Edict of Nantes, granting religious liberty to the French Protestants, a protection they enjoyed for almost 90 years, until revoked in 1685. Henry was sometimes called 'Henry the Great' or 'good king Henry.' Though he did succumb to the immoral sexual life of the French court as his mother had feared, the influence of his Christian mother and grandmother could be seen in Henry's protection of the French Protestants and his interest in the common people of France.

---

36   As quoted in *Great Women of the Christian Faith*, p. 88.

37   Ibid., p. 89.

A Huguenot Mother to Her Son

Among those Protestants who managed to survive the St. Bartholomew's Massacre was Charlotte du Plessis de Mornay. In Paris for Henry of Navarre's wedding, Charlotte was warned of the killings by a kitchen maid. Charlotte escaped and managed to find refuge with a friend and was able to find a hiding place when soldiers came to the house looking for her. Escaping to another refuge nearby, she hid in the hollow space under the roof of an outhouse, listening to the cries of men, women, and children being murdered in the street. Charlotte's mother and brothers gained safety by attending a Catholic mass, but Charlotte refused such a compromise and continued her flight, narrowly escaping capture or discovery on several occasions.

Charlotte later married Philip du Plessis de Mornay, who shared her strong Biblical convictions. Philip was a friend of Henry of Navarre, serving as his secretary and going on diplomatic missions for him to England and Flanders. When Henry became King, Philip was the primary author of the Edict of Nantes, giving liberty to French Protestants. Philip later fell out of favor with the King, however, for his unwillingness to compromise his religious convictions for French policy.

Charlotte wrote the memoirs of her husband's life for her son. In her opening address she wrote:

> 'Now that I behold you ready to start off into the world, to see it, and to study in it the
> manners of men and the state of nations, not being able to follow you with my eyes, I will
> follow you however with the same care, and pray God that you may increase in the fear
> and love of God ... He has made you to be born of a father of whom in these days He has
> made use (and will again serve to his glory), and who has since your infancy dedicated you
> to His service ...But to the intent that you should never want [lack] a guide, here is one
> under warranty of my own hand to go with you; this is the example of your father, which
> I adjure you to have ever before your eyes, to the which end I have taken the trouble to
> discourse to you what I have been able to know of his life ... you have enough here to know
> what graces God has given him, as well as the zeal and affection with which he has ever
> used them; and you may hope for the like help whenever you too are resolved to serve Him
> with all your heart...In whatever place you are, serve God, and follow your father ...'*

Charlotte's son died in battle before she had finished her memoir. She herself died within the year.

---

* 'Memoirs of Madame du Plessis-Mornay,' *Littel's Living Age*, 598.

Christian Women in the Counter-Reformation and the English Reformation: *The Household of Faith*

Galatians 6:10

During the fifteenth and sixteenth centuries, many recognized that the Roman Church was failing to reflect the spirit of Christ. The Roman Church's hierarchy had accumulated tremendous wealth for itself and often administered its holdings and patronage for selfish gain. Bishops and popes seemed more involved in political intrigues than spiritual ministrations. Scholastic theologians had become sterile in their vain disputations, and the lower clergy were often illiterate, ignorant, and superstitious. While many recognized that correction was needed, they differed on the nature of the desired reforms. Protestant Reformers believed the power and tradition of the Church had supplanted the authority of the Scriptures. They sought to return the Church to the Biblical foundation of the apostolic teaching, stripped of the centuries of accumulated accretions of Church traditions. Others, however, sought to maintain the authority and tradition of the Church while bringing about a moral reformation. These latter became part of the Catholic Reformation. The Catholic Reformation, also called the Counter-Reformation, attacked the teachings of the Protestant Reformation while seeking to purify and strengthen the authority and hierarchy of the Roman Church.

One important leader of the Counter-Reformation was the Spaniard Ignatius of Loyola (1491-1556), founder of the Society of Jesus, or Jesuits. The Jesuits became teachers and leaders of reform within the Roman Church. Ignatius proclaimed such loyalty to the Church that his Rule 13 of 'Rules for Thinking with the Church' stated, 'I will believe that the white that I see is black if the hierarchical Church so defines it.' Ignatius coupled this unquestioning obedience to the Church with a self-denial and mysticism which he described in his *Spiritual Exercises*. Ignatius' contemporary and fellow-Spaniard, Teresa of Ávila (1515-1582), also cultivated a mystical devotion and sought reformation within the Roman Church.[1]

---

1   *Other Women's Voices*, http://home.infionline.net/~ddisse/teresa.html.

Return to Mystical Contemplation

Teresa was born in the Spanish town of Ávila two years before Luther began
the Reformation in Germany. Her parents were both devout, and from an
early age Teresa was interested in the religious books her father read. In
her room was a picture of the Woman at the Well, and Teresa frequently
repeated as a prayer the Samaritan woman's words, 'Give me this water that
I thirst not' (John 4:14-15). Teresa's education in a convent reinforced her
religious yearnings. When she read some of St. Jerome's letters to Christian
women at Rome, Teresa decided to similarly consecrate her life to Christ.
In 1534, she entered the Carmelite Monastery of the Incarnation, at Ávila.

Teresa suffered much sickness from the austerities in the monastery, but she
cultivated a mystical devotion which brought periods of great ecstasy as well.
Through self-concentration and an inner contemplation, she sought to bring
herself into absolute subjection to God. By withdrawing into her inner self, she
believed God would be brought inside the soul as well. Teresa described four
stages to this spiritual communion. First was mental prayer or the devotion
of the heart. By devout concentration or contemplation, the soul withdrew
from the outward world and penitentially observed the passion and suffering
of Christ. The second stage was the devotion of peace. Here the human will
was lost in God, though other faculties of memory, reason and imagination
might still be distracted by the world. In the third stage, the devotion of union,
the reason was absorbed in God and experienced a supernatural ecstatic state,
a conscious rapture in the love of God. In the final state of ecstasy or rapture,
the soul was passive, and all consciousness of being in the body disappeared. All
was absorbed in and intoxicated with God:

> Body and spirit are in the throes of a sweet, happy pain, alternating
> between a fearful fiery glow, a complete impotence and unconsciousness,
> and a spell of strangulation, intermitted sometimes by such an ecstatic
> flight that the body is literally lifted into space. This after half an hour
> is followed by a reactionary relaxation of a few hours in a swoon-like
> weakness, attended by a negation of all the faculties in the union with
> God. From this the subject awakens in tears; it is the climax of mystical
> experience, productive of the trance.[2]

Like earlier medieval mystics, Teresa experienced personal visions.
Beginning in 1559, she became convinced that Christ was present to
her in bodily form, though invisible to others. This vision lasted without
interruption for two years. Teresa was consumed with the suffering of
Christ and willing to share in that suffering in service for others. In one
vision, an angel drove a lance repeatedly into Teresa's heart, and she
prayed, 'Lord, either let me suffer or let me die.'

2   'Theresa, Saint,' *The New Schaff-Herzog Religious Encyclopedia*, Vol. 11, p. 413.

Grieved by the corruptions in the Church, Teresa sought to reform her own Carmelite order, returning the nuns to the original Carmelite ideal of an austere and contemplative life. Her reformed order, known as the Barefoot Carmelites, adopted a stricter rule than the original order. Leather or wooden sandals replaced shoes, and the nuns practiced flagellation three times a week. Teresa established sixteen convents of her Order and fourteen monasteries of Carmelite Friars. The Order spread throughout Europe, to Spanish America, and to Persia and India in the East.

Teresa's confessor, Peter of Alcantara, encouraged her to write her *Autobiography* and other works about her contemplative life. *The Way of Perfection* (1559) described the process of mental prayer. *The Interior Castle* (1577) compared the contemplative soul to a castle with

---

Vittoria Colonna (1490-1547)

Vittoria Colonna was an Italian writer of religious verse as well as a friend and encourager of Michelangelo. Michelangelo claimed that Vittoria's conversation and the examples of her life, in the midst of Rome's corruption, made him a better Christian. Married at nineteen, Vittoria endured many years of separation from her husband, who was a heroic Italian commander in the wars against France. Vittoria belonged to the Oratory of Divine Love, which sought to bring moral reform and evangelical simplicity to the Catholic Church. She also wrote a series of sonnets called *The Triumph of Christ*, reflecting on the Crucifixion and Resurrection, by which Christ brought salvation.*

Other Women's Voices, http://home.infionline.net/~ddisse/colonna.html.

---

seven successive interior courts or chambers, analogous to the seven heavens. These works continue to be read and offer spiritual guidance to some today. These writings led the Roman Catholic Church to name Teresa among the 'Doctors of the Church.' This rare honor is given by the Pope to those saints whose writings can bring great benefit to the whole Church and whose life was marked by great holiness. Among the thirty-three 'Doctors of the Church,' only three are women. Teresa of Ávila, along with Catherine of Siena, was so named in 1970.[3]

Teresa's life of inward-looking, contemplative mysticism contrasted greatly with the lives and thinking of those who were part of the Protestant Reformation. The women of the Reformation knew God from His revelation of Himself in the Scriptures, not through visions or mysticism. They lived their Christian lives in communities and families, not in austere isolation or ascetic flagellation. They came to know God in a deeper way by a greater knowledge of the Scriptures and obedience to God's Word, not through a self-imposed abnegation of the body and extra-Biblical meditative techniques.

---

3   The third female 'Doctor of the Church,' is Teresa of Lisieux (1873-1897), proclaimed a Doctor in 1998.

High Drama at the English Court

During the Renaissance and Reformation, women rulers of great influence could be found on thrones throughout Europe:

> Never before (and seldom after) was Europe ruled by so many learned ladies: Elizabeth of England, Mary of Scotland, Marguerite of Navarre, Catherine de Medici and Louisa of Savoy in France, Margaret of Austria, Mary of Hungary, Catherine Cornaro, queen of Cyprus, Eleanor of Aragosa, and Isabella of Spain.[4]

Catherine of Aragon, Isabella's daughter, did not attain the influence of some of the other queens, but she was important to the high drama of the court of England during this period. The royal court of Tudor England was full of drama, and not just because Shakespeare wrote his plays during this time. The court itself was filled with passion, plots, and powerful personalities performing on an international stage for high stakes. Religion and the nature of the Christian faith were also underlying currents pulsating through the events and discussions of this period. Reminiscent of a millennium earlier when Christian queens influenced the gospel's establishment on the British Isles, the establishment of the Reformation's evangelical teaching gained support in the sixteenth century, in part, through the influence of English queens and noblewomen.

Among royalty, marriages were usually tools of political alliances. The alliance between England and Spain was sealed by the betrothal of the young English prince and Spanish princess. Catherine of Aragon (1485-1536), daughter of Ferdinand and Isabella of Spain, was betrothed at the age of three to Prince Arthur of England, who then was not yet two. When she was sixteen Catherine sailed to England, with an appropriately impressive entourage, for her wedding with Arthur, who died six months after the wedding. The English King Henry VII, eager to maintain the Spanish alliance, was able to betroth the young princess to his next son, Prince Henry, who was six years Catherine's junior and not yet old enough to marry. When Henry was eighteen, his father died. The young King Henry VIII promptly married Catherine of Aragon and made her his queen. The two were happy and beloved by their countrymen, but Catherine was unfortunate in childbirth. Though she had six children, only daughter Mary survived.

Juan Luis Vives, a Spanish humanist and friend of Erasmus, wrote an instruction manual for the education of Mary. This *Instruction of a Christian Woman*, first published in 1523, went through over thirty editions, continued to be published well into the next century, and was translated

---

4   Katherina M. Wilson. *Women Writers of the Renaissance and Reformation*. Athens, Georgia and London: University of Georgia Press, 1987, xxii.

into at least six languages. In thirty-eight chapters Vives wrote of the life of a Christian woman from childhood to widowhood, treating of everything from her apparel to sex with her husband. Throughout, Vives emphasized the importance of virtue. Learning and education were important only as they increased virtue. Vives wrote that women were easily led astray and should occupy themselves with wholesome thoughts and occupations. Vives commended spinning as a noble way to occupy the hands, and reading religious material (not romances of courtly love) was encouraged. Chastity was of the highest importance to a woman, and she was expected to restrict her behavior and activities to protect this most precious virtue. Vives also discussed in detail women's outward adornment. He was adamant that women should not use cosmetics or dye their hair; flashy jewelry and lavish clothes were to be avoided.

Erasmus Extols Companionship in Marriage

Like the Reformation leaders, Erasmus and other leading humanists of the day extolled marriage as superior to the celibate, ascetic life esteemed throughout the Middle Ages. The humanists valued companionship as a goal in marriage, in addition to procreation and the prevention of fornication. Erasmus called monastic celibacy 'a form of living both barren and unnatural.' He even equated celibacy with abortion, noting 'there is small diversity [little difference] between him that murders that which begins to be born, and him which procures that nothing can be born.' In his *Praise of Matrimony*, Erasmus wrote that it was 'an especial sweetness to have one with whom you may communicate the secret affections of your mind, with whom you may speak even as it were with your own self.'

The second book of Vives' *Instruction of a Christian Woman* was devoted to the superiority of marriage. Like his friend Erasmus, Vives saw companionship as an important purpose of marriage. He wrote that the husband should consider his wife 'as a most faithful secretary of your cares and thoughts, and in doubtful matters a wise and a hearty counselor. This is the true society and fellowship of man …'[5] The Council of Trent (1545-1563), which officially formalized the Catholic response to the Protestant Reformation, repudiated the Renaissance humanist and Reformation teachings on the superiority of marriage to celibacy. The 24th session of the Council adopted a canon stating, 'If anyone says that the married state excels the state of virginity or celibacy, and that it is better and happier to be united in matrimony than to remain in virginity or celibacy, let him be anathema.'[6]

---

5   'Spiritualized Household,' p. 21.

6   Ibid., p. 32.

Queen Catherine's personal virtues, chastity, and companionship were not enough to keep King Henry's eyes and heart from straying, however. As Catherine approached the post-childbearing years, her failure to produce a male heir for her husband led to the couple's separation. Based upon Leviticus 20:21, 'If a man takes his brother's wife it is impurity... they shall be childless,' Henry began to think his marriage with Catherine was forbidden in Scripture and cursed. Catherine insisted her marriage with Henry's brother Arthur had never been consummated. Nevertheless, Henry sought from Pope Clement VIII an annulment of his marriage with Catherine. Politically, the Pope could not favor such a request. Charles V, Catherine's nephew and the Holy Roman Emperor, had armies in Italy and held the Pope a virtual captive. Yet, the Pope did not want to anger the King of England either. Caught between the two powers, the Pope delayed and did nothing for several years. Henry, however, had convinced himself that his seventeen-year marriage to Catherine had not been a legitimate marriage at all and acted as if the marriage were invalid.

The King's wandering eye was drawn to one of Catherine's ladies-in-waiting, Anne Boleyn.[7] Anne's sister Mary had been Henry's mistress for a time, and Henry apparently expected to easily enjoy Anne's favors. However, Anne sought to preserve her honor and would not give herself to the King except in marriage.

From the age of twelve or thirteen, Anne Boleyn (1501?-1536) had been educated at the French court. There she became skilled in music, poetry, and courtly graces. She gained a sense of fashion and elegance, wit and grace, which quickly brought her to the notice of the English king when she appeared at the English court. Though she enjoyed the fashion, finery, music, and gaiety of the French court, Anne did not partake of the court's immorality. She had a more serious side and was attracted to the evangelical ideas of the Reformation. She first learned of evangelical teachings while at the court of Queen Claude of France. She read Lefevre's French translation of the Bible and studied French commentaries on Scripture. The books of Anne's which survive today give evidence of her evangelical faith: a 1534 Lefevre Bible in French, inscribed with Romans 5:12-18 and John 1:17; a copy of William Tyndale's 1534 English New Testament (Anne's copy of this banned book is now in the British Library); a book of Huguenot poetry by Clement Marot, and a commentary on Ecclesiastes. Contemporary accounts also indicate that Anne's choice of reading material frequently included works written by those following evangelical perspectives.

---

7   Much has recently been written about the religious faith and evangelical beliefs of Anne Boleyn, as well as her influence on the Reformation in England and the cause of her execution. See Eric Ives' *The Life and Death of Anne Boleyn* (Blackwell Publishing, 2005).

When Anne returned to England, she became lady-in-waiting to Queen Catherine, and King Henry soon noticed her at court. The cultivated, elegant ways Anne learned in France distinguished her from the Englishwomen at court. She was talented in the dances and elaborately staged tableaux of the court, as well as being witty and intelligent in conversation. Though in the popular mind Anne has often been portrayed as a woman of loose morals consumed with ambition to be queen, the facts speak otherwise. For six years King Henry assiduously pursued Anne, but she refused to become his mistress. Her refusal made her more attractive to Henry. Only when Henry's divorce from Catherine seemed a certainty and Henry presented Anne as his intended wife, did Anne yield to Henry. Henry swiftly married Anne when she became pregnant, though he kept the marriage secret until the Parliament completed its formal approval of the King's divorce. Despite Henry and Anne's high expectations for a boy, Anne gave birth to a baby girl. They named her Elizabeth, a name shared by the mothers of both Anne and Henry. Anne's two later pregnancies ended in miscarriages – the latter one was a son.

Henry's divorce of Catherine and marriage to Anne led to his excommunication by the Pope and the establishment of the Church of England with the King at its head. Anne encouraged Henry in England's separation from the papacy. Though it is often said that Anne was the cause of the break-up of Henry's marriage with Catherine, the facts indicate that Henry questioned the validity of his marriage to Catherine before he ever met Anne. Assured of Henry's impending divorce with Catherine, Cardinal Wolsey traveled to France to arrange a marriage between Henry and the daughter of the French King. He returned to England unsuccessful in his quest only to find Henry intent on securing Anne's consent to marriage.

Though no records remain revealing Anne's personal beliefs with certainty, there is evidence that she used her influence to encourage the Reformation in England. Both in England and on the Continent, she was widely regarded as a catalyst in the reform of the Church of England. The historian and martyrologist John Foxe wrote that the papal power and authority in England

> began utterly to be abolished, by the reason and occasion of the most virtuous and noble lady, Anne Boleyn, who was not as yet married to the king (howbeit in great favor) by whose godly means and most virtuous council, the king's mind was daily inclined better and better…[Anne] without all controversy was the private and open comforter and aider of all the professors of Christ's Gospel…her life being also directed according to the same.[8]

---

8   Quoted in Thomas S. Freeman, 'Research, Rumour and Propaganda: Anne Boleyn in Foxe's "Book of Martyrs,"' *The Historic Journal*, Vol. 38, no. 4 (Dec. 1995), p. 801. Spelling has been modernized.

Anne knew how to use her influence to shape the thinking of the King as well as secure positions for those with an evangelical bent. Anne patronized Protestant publishers and writers and protected merchants involved in the importation of English Bibles and evangelical works. She tried to convince Henry, whose theology was still very much Catholic though he had broken with the Pope, that William Tyndale, the scholar forced to translate the Bible into English while in exile, was his friend. Anne was behind Henry's appointment of several evangelical bishops and deans. Historians recognize that the impact of the ecclesiastical appointments made under Anne's influence 'was crucial to the future of the Reformation.'[9] The Boleyn family's chaplain, Thomas Cranmer, became Archbishop of Canterbury and a molder of the Church of England through the liturgy he composed, particularly the *Book of Common Prayer*.

Anne's personal chaplains included Hugh Latimer and Matthew Parker. Latimer was appointed a bishop through Anne's influence and later was martyred for his faith under Queen Mary. Matthew Parker became Archbishop of Canterbury and a leader of the Reformation under Anne's daughter, Queen Elizabeth. The sincerity of Anne's humility and desire to be true in her faith was evident by her exhortation to her chaplains to freely tell her what they 'saw in her amiss.'

Anne was very much interested in helping the poor. In the year before her coronation, she distributed a hundred pounds of clothing to the poor each week. Until the time of her arrest, she regularly gave help to poor families and householders. Her charity was not simply bestowed on beggars and vagrants; she sought out families in need and found meaningful ways to help them. She organized the ladies at court to sew clothes for the poor, believing that there should be no idleness among them. With her brother and father she maintained poor scholars at Cambridge, including several who later became archbishops and bishops. Anne also was instrumental in obtaining release from prison for those with evangelical views, such as the merchant who smuggled in copies of Tyndale's English New Testament and scholars imprisoned for writing evangelical works. When the monasteries were dissolved, Anne worked to have the funds used for the poor and to support education. She believed that since the monasteries originally were founded from charitable gifts, funds from the dissolution of the monasteries should only be used for charitable purposes. That she encouraged the money to be used for charity, rather than appropriated for political favorites or the royal treasury, was a cause for some, particularly the powerful minister Thomas Cromwell, to turn against her.

Anne accumulated both political and religious enemies during her reign of 'One Thousand Days' and was not always able to keep Henry's devotion.

---

9   Ives. *Anne Boleyn*, p. 261.

Henry's attraction to Anne's wit, grace, independence, and charm did not prevent him from having several affairs during their marriage, affairs which Anne always vehemently protested. She was known as a woman with a sharp tongue and temper. The death of Catherine of Aragon in 1536 somewhat removed the 'divorce' stigma from Henry. Some advisors thought the removal of Anne would make possible a rapprochement between Henry, Pope Clement, and Emperor Charles V (who was also King Charles I of Spain). That Anne had only produced a daughter followed by two miscarriages, but no male heir, made it easier for others to persuade Henry that Anne would be better out of the way. Besides, Jane Seymour had now moved into Henry's favor. Thomas Cromwell, Henry's chief minister, told the Spanish ambassador that he engineered Anne's downfall to promote England's alliance with Charles V.

Anne's fall was swift. She was arrested on May 2, 1536, on charges of adultery, incest, witchcraft, and high treason. Also arrested were Sir Francis Weston, Sir Henry Norris, Mark Smeaton, William Brereton, and Anne's brother, George Boleyn. Under torture, Mark Smeaton confessed his guilt. All others vehemently maintained their innocence, as did Anne. It was difficult to believe that Anne, noted for her Christian spirit, could be guilty of adultery with five men. Most historians today recognize that there was no truth in any of the charges, and that Anne's death was engineered for political and religious reasons.[10]

Anne Boleyn was executed at the Tower of London on May 19, seventeen days after her arrest. King Henry allowed her to be beheaded by the sword, which would be the most swift and painless death. John Foxe recorded Anne's last words:

> Good Christian people! I am come hither to die, for according to the law, and by the law, I am judged to death; and therefore I will speak nothing against it. I come hither to accuse no man, nor to any thing of that whereof I am accused and condemned to die; but I pray God save the king, and send him long to reign over you, for a gentler, or a more merciful prince was there never; and to me he was ever a good, a gentle, and a sovereign lord. And if any person will meddle of my cause, I require them to judge the best. And thus I take my leave of the world, and of you all, and I heartily desire you all to pray for me. O Lord have mercy on me! To God I commend my soul.[11]

---

10   Historian Eric Ives has the interesting theory that Shakespeare's *A Winter's Tale* is a retelling of Anne Boleyn's false accusations and trial. Hermione represents Anne, and the daughter who is whisked away from danger and survives represents Queen Elizabeth.

11   John Foxe. *Acts and Monuments*, Book III, p. 529 of 1563 edition, http://www.hrionline.ac.uk/johnfoxe/main/3_1563_0529.jsp.

So she knelt and repeated several times, 'To Christ I commend my soul, Jesus, receive my soul.' Foxe added:

> ... her last words, declared no less the sincere faith, and trust that she had in Christ, then her modesty also did utter the goodness of her cause and matter. There were in this Queen besides the comeliness of her form and beauty, many other giftes of a well instructed mind, as gentleness, modesty, and piety toward all men, besides a fervent desire in her heart unto the true and sincere religion, so that during her life, religion happily flourished and went forward. But I know not by what unhappy destiny, it is given unto this world, that those things which are most excellent, are soonest violently taken away as unworthy for the world.

Foxe was amazed that the Parliament, which had three years before confirmed Anne's marriage with King Henry as most lawful, should suddenly repeal its own doings and declare the marriage unlawful. Not satisfied with that, the Parliament proceeded to accuse her of the most carnal desires, even with her own brother, 'being so contrary to all nature, that no natural man will believe it.' Foxe did not know the 'great mystery' behind such changes in Parliament, but he could not help but believe it was a secret plot of the Catholic faction:

> Considering what a mighty stop she was to their purposes and proceedings, and on the contrary side, what a strong bulwark she was for the maintenance of Christ's Gospel, and sincere religion, which they then in no case could abide....

Bible Study in the Palace

At the time of Anne's death, a number of the English Reformers were concerned that the reformation of the Church in England would die without Anne's influence and prodding. Nicholas Shaxton, Bishop of Salisbury, encouraged Thomas Cromwell to more diligently promote 'the honour of God and his Holy Word than when the late queen was alive and often incited you thereto.'[12] The Scottish Lutheran Alexander Ales, who was acquainted with Martin Luther and Philip Melanchthon from his exile in Germany, later wrote Anne's daughter Elizabeth that 'True religion in England had its commencement and its end with your mother.'[13]

The day after Anne's May 19th execution, Henry was betrothed to Jane Seymour. Eleven days after Anne's execution, Henry and Jane were married. Many of the conservative faction opposing Anne, and the Catholic supporters of Princess Mary (Catherine of Aragon's daughter) were

---

12   Ives. *Anne Boleyn*, p. 264.

13   Ibid., p. 264.

hopeful that with Anne out of the way, England would be restored to the Roman Church. They were to be disappointed. Henry was convinced of the rightness of his divorce from Catherine, separation from the Pope, and his position as head of both the government and Church in England. There was to be no turning back to the old ways.

King Henry's third wife, Jane Seymour, produced for Henry the son he had long desired. Jane herself died within days of her son Edward's birth. Henry was to marry three more times – briefly to Anne of Cleves, whom he divorced; to Catherine Howard, who was executed for adultery and treason; and finally to Katherine Parr. Katherine, Henry's last wife, had a powerful effect on the English court ladies through palace Bible studies and on the future Queen Elizabeth through her caring, motherly attention.

Curiously, Katherine Parr (1514-1548), Henry VIII's sixth wife, was named after his first wife, Catherine of Aragon! Katherine's mother had been a lady-in-waiting to the first queen. Katherine was intelligent and loved learning. Fluent in French, Latin, and Italian, she began learning Spanish after she became queen. After Katherine's first two husbands had died, Thomas Seymour, brother of the former queen Jane Seymour, showed an interest in marrying her. However, King Henry VIII claimed her for himself. Katherine felt she must heed the King's wishes and was married to the king in a quiet ceremony in 1543.

Katherine was very much interested in Bible study and the teachings of the Reformation. Her chaplain was Miles Coverdale, an early Bible translator who had printed the first complete English translation of the Bible in 1537, based largely on the work William Tyndale had done before his execution. Coverdale also edited the 'Great Bible' of 1539, a copy of which King Henry proclaimed should be placed in every church in England. The times had changed somewhat since the days of Queen Anne, whose copy of Tyndale's English translation of the New Testament was a forbidden book. Queen Katherine Parr had a Bible translator for a chaplain!

Despite such changes, there were still limitations on religious discussions and Bible study. England's break with Rome and the papacy did not mean that reform had fully come to the Church of England. The doctrines of the Roman Church to which many of the Reformers objected, doctrines such as purgatory, transubstantiation, and the practice of praying to the saints, were still official doctrines of the Church of England. The Six Articles of 1539 confirmed the Church of England in Roman Catholic beliefs. Books which did not support the beliefs in the Six Articles were considered heretical. These would have included many of those published by the continental Reformers. Though the Bible was now available in the English language, reading it was not encouraged. The Act for the Advancement of True Religion, enacted May 12, 1543, restricted Bible reading to clerics, noblemen, gentry, and rich merchants. Noblewomen were only allowed to read the Bible in private.

Nevertheless, Katherine Parr gathered around her court a number of ladies-in-waiting keenly interested in theology and Bible study. One of these was Anne Askew (1521?-1546).[14] Anne was the second daughter of Sir William Askew of South Kelsey, Lincoln. Her older sister had been betrothed to marry Thomas Kyme, but died before the marriage took place. Anne was then forced to marry Kyme. The couple had two children, but it was not a good marriage. Kyme was a firm Catholic, while Anne was evangelical in her faith. Her intense devotion was certainly impressive, but Kyme finally forced Anne out of the house. She went to London, where she became a part of the small group of evangelicals surrounding the Queen. She was active in sharing the gospel throughout London, primarily through the distribution of the Bible, tracts and religious books. Anne was first arrested in 1545 and particularly examined about her attitude toward the mass. The Catholic doctrine of transubstantiation included the belief that during the sacrament of the mass, the bread and wine were transformed into the literal body and blood of Christ. Anne contended that Christ died once for our sins, was buried, resurrected, and then seated at the Father's right hand. To claim that the mass was a re-sacrifice of the body and blood of Christ was contrary to Scripture and negated the very salvation which Christ brought. She was arrested and interrogated again in 1546, followed by another arrest and interrogation under torture a few months later. Anne's answers to her examiners showed an extensive knowledge of Scripture, ready wit, boldness, and courage to maintain her faith under intense persecution and the possibility of death.

An examining priest asked Anne if she didn't think that private masses helped departed souls. Anne replied, 'it was great idolatry to believe more in them than in the death which Christ died for us.' When repeatedly asked if she believed that the sacrament of the mass was indeed the body of Christ, Anne replied, 'I believe as the Scripture doth teach ... I believe that so oft as I, in a Christian congregation, do receive the bread in remembrance of Christ's death, and with thanksgiving according to his holy institution, I receive therewith the fruits also of his most glorious passion.' When exhorted to believe that at the mass the priest transformed the bread and wine into Christ's body and blood, Anne replied, 'I have read that God made man; but that man can make God, I never read, nor, I suppose, ever shall read.' She further asserted that 'my God will not be

14   Marie Gentert King ed. *Foxe's Book of Martyrs*. Tappan, N.J.: Fleming H. Revell, 1968, pp. 162-8.

eaten with teeth, neither yet dieth he again, and upon these words that I have now spoken will I suffer death.'

Her examiners tried to persuade Anne her views were heretical, but Anne clung to her understanding of Scripture. She was finally taken to the Tower, where she was commanded to tell the names of other ladies who shared her beliefs – whether Lady Suffolk, Lady Sussex, Lady Hertford, Lady Denny, or Lady Fitzwilliam. Anne would not provide any names. Since she wouldn't confess any names, the examiners, including the Bishop of London, put her on the rack, where she was stretched to try to break her will. This was illegal, since the racking of women was forbidden, and Anne was a 'gentlewoman' besides. But, Anne was isolated from her family, and her friends at court were unable to help her. Several of her bones were dislocated and broken, yet Anne remained silent, not even crying out in pain. As she later wrote, 'my Lord God, I thank his everlasting goodness, gave me grace to persevere.' She was promised that she could have anything she wanted if she recanted, but if she did not, she would be burned. Anne replied that she could find nothing in Scripture about Christ or the apostles putting anyone to death. She saw this as another example of the Romish Church going against God's Word. Anne said she would rather die than break her faith.

Anne's strength did not come from visions or mysticism; Scripture was her pathway to God. John Bale, Anne's biographer, recognized that it was precisely Anne's spiritual strength in her weakened physical condition which showed God was with her. 2 Corinthians 12:9 told that the strength of God was made perfect in weakness. Bale saw that when Anne 'seemed most feeble, then was she most strong...and gladly she rejoiced in that weakness, that Christ's power might strongly dwell in her.'[15] Bale compared Anne's martyrdom in detail with that of the second-century martyr Blandina. Both were young and tender yet never fainted under their torments. Both were not terrified at their painful death, for the Spirit of Christ gave them joy. The martyrdom of each led to the conversion of many.

Anne was so broken in body by her tortures that when she was taken to Smithfield to be burned, she was unable to walk and had to be tied in a chair and carried. Anne Askew was chained to the stake and burned, along with three others, on July 16, 1546. She was twenty-five years old. In her account of her trials, she concluded with this prayer:

O Lord, I have more enemies now than there be hairs on my head. Yet, sweet Lord, let me not set by them which are against me, for in thee is my whole delight; and, Lord, I heartily desire of thee that thou wilt, of thy most merciful goodness, forgive them that violence which they do

15   Elaine V. Beilin. *Redeeming Eve: Women Writers of the English Renaissance*. Princeton University Press, 1987, p. 33.

and have done unto me. Open also thou their blind hearts that they may hereafter do that thing in thy sight which is only acceptable before thee, and set forth thy verity aright, without all vain phantasy of sinful men. So be it, O Lord, so be it.

King Henry was ill, and competing factions vied for his interest as they looked to his successor. Prince Edward was yet a child, and whoever became the young king's regent could direct the future of the country. Both conservative and reformed factions sought control of the future regency. The religious debate and attack on Anne Askew was part of this power struggle. Anne's refusal to name, even under the greatest torture, any other women at court who shared her beliefs protected others and undoubtedly kept the persecution from spreading. Anne certainly protected Queen Katherine Parr.

Katherine was a patient, caring wife for King Henry. Often the King would sit with his bad leg pillowed in Katherine's lap, and he seemed soothed by her mild manner and words. The King's trust in Katherine was so complete, that when he was in France for some months, he appointed her as regent. She was an able executive during that time. On one occasion, however, the king became irritated at Katherine's theological discussion, and left the room in a huff, muttering, 'A good hearing it is when women become clerks [or clergy]; and a thing much to my comfort, to come in my old days to be taught by my wife!'

Bishop Stephen Gardiner overheard the King's remarks and eagerly built upon them to remove Katherine. Gardiner insinuated that Katherine was a heretic, did not follow the Six Articles, and was promulgating reform among her ladies-in-waiting, with Bible studies and illegal evangelical books being read at court. Gardiner drew up charges against Katherine for the King's approval and sought to have her arrested. An unknown Protestant got wind of the plan and was able to drop a copy of the impending charges at Katherine's door. Katherine turned white and collapsed in a fit of anxiety, realizing the danger she and the evangelical cause were in. If the Catholic conservatives gained the upper hand, they would control the future regency of Edward, and the reformation of the Church of England would be forestalled. Katherine composed herself and went to the king with a masterful apology:

> Your Majesty doth right well know, neither I myself am ignorant, what great imperfection and weakness by our first creation is allotted unto us women, to be ordained and appointed as inferior and subject unto men as our head, from which head all our direction ought to proceed, and that as God made man to his own shape and likeness, whereby he being endued with more special gifts of perfection, might rather be stirred to the contemplation of heavenly things, and to the earnest endeavor to obey his commandments; even so also made he woman of man, of

whom and by whom she is to be governed, commanded, and directed. Where womanly weakness and natural imperfection, ought to be tolerated, aided, and borne without, so that by his wisdom such things as are lacking in her, ought to be supplied.[16]

With this humble beginning, Katherine went on to say that she was seeking to be directed and taught by him and in no way sought to instruct the King. Katherine did believe that, in his better moments, Henry was as Moses leading England from the Pharaoh of the Roman pontiff. Henry was totally forgiving of Katherine and accepted her humble apology.

A few days later, unaware of the peace which had been restored between Katherine and the King, leaders of the Catholic conservative party led a troop of soldiers in to arrest Katherine. Henry was furious at their plotting and attempts to fill his mind with lies and deceit about Katherine. He dismissed them all and never trusted them again. In the King's will, the Protestants were given control over young King Edward's future regency.

Katherine had a powerful mothering influence over Henry's children, particularly Edward and Elizabeth. Elizabeth was only two years old when her mother was executed; Edward's mother died shortly after his birth. The kindness, warmth, and intelligence of Katherine, as well as her evangelical faith, were good for the children. Elizabeth herself, an adolescent at the time of Katherine's reign, especially seemed to have benefited from Katherine's interest. The Bodleian Library contains eleven-year-old Elizabeth's very personal 1544 New Year's Eve present to Katherine. Elizabeth made an English translation of Marguerite of Navarre's *Mirror or Glass of the Sinful Soul.* Marguerite had been an acquaintance of Anne Boleyn's, and Elizabeth very possibly used her mother's French edition of the work when making the translation. Elizabeth embroidered the cover of her translation and wrote an introduction for Katherine, noting the 'affectious will and fervent zeal which your highness hath towards all godly learning.' According to Elizabeth, in *The Mirror* Marguerite:

> doth perceive how of herself and of her own strength she can do nothing that good is or prevaileth for her salvation, unless it be through the grace of God, whose mother, daughter, sister, and wife by the Scriptures she proveth herself to be. Trusting also that through His incomprehensible love, grace, and mercy, she (being called from sin to repentance) doth faithfully hope to be saved.[17]

The following year, as her New Year's gift for Katherine, Elizabeth translated the first chapter of John Calvin's *Institutes* into English.

---

16   As quoted in Paul F.M. Zahl, *Five Women of the English Reformation*, (Grand Rapids, Michigan: William B. Eerdmans Pub. Co., 2001), p. 44.

17   Elizabeth I. *Collected Works*. Chicago & London: The University of Chicago Press, 2000, p. 7.

After Henry's death, Katherine married Thomas Seymour, though the man was not faithful and was ruled by his personal ambition. Katherine wrote and published a work with the lengthy, descriptive title: *Lamentation or Complaint of a Sinner Made by the Most Virtuous and Right Gracious Lady Queen Katherine (Parr), Bewailing the Ignorance of Her Blind Life, Led by Superstition.* The briefer subtitle was *Very Profitable to the Amendment of Our Lives.* Though Katherine lived at the highest levels of society in Tudor England, her work reflected the true Christian experience of men and women at every level of society.

Excerpts from Katherine Parr's
Lamentation or Complaint of a Sinner

On her repentance:

'Christ was innocent, and void of all sin; and I wallowed in filthy sin, and was free from no sin. Christ was obedient unto his Father...and I disobedient, and most stubborn even to the confession of truth...Christ despised the world, with all the vanities thereof, and I made it my god, because of the vanities. Christ came to serve his brethren, and I coveted to rule over them. Christ despised worldly honour, and I much delighted to attain the same...By this Declaration, all creatures may perceive how far I was from Christ, and without Christ.'

On her conversion:

'What! Shall I fall in desperation? Nay, I will call upon Christ, The Light of the world. The Fountain of life, the Relief of all careful consciences, the Peacemaker between God and man, and the only health and comfort of all repentant sinners....'

'I have certainly no curious learning to defend this matter..., but a simple zeal and earnest love to the truth inspired of God, who promiseth to pour his Spirit upon all flesh; which I have, by the grace of God...felt in myself to be true...'

On the matchless Christ:

'When I look upon the Son of God..., so unarmed, naked, given up, and alone, with humility, patience, liberality, modesty, gentleness, and with all other his divine virtues, beating down to the ground all God's enemies, and making the soul of man so fair and beautiful; I am forced to say that his victory and triumph are marvelous; and therefore Christ well deserved to have this noble title, Jesus of Nazareth, King of the Jews...'

On the last Judgment:

'We shall have no man of law to make our plea for us, neither can we have the day deferred; neither will the Judge be corrupted with affection, bribes, or reward; neither will he hear any excuse or delay, neither shall this saint, or that martyr, help us, be they ever so holy; neither shall our ignorance save us from damnation; but yet willful blindness, and obstinate ignorance, shall receive greater punishment, and not without just cause. Then shall it be known who hath walked in the dark.'

As quoted in Paul Zahl's *Five Women of the English Reformation*, pp. 50-2.

At the age of ten, Jane Grey became the ward of Katherine Parr, whose mothering encouraged Jane's Christian faith and devotion. Jane, a great-niece of Henry VIII and named after his wife Jane Seymour, shared Katherine's Protestant faith and even corresponded with leading Reformers in Europe. She was a precocious, well-educated child who not only learned traditional womanly skills in needlework and music, but was accomplished in Latin, Greek, French, and Italian, as well as having some knowledge of Hebrew, Chaldee, and Arabic!

Henry VIII's will stipulated that the succession to the throne should fall on his three children – Edward, then Mary, then Elizabeth, even though the two daughters were by law illegitimate. Next in line after Elizabeth were the legitimate children of Henry VII's younger sister, which included Lady Jane Grey. Young King Edward was never a healthy lad. As his health declined further, he and his regents attempted to change the succession to keep the throne in Protestant hands, in the likelihood of the young king's death. The line of succession was altered to go to Lady Jane Grey, rather than to Henry VIII's Catholic daughter Mary. Lady Jane resisted the move, but her parents and powerful leaders around King Edward, especially the Duke of Northumberland, finally obtained her acquiescence At the will of her parents, Jane married Northumberland's son, Guilford Dudley.

Four days after Edward died, Jane was declared Queen. She and Dudley went to the Tower of London to prepare for their coronation. The change in succession was not popular with the people, however, and after nine days Henry VIII's daughter Mary was able to garner sufficient support to enter London as Queen. Lady Jane and her husband were arrested and became prisoners in the Tower.

Queen Mary sent her personal chaplain to Jane to try to convert her to Catholicism. But Jane staunchly maintained her Protestant faith. On February 12, 1554, at the age of sixteen, Lady Jane was beheaded on Tower Green. On the scaffold, before her execution, Jane addressed the crowd:

> Good people, I am come hither to die, and by a law I am condemned to the same. The fact [that Jane was declared queen], indeed against the Queen's highness was unlawful, and the consenting thereunto by me; but touching the procurement and desire thereof by me or on my behalf, I do wash my hands thereof in innocency, before God, and the face of you, good Christian people, this day.

She then recited Psalm 51 in English. Jane had become a pawn in England's religious and political struggles. Her youth, innocence, and submissive spirit created much sympathy and compassion. One of the first Protestants executed under Queen Mary, Lady Jane Grey continues to be viewed as a Christian martyr by many today.

Queen Elizabeth I (1533-1603) came to the throne when she was twenty-five. She had lived through much during her young life — her mother beheaded, herself declared illegitimate, isolation and fear under the changing political and religious regimes, and imprisonment in the Tower of London. On the day of her coronation in 1559, she made a heartfelt prayer:

> O Lord, almighty and everlasting God, I give Thee most hearty thanks that Thou hast been so merciful unto me as to spare me to behold this joyful day. And I acknowledge that Thou hast dealt as wonderfully and as mercifully with me as Thou didst with Thy true and faithful servant Daniel, Thy prophet, whom Thou deliveredst out of the den from the cruelty of the greedy and raging lions. Even so was I overwhelmed and only by Thee delivered. To Thee (therefore) only be thanks, honor, and praise forever, amen.[18]

In 1533, when Pope Clement refused to recognize Parliament's decree of divorce of Henry VIII from Catherine, England broke with Rome. Parliament's Act of Supremacy in 1534 established the Church of England and made the king its supreme head. For the rest of the century, excepting the five-year reign of Mary (1553-1558) when England was restored to the Catholic fold, the courts of Henry, Edward, and Elizabeth provided fertile soil for the seeds of Europe's Protestant Reformation to grow. Many of the women at the English court found strength in their evangelical faith and in reading the Bible. From the Scriptures they learned they had access to God through Christ alone. Their unmediated access to God gave them courage, strength, and freedom to face death as well as life.

---

18   Elizabeth I. *Collected Works* (eds. Leah S. Marcus, Janel Mueller, Mary Beth Rose). Chicago & London: The University of Chicago Press, 2000, pp. 54-5. Throughout her life Elizabeth wrote private prayers (in English, French, Italian, Spanish, Greek, and Latin!), some of which were collected and published during her lifetime.

Heiresses of the Reformation:
Joint Heirs with Christ

Romans 8:17

Elizabeth I's ascension to the English throne in 1558 followed years of religious upheaval and political turmoil. Elizabeth's father, Henry VIII, had separated the Church of England from papal authority and placed the English monarch at the head of the English Church. Henry, however, did not embrace the evangelical beliefs of the Reformation, and the English Church's doctrines and practices largely continued to be those of the Roman Church. Henry's son and heir, the young King Edward VI, was a Protestant, and his regents encouraged the evangelical faith within England. During Edward VI's reign, Thomas Cranmer's *Book of Common Prayer* became the standard of Anglican worship. English Bibles were permitted among the people, transubstantiation (the worship of bread and wine as the body and blood of Christ) was rejected, clerical marriage became legal, and ritual images were removed from the churches. Edward's brief reign of six years was followed by the five-year reign of his sister Mary. Queen Mary zealously sought to return England to the Catholic fold, repealing the Act of Uniformity passed under Edward. Many English Protestants fled to the Continent for safety. Protestants remaining in England were persecuted; nearly 300 were executed under Mary.

When Elizabeth came to the throne, the Acts of Supremacy and Uniformity once again placed the Church under the monarchy's governance and established the *Book of Common Prayer* as the Anglican liturgy. The English Bible was once again freely allowed in the country and recognized as the determining authority in matters of faith. The Thirty-Nine Articles defining the beliefs of the Church of England were essentially Protestant; however, many elements of Catholic liturgy remained. By following a *via media*, Queen Elizabeth sought to avoid the extremes of the competing religious groups in her realm. Many who had been exiles in Geneva under Queen Mary wanted to purify the Church of England along the lines of Calvin's Geneva. These Puritans wanted to go beyond the *via media* of Elizabeth and bring a complete reformation to England. They were to be a key force in shaping the face of England and America for the next century.

177

Women of Puritan Times

As heirs of the Reformation, Puritans abjured the medieval idea of celibacy and placed a high value on marriage and the family. Their ideas of sex and marriage were truly revolutionary. Professor Leland Ryken summarized their stance: 'The Puritans devalued celibacy, glorified companionate marriage, affirmed married sex as both necessary and pure, established the ideal of wedded romantic love, and exalted the role of the wife.'[1]

The prominent medieval notion that women were in some way more evil, lustful and irrational than men had no place in Puritan thought. Puritan Richard Cleaver wrote:

> Most true it is that women are as men...reasonable creatures, and have flexible wits, both to good and evil...And although there be some evil and lewd women, yet that doth no more prove the malice of their nature than of men, and therefore the more ridiculous and foolish are they that have inveighed against the whole sex for a few evil.

John Cotton wrote as follows:

> Women are creatures without which there is no comfortable living for man: it is true of them what is wont to be said of governments, *That bad ones are better than none*: They are a sort of Blasphemers then who despair and decry them, and call them a *necessary Evil*, for they are a necessary Good: such as it was not good that man should be without.

Based on Genesis 2:18, 'it is not good that the man should be alone; I will make him a help meet for him,' the Puritans saw the main purpose of marriage as companionship. Famed Puritan Richard Baxter wrote:

> It is a mercy to have a faithful friend that loveth you entirely...to whom you may open your mind and communicate your affairs...And it is a mercy to have so near a friend to be a helper to your soul and...to stir up in you the grace of God.

Daniel Rogers further expounded:

> Husbands and wives should be as two sweet friends, bred under one constellation, tempered by an influence from heaven whereof neither can give any reason, save mercy and providence first made them ... and then made their match; saying, see, God hath determined us out of this vast world each for [the] other.[2]

The Puritans saw the family as the foundational institution of society, both spiritual and secular. The family was called the 'seminary of all other societies,' a foundation of both the Church and the state. The husband and wife were the king and queen of this little commonwealth, and as such both

---

1   Leland Ryken. *Worldly Saints: The Puritans as They Really Were*. Grand Rapids, MI: Zondervan Acadamic Books, 1986, p. 53.

2   Quotes of Puritan authors on marriage found in *Worldly Saints*, pp. 50-2.

were responsible for the governance of the family. There was a hierarchy in the family, with the husband as the head and the wife in submission to him. The husband's headship was not a tyranny, but he was, like Christ, to rule in love and wisdom. Samuel Willard wrote that a good husband will rule 'as that his wife may take delight in [his headship] and not account it a slavery but a liberty and a privilege.' One Puritan preacher said that the wife's responsibility is to 'guide the house and not guide the husband.' The Scriptures called upon the wife to submit to the husband, but this was to be of the wife's own will, not through any force from the husband. John Winthrop said that the Christian wife's submission was 'her honour and freedom... Such is the liberty of the church under the authority of Christ.' The husband and wife shared a spiritual equality, but they had differing stations in the governance of the home and family. The wife was as the husband's assistant in authority, office, advice and counsel in the home.

An important aspect of the Puritan home was the responsibility of caring for the spiritual welfare of those in the family, both children and servants. Daily Bible reading and prayers, with the father serving as the 'priest' of the family congregation, were routine. Puritan domestic manuals of the day especially developed the importance of parents instructing the children in spiritual truths. One indicator of the importance placed on home instruction was that in the last half of the sixteenth century in England, over 100 editions of catechisms for household use were published. The Geneva Bible, most used by the Puritans, included a marginal note to Deuteronomy 21:18 stating, 'it is the mothers [sic] dutie also to instruct her children,' and, in practice, the instruction of children was often overseen by the mother in the family. If women were to educate their children, it followed that the education of women was considered a necessity. Puritans recognized that in their domestic sphere as wife and mother, women had an important role in shaping the spiritual education of the nation. The woman's spiritual calling in the home was as significant as any public function in the Church or government.

Evidence of women's concern for the spiritual education of their children is abundant in the many advice books written by women for their children at this period. Dorothy Leigh's *The Mother's Blessing* set the pattern. First published in 1616, the work went through twenty-three editions between 1616 and 1674, including seven editions in its first year, easily making it the best-selling book written by a woman in the seventeenth century. Leigh's husband had died, and in his will he had urged her to see their three sons 'well instructed and brought up in knowledge.' Sensing that her own life would soon come to an end, Dorothy Leigh wrote down her advice to her sons as a way of carrying out her husband's wish. Her work was published shortly after her death. The book's typically lengthy subtitle explained more fully Dorothy's purpose: *The godly counsaile of a Gentle-woman not long since deceased, left behind her for her Children: containing many good exhortations, and godly admonitions, profitable for all Parents to leave as a Legacy to their Children, but especially for those, who by reason of their young yeeres stand most in need of*

Instruction. The title page also had Proverbs 1:8 written under Dorothy Leigh's name, 'My sonne, heare the instruction of thy father, and forsake not the lawe of thy mother.'

Dorothy Leigh told her sons she wrote out of motherly affection for them:

> neither care I what you or any shall think of me, if among many words I may write but one sentence, which may make you labour for the spiritual food of the soul, which must be gathered every day out of the word, as the children of Israel gathered Manna in the wilderness ... For as the children of Israel must needs starve, except they gath'red every day in the wilderness and fed of it, so must your souls, except you gather the spiritual Manna out of the word every day, and feed of it continually: for as they by this Manna comforted their hearts, and strengthened their bodies, and preserved their lives; so by this heavenly Word of God, you shall comfort your souls, make them strong in Faith, and grow in true godliness, and finally preserve them with great joy, to everlasting life, through Faith in Christ; whereas, if you desire any food for your souls, that is not in the written Word of God, your soul die with it even in your hearts and mouths; even as they, that desired other food, died with it in their mouths [Num. 11:33] were it never so dainty: so shall you, and there is no recovery for you.[3]

Yet, Dorothy also wrote for publication, encouraging other mothers to teach and care for their children and write their instructions to them. She discussed a multitude of topics: how to further a reformation of manners, morals and religion; the importance and method of prayer; the proper and improper use of worldly wealth; the need to restrict business dealings and marriage to the godly; and the faults of worldly ministers. Her writing was permeated with Scripture as well as simple analogies. When describing the advantages of casting all cares upon God, Dorothy warned of the devil as a 'cunning fisher':

> When the devil makes all his poisonous baits, wherewith he draws an innumerable company of souls to hell, he covers them all with some worldly thing or other, that they may not see the hook; some he covers with gold, some with silver, some with earth, some with clay, some with honor, some with beauty, some with one thing, and some another.[4]

She further developed the fisher/bait analogy for some pages. In a chapter on 'the way to rule our corruptions,' she began to develop the importance of the Holy Spirit in the Christian life, which she enlarged upon in the ensuing chapter:

> ... without [the Holy Spirit] we are like a house which is built fair on the outside: but there are no windows to show any light at all into it, and then

---

3   *The Mother's Blessing*, ch. 2, All quotes from *The Mother's Blessing* are as found in Sylvia Brown, ed. *Women's Writing in Stuart England*. Sutton Publishing, 1999. (Was the 20th-century Christian humanist Dorothy Leigh Sayers named after the popular woman writer of the 17th century?)

4   Ibid., ch. 38.

the house is good for nothing, because there remains nothing but darkness
in it: even so dark is the earth of *Adam*, which we are made of ... [5]

One of Dorothy's sons, William, did become a minister as she wished. He
became rector at Groton, Suffolk, under the patronage of Puritan John
Winthrop, who later led the Puritan migration to America and became
governor of Massachusetts. By putting her motherly advice in writing,
Dorothy Leigh not only passed on important Biblical truths to her sons,
but taught other women how to teach spiritual truths to their children,
thus encouraging them to do the same. *The Mother's Blessing* became
a pattern for other motherly advice books.

Lady Grace Mildmay (1552-1620) not only wrote an important motherly
advice work, she also wrote the first autobiography in English written by
a woman. Grace Mildmay had been educated at home with her three sisters
by her mother and a governess, a niece of her father's. Her education was
a general one, focusing on basic academics, deportment, domestic skills,
and religion. Among the domestic accomplishments in which Grace came to
excel was medicine. She became quite skilled in herbal treatments, and later
kept extensive notes on various cures and their effectiveness.

Grace called her mother an 'Angell of God' and throughout her life
honored and treasured her teachings and example. Shortly before her
death at the age of eighty-four, Grace's mother encouraged her daughters
to daily read chapters in the Bible, as she had done all her life and as her
own godly mother had done. Grace followed this advice and throughout
her life daily opened her Geneva Bible and read one chapter each in Moses,
the Prophets, the Gospels, and the Epistles, in addition to the Psalms for
the day. She also regularly read three other books her mother had given
her – John Foxe's *Book of Martyrs*, Wolfgang Musculus' *Common Places*, and
Thomas à Kempis' *Imitatio Christi*. Daily she went into her room, cast all
earthly things from her mind, and submitted herself to God and His Word.
In humility she looked to God's leadership and learned to rely on God,
whatever troubles came her way, as they inevitably did.

When she was fifteen, Grace was married to Anthony Mildmay, then
eighteen or nineteen. The match was negotiated between the parents, and
Anthony was not particularly interested in the marriage. He was often
away from home on diplomatic missions for the Queen. When he was
home, Anthony could sometimes be quite harsh, though he would later
apologize for his rudeness. Grace could have lived at the royal court,
but she thought the temptations for her there would be too great, so she
remained at her home, Apethorpe Manor, in Northamptonshire. There she
used her medical abilities, as well as her financial means, to help the poor

---

5   *The Mother's Blessing*, ch. 30.

and suffering. The first ten years of her marriage she was childless, which undoubtedly was a sorrow and difficulty for her. Yet, whatever difficulties she faced, she found strength in her faith in God. This was the lesson Grace wished to convey in her autobiography and meditations.

While in her sixties, after her husband had died, Grace wrote her autobiography for her only daughter and her grandchildren. Her work was not simply an accounting of her life, but was the story of her spiritual growth since childhood. The autobiography was an introduction to her spiritual meditations, which she called the 'consolation of my soul, the joy of my heart, and the stability of my mind.'[6] She had kept a journal of her spiritual meditations and edited some of these specifically for her descendants' edification. Because of her deep, personal relationship with Christ, her life had a strength and peace which became a testimony of her faith to her daughter and grandchildren. Her life was an example of the results of daily reading and meditation on the Scripture. As she wrote her granddaughter:

> Whosoever in the beginning of his life sets the word of God always before his eyes and makes the same his delight and counselor, and examines all that he sees, all that he hears, all that he thinks, and all that he loves, wishes or desires by the said word of God, he shall be sure to be preserved in safety.[7]

Elizabeth Knevet Clinton, the Countess of Lincoln (1574-1630?), gave her advice on child-rearing to her daughter-in-law. She held that the obligation to 'marry and bear children' included not just pregnancy and giving birth but nurturing the child through breastfeeding. A mother who did not nurse her own child showed 'unmotherly affection, idleness, desire to have liberty to gad from home…and the like evils.' According to Clinton, the child at the breast 'is the Lord's own instruction…instructing you to show that you are his new born babe by your earnest desire after his word.'[8]

Elizabeth Joscelin (1596-1622) died after six years of marriage to Towrell Joscelin and only a few days after her child was born. She had a premonition that she would die in childbirth and left her 'Mother's legacies to her unborn child' with her husband before she died. He printed the tract after her death, and it became among the most popular of the 'mother's advice' books. Not knowing whether she would bear a son or a daughter, Elizabeth wrote instructions and advice for each. If a son, she wrote, 'I humbly beseech Almighty God … that

6   Retha M. Warnicke, 'Lady Mildmay's Journal: A Study in Autobiography and Meditation in Reformation England,' *Sixteenth Century Journal*, vol. 20, No. 1 (Spring 1989), p. 57.

7   Quoted in Norman Leslie Jones, *English Reformation*, (Blackwell Publishers, 2002), p. 25.

8   Betty Travitsky, 'New Mother of the English Renaissance,' Cathy N. Davidson and E.M. Broner, eds. *The Lost Tradition: Mothers and Daughters in Literature*. New York: Frederick Ungar Publishing Co., 1980, p. 36.

thou may serve him as his Minister, if he make thee a man.' If the child were a daughter, she wrote her husband:

> I desire her bringing up may be learning the Bible, as my sisters doe, good housekeeping, writing, and good workes: other learning a woman needs not: though I admire it in those whom God hath blessed with discretion, yet I desired not much on my owne, having seen that sometimes women have greater portions of learning than wisdom....But where learning and wisdom meet in a virtuous disposed woman she is the fittest closet for all goodness...Yet I leave it to thy will...If thou desire a learned daughter, I pray God give her a wise and religious heart, that she may use it to his glory, thy comfort, and her own salvation.

Elizabeth's concerns for her child were primarily spiritual: 'I never aimed at so poor an inheritance for thee as the whole world: ...the true reason I have so often kneeled to God for thee, is, that thou might be an inheritor of the Kingdom of Heaven.'[9]

This new emphasis on motherhood has come to be known by scholars as the 'new mother' idea and is well documented not only in Puritan writings, but in the writings of the Renaissance humanists. Though the Puritans developed and held on to the ideal longest, the concept and practice of the family as a spiritual household and place of spiritual instruction was something espoused by Erasmus and other humanists, including the Catholic Thomas More. That the practice of the spiritual household died out in Catholic and Anglican circles but continued in Puritan circles was due in large part to the Council of Trent. The Council of Trent (1545-1563), which established the norms for Catholic orthodoxy and practice after the Reformation, not only proclaimed the married state inferior to celibacy, but also made the catechism and instruction of children the responsibility of the bishops, not the family. The Council seemed to have thought that religious instruction within the household would subvert the purity of doctrine and the authority of the Church hierarchy. Teaching the priesthood of all believers, and even speaking of the father as a kind of priest in his family, was regarded as a form of insubordination to the clerical order of the Church.[10]

Besides the home being a place of religious instruction, Puritan women also used their homes as places of hospitality for the saints. Separatist or Independent churches often met in private homes, and lodgings were provided for nonconformist ministers. Women were an important part of the spiritual networking of the Puritan household meetings. Women of position used their influence to plead at court for the protection of Puritan ministers. As in the days of the earliest Church, wealthier Christian women provided patronage and

---

9   'New Mother of the English Renaissance,' pp. 39-40.

10   Margo Todd in 'Humanists, Puritans and the Spiritualized Household,' *Church History*, Vol. 49, No. 1 (March 1980), pp. 18-34.

support for the clergy, including financing the publication of tracts and religious works. Educated women also published works of their own, though many of the works published by women before the mid-seventeenth century were translations. As seen in chapter six, Anne Locke translated Calvin's sermons. Mary Sidney Herbert, the Countess of Pembroke, joined her brother Sir Philip Sidney in translating the psalms into English poetry.

Mary Sidney (1561-1621) was born into an aristocratic Tudor family which held positions of prominence during the reigns of Henry VIII and his daughter Elizabeth. Mary's father, Sir Henry Sidney, was lord president of Wales and lord deputy of Ireland; her mother, Mary Dudley, was daughter of the Duke of Northumberland. Together the Dudley and Sidney families controlled two-thirds of the lands ruled by Queen Elizabeth. Mary Sidney was given an excellent education, comparable to that of Queen Elizabeth herself. In addition to traditional training in household medicine and administration and the feminine skills of music and needlework, Mary Sidney was taught the Scriptures and the classics. She was fluent in French, Italian and Latin, and probably knew some Greek and Hebrew. In 1577, at the age of fifteen, she married Henry Herbert, the wealthy Earl of Pembroke. Four children were born to the couple before Mary was twenty-three. In 1586, both of Mary's parents died. The same year, her older brother Philip died fighting against the Spanish in the Netherlands. Mary was overcome by illness and grief, as well as with fear at the prospect of the invasion of the Spanish Armada.

Mary recovered after the defeat of the Armada, returned to London, and became an important patroness of literature. She supervised the publication of her brother Philip's unpublished works. Most notable was her completion of a metrical paraphrase of the psalms which Philip had begun. Philip had translated Psalms 1–49 into English verse; Mary completed the 150 Psalms. Others had turned various psalms into English verse, but the Sidneys together were the first to provide English verses for the entire psalter. Mary used an amazing variety of verse forms and rhetorical figures. Her psalms reflected her scholarship and her careful reading of commentaries in English, French, and Latin. An artistic achievement in its own right, the Sidney verse translation of the psalms influenced the devotional poets of the next century, especially George Herbert and John Donne. Donne called Philip and Mary Sidney 'this Moses and this Miriam' and said, 'They show us Islanders our joy, our King, / They tell us *why*, and teach us *how* to sing.'[11] Through the fame of her contribution to the 'Sidnean Psalms,' Mary Sidney became the first Englishwoman to receive recognition as a poet.

Under both Elizabeth and the Stuart monarchs, Puritans endured imprisonment and persecution, most often for not conforming to the Church of England's liturgy and ceremonial requirements. Puritan women were imprisoned as well as men, and the women could be the most vocal in protesting Anglican practices. From 1565 to 1567, when Queen Elizabeth

---

11   Margaret P. Hannay, 'Mary Sidney Herbert, Countess of Pembroke (1561-1621),' www.
English.cam.ac.uk/sidney/pembroke_biography.htm, accessed 10-28-2007.

women led the protests!

and Archbishop Matthew Parker sought uniformity in vestments and liturgy, the women of London led in defending their preachers. When John Bartlett was suspended as a lecturer at St. Giles Cripplegate, sixty women defended him and surrounded the house of Bishop Grindal in protest. When pastors John Gough and John Philpot were removed from their London pulpits, over two hundred women accompanied them over London Bridge into exile in the country. During this period, more women than men were imprisoned in London's Bridewell prison for their Puritan convictions.

Lucy Hutchinson, Puritan Writer

Lucy Hutchinson (1620-1680) was a Puritan whose writings help illumine Puritan ideals. Her *Order and Disorder* was the first epic poem written by an Englishwoman and has been favorably compared to *Paradise Lost* both in the quality of its composition and in its subject matter.

Lucy's husband was Colonel John Hutchinson, a trusted officer of Oliver Cromwell. Colonel Hutchinson was one of the commissioners of the trial of Charles I and a signer of his death warrant. Under the Commonwealth he continued to be an active member of Parliament. At the Restoration, he was imprisoned and died during his imprisonment. After her husband's death, Lucy wrote *Memoirs of the Life of Colonel John Hutchinson* especially to record the character of their father for her eight children, but also as a record from the Puritan perspective of the momentous events surrounding her husband's life. Her descriptions belie the picture of the Puritans as narrow and dour. Lucy's description of her husband's love for her follows the Puritan conceptions of marriage:

> Man never had a greater passion or a more honorable esteem
> for woman; yet he was not uxorious, and never remitted that
> just rule which it was her honor to obey; but he managed the
> reins of government with such prudence and affection, that
> she who would not delight in such honorable and advantageous
> subjection must have wanted a reasonable soul. He governed
> by persuasion which he never employed but in things profitable
> to herself. He loved her soul better than her countenance; yet
> even for her person he had a constant affection, exceeding the
> common temporary passion of fond fools. If he esteemed her at
> a higher rate than she deserved, he was himself the author of the
> virtue he doted on; for she was but a faithful mirror, reflecting
> truly, but dimly, his own glories upon him. When she ceased
> to be young and lovely, [Lucy became disfigured by smallpox
> shortly before her marriage] he showed her the most tenderness.
> He loved her at such a kind and generous rate as words cannot
> express, yet even this, which was the highest love any man could
> have, was bonded by a superior feeling; he regarded her, not as
> his idol, but as his fellow-creature in the Lord, and proved that
> such a feeling exceeds all the irregularities in the world.*

---

*As quoted in Sarah J. Hale, *Lessons from Women's Lives*, (London: William P. Nimmo, 1877), p. 52.

In the following century, when Civil War between Parliamentary and Royalist forces broke out, women offered their support in a number of ways. A large body of middle-class women, led by Ann Stagg, a brewer's wife, presented a petition supporting Parliament at the door of the House of Commons. Ann Stagg prefaced the presentation by saying

> It may be thought strange and unbecoming our sex to show ourselves here, bearing a petition to this honourable assembly; but Christ purchased us at as dear a rate as he did men, and therefore requireth the same obedience for the same mercy as of men; we are sharers in the public calamities.[12]

The women were received courteously; John Pym encouraged them, telling them, 'Repair to your houses, we entreat, and turn your petitions into prayers at home for us.' The women not only prayed, but contributed materially to the Parliamentary forces. The wealthier contributed their jewels, while the poorer women brought their silver thimbles, spoons, and bodkins. The Royalists scoffingly called the Parliamentary army the 'thimble and bodkin army.' Women also helped defend ports and castles besieged by Royalists

The political upheaval of the time brought many into personal peril and difficulty. Christian women affected by the political fortunes of their husbands showed a level of courage and fortitude unknown to the secular world. Perhaps Mary Love, wife of pastor Christopher Love, best illustrated this Christian courage and consecration. Christopher Love, a London pastor and writer of many Christian works, opposed the execution of Charles I and the Protectorate of Oliver Cromwell. In 1651, he and five other prominent ministers were accused of high treason, charged with plotting to reinstate the monarchy under Charles II. Love was sentenced to be executed, and while in the Tower of London, he sent letters to his wife, as she did to him. Their letters reveal a love and Christian bond with roots in and eyes on eternity. On August 21, 1651, the day before Christopher's execution, Mary wrote her husband:

> My Heavenly Dear, I call thee so because God hath put heaven into thee before He hath taken thee to heaven. Thou now beholdest God, Christ, and glory as in a glass; but tomorrow, heaven's gates will be opened and thou shalt be in the full enjoyment of all those glories which eye hath not seen, nor ear heard, neither can the heart of man understand...O lift up thy heart with joy when thou layest thy dear head on the block in the thought of this: that thou are laying thy head to rest in thy Father's bosom which, when thou dost awake, shall be crowned not with an earthly

---

12   James Anderson. *Memorable Women of the Puritan Times*, vol. 1. Soli Deo Gloria Publications, 2001 (reprint of 1862 London edition by Blackie and Son), p. 15.

fading crown but with a heavenly eternal crown of glory...O let not one troubled thought for thy wife and babes arise within thee. Thy God will be our God and our portion. He will be a husband to thy widow and a father to thy children; the grace of thy God will be sufficient for us...Now my dear, I desire willingly and cheerfully to resign my right in thee to thy Father and my Father, who hath the greatest interest in thee. And confident I am, though men have separated us for a time yet our God will ere long bring us together again where we shall eternally enjoy one another, never to part more...Farewell, farewell, my dear, till we meet there where we shall never bid farewell more; till which time I leave thee in the bosom of a loving, tender-hearted Father. And so I rest till I shall forever rest in heaven.[13]

Mary certainly exhibited the 'peace of God which surpasses all understanding.'[14]

Puritan Women in America

During the political and religious turmoil in England under Charles I, the King was intent on asserting his 'divine right' in Church and state, while the Puritans sought to follow a Biblical pattern in both. As the possibility of their successfully influencing the King to their way of thinking waned, many Puritans considered the possibility of establishing a new England in America. With the tension between the King and the Puritans mounting, it seemed little short of a miracle that the King granted the Massachusetts Bay Charter to a group of Puritans, giving them the right to establish and rule a colony in America. When the Massachusetts Bay Charter was granted in 1628, John Winthrop led the organization of the migration and establishment of the colony.

A businessman and man of affairs, John Winthrop had a heart for God. In his work, as in all of life, he sought to live in a God-honoring way. His wife Margaret (1591-1647) similarly looked for God's hand in all of life's events. First as one of three attorneys to the Court of Wards and Liveries (which oversaw estates which had reverted to the King) and then when planning the Great Puritan Migration, Winthrop often had to be away in London. Margaret remained at Groton Manor, Suffolk, overseeing the family and the estate. The loving letters each wrote to the other revealed much of the Winthrops' heart and thoughts. Written in the rough and tumble of political and domestic life, the letters were full of relations of mundane affairs – children's illnesses, deaths in the community, the making of cheeses, supervision of help, transportation problems, effects of political maneuvers, etc. Inextricably woven throughout the mundane,

---

13   Don Kistler. *A Spectacle unto God: The Life and Death of Christopher Love (1618-1651).* Soli Deo Gloria Publications, 1998, pp. 84-5.

14   Philippians 4:7.

however, were the expressions of the deepest affection for each other and a Christian outlook on all that transpired. The human elements and earthly affairs were seamlessly blended with spiritual reflections and prayerful thoughts. Both Margaret and John selflessly sought God's will and path for the other during the many times they were apart. Each viewed difficulties as trials which were part of God's larger plan for their lives.

When the children and servants were ill and troubles seemed to multiply, Margaret wrote John of the news and concluded, 'Thus it pleases the Lord to exercise us with one affliction after another in love; lest we should forget ourselves and love this world too much, and not set our affections on heaven where all true happiness is for ever.' In the next letter, she continued in the same vein:

> I hope the Lord will hear our prayers and be pleased to stay his hand in this visitation, which if he please to do we shall have great cause of thankfulness. But I desire in this and all other things to submit unto his holy will. It is the Lord, let him do what seems good in his own eyes. He will do nothing but that shall be for our good if we had hearts to trust him, & all shall be for the best whatsoever it shall please him to exercise us withal...[15]

John and Margaret each encouraged the other in their Christian faith and hope throughout their lives.

When John sailed for America in 1630, leading 700 Puritans in eleven ships, Margaret remained behind in England. She was pregnant and planned to rejoin her husband in America the following year. Before John sailed on the *Arabella* with two sons Stephen and Adam, he wrote Margaret:

> My dear wife be of good courage, it shall go well with you and us. The hairs of your head are numbered. He who gave his only beloved to die for you, will give his Angels charge over you. Therefore raise up your thoughts, & be merry in the Lord. Labor to live by your Faith. If you meet with troubles or difficulties, be not dismayed. God does use to bring his children into the straights of the Red Sea &c, that he may show his power and mercy in making a way for them. All his course towards us are but to make us know him & love him.[16]

Margaret did arrive in America in 1631, accompanied by their young son Samuel and the oldest Winthrop son, John Jr. Baby Ann died a week after Margaret set sail to rejoin John, who had never seen his infant daughter. After a ten-month voyage, Margaret's ship arrived in New England. The people welcomed her with abundant gifts of provisions and food, showing their love for Governor Winthrop and his wife. Margaret and John lived

---

15   Diana Severance, ed. *A Cord of Three Strands*. Xulon Press, 2004, p. 58.

16   Ibid., p. 68.

together in Boston for fifteen years. It seems that their strong spiritual union had only grown stronger through their years of separation and difficulties. In 1647, an epidemic swept through the colony. Margaret Winthrop fell sick June 13 and died the next morning. John wrote in his diary, '14. In this sickness the governor's wife, daughter of Sir John Tindal, knight, left this world for a better, being about fifty-six years of age; a woman of singular virtue, prudence, modesty, and specially beloved and honored of all the country.'[17]

In many ways the relationship between John and Margaret Winthrop was a model of the Puritan family. The husband was the head of the family. Though the wife was submissive to the husband's leadership, she was his equal in companionship and had important responsibilities in managing the household and children. In a primarily agricultural economy, managing the household often included the farming business of the family. One historian called Puritan wives 'deputy husbands,' who were empowered to act for their husbands in legal and financial matters.[18] This was especially true when John was away in London or in America establishing a new colony.

The First Native American Christian Woman

The first known Native American Christian was Pocahontas, a daughter of the Indian chief Powhatan, in what became the colony of Virginia. Pocahontas was early attracted to the English settlers and befriended these visitors to her land. Though often remembered for saving the life of John Smith, Pocahontas married English settler John Rolfe. Rolfe had prayerfully considered whether or not he should marry Pocahontas, and gathered together numerous Scriptures persuading himself his love for her could be a means of bringing her people to Christ. Pocahontas converted to the Christian faith and was instructed in the Scriptures by Rev. Whitaker.

When Pocahontas converted to Christianity, she took the Christian name of Rebecca at her baptism. After her marriage to John Rolfe, the couple traveled to England, where Rebecca became the sensation of London society and was received by the Queen (but not received by King James. The King, displeased with Rolfe for marrying a princess without his permission, refused to see the Native American).

Before returning to America, Rebecca took ill and died. She was buried at St. George's church at Gravesend. The church today contains two stained glass windows commemorating the young American woman. One is of the Old Testament matriarch Rebecca, with a smaller picture depicting Pocahontas' baptism. The other window is of Ruth, the Moabitess who left her native people to follow the God of Israel. Did Pocahontas/Rebecca know of Ruth's famous words to Naomi–'Intreat me not to leave thee, nor to depart from thee, for whither thou goest, I will go: and where thou dwelleth, I will dwell: thy people shall be my people, and thy God my God'?

---

17   Robert C. Winthrop, ed. *Life and Letters of John Winthrop*. New York: De Capo Press, 1971 (reprint of 1864-1867 ed.), Vol. II, p. 362.

18   Laurel Thatcher Ulrich. *Good Wives: Image and Reality in the Lives of Women in Northern New England, 1650-1750*. New York: Alfred A. Knopf, 1982.

The spiritual companionship of husband and wife, as well as their recognition that the primary fealty of each was to their God, were important hallmarks of the Puritan marriage. In his famous address on board the *Arabella* en route to New England in 1630, Winthrop spoke at length about the importance of love among the Christians in the new settlement. He noted that 'love among Christians is a real thing, not imaginary,' and that the 'state of wedlock' was the closest thing on earth to heaven.

The first English poet in America, Anne Bradstreet (1612-1672), also held this Puritan view of marriage and of woman's position. In 1630, when she was eighteen, Anne, along with her parents Thomas and Dorothy Dudley and husband Simon, sailed to America with John Winthrop's fleet. Thomas Dudley, who had been steward to the Earl of Lincoln, left behind wealth in England to serve God in America. Anne had been tutored since she was seven in dancing, languages, music, and the skills expected of a lady of piety and some station in life. At sixteen she married Simon Bradstreet, the son of a Puritan minister and part of the Earl of Lincoln's household. Both Anne's father and her husband served as governor of Massachusetts several times, so she was among the leading families of the young colony. In the midst of her many household duties and raising eight children, Anne wrote poetry.[19] Many of Anne's poems were descriptions of events in her life, which led her to spiritual meditations and Christian reflections on the event. Anne's poems were a way of focusing her attention upon God in times of hardship. The poem entitled 'Verses upon the burning of our house, July 18th, 1666' described the burning of her house with its pleasant things and memories, but reflected on the house built in heaven gloriously furnished by a mighty Architect. The poem concluded

> Farewell, my pelf, farewell, my store.
> The world no longer let me love;
> My hope and Treasure lies above.

In the epitaph Anne wrote for her mother, Dorothy Dudley, she pictured the Puritan ideal of woman:

> A worthy matron of unspotted life,
> A loving mother and obedient wife,
> A friendly neighbor, pitiful to poor,
> Whom oft she fed and clothed with her store;
> To servants wisely awful, but yet kind,
> And as they did so regard did find.
> A true instructor of her family,
> To which she ordered with dexterity.

---

19   Selected poems by Anne Bradstreet may be found at *The Celebration of Women Writers*, http://
digital.library.upenn.edu/women/bradstreet/1678/1678.html.

Within a span of about ten years, Anne had eight children, all of whom lived to adulthood, a very rare occurrence in a day when most families lost several children to disease. Though Anne's children did become seriously ill, they recovered, as Anne wrote in 'Upon My Daughter Hannah and Her Recovering from a Dangerous Fever:'

> Bles't be Thy Name who dids't restore to
>   health my Daughter dear
> When Death did seem ev'n to approach
> And life was ended near.
> Grant she remember what thou'st done
> And celebrate thy praise
> And let her conversation say
>   She loves Thee all her days.

Having eight children, Anne was wise enough to recognize that each child was different and required different parenting:

> Diverse children have their different natures; some are like flesh [or meat] which nothing but salt will keep from putrefication; some again like tender fruit that are best preserved with sugar; those parents are wise that can fit their nurture according to their Nature.

Several of Anne's poems were about her husband Simon, who frequently was absent on government business. 'To My Dear and Loving Husband' reads:

> If ever two were one, then surely we.
> If ever man were loved by wife, then thee;
> If ever wife was happy in a man,
> Compare with me, ye women, if you can.
> I prize thy love more than whole mines of gold
> Or all the riches that the East doth hold.
> My love is such that rivers cannot quench,
> Nor ought but love from thee, give recompense.
> Thy love is such I can no way repay,
> The heavens reward thee manifold, I pray.

Unknown to her, Anne's early poems were collected by her father and brother-in-law and taken to England, where in 1650 they were published as *The Tenth Muse Lately Sprung Up in America*. In the preface, Anne's brother-in-law wrote that the poems were

> the Word of a Woman, honoured, and esteemed where she lives, for her gracious demeanor, her eminent parts, her pious conversation, her courteous disposition, her exact diligence in her place, and discreet, managing of her Family occasions, and more than so, these Poems are

but the fruit of some few hours, curtailed from her sleep and other refreshments.

In later years, Anne also wrote more lengthy poems, treating of learned subjects, such as the four kingdoms of Daniel, the seasons, or the ages of men. These, however, were read by friends and family and were not published until after her death. Though remembered today for her poetry, Anne did not consider poetry-writing her primary occupation. Her life before God was primarily as a wife and mother. When Anne wrote an autobiography for her children, she never mentioned her poetry. Writing in her journal near her death she concluded, 'Upon the Rock Christ Jesus will I build by faith, and if I perish, I perish. But I know all the powers of Hell shall never prevail against it. I know whom I have trusted, and whom I believe and that he is able to keep what I have committed to his charge.'

While Margaret Winthrop and Anne Bradstreet modeled the role of the Puritan woman, wife, and mother, their names are not as well recognized as that of Anne Hutchinson, a rebel to the Puritan ideals and government. Anne Hutchinson (1591-1643) and her husband were part of Rev. John Cotton's church in Boston, Lincolnshire, and they immigrated to New England in 1634-5, along with Cotton and other members of the congregation.

The Boston church in England had emphasized two different ways of measuring the reality of a person's conversion. One said that works were evidence of salvation; the other said personal union with the Holy Spirit was evidence of salvation. The tension between these two views was brought to the colony when many of the Boston church immigrated with Pastor Cotton. In New England, Anne began holding weekly meetings in her home to discuss Rev. Cotton's sermons. The meetings grew, and another meeting started with both men and women attending. Anne began going beyond simply reviewing the sermons and began teaching her own views of Scripture, attacking leaders of the Massachusetts colony who disagreed with her.

When Anne had a conversion experience early in the 1630s, she sensed God's love in a special way. When this sense later faded, she sought to recapture it by her works, especially fasting and opening herself to the random association of the words of Scripture, which she believed came from the Holy Spirit. Many Puritans taught that works or sanctification were signs of conversion, evidences of grace and justification. Anne believed this at first, but came to think that this was legalistic and that the personal presence of the Holy Spirit was a better proof of conversion. Anne's brother-in-law, Rev. John Wheelwright, taught that every Christian could receive the direct inspiration of the Holy Spirit. Anne came to believe

Those Salem Witches

When many think of the Puritans of Massachusetts, they think of the Salem Witchcraft trials of 1692. Yet, Salem's witchcraft hysteria was an example of the Puritans' succumbing to outside cultural influences rather than being true to their Puritan beliefs.

In the seventeenth century, witchcraft was widely acknowledged as an evil in England and throughout Europe. Witchcraft trials and even the burning of witches were a part of the culture of the day. According to the Renaissance theory of witches, women were particularly susceptible to the devil's wiles, and witches were recognized as an evil which should be purged from society.

In Salem, the problem began with some teenage girls accusing citizens of the town of bewitching them. Even if witnesses could testify that the accused had not even come near the girls, the idea that the 'specter' of the individual could be persecuting the girls was accepted. The acceptance of 'spectral evidence' rather than true forensic evidence by the courts allowed a great injustice to be done in Salem. At one time, 150 people were imprisoned as being suspected witches. Many of the accused were social misfits or middle-aged women; few were young or middle-aged men. Nineteen people were eventually hanged (no witches were burned in the colonies), and one was pressed to death for refusing to testify.

Scholars have noted several causes for the witchcraft hysteria at Salem, including the following:

- A West Indian slave was practicing voodoo in the village and enticing the girls with superstitions
- Judges and ministers were nervous about the colony's spiritual decline and were eager to find ways to check it
- There was simmering community hostility against a few lonely old women and a few new families
- A wide range of occult practices were being secretly practiced in the village
- The adolescent hysteria of a few teenage girls was accompanied by the judicial hysteria of a few older men.

The witch trials at Salem came about because the villagers accepted contemporary theories of witches rather than looking to the Bible for the criteria for who was a witch and what the punishment should be. Leading Puritan ministers, such as Increase Mather, spoke out against the trials. Most of the clergy recognized the real evil was with the accusers; when the girls began accusing people of spotless character, the trials were ended. Five years after the trials, one of the judges, Samuel Sewell, confessed his guilt for the judgment at the trials. The trials showed the vulnerability of the people to mass suggestion and their failure to follow the Scriptures, which they claimed to be their guide.

that those who believed works were evidence of salvation were teaching a covenant of works and were bound by the law that Christ came to abolish. The entire controversy became known as the Antinomian (anti-law) controversy, implying that Anne and her followers wanted to throw off the requirements of the law entirely and lead a life of absolute freedom and licentiousness. Rev. Wheelwright and Anne attacked the ministers of the colony, even calling them antichrists, and saying that only Rev. Cotton and Rev. Wheelwright were teaching the truth. When the Pequot War broke out, Anne and Rev. Wheelwright discouraged Bostonians from volunteering and serving under the leadership of such false ministers.

Anne's meetings and attacks upon the ministers were looked upon as attacks upon the leadership of the colony in a time of war and considered a threat to the safety and stability of the colony. The Court of Massachusetts disbanded Anne's twice-weekly meetings saying,

> women might meet (some few together) to pray and edify one another; yet such a set assembly (as was then in practice in Boston), where sixty or more did meet every week and one woman (in a prophetical way), by resolving questions of doctrine and expounding scripture took upon her the whole exercise, was agreed to be disorderly, and without rule.[20]

Yet Anne continued the meetings. In doing so she disrupted the peace and harmony of the colony and threatened the very religious basis of the Massachusetts government. Anne claimed her meetings were in accord with the apostle Paul's instructions – they were in her private home, not in church. Paul had told the older women to teach the younger, and there was nothing amiss in her privately teaching and counseling men. Since both male and female were one in Christ, she claimed she had done nothing wrong.

The Massachusetts Bay Colony had been established as a covenantal society with the goal of building a civil and ecclesiastical society to improve the residents' lives and allow them to serve the Lord. Anne's views were outside the agreed-upon covenant, and thus were a threat and danger to the colony itself. To protect the colony, laws were passed restricting new immigrants to those approved by the council or magistrates. In a commonwealth founded by free consent, the people must have a common interest in each other. Those whose dispositions would be hurtful to the commonwealth should be excluded. No person could be a part of the commonwealth without the consent of the magistrates and leaders. Accordingly, some who came from Lincolnshire and shared the views of Hutchinson were allowed to stay only four months before they were required to return to England. Those responsible for governance maintained that the colony should not have to receive those who made out the ministers and leaders of the colony to be the enemy of Christ.

---

20   Marilyn J. Westerkamp. *Woman and Religion in Early America, 1600-1850: The Puritan ad Evangelical Traditions*. London and New York: Routledge, 1999, p. 39.

Governor John Winthrop and pastor John Cotton tried to moderate the differences, but Anne Hutchinson and Rev. Wheelwright refused to admit any error or modify their views.

In October 1636, at a meeting of the General Court, the clergy met with Rev. John Cotton. He said he had taught that the Holy Spirit indwelt the saints, but that this teaching was distinct from the personal union and inspiration of the Holy Spirit Rev. Wheelwright had preached; the latter had more in common with Quakerism. In November 1637, John Wheelwright was banished from the colony; a trial of Anne Hutchinson followed. Anne, a woman of intelligence and extensive knowledge of the Scripture, was able to think circles around the leaders of the General Court, answering them repeatedly with Scripture. She incriminated herself, however, when she began to speak about her personal revelation, like the prophet Daniel. She 'prophesied' that the colony and the court would come to ruin because of their treatment of her. At the trial, Hugh Peter, for the Court, told Anne, 'you have stepped out of your place, *You have rather bine a Husband than a Wife and a preacher than a Hearer; and a Magistrate than a Subject.'* [21] The court accordingly banished her 'for traducing the ministers and their ministry in this country, [for which] she declared voluntarily her revelations for her ground, and that she should be delivered and the Court ruined, with their posterity.'[22] If Anne did not support the leadership and government of Massachusetts, she must find somewhere else to live. After the civil proceedings were over, Anne Hutchinson was brought before the Boston church on charges of heresy and excommunicated.

John Winthrop had little charity for Anne Hutchinson because she never would admit her error. She was uncompromising in her negative attitude towards the clergy and seemed to have a grandiose sense of her own self-importance. Her arrogance and impulsiveness itself were a threat to the social order of this Puritan experiment on the edge of the American wilderness. Unable to respect a woman asserting such religious leadership outside of the home, Winthrop called Anne an 'American Jezebel' and an agent of the devil. Winthrop was probably also embarrassed by Anne's brilliant answers in court. When Anne moved to Rhode Island and gave birth to a deformed child prematurely, Winthrop took this as a curse of God upon her. English correspondents complimented Winthrop on dealing with the seriousness of the issues, saying such upstart opinions as Anne Hutchinson's were not held in England.

---

21   Lyle Koehler, 'The Case of the American Jezebels: Anne Hutchinson and Female Agitation during the Years of Antinomian Turmoil, 1636-1640,' *The William and Mary Quarterly*, 3rd Ser., Vol. 31, No. 1 (Jan. 1974), p. 64.

22   Francis J. Bremer. *John Winthrop*. Oxford University Press, 2003, p. 298.

When she was banished, Anne and her family moved to Rhode Island, where Anne became an Anabaptist and against all civil authority among Christians. She also denied that there were not, nor could there be, any true churches since the time of the apostles and evangelists. After Anne's husband died in 1641, Anne became disgruntled with affairs in Rhode Island. She and her five children moved to New Netherlands (New York) the following year. Within months she and her children were massacred by Indians. The Massachusetts authorities saw this as God's punishment for her heresies.

In 1987, Massachusetts Governor Michael Dukakis pardoned Anne Hutchinson and revoked Winthrop's edict of banishment 350 years earlier, and some recent writers have elevated Hutchinson as a feminist proponent of religious liberty and freedom of conscience. In her day, however, she did not espouse broad and wide-ranging principles of liberty or women's rights. Hers was a personal struggle against an authoritarian society trying to bring religious and civil order out of a wilderness. Her individual charm, coupled with her intellect and brilliance, led to a band of supporters gathering around her and made her a powerful opponent to the civil and religious leaders of her day. Her pride and arrogance prevented her from having a more positive influence on those same leaders or being a positive instrument for change on her society. Some of her followers became members of the Quakers, a group who from the beginning espoused the right of women to preach freely, or lead in all the meetings of the Church.

Women and the Society of Friends

England of the seventeenth century underwent important transformation both religiously and politically. Queen Elizabeth had established the Anglican Church along a *via media*, but many yearned for a Church whose forms and practices, as well as its doctrines, conformed to a strictly Biblical pattern. James I and Charles I, the Stuart monarchs who followed Elizabeth, favored a more formal liturgy, vestments, and hierarchical structure to the Church. They also believed firmly in their divine right to rule and found it easy to ignore the power of Parliament and the legal constraints which had been placed on the monarchy over the centuries. Such religious and political conflict resulted in the English Civil War (1642-1651) between the Royalist and Parliamentarian forces. King Charles I was executed for high treason in ignoring English law, and a republic or Commonwealth was declared in 1649. With the Royalist forces defeated, the Parliamentary and independent forces became more fractious, causing the Protectorate under Oliver Cromwell to be established in 1653 as an attempt to preserve order in the nation.

George Fox (1624-1691) lived during this tumultuous time in England's history. He tired of the ever-changing state-controlled religion. The English Church had been successively Roman Catholic, Anglican,

Presbyterian, and Independent, yet, for Fox, none of these forms seemed to embody the truth. He rejected all forms of institutional Christianity and became convinced that Christ was not solely contained in either the Mass or the Bible, but should be personally experienced. Fox himself believed God had spoken to him, and he began to speak in the open air, outside the churches, of the Divine Light and true Christianity as he knew it. Fox's movement swiftly spread throughout England and beyond. Some of his followers seemed fanatical when 'moved by the Spirit' – gaining the group the name of 'Quakers' for their trembling and enthusiasm. Fox, however, learned to check behavior by Scripture, and emphasized that the liberation from sin found in Christ should lead to an individual's obedience to Christ.

Fox taught an equality of Christians totally unknown at the time. Servant girls and aristocrats equally came and sat side by side in the meetings of the Society of Friends, as Fox's followers called themselves. The Friends or Quakers refused to show any deference to people of position in society, declining even to take off their hats to judges or people in authority. They did not pay the obligatory tithes to the state Church or take oaths of any kind. Because of the state-sanctioned Church, Quaker religious meetings were forbidden and illegal. Fox had an audience with Oliver Cromwell as he tried to obtain religious freedom. He told Cromwell that Christians must not only have the Scriptures, they must live by the Scriptures. He encouraged Cromwell to reject the military weapons on which he relied and take up the armor of the Spirit. Though Cromwell had respect and sympathy for Fox, fearing chaos and disorder in the kingdom, he did not permit the religious freedom Fox requested. With the threats of rebellion against the government materializing towards the end of the Protectorate, thousands of Quakers were imprisoned for their failure to take oaths or show loyalty to the government. Fox himself was imprisoned on many occasions. On at least one occasion he was imprisoned with the woman who became his wife.

Margaret Askew (1614-1702) was related (possibly a great-granddaughter) to the martyr Anne Askew, burned at the stake during the days of Henry VIII. When she was eighteen, Margaret married Thomas Fell, a lawyer and Member of Parliament. The couple had eight children, seven daughters and a son, and lived in Swarthmoor Hall in Lancashire. In 1652, Margaret heard George Fox speak and became a follower and supporter of his. Later she wrote that when she listened to Fox, he opened to her 'a book that we had never read in, nor indeed had ever heard that it was our duty to read in...And he turned our minds toward the light of Christ as they had never been turned before.'[23] The 'book' Margaret

---

23   Quoted in Deen, *Great Women of the Christian Faith*.

referred to was simply the 'inner light of the soul.' Though George Fell never joined the Quakers himself, he supported his wife in her religious work with the Quakers. Swarthmoor Hall became a center of Quaker life, and Margaret became the unofficial secretary of the society, writing letters for Fox and others, as well as writing tracts herself. Her organizational skills in themselves were important to the fledgling group.

In 1658, George Fell died, leaving Swarthmoor and his estate to Margaret. When Charles II was brought to the throne at the Restoration in 1660, he sought to restore a high Anglican Church to power, and government forces raided Swarthmoor to stop the illegal religious meetings held there. Margaret petitioned the king for freedom of conscience, promising persuasion, not violence, to bring about change in government or religion. However, in 1664, Margaret was arrested for having Quaker meetings in her home and for not taking the oath of loyalty to the Anglican Church. She was imprisoned in the Lancaster jail and finally sentenced to life imprisonment and forfeiture of her property.

While in prison she wrote books and pamphlets, including one in 1666 entitled 'Women Justified, Proved, and Allowed of by the scriptures, all such as Speak by the Spirit and Power of the Lord Jesus.'[24] Margaret tried to show from Scripture that women should speak and preach freely. She contended that men and women equally bore the image of God and that limitations on a woman's freedom were not made until after the Fall of Adam and Eve. The Church was described as a woman in Scriptures; to limit the speech of women was to limit the speech of the Church. Numerous women mentioned in Scripture showed that women were to preach the gospel – including the Samaritan woman, Martha and Mary, the women with Christ during His ministry, Mary Magdalene, Priscilla, Hannah, Esther, Jesus' mother Mary and her cousin Elizabeth (both prophesied clearly). In support of women prophesying, Margaret quoted Joel 2:29, 'And also upon the servants and upon the handmaids in those days will I pour out my spirit.' Neither men nor women were to speak without the Spirit of God, but it would be wrong to limit the speech of a woman when the Spirit clearly was prompting her. Christ worked through the weak to accomplish His purposes, and He could work through a preaching woman.

Margaret examined the Scriptures in 1 Corinthians and 1 Timothy 2 where Paul enjoined the women to keep silence and not exert authority over men. She decided these Scriptures were intended for unruly women in the early Church who were disrupting meetings and adorning themselves with worldly ways and fashions. She believed the Scriptural admonitions had nothing to do with Christian women of later centuries

---

24   Available at www.qhpress.org/texts/fell.html.

who, under the power of the Spirit, preached to others. George Fox, who was in prison with Margaret when she wrote this tract, later wrote and spoke similarly about the freedom of women to preach and minister. From the earliest days of the Quaker meetings, women spoke freely. The Quakers had no ordained ministers. All who spoke in the Quaker meeting were lay people and were to speak only by the direct inspiration of the Divine Light, including women. Ultimately, Quakers looked to the Inner Light more than the Scriptures for their authority and guidance. Looking to personal inspiration rather than Scripture as their ultimate authority, Quakers easily developed a diversity of beliefs distinct from the truth found in Christ.

In 1668, Margaret was released from prison by the order of the King and Council. Her property had been protected by her daughters and had not been confiscated; she was able to return to life at Swarthmoor. In 1668, Margaret Fell married George Fox, ten years her junior. This was a marriage for spiritual purposes. During their twenty-two years of marriage, they were apart more often than they were together. George was imprisoned several more times for illegal religious assembly, and also traveled to America. In later years he lived in London, staying with one of Margaret's four married daughters, while Margaret remained at Swarthmoor with her youngest daughter and son-in-law. Gulielma Penn, wife of Pennsylvania founder William Penn, kindly wrote Margaret, 'methinks if thou foundest a Clearness and Freedom in the Lord, it would be happie thou wert nearer thy dear Husband and children, but that I leave [to] the Lords ordering, and thy Freedom.'[25] Yet Margaret maintained her independence and remained at Swarthmoor. She used her wealth and higher social position to enhance George Fox's position and elevate the Quaker cause whenever possible.

Margaret was important in establishing women's meetings among the Quakers, which expanded the role of women in the Church. These meetings had a role in governing the Church, disciplining women, and controlling the Church's membership. George Fox wrote a pamphlet encouraging the meetings. The women's meetings collected money to distribute to the poor and helped train women in midwifery, social welfare, and how best to help and minister to others. The women's meetings were also the first to rule on a couple's intention to marry. Both man and woman would need to be Quakers, and if one was outside the community, his Quaker credentials and his suitableness for marriage, both materially and spiritually, were examined by the women.

---

25   Bonnelyn Young Kunze, 'Religious Authority and Social Status in Seventeenth-Century England: The Friendship of Margaret Fell, George Fox, and William Penn,' *Church History*, Vol. 57, No. 2 (June 1988), p. 181.

In the seventeenth century, the majority of the traveling ministers who spread the Quaker teachings throughout Britain, America, the Continent, and Turkey, were women. One historian estimated that from 1700 to 1775, there were between 1300 and 1500 female preachers among the Quakers. Usually two women traveled together, an older and a younger one. The women were approved by first monthly and then quarterly meetings of Friends before being permitted to travel and minister in the Friends' name.

One of the pioneering Quaker missionaries was Mary Fisher (1623?-1698?), a Yorkshire servant girl. Mary was a servant in the home of Richard Tomlinson and his wife Pontefract when she first heard George Fox. The entire household converted to Quakerism, and Mary began preaching the Quaker faith to the parish minister. For sixteen months she was imprisoned in York Castle with other Quakers, from whom she learned and grew in the faith. Quakers believed that ministers of Christ became such from knowledge of Christ's life and work, not merely by knowledge of Greek, Hebrew, and Latin. When released from prison, Mary Fisher and a friend went to preach to the students at Sidney Sussex College. For this they were arrested and whipped publicly at the Market-Cross. Mary and her friend showed the utmost courage under persecution. In 1655, Mary set out for America with Anne Austin, arriving in Boston in May 1656.

The Puritan leaders in Massachusetts believed the Quaker preachers challenged the colony's order and threatened the pure doctrine and practice of the colony. If allowed to continue, they feared Quaker beliefs would bring anarchy and undermine the moral fabric of their fragile society in the American wilderness. Massachusetts accordingly had passed laws against the Quakers. Quakers were banished from the colony, and if they returned they could be physically punished. If they persisted in returning to the colony, they could be executed. When Mary and Anne arrived in Boston, they were kept prisoner aboard the ship, their trunks were searched and all their books were burned. They were shipped back to Barbados and then England without ever being able to preach in Boston.

In 1657, when she was thirty-four, Mary journeyed to Turkey with five other Quaker missionaries, three men and two women. She told people along the way she had a 'message to the king from the Most High God.' Fearlessly, Mary came to speak to the Ottoman Sultan, whose court was then at Adrianople with an army of twenty thousand men. Quaker historian William Sewel, writing in 1795, described the scene:

> The Sultan bade her speak the word of the Lord to them, and not to fear, for they had good hearts and could hear it. He also charged her to speak the word she had to say from the Lord, neither more nor less, for they were willing to hear it, be it what it would. Then she spoke what was

upon her mind. The Turks hearkened to her…Then the Sultan desired her to stay in the country, saying that they could not but respect such a one, as should take so much pains to come to them so far as from England, with a message from the Lord God. He also proffered her a guard to bring her into Constantinople…But she, not accepting this offer, he told her it was dangerous traveling, especially for such a one as she; and wondered that she had passed so safe so far as she had; saying also that it was in respect to her, and kindness that he proffered it, and that he would not do anything that she should come to the least hurt in his dominions. She, having no more to say, the Turks asked her what she thought of their prophet Mahomet and she answered she knew him not, but Christ the true prophet, the Son of God, who was the Light of the World, and enlightened every man coming to the world, Him, she knew.

Though Mary's words are not known to have changed any Turkish heart, they did give courage to the Quakers back in England. Mary later wrote to another Quaker:

I bore my testimony for the Lord before the King unto whom I was sent, and he was very noble unto me … and he and all that were about him received the words of truth without contradiction … There is a royal seed amongst them which in time God will raise. They are more near truth than many nations. There is a love begotten in me towards them which is endless.[26]

A continent away, another Quaker preacher was boldly speaking her faith with a more direful end. Mary Dyer was a Puritan who settled in Boston, Massachusetts, with her husband in 1635. She became a strong supporter of Anne Hutchinson and followed her to Rhode Island when she was banished from Massachusetts. The Puritans thought Mary was infected with the same erroneous doctrines as Anne. In 1652, Mary accompanied her husband when he returned to England with Roger Williams to procure a charter for the colony of Rhode Island. While in England, Mary converted to Quakerism. When her husband returned to America, Mary remained in England four more years growing in her Quaker beliefs.

When Mary Dyer and fellow-Quaker Ann Burden returned to New England in 1656, they were arrested in Boston and placed in jail. Mary Fisher and Anne Austin had been deported only days before. When he heard she was in prison in Boston, Mary Dyer's husband came from Rhode Island to procure Mary's release on the promise that she would not remain in Massachusetts Bay Colony. The next year, however, Mary went to the colony of New Haven to preach and was expelled. A month later she returned to Boston to visit some Quakers in prison. She was arrested again by the authorities. Mary and two other Quakers were brought

26   Quotes from William Sewel's *History of the Rise, Increase, and Progress of the Christian People Called Quakers*, 1795, in Deen's *Great Women of the Christian Faith*, pp. 128-9.

before the Massachusetts governor, who asked why they had returned to the colony after they had been banished from it. They contended they were obeying the Lord in coming and preaching. For the repeated offense of returning to Boston and not respecting her banishment, Mary Dyer and the others were sentenced to hang on October 27, 1659. Mary's husband's petition for clemency for his wife brought a reprieve, and Mary once again was banished from Massachusetts. Less than six months later, however, she returned to preach in Boston. She felt this was her duty before God, even though she knew it meant death. Mary Dyer was hanged June 1, 1660. Her former pastor in Boston urged her to repent, but Mary said, 'Nay, I cannot, for in obedience to the will of the Lord God I came, and in His will I abide faithful to the death.'[27] Women continued to be an important part of Quakerism in ensuing centuries. In the nineteenth century, Quaker women became important leaders of the women suffrage movement. Many of the principles and practices of this later movement can be seen in the early Quaker women.

Daughters of Zion
Cotton Mather, the American Puritan pastor and prolific writer, wrote a work on Christian women published in 1692 as *Ornaments for the Daughters of Zion*, subtitled 'The character and happiness of a virtuous woman: in a discourse which directs the female sex how to express the fear of God at every age and state of their life and obtain both temporal and external blessedness.'[28] The book was written specifically for 'promoting the Fear of God in the Female Sex.' The basic organization of Mather's work followed Jean Vives' 1529 work written at the request of Catherine of Aragon for her daughter Mary, but Mather provides a distinctively Puritan reflection on womanhood.

Mather began by discussing the character of a virtuous woman. The foundation of all in a virtuous woman's life was the conviction that there is a God. In creation she saw the wisdom, power, and goodness of God throughout the universe, and this produced in her a reverence. She saw God's providence preserving all things to His purposes and recognized that God was a wise General over all the quarrelsome and contentious things in the world. She had the most respect and reverence for all connected with the Name of God, especially the Word of God. She had a fear of God and sought to avoid anything which might bring displeasure to Him. Not only did she not want to offend, but she sought to please and serve the great God and considered being a servant of God the highest of all callings. The worship of God was her greatest delight. She perfumed every room of

---

27   Quoted in Deen, *Great Women of the Christian Faith*, p. 346.

28   Cotton Mather. *Ornaments for the Daughters of Zion*. Cambridge: S.G. & B.G., 1692.

her house with prayer. Scriptures and sermons were very dear to her, 'and it is not every trifle (as the want of a Garment or a dread of the weather) that she will make her excuse for her absence from the *Means of Grace*' and Sabbath worship.

Mather secondly dealt with the happiness of the virtuous woman. While volumes had been written on the evils of the female sex, Mather wrote that the virtuous woman would be praised for her fear of God and the wisdom and benefits which came from the fear of the Lord:

> The fear of God will soon make it evident, that you are among the excellent in the Earth. If any Men are so wicked (and some sects of Men have been so) as to deny your being rational Creatures, the best Means to confute them, will be by proving yourselves religious ones. I do assure you, and I have more than Luther to consent and concur with me, in this Assertion, That the Actions of even the meanest Milk-maid or Cook-maid, when done in the fear of God, are in the Account of God more noble Things than the Victories of a Caesar! Thus do I set before you, the Way for you to be ennobled; thus ennobled, many of you already are.

Mather noted that there were more women in Church than men. Possibly this was because there were more women in the world than men, though Mather didn't think so. More likely it seemed to him that

> The Curse in the Difficulties both of Subjection and of Childbearing, has been turn'd into a Blessing, by the free Grace of our most gracious God. God sanctifies the chains, the Pains, the Deaths which they meet withal; and furthermore, make the Tenderness of their Disposition, a further Occasion of serious Devotion in them ... most of you have more Time to employ in the more immediate Service of your souls, than the other Sex is owner of. You are ordinarily more within the House, and so may more mind the Work within the Heart than we ...

The longest portion of Mather's work dealt with counsel and advice. Some of the advice was suited for either sex: pray constantly that the fear of God may be implanted in your soul; let every action in the day be done in fear of God; begin and end the day in communion with God:

> Throughout all the Day, interweave a conscience of Duty into all your Motions, all your affairs. Let every meal, every sleep, every visit, and all your domestick business, though it be but the rocking of a cradle, be done with an eye to this, *This is the thing wherein I may perform a Service to God, and expect a Blessing from God; This is what my God would have me to be about.*

Other areas of advice Mather deemed especially suitable to the female sex. Women should be cautious about those who would seduce them from the fear of God. The devil designed to use the weaker sex to reach their husbands. A poison is most effective when placed in woman's milk! Though women were often accused of misusing the tongue, Mather thought it unfair that all women should be accused of such weakness. He also devoted some space to the importance of proper speech, citing many appropriate Scriptures:

> Proverbs 10:20, 'The Tongue of the Just, is as choice Silver.' So your speech ought likewise to be rare, like silver, which is not so common as copper or iron is. Be careful that you don't speak too soon, because you cannot fetch back and eat up, what is uttered; but study to answer. And be careful that you don't speak too much ...

A consecrated Christian woman should exercise discernment in the clothing she wore.

A woman's fashion should not prejudice her health. Her dress should be consistent with modesty and sobriety and should be according to her rank in society. She should not over-expose parts of her body. An old woman should not dress as a young woman. If a woman spent more time on her clothes than she did in praying or working out her own salvation, then the clothes became a snare to her soul.

Mather recognized that the most important thing for a virtuous woman was her faith in Christ: 'Whoever pretends to write the calling of a Virtuous Woman, and forgets to urge Faith in the Lord Jesus Christ as the Root and Source of all true Virtue, has finely left out the one Thing needful.' Such a woman maintained the fear of God in every condition and stage of life. Mather described in detail how the maid, the virtuous wife, the virtuous mother, and the virtuous widow each in her own way and station lived out and manifested the fear of the Lord. Mather concluded his work with the prayer:

> I praise thee, O my God, for thy assisting my Endeavors to describe the Praises of the virtuous Woman; and rely upon thy Grace in the Son, that these my poor Labours may be accepted and succeeded among the Daughters of the People. Amen.

9

Reform and Revival:
Renewed Day by Day

2 Corinthians 4:16

Throughout the seventeenth and eighteenth centuries, women from all social classes and levels of wealth were finding avenues for expanding their influence for the gospel. While the role of wife and mother continued to be emphasized as an important area of Christian influence, women were also involved in evangelism, education, and missionary enterprises. Women were part of the growing trans-continental Christian world, with connections in Europe, the Americas, and Africa.

Reform in Europe

One of the most learned women of the seventeenth century was Anna Maria van Schurman (1607-1678).[1] Anna Maria was the only daughter of a family belonging to the German lesser nobility and was educated at home with her two brothers. Something of a child prodigy, Anna Maria corresponded with literati throughout Europe and was the first woman to attend a Dutch university (While attending the University of Utrecht, she listened to the lectures behind a curtain, so as not to distract the male students!). Her correspondents not only included leaders of thought throughout Europe, but revealed a network of intellectual women corresponding with each other.

Anna Maria, a skilled linguist, was translating Latin by age 10. Besides her native language, she spoke French, English, and Spanish fluently; she also knew Greek, Hebrew, Arabic, Chaldaic, Syriac, Ethiopian, Turkish and Persian. As a teenager, her poetry was praised by leading poets of the day. Yet, Anna was most interested in art, and she became skilled in painting and etching. Even with her precocious gifts and talents, Anna managed to remain humble.

---

1   *Other Women's Voices*, http://home.infionline.net/~ddisse/schurman.html.

Raised in a Dutch Reformed family, Anna was drawn to Christian truth at a young age. In her autobiography she recalled a time when she was barely four years old:

> While collecting herbs with the maid whose chore this was, I sat down on the bank of a certain stream. When she suggested it, I recited from memory the response to the first question of the Heidelberg Catechism. At the words 'that I am not my own but belong to thy most faithful servant Jesus Christ,' my heart was filled with such a great and sweet joy and an intimate feeling of the love of Christ that all the subsequent years have not been able to remove the living memory of that moment ... I thirsted constantly from childhood on with an honest and sincere desire for the true practice of devotion.[2]

In 1638 her dissertation on *Whether a Christian Woman Should be Educated,* written for the theologian André Rivet, was published; it became her most famous work. Anna considered the old question debated since at least the days of Tertullian of whether a classical education interfered with spiritual growth – whether Athens could coexist with Jerusalem. She developed fourteen very logical arguments for the education of women, which can be summarized as follows:[3]

1. Woman has reason, so she is fitted to understand the arts and sciences.

2. Woman desires to learn the arts and sciences and so is fit to study.

3. Woman, unlike beasts, has a countenance raised to heaven, suitable for knowledge and contemplation.

4. Study is a suitable occupation for anyone wanting to avoid idleness.

5. Study is suited for those with a more tranquil and carefree life (i.e. those women with some wealth who are not consumed with the chores of their family and household).

6. Women were to be homemakers, and education and study is suited to woman at home by herself.

7. Education is suitable for pursuing virtue.

8. Whatever perfects and adorns the mind is fitting for a Christian woman.

9. Whatever arouses a greater love and reverence for God is fitting for a Christian woman.

10. Education and right reason can help fight against heresies.

---

2   From *Eukleria* 2.1 in Anna Maria van Schurman. *Whether a Christian Woman Should be Educated and other writings from her intellectual circle* (ed. and trans. Joyce L. Irwin). (Chicago and London: The University of Chicago Press, 1998), pp. 79-80.

3   *Whether a Christian Woman Should be Educated and other writings from her intellectual circle*, pp. 25-37.

11. All things which teach prudence are suitable for a Christian woman.

12. Whatever leads to true greatness of soul is suitable for a Christian woman.

13. Whatever fills the human mind with exceptional and honest delight is suitable to a Christian woman.

14. Ignorance is not fitting for a Christian woman.

Anna Maria contended that education was not just for those with a public function or sphere of activity. Following the Scriptures, she did not believe women were suited for political or ecclesiastical leadership. However, she did believe that since education was compatible with private goals, parents should educate their daughters. She held up Elizabeth I and Jane Grey as key examples of educated Christian women. Women were not just to learn spinning and weaving, but theology, nature, Scripture, history, languages, and biographies.

After the death of her parents, Anna Maria was left to care for two elderly blind aunts, and her studies could no longer occupy her time. She became actively involved in charity and hospital work. Drawn out of her studies and more involved in the daily, ordinary affairs of life, she began to think perhaps she had spent too much time on classical learning and

> worthless matters.... I did not always give first place to the things that could glorify God, edify my neighbor, and make a soul more pleasing to God ... I clung with too much affection to various sciences and arts and in them sought, even if I did not find, some pleasure and repose.[4]

She had tried to study everything too much, when she should have spent more time learning the 'one thing necessary' of which Jesus spoke.[5]

Anna Maria's contemporary in France, Madame Jeanne Guyon (1648-1717), became noted for her spiritual writings. Jeanne was a French aristocrat who moved in the highest of court circles. Educated in a convent, she always had a heart for God, though she was often surrounded by fear. When only ten years old, she happened upon a Bible in the convent. She was consumed with a desire for reading the Bible and memorized large portions of Scripture. She wanted to become a nun, but her father opposed this. When she was fifteen, he arranged her marriage to a man of great wealth, M. Jacques Guyon.

Madame Guyon's mother-in-law governed the household like a tyrant and was constantly humiliating her daughter-in-law and criticizing her to her son. Though young, Madame Guyon realized that God could use this

---

4   From 'Eukleria,' in *Whether a Christian Woman Should be Educated*, pp. 89-90.

5   i.e., to learn God's Word (Luke 10:42).

adversity for good in her own soul, just as God had meant it for good when Joseph was sold into slavery in Egypt (Gen. 50:20). She knew that God used her mother-in-law to bring humility to her own spirit. She turned to prayer and books of devotion, particularly Thomas à Kempis' *Imitation of Christ*. Through sickness, suffering, and the death of two of her children Jeanne learned to trust God's comforting hand. She learned that by outward suffering God strengthened the inner soul.

When she was 28, Madame Guyon's husband died, leaving her with three children, including one born just months before her husband's death. Though her husband's estate left her well off for the rest of her life, her mother-in-law continued adamantly in her hostility, and Madame Guyon had to leave her home. She began using her fortune to help others, dispensing food, nursing the sick, and establishing hospitals. After a few years of widowhood, she began traveling throughout France and Switzerland with her daughter and a small group of servants, teaching the importance of seeking Christ by a quiet faith, not by outward ceremonies. Practicing an extreme asceticism, she sought to totally lose herself in God.

Madame Guyon wrote 40 books developing the importance of an inward, Christ-transformed life. Her lengthy autobiography has been compared to Augustine's *Confessions* in its examination of the inner soul. Her most influential book, *The Method of Prayer*, was based upon St. Paul's instruction to 'Pray without ceasing' (1 Thess. 5:17). She taught that perfection is reached when the soul is lost in God and moves as one with Him. Such beliefs were known as Quietism and were considered heresy by the Church. Madame Guyon was imprisoned for seven years, first in a monastery and then in the Bastille. She was released after signing a retraction of her views. The imprisonment broke her physically, and she suffered much from her infirmities the remaining fifteen years of her life. Her total surrender to God remained firm to the end, however, and in her last will and testament she wrote,

> It is to Thee, O Lord God, that I owe all things; and it is to thee, that I now surrender up all that I am. Do with me, O my God, whatsoever Thou pleasest. To Thee, in an act of irrevocable donation, I give up both my body and my soul, to be disposed of according to thy will. Thou seest my nakedness and misery without Thee. Thou knowest that there is nothing in heaven, or in earth, that I desire but Thee alone. Within Thy hands, O God, I leave my soul, not relying for my salvation on any good that is in me, but solely on Thy mercies, and the merits and sufferings of my Lord Jesus Christ.[6]

Madame Guyon and her writings are not without controversy today. Certainly her mystical visions sought a revelation beyond the Scriptures.

---

6   As quoted in *Great Women of the Christian Faith*, p. 140.

Her teaching that the Christian should abandon his whole existence to God could produce a mindless passivity rather than a true submission to God's will and purposes. Yet her teachings on meditatively praying the Scripture and of an inward holiness which comes through God's personal work in the soul encouraged a godly Christian life independent of human works and institutional Church rituals. Numerous Protestants have been enriched in their Christian walk by her writings and life-story. Finding no spiritual sustenance in the outward, institutional elements of the Catholic Church, Guyon focused on her inward, personal spiritual life. Though she remained in the Catholic Church, she had learned the importance of divine grace. She learned that God was working in both the good and bad events of her life to work His will in her soul. Her writings, especially *Experiencing the Depths of Jesus Christ*, and her personal example of total surrender to God influenced many, including the holiness and deeper life movements in England and America. While in prison in Burma, missionary Adoniram Judson was consoled by William Cowper's translation of her verses:

> No bliss I seek, but to fulfill
> In life, in death, Thy lovely will;
> No succour in my woes I want,
> Except what Thou art pleased to grant.
> Our days are numbered – let us spare
> Our anxious hearts a needless care;
> 'Tis Thine to number out our days,
> And ours to give them to Thy praise.[7]

Charles Spurgeon found inspiration in Madame Guyon's peace and joy in suffering. In his 'Lily among Thorns' sermon in 1880 he preached:

> You that are kept from roaming by sickness or by family trials need not regret these things, for perhaps they are the means of making you more completely your Lord's. How charmingly Madame Guyon wrote when she was immured in a dungeon. Her wing was closely bound, but her song was full of liberty, for she felt that the bolts and bars only shut her in with her Beloved, and what is that but liberty? She sang,

> > 'A little bird I am,
> > Shut from the fields of air;
> > And in my cage I sit and sing
> > To him who placed me there;
> > Well pleased a prisoner to be,
> > Because, my God, it pleases thee.
> > Nothing have I else to do,
> > I sing the whole day long;
> > And he whom I love to please
> > Does listen to my song;

---

7   *Great Women of the Christian Faith*, p. 130.

He caught and bound my wandering wing,
But still he bends to hear me sing.'[8]

'As the lily among thorns' she lived in prison shut in with her Lord, and since the world was quite shut out, she was in that respect a gainer .

John Wesley, the founder of Methodism, praised Madame Guyon, finding in her a rare example of true holiness.

Wesley was also strongly influenced by the Moravians, a group in which women found positions of prominence. Moravians were the spiritual heirs of John Huss, the proto-Reformation Czech leader who was burned at the stake by the Council of Constance in 1415. Fleeing persecution in their native land, the Moravians found safety on the lands of Count Zinzendorf in what is now eastern Germany. Niklaus Ludwig von Zinzendorf was among the nobility of Europe who reached out to help the lowly in the name of Christ. Since a child Zinzendorf had strong Christian leanings, but when he was twenty he was particularly moved by a painting of Christ. Underneath the painting were the words, 'I have done this for you, what have you done for me?' From that moment, Zinzendorf sought to do whatever Christ led him to do. When the Moravians fled persecution in 1722, he offered them a place of refuge on his lands and in the community of Herrnhut.

Zinzendorf not only offered a place of refuge, but became a leader of the Moravians. He organized them into small groups or 'choirs' that met together to encourage each other spiritually. The sexes were separated in the community, and each individual was assigned to a particular group – Little Boys, Little Girls, Older Boys, Older Girls, Single Brothers, Single Sisters, Married Brothers, Married Sisters, Widowers, or Widows. Worship services for each group emphasized aspects of the life of Jesus most appropriate to that group, and each group had its own set of leaders. Within a few years, however, dissensions sprang up in the community. The leaders prayed about the growing disharmony; after a communion service on August 13, 1727, a spiritual awakening spread among the people. They all sensed a need to repent of their selfish attitudes and seek God's calling in a fresh way. One member of the community deeply affected by the Herrnhut revival was Anna Nitschmann (1715-1760), a girl of twelve.

Anna had come with her family to Herrnhut in 1725. Her father and older brother had been imprisoned for their Christian faith while they were still in Moravia. During the revival in 1727, Anna dedicated her life to the Lord's service and began organizing the young women for worship and ministry. Because of the separation of the sexes in the Moravian community, women had leadership positions over groups of other women in the Moravian Church. The community's leaders noticed

---

8   C.H. Spurgeon. *The Metropolitan Tabernacle Pulpit: Sermons preached and revised by C.H. Spurgeon during the year 1880*, vol. 26. London: Passmore & Alabaster, 1881, p. 138.

Anna's excellent work among the Single Sisters and nominated her for the position of 'chief eldress' for all of the women at Herrnhut. Three other women were also nominated, but Anna Nitschmann's name was chosen by lot. At fourteen she became leader of the Moravian women!

Moravians were the first Protestants to send out evangelistic missionaries, and Anna became part of the 'Pilgrim congregation' ready to carry the message of Christ anywhere. She traveled to many foreign lands, including America, where she helped found Bethlehem and Nazareth, Pennsylvania. Anna was twice offered marriage, but she refused. However, a year after Count Zinzendorf's wife died, he asked Anna to marry him, and she agreed. They were married in 1757, a nobleman and a commoner united together in Christ.

The first Moravian missionaries went to work among the slaves of St. Thomas in 1732. One of the slaves most receptive to their gospel message was Rebecca (1718-1780). Rebecca was born around 1718 on the British island of Antigua, the child of a white father and an African, slave mother. When about seven she was kidnapped and sold to Dutch planter Lucas van Beverhout of St. Thomas. The child had a strong desire to become a Christian and sought out a Catholic priest, who baptized her under the name of 'Rebecca.' About the same time, her master's son and heir freed her. Possibly he did not want to keep her in slavery since she had become a Christian.

In 1736, Moravian missionary Friedrich Martin joined the Moravian missionary enterprise on St. Thomas. Rebecca responded to the gospel presented and the spiritual equality the Moravians so clearly believed and practiced. Rebecca and other blacks, free and enslaved, established the first black church in the Americas on St. Thomas. In 1738, Martin officiated at the marriage of Rebecca and another German Moravian missionary, Matthäus Freundlich. Rebecca traveled about the island evangelizing and encouraging slaves in their Christian faith.

The planters were displeased with the social equality being practiced by the Moravians, fearing they would stir the slaves to rebellion. Martin, Rebecca, and her husband were arrested on the premise that the Freundlichs' marriage was invalid. Rebecca showed great courage during her imprisonment and gave eloquent testimony of her Christian faith at her trial. When Count Zinzendorf arrived on the island, he intervened to prevent the heavy fines, further imprisonment and possible re-enslavement of Rebecca. Rebecca and her husband, with some of the other Moravian missionaries, went to Germany in 1742. Matthäus soon died, leaving Rebecca with a two-year-old daughter who died two years later. After a few years, Rebecca married Christian Jacob Protten, also of the Moravian Brethren and the son of an African woman and a Danish seaman. In the Moravian community, Rebecca was ordained as a leader of the group of married women, giving a black Christian woman authority over white European women.

While Rebecca gained a position of leadership among the Moravians, her husband's pride and alcoholism were the probable causes for the couple's being expelled from the community. They went to Christian's ancestral home at Christiansborg on the Gold Coast of Africa, where they opened a school. Rebecca never returned to the Church she helped begin in the Americas, but died in the home of her ancestors.

The Wesleyan Revivals in England

Early eighteenth-century England had degenerated into a moral cesspool. Thomas Carlyle remarked that the stomach was well alive but the soul was extinct. The strong Christianity of the earlier Puritan period was in decline, and Deism was rampant. A philosophical moralism permeated the churches. Lawyer Sir William Blackstone visited the church of every major clergyman in London but 'did not hear a single discourse which had more Christianity in it than the writings of Cicero.'[9] In most sermons, he found it would have been impossible to tell whether the preacher was a follower of Cicero, Mohammed, or Christ! Bishop Berkeley believed that morality and religion in the country had collapsed 'to a degree that was never known in any Christian country.'[10] William Hogarth's print of 'Beer Street and Gin Alley' illustrated the rampant drunkenness. Gambling was so extensive that one historian called England a vast casino. Newborns were left exposed to die in the streets; 97% of the infant poor in workhouses died as children. Bear-baiting and cockfighting were accepted sports. Tickets to public executions were sold as to a theater. The slave trade further coarsened the nation's conscience. Historians recognize that the nation of England changed course in the eighteenth century largely through the Great Awakening and the ministry of John Wesley, George Whitefield, and others.

Because of the tremendous moral change in England brought about by the evangelical awakening, Wesley has been recognized as one of the most influential men in eighteenth-century England. Historians also recognize that Wesley became the leader he was largely through the influence and prayers of his mother Susanna. Susanna Wesley (1669-1742) was the youngest of twenty-five children. Her father, Dr. Samuel Annesley, was a famous Nonconformist minister who preached to one of the largest congregations in London. Her mother, Dr. Annesley's second wife, was

9   Charles J. Abbey and John H. Overton. *The English Church in the Eighteenth Century*. London: Longman, Green, & Co., 1896, p. 681.

10   *The Works of George Berkeley, D.D. Bishop of Cloyne*. G. Bell & Sons, 1898, p. 194.

the daughter of a Member of Parliament. When she was twenty, Susanna married Samuel Wesley, a Church of England minister.

Susanna faced many hardships after her marriage. She had nineteen children, only nine of whom lived to adulthood. One daughter was deformed for life. Susanna's husband Samuel had an impractical bent and could be obstinate and stubborn. He considered himself a poet and scholar, and spent much time and energy in the production of several mediocre works which were soon forgotten. In his quest for preferment in the Church of England, he often undertook lengthy stays in London attending ecclesiastical conferences at his own expense, piling up debt for himself and his family. Sometimes he was able to find financial help from wealthy patrons, but he also spent time in debtors' prison while Susanna somehow kept the home and family together.

After twelve years of marriage, Samuel provoked a quarrel with Susanna and almost left her. After evening prayers one day, Samuel noted that Susanna had not said 'Amen' to the prayers for the King. Susanna replied that she believed King James II, not King William of Orange, was the rightful King, and she could not in good conscience say 'Amen' to this prayer. Samuel demanded her obedience. When Susanna would not conform her opinion to his demands, he immediately knelt and vowed to God he would not come near her or join her in bed until she had changed her opinion. Samuel soon left for London, giving Susanna time to submit to his judgment. When he returned some months later and she still could not in good conscience submit, he decided to leave her, never to see her again. He said he was taking a chaplaincy in the Navy and would care for the children. On his way out of town, Samuel met a clergyman who in some manner must have persuaded Samuel that the oath he had taken not to touch Susanna was of no effect, since it was contrary to his marriage vows taken earlier. On his way back to the house, Samuel discovered that the parsonage was on fire. Susanna barely escaped with the three children. The incident not only reveals something of Susanna's strong will and conscience but also shows the foolishness, obstinacy, and desperation under which Samuel sometimes operated. Why did Samuel suddenly become concerned about Susanna not saying 'Amen' when it had not been an issue with him in years past? Apparently under financial difficulties, Samuel perhaps thought he would not be able to receive hoped-for patronage from King William if Susanna did not appropriately swear allegiance to the sovereign. A year after Samuel and Susanna reconciled, their fifteenth child, John Wesley, was born.

Some years later, when Samuel was again away attending the ecclesiastical convocation, on Sunday evenings Susanna read to the family from the best sermons in the library. The servants attending these readings asked if they could invite other family members, and before long over two hundred people were attending the meetings. The local curate was quite jealous that Susanna's readings and explanations were attracting a larger crowd than was attending his church services. After the curate's complaint, Samuel wrote Susanna for her to discontinue the meetings. Susanna wrote back saying that the meetings had helped so many people and were only opposed by the curate and one of his friends. She concluded by saying,

> If after all this you think fit to dissolve this assembly do not tell me you *desire* me to do it, for that will not satisfy my conscience; but send your *positive command* in such full and express terms as may absolve me from all guilt and punishment for neglecting this opportunity for doing good when you and I shall appear before the great and awful tribunal of our Lord Jesus.[11]

Samuel never sent his positive command, and Susanna continued her Sunday evening readings.

Through personal sorrows, financial strain, and a difficult husband, Susanna was still able to see God's mercy:

> Though man is born to trouble, yet I believe there is scarce a man to be found upon earth but, take the whole course of his life, hath more mercies than afflictions, and much more pleasure than pain. All my sufferings, by the admirable management of Omnipotent Goodness, have concurred to promote my spiritual and eternal good ... Glory be to Thee, O Lord![12]

With such a large household, Susanna learned her days had to be organized and methodical if she was to accomplish anything. She spent at least an hour of every day in her private devotions; six hours a day, six days a week she set aside for the education of her children, even writing some of the textbooks and study materials herself. She instructed the children in both academic subjects and Christian truth. At least once a week she had a personal, spiritual conversation with each one of her children. When an adult, Susanna's son John asked his mother to write down her advice and instructions on child rearing. She acceded to his request while also noting that

> No one can, without renouncing the world in the most literal sense, observe my method. There are few, if any, who would devote about twenty years of the prime of life in hopes to save the souls of their children.[13]

---

11   J.B. Wakely, 'Susanna Wesley and the Unauthorized Meetings,' *John Wesley: Holiness of Heart and Life*, at http://gbgm-umc.org/umw/Wesley/susannawesley.stm.

12   *Great Women of the Chirstian Faith*, p. 143.

13   Arnold A. Dallimore. *Susanna Wesley: The Mother of John & Charles Wesley*. Grand Rapids, Michigan: Baker Book House, 1993, p. 57.

Susanna summarized for her son her principles for childhood education:

> I insist upon conquering the will of children ... because this is the only strong and rational foundation of a religious education, without which both precept and example will be ineffectual. But when this is thoroughly done, then a child is capable of being governed by the reason and piety of its parents, till its own understanding comes to maturity and the principles of religion have taken root in the mind.

She also formulated eight rules that gave structure to this principle. These can be summarized as follows:

1. A child guilty of a fault should not be beaten, if there is a full confession of the fault, with a promise to correct it. This would eliminate lying and needless beatings.

2. No sinful act should pass without punishment.

3. No child should be beaten twice for the same fault.

4. A significant act of obedience should be recognized and even, on occasion, rewarded.

5. An intention toward obedience, even if the performance was not as well as it should have been, was to be accepted and encouraged.

6. The privacy and the property of others were to be respected.

7. Promises were to be strictly enforced and observed.

8. No girl was to be put to work (e.g. sewing) before she could read.[14]

Susanna and the children began and ended every school day with the singing of a psalm and the reading of the Scriptures. Susanna gave her children an emphasis on the worth of spiritual things, and they continued to seek her counsel when they were adults and she was an old woman. In 1709, Susanna wrote to her oldest son Samuel, 'There is nothing I desire to live for, but to do some small service to my children: that, as I have brought them into the world, I may, if it please God, be an instrument of doing good unto their souls.'[15]

Susanna's son Samuel was a promising minister who died early. Sons John and Charles became the leaders of Methodism, with Charles writing

---

14 Nehemiah Curnock (ed.), *The Journal of the Rev. John Wesley*. London: Charles H. Kelley, 1909-1916, III, 36-9, as quoted in Samuel J. Rogal, 'The Epworth Women: Susanna Wesley and Her Daughters,' *Wesleyan Theological Journal*, Volume 18, Number 2, Fall, 1983,http://wesley.nnu.edu/fileadmin/imported_site/wesleyjournal/1983-wtj-18-2.pdf. accessed June 2, 2011.

15 'The Epworth Women: Susanna Wesley and Her Daughters.' See website in previous footnote.

hymns which continue to influence people the world over. Susanna's daughters, however, suffered much through unfortunate marriages, bringing great sorrow to Susanna herself in her later years. After her husband's death, Susanna went to live with various of her children, making a home at last with John at The Foundry in London. She died surrounded by her children. Her last words were, 'Children, as soon as I am released, sing a psalm of praise to God.' Charles wrote the epitaph placed on her gravestone:

> In sure and stedfast hope to rise
> And claim her mansion in the skies,
> A Christian here her flesh laid down,
> The cross exchanging for a crown.
>
> True daughter of affliction, she,
> Inured to pain and misery,
> Mourned a long night of griefs and fears,
> A legal night of seventy years.
>
> The Father then revealed his Son,
> Him in the broken bread made known;
> She knew and felt her sins forgiven
> And found the earnest of her heaven.
>
> Meet for the fellowship above,
> She heard the call, 'Arise my love!'
> 'I come,' her dying looks replied,
> And lamb-like as her Lord she died.[16]

From its earliest days, women played an important part in the Methodist movement begun by Susanna's sons John and Charles. Many of the earliest leaders of the Methodist classes were women; some women also became lay preachers. Undoubtedly the most important woman among the early Methodists was Selina Hastings, Countess of Huntingdon (1707-1791). A member of the aristocracy, Lady Huntingdon was converted through the testimony of her sister-in-law and the preaching of Benjamin Ingham, a Methodist evangelist. She then began to work diligently to bring the gospel to everyone in her sphere of contacts, from her aristocratic social circle to the servants in her house and the poor in her community. She established classes for women, teaching them the Scripture and encouraging them to live their faith out in showing the love of Christ to others.

Lady Huntingdon actively supported the Wesleys and numerous other evangelicals of the day, holding meetings in her various homes for her aristocratic friends to meet the Wesleys and hear them preach.

---

16 *Susanna Wesley*, pp. 166-7.

She appointed George Whitefield her personal chaplain, supported his many preaching tours, and aided Whitefield in establishing the Bethesda Orphanage in Georgia. She worked and supported people of evangelical persuasion regardless of denominational affiliation – Anglican, Moravian, Dissenter, or Methodist. Evangelistic preaching could not always be heard in Anglican Churches, so she took advantage of her right as a 'Peer of the Realm' to establish chapels in her homes and estates. Owning much property, she established over one hundred chapels for evangelistic preaching in areas where she had lands. Preachers in the chapels were not required to be ordained by the Church of England. With great managerial skills, she oversaw the chapels, arranging for evangelical ministers to fill the pulpits and scheduling them so as not to conflict with the Anglican services of the parishes.

To train ministers for the chapels, she, in consultation with Welsh evangelist Howell Harris, established Trevecca College, with John Fletcher as president. Lady Huntingdon worked closely with Fletcher on the procedures and curriculum of the college. She also kept up a steady correspondence with the students and the itinerant Methodist ministers, encouraging them in the gospel work. In one letter she wrote that, 'The salvation of souls and exalting the praises of our Blessed Lord and Saviour has alone [been] the ground of my heart.'[17] Often she described herself as part of 'this present Reformation' of England. Lady Huntingdon had a passion for the spread of the gospel, and at one point struggled with her personal role in the gospel's proclamation. Was she not to go into the highways and fields to preach the Good News to the lost? From the Scripture, she could not approve of a woman preaching and never sought such a position or role. She truly believed that the Lord favored her with Trevecca College 'when many more voices than mine could breathe still better the longing of my heart.'[18]

Lady Huntingdon's own suffering and hardship increased her empathy for others in difficulties and distress. Two of her sons died of smallpox; her husband died suddenly and early; only one of her seven children survived her. She reached out to others, small and great, to minister to them in their time of need. When Charles Wesley's wife Sally contracted smallpox, Lady Huntingdon nursed her to health again. She spent time with George Frederick Handel during his last illness, encouraging him in the Lord. In an age of England's colonial expansion across the globe, Lady Huntingdon was concerned about the souls of the native Africans and Americans and sought to send out missionaries. In her seventies she

17   John R. Tyson. 'Lady Huntingdon's Reformation,' *Church History*, Vol. 64, No. 4 (Dec. 1995), p. 584.

18   'Lady Huntingdon's Reformation,' p. 590.

seriously contemplated a trip to America to work among the Native Americans herself.

Difficulties also came in the form of discord with other Christians. Lady Huntingdon had a firm conviction in the truth of the Reformation principle of justification by faith. When John Wesley turned more towards an Arminian theology, writing that salvation was not 'by the merit of works, but works as a condition' of salvation, Lady Huntingdon believed Wesley was 'establishing another foundation, repugnant to the whole plan of man's salvation under the new covenant of grace, as well as the clear meaning of our Established Church and all other Protestant Churches.'[19] She no longer allowed Wesley to preach in 'her' chapels or home classes, breaking a long association and friendship.

In 1779, an ecclesiastical court stipulated that though she had the right to appoint personal chaplains, the service of those chaplains was to be private, and they could not conduct public worship. This compelled Lady Huntingdon to break with the Church of England and license her chapels and preachers as Dissenters. No longer could 'The Countess of Huntingdon's Connexion' be an evangelical 'lump of leaven' within the Anglican Church. However, 'The Countess of Huntingdon's Connexion' continues today and includes active chapels in England and Sierra Leone[20].

Lady Huntingdon gave over £100,000 to Christian work, an amount equivalent to many millions of dollars today. Even more, she gave herself to the work of the ministry. Thomas Wills, a contemporary Methodist minister, described her as one of the brightest lights for the gospel:

> Thousands, I say tens of thousands, in various parts of the kingdom have heard the gospel through her instrumentality that in all probability would never have heard it at all; and I believe through eternity will have cause to bless God that she ever existed. She was truly and emphatically a Mother in Israel...[21]

Though not of the aristocracy, Hannah More (1745-1833) mingled with the highest of society and exerted a tremendous moral influence in her day through her writings and philanthropy. Hannah was the fourth of five daughters born to a schoolmaster in a village near Bristol, England. She learned to read by the age of four, learned Latin at an early age, and later learned French, Italian, and Spanish. Her older sisters established a boarding school in Bristol, and Hannah went to teach there. Hannah was a clever writer and conversationalist, and she made the acquaintance of several learned men when they were in Bristol. They

---

19   Ibid., p. 589.

20   'The Countess of Huntingdon Connexion' website at http://www.cofhconnexion.org.uk/.

21   Faith Cook. *Selina, Countess of Huntingdon: Her Pivotal Role in the 18th Century Evangelical Awakening.* Banner of Truth Trust, 2001, pp. 79-80.

in turn introduced her to other leaders of London society. Hannah was in the social circle of writer Samuel Johnson, painter Sir Joshua Reynolds, actor David Garrick, and statesmen Edmund Burke and Horace Walpole. When she was still in her twenties, literary leaders praised her poetry and plays, which sold so well that Hannah was able to support herself by her writings.

In time, Hannah tired of fashionable society and bought a little cottage, Cowslip Green, near Bristol. She continued to write, but with a stronger Christian purpose. She corresponded with Christian leaders, including John Newton, and became more friendly with the evangelical Clapham Sect, a group of Anglican social reformers which included William Wilberforce and Zachary Macaulay. The Clapham Sect financed many of her later writings on Christian morality. Han-

> **From Thomas Scott's *Commentary* on Genesis 2:24 (1788)**
>
> 'The mutual inclinations of the sexes for each other (which however debased by sin, was originally implanted by the Creator) when regulated by the law of God, and free from other restraints, becomes the foundation of all the religions of life, the source of the most rational of our earthly comforts, and equally beneficial to individuals, families, and nations: like a river, which, gliding in its banks, beautifies and enriches the neighboring plains. But when unscriptural restraints are imposed, or when it bursts through the appointed bounds, it diffuses vice, discord, disease, and misery with horrible rapidity; like the same river, obstructed in its natural channel, overflowing its banks, inundating and desolating the fields, and converting the neighboring country into a noxious marsh or fen. — "Go among the enemies of the gospel, and you shall see the woman either reduced to abject slavery, or basely flattered for the vilest of purposes: but in Christian families, you see her trusted with honor and respect; as a friend, as naturally an equal, a soother of man's cares, a softener of his grief, and a partner of his joys."'

nah sought to reform fashionable society by showing the folly of its worldly pleasures in works such as *Manners of the Great* and *Estimate of the Religion of the Fashionable World.* Hannah also focused her reforming efforts on the lower classes. She began a number of schools for the poor in her own neighborhood, raising money for them and directing them. These Sunday Schools taught basic reading and instructed the students in the Christian faith. When Hannah first began distributing Bibles and establishing Sunday Schools in the Vale of Cheddar, farmers opposed education, thinking that education and learning to read would take away their agricultural workers. In time, however, the district was morally transformed by Hannah's efforts. Discovering that thirteen neighboring parishes did not have a resident minister, Hannah established nine schools in the area to remedy this lack of Christian education.

Hannah's writing, by extolling Christian morality, was a politically stabilizing influence on the lower classes. *Village Politics, by Will Chip a Country Carpenter* ably exposed the foolishness of revolutionary ideas then popular in France and gaining attention in England. The British government purchased thousands of copies for distribution, and the work was translated into French and Italian. Hannah also published a series of tracts focusing on the virtues of contentment, sobriety, humility, hard work, and the importance of trusting God. Her Christian and moral works were best-sellers in both England and America.

In 1799 Hannah published *Strictures on the Modern System of Female Education*, which went through twenty editions in just a few years.[22] In her work Hannah emphasized the importance of Christian instruction in education. Women owed their elevation in society to Christianity, whose principles exalted the soul as well as the mind. Only Christianity taught the ultimate laws of morals which were the foundation for true and desirable knowledge. Hannah did not separate education and religion, but believed that every pursuit or object of study should be subject to the moral laws of Christianity. She believed a woman properly educated in a Christian manner could be a woman of influence. Women should not become rivals with men for power, but should cooperate with them in the moral reform of society.

In Hannah's outline of a suitable course of instruction for young ladies, she inveighed against women being preoccupied with external appearance and frivolity. External beauty soon fades and is lost; females should receive an education which went beyond the fleeting and temporal. Girls should only read what is of lasting value, not books which were frivolous or contained only a superficial knowledge. Hannah had contempt for English sentimentality, French philosophy, German mysticism and Italian poetry. Imagination should never be cultivated to the neglect of judgment. History was the most improving of all studies, because it revealed the ways of providence and enlarged the mind. The last three chapters of her work were especially devoted to the importance of Christianity. She noted that a worldly spirit was incompatible with the spirit of Christianity. She briefly covered the leading doctrines of Christianity, showing how an understanding of human nature's corruption, the doctrine of redemption, and the necessity for a changed heart produced by divine influence were important in producing a truly Christian character. She concluded by providing instructions on the duty and efficacy of prayer.

Hannah More's moral and evangelical writings and works exemplified the best in the movement known as the Wesleyan revival in England. Her religious tracts and the establishment of Sunday Schools contributed to the development of literacy and Christian knowledge. Her works dealing with the education of the young, especially women, indicated the importance of Christian teaching as the very foundation of education and learning. Her bestowal of thousands of pounds of money she had earned from her

---

22 Hannah More's *Strictures on Female Education* can be found at http://books.google.com/boo ks?hl=en&id=WaQWAAAAIAAJ&dq=Strictures+on+the+Modern+System+of+Female +Education&printsec=frontcover&source=web&ots=06UcT_1cUi&sig=RGULChgARP rKdJDatS1FZI4F0AU&sa=X&oi=book_result&resnum=1&ct=result .

writings on charities for the poor showed the importance she placed on Christians caring for their neighbors.

The Great Awakening in America

The religious revival in eighteenth-century England had its counterpart across the Atlantic, and there were important transatlantic connections to the revival. When Jonathan Edwards became pastor in Northampton, Massachusetts, in the 1730s, he found a spiritually dead Church. The ardor of the earliest Puritans had cooled, and their descendants a century later were more concerned with increasing wealth and comfortable living than with furthering the Kingdom of God. A spiritual malaise had set in. Edwards began preaching a series of sermons on justification by faith, and within a few months the Spirit of God brought hundreds to faith in Christ. Edwards wrote a number of works giving his thoughts on the revival. *Narratives of Surprising Conversions* described the revival and its effects on the life of the town of Northampton. *Treatise Concerning Religious Affections* showed that true religion must affect the heart, not consist merely in the outward observance of religious forms. *Distinguishing Marks of the Spirit of God* carefully examined 1 John 4 to see what the evidences of a true revival and work of the Spirit of God would be. These works were read on both sides of the Atlantic and stimulated ministers and others to begin praying and looking for a revival.

George Whitefield first began preaching in the open-air fields of England, encouraging John Wesley and others to take the gospel to the people beyond the walls of the church buildings. His ministry in America was even more far-reaching. Making seven evangelistic trips to America between 1738 and 1770, Whitefield preached over 18,000 sermons in America alone. He was the most well-traveled as well as the most well-known man in the colonies, drawing large crowds wherever he spoke. The people were ready for a personal religion, distinct from the cold formalism of the churches.

When Whitefield preached in New England, Jonathan Edwards' wife Sarah wrote,

> It is wonderful to see what a spell he casts over an audience by proclaiming the simplest truths of the Bible. I have seen upward of a thousand people hang on his words with breathless silence, broken only by an occasional half-suppressed sob. He impresses the ignorant, and not less the educated and refined . . . our mechanics shut up their shops, and the day-labourers throw down their tools to go and hear him preach, and few return unaffected. . . . Many, very many persons in Northampton date the beginning of new thoughts, new desires, new purposes and a new life, from the day they heard him preach of Christ.[23]

---

23   Arnold Dallimore. *GeorgeWhitefield*. Crossway Books, 1990.

Sarah Edwards was not only impressed with Whitefield, but Whitefield was impressed with Mrs. Edwards. Whitefield stayed with the Edwards during his travels and later wrote

> A sweeter Couple I have not yet seen... She ... talked feelingly and solidly of the Things of God, and seemed to be such a Help meet for her Husband that she caused me to ...[pray] God, that he would be pleased to send me a Daughter of Abraham to be my wife.[24]

Whitefield made a point to find a wife to marry as soon as he returned to England.

Sarah Edwards (1710-1758) was the daughter of James Pierpont, minister of the church at New Haven, Connecticut, for thirty years and one of the founders of Yale. Sarah was nine when Jonathan Edwards first attended Yale and her father's church. Soon after Edwards graduated from Yale, when he was twenty and Sarah was thirteen, Edwards gave Sarah a book in which he wrote:

> They say there is a young lady in [New Haven] who is beloved of that Great Being, who made and rules the world, and that there are certain seasons in which this Great Being, in some way or another invisible, comes to her and fills her mind with exceeding sweet delight, and that she hardly cares for anything except to meditate on him — that she expects after a while to be received up where he is, to be raised out of the world and caught up into heaven; being assured that he loves her too well to let her remain at a distance from him always. There she is to dwell with him, and to be ravished with his love, favor, and delight forever. Therefore, if you present all the world before her, with the richest of its treasures, she disregards it and cares not for it, and is unmindful of any pain or affliction. She has a strange sweetness in her mind, and singular purity in her affections; is most just and praiseworthy in all her actions; and you could not persuade her to do anything thought wrong or sinful, if you would give her all the world, lest she should offend this great Being. She is of a wonderful sweetness, calmness and universal benevolence of mind, especially after those times in which this great God has manifested himself to her mind. She will sometimes go about, singing sweetly, from place to [place]; and seems to be always full of joy and pleasure; and no one knows for what. She loves to be alone, and to wander in the fields and on the mountains, and seems to have someone invisible always conversing with her.[25]

Edwards courted Sarah for four years; they were engaged in 1725 and married in 1727. Five months before their marriage, Jonathan was ordained as assistant minister to his grandfather Solomon Stoddard in

24   Elisabeth D. Dodds. *Marriage to a Difficult Man: The Uncommon Union of Jonathan and Sarah Edwards*. Laurel, MI: Audobon Press, 2003, p. 74.

25   George Marsden. *Jonathan Edwards*. New Haven and London: Yale University Press, 2003, p. 93.

Northampton, Massachusetts. In Northampton the young couple were provided with an ample house, a large garden plot of ten acres, and fields outside the village for raising sheep, pigs, and cows. Sarah was the perfect match for Jonathan. She managed all the affairs of the house, fields, and cottage industries and provided a home of calm and stability for his studies and work. Edwards' friend and first biographer, Samuel Hopkins, wrote

> It was a happy circumstance that he could trust everything ... to the care of Mrs. Edwards with entire safety and with undoubting confidence. She was a most judicious and faithful mistress of a family, habitually industrious, a sound economist, managing her household affairs with diligence and discretion.
>
> While she uniformly paid a becoming deference to her husband and treated him with entire respect, she spared no pains in conforming to his inclination and rendering everything in the family agreeable and pleasant; accounting it her greatest glory and there wherein she could best serve God and her generation, to be the means in this way of promoting his usefulness and happiness ...
>
> And no person of discernment could be conversant in the family without observing and admiring the perfect harmony and mutual love and esteem that subsisted between them.[26]

Sarah and Jonathan had eleven children. That all of them survived childhood was itself a testimony to the Edwards' well-regulated household. Edwards believed the family was a place to better learn the love of God and that 'the whole world of mankind are chiefly kept in action from day to day ... by love.' He wrote that

> Every family ought to be...a little church, consecrated to Christ and wholly influenced and governed by His rules. And family education and order are some of the chief means of grace. If these fail, all other means are like to be ineffectual.[27]

All the children were taught obedience at the earliest age, with Jonathan taking the lead in establishing parental authority. A rebellious will and stubbornness were subdued early, with calmness and firmness. Once submission was firmly established in the child, then a sweet obedience followed in later years which Sarah especially reinforced. Samuel Hopkins, a student of Edwards who spent several months with the family, praised the Edwards' well-behaved children and Sarah's mothering skills:

> She had an excellent way of governing her children; she knew how to make them regard and obey her cheerfully, without loud angry words, much less heavy blows. She seldom punished them: and in speaking to them, used gentle and pleasant words. If any correction was necessary,

---

26   *Marriage to a Difficult Man*, pp. 29-30.

27   Ibid., p. 45.

she did not administer it in a passion; and when she had occasion to
reprove and rebuke she would do it in a few words, without warmth and
noise … In her directions in matters of importance, she would address
herself to the reason of her children, that they might not only know her
… will, but at the same time be convinced of the reasonableness of it.
She had need to speak but once; she was cheerfully obeyed; murmuring
and answering again were not known among them.

In their manners they were uncommonly respectful to their parents.
When their parents came into the room they all rose instinctively from their
seats and never resumed them until their parents were seated; and when
either parent was speaking … they were all immediately silent and attentive.
The kind and gentle treatment they received from their mother, while she
strictly and punctiliously maintained her parental authority, seemed naturally
to … promote a filial respect and affection, and to lead them to a mild tender
treatment of each other. Quarrelling and contention, which too frequently
take place among children, were in her family unknown….

Her system of discipline was begun at a very early age and it was her
rule to resist the first, as well as every subsequent exhibition of temper
or disobedience in the child…wisely reflecting that until a child will
obey his parents he can never be brought to obey God.[28]

The Edwardses had devotions at each meal. During the morning devotions,
Jonathan quizzed the children with spiritual questions, on a level each child
could understand. On Saturday evenings, he instructed the children in the
Westminster catechism, which each child memorized. Sarah's management
of the household allowed Jonathan to spend thirteen hours a day in his study.
At 4 p.m. he would come from his study, and Sarah and he would go riding
or walking together. Other times throughout the day, Sarah joined Jonathan
in the study for conversation. Their union was one of soul as well as body,
and Jonathan and Sarah could confide their deepest thoughts with each other.

Sarah, as did Jonathan, had bouts of melancholy and depression, which
she was able to overcome by her trust in God. In 1742, for two weeks, she
experienced a spiritual ecstasy which at times was physically overwhelming.
She was rational throughout this time and able to go about her duties (which
were many, considering there were then seven children, servants, and guests in
the house!), but she was overcome by joy and full of praise to God. Jonathan
was away at the time on a preaching tour, but when he returned she was able to
describe everything to him. He wrote up and published her experience (with
her name and personally identifying references removed) as *Some Thoughts
Concerning the Present Revival of Religion*. Sarah's experience was an example that
physical effects could accompany a mature expression of spiritual revival and
renewal. Before this experience, Sarah had too highly regarded the opinion
of others and her own reputation. She had also been too solicitous for her
husband's high esteem and kindnesses. When she felt 'entirely swallowed up
in God,' she realized that these were petty concerns. By submitting her will

entirely to God's, she became weaned from this present world and absorbed by God's own wondrous love. All the cares of the world she could submit to Him. The more she submitted herself to God, the freer she became of earthly cares, and the more joyous her feeling of her acceptance with God.[29]

Sarah shared the hardships with her husband. After 23 years in Northampton, the congregation voted to remove Jonathan Edwards as pastor. Offered numerous positions elsewhere in America and abroad, Edwards chose to settle in the missionary outpost of Stockbridge, ministering to the Native Americans. Five years later Edwards was offered the presidency of the College of New Jersey at Princeton. The previous president, Aaron Burr, Sr., had married the Edwards' daughter Esther. He became ill and died at the age of forty-one. Esther was left alone with two small children. After the funeral, Esther wrote her mother, 'God has seemed sensibly near … I think God has given me such a sense of the vanity of the world, and uncertainty of all sublunary enjoyments, as I never had before. The world vanishes out of my sight! Heavenly and eternal things appear much more real and important, than ever before.'[30]

When Jonathan Edwards finally accepted the post of president of the College, he stayed with his daughter Esther. Smallpox was rampant, and Jonathan decided to submit to the new process of inoculation, persuading Esther to be inoculated with her two children at the same time. Though Esther and the children recovered from the inoculation, a secondary fever afflicted Jonathan. When he realized he was facing death, he called his daughter Lucy to his side, who wrote down his last requests:

> Dear Lucy, it seems to me to be the will of God that I must shortly leave you; therefore give my kindest love to my dear wife, and tell her, that the uncommon union, which has so long subsisted between us, has been of such a nature, as I trust is spiritual, and therefore will continue forever: and I hope she will be supported under so great a trial, and submit cheerfully to the will of God. And as to my children, you are now like to be left fatherless, which I hope will be an inducement to you all to seek a Father, who will never fail you.[31]

Sarah herself was ill at the time in Stockbridge, but wrote Esther:

> O My Very Dear Child,
>   What shall I say? A holy and good God has covered us with a dark cloud. Oh that we may kiss the rod, and lay our hands on our mouths! The Lord has done it. He has made me adore his goodness, that we had him so long. But my God lives; and he has my heart. Oh what a legacy my husband, and your father has left us! We are all given to God: and there I am, and love to be.[32]

---

29   *Jonathan Edwards*, pp. 240-7.

30   Ibid., pp. 428-9.

31   *Jonathan Edwards*, p. 494.

32   Ibid., p. 495.

Esther never received her mother's letter. She contracted a fever and died less than two weeks after her father. Sarah decided she should raise the two orphaned children of Esther and Aaron Burr. On her way to Princeton to pick up the children, while staying in Philadelphia, Sarah was afflicted with dysentery and died, October 2, 1758. Within a year, the Edwards family had suddenly lost four members.

The 'uncommon union' of Sarah and Jonathan Edwards was indeed a spiritual one as well as physical. The writings of Jonathan Edwards continue to influence Christians today; the descendants of Sarah and Jonathan's eleven children have been influential as well. By 1900, this single marriage produced 13 college presidents, 65 professors, 100 lawyers, a dean of a law school, 30 judges, 66 physicians and a dean of a medical school. Also by 1900, Sarah and Jonathan Edwards' descendants included 80 holders of public office, including three U.S. Senators, mayors of three large cities, governors of three states, a Vice-President of the United States, and a controller of the United States Treasury. Members of the family wrote 135 books, ranging from *Five Years in an English University* to *Butterflies of North America*. They edited 18 journals and periodicals. Many were ministers and 100 missionaries went overseas; others became members of mission boards. Still others were directors of banks or owners of large business corporations.

The evangelical preaching of the colonial revivals affected women of all classes throughout the thirteen English colonies in America. When she was about seven years old, Phillis Wheatley (1753-1784) was brought from Africa to America and sold as a slave. John Wheatley of Boston purchased the little girl to be trained for domestic work. Phillis was an amiable and intelligent child, and a daughter in the family taught the little girl to read. Mrs. Wheatley allowed Phillis time to study, and she learned quickly. Phillis's intelligence was accompanied by an affectionate, meek and humble spirit. Clergymen and people of high society would come to visit this unusual African native. When she was sixteen, in 1770, Phillis joined the Old South Meeting House in Boston. When she became ill in 1773, the Wheatleys sent Phillis to England for her health, accompanied by the Wheatleys' son. In England she met Lord Dartmouth, Secretary of the Colonies, and the Countess of Huntingdon. While in England, a book of her poems, originally written for herself and her family, was published. When the poems became a great success, the Wheatleys gave Phillis her freedom. She continued to live with the family until Mr. & Mrs. Wheatley's death. She then married a free black grocer and had three children, but two of the children died early and her husband left her. Phillis fell into poverty, unable to care for herself or her remaining child. She was working on a second book of poetry when she died at the age of 31, her child dying soon after. Phillis' poems continue to express the beauty of soul and Christian faith of America's first published black poet.[33]

The evangelicalism which arose from the revivals of the eighteenth century, with its emphasis on the need for personal conversion to Christ, had the effect of giving women a spiritual freedom which did not always match their social standing or legal positions. Yet, whether slave or free, whether poor or from the wealthiest ranks, Christian women had an equality in Christ which enabled them to have a peace and joy. Many also used their freedom in Christ to serve others and to work for the improvement and betterment of their society. Women especially became leaders in the social reform movements in the following century.

Poems by Phillis Wheatley*

On Being Brought from Africa to America

'Twas mercy brought me from my pagan land,
Taught my benighted soul to understand
That there's a God – that there's a Saviour too;
Once I redemption neither sought nor knew.
Some view our sable race with scornful eye –
"Their color is a diabolic dye."
Remember, Christians, Negroes black as Cain
May be refined, and join the angelic train.

On the Death of the Rev. Mr. George Whitefield. – 1770

Hail, happy saint! On thine immortal throne,
Possest of glory, life, and bliss unknown:
We hear no more the music of thy tongue;
Thy wonted auditors cease to throng.
Thy sermons in unequalled accents flowed,
And ev'ry bosom with devotion glowed;
Thou didst, in strains of eloquence refined,
Inflame the heart, and captivate the mind.
Unhappy, we the setting sun deplore,
So glorious once, but ah! It shines no more.

    Behold the prophet in his towering flight!
He leaves the earth for heaven's unmeasured height,
And worlds unknown receive him from our sight.
There Whitefield wings with rapid course his way,
And sails to Zion through vast seas of day.

---

33   Phillis Wheatley's poems can be found at http://www.gutenberg.org/etext/409.

Thy prayers, great saint, and thine incessant cries,
Have pierced the bosom of thy native skies.
Thou, moon, hast seen, and all the stars of light,
How he has wrestled with his God by night.
He prayed that grace in ev'ry heart might dwell;
He longed to see America excel;
He charged its youth that ev'ry grace divine
Should with full luster in their conduct shine.
That Saviour, which his soul did first receive,
The greatest gift that ev'n a God can give,
He freely offered to the numerous throng,
That on his lips with list'ning pleasure hung.

'Take him, ye wretched for your only good,
'Take him, ye starving sinner, for your food;
'Ye thirsty, come to this life-giving stream,
'Ye preachers, take him for your joyful theme;
'Take him, my dear Americans,' he said,
'Be your complaints on his kind bosom laid:
'Take him, ye Africans, he longs for you;
'Impartial Saviour is his title due:
'Washed in the fountain of redeeming blood,
'You shall be sons, and kings, and priests to God.'

Great Countess,** we Americans revere
Thy name, and mingle in thy grief sincere;
New-England deeply feels, the orphans mourn***,
Their more than father will no more return.

But though arrested by the hand of death,
Whitefield no more exerts his lab'ring breath,
Yet let us view him in the eternal skies,
Let ev'ry heart to this bright vision rise;
While the tomb, safe, retains its sacred trust,
Til life divine reanimates his dust.

---

*Poems of Phillis Wheatley, a native African and a slave. Bedford, Massachusetts: Applewood Books, 1995 [revised edition of Memoir and poems of Phillis Wheatley, a native African and a slave, 1838], 12, pp. 16-18.

**The Countess of Huntingdon, to whom Mr. Whitefield was chaplain.

***Orphans from the Bethesda orphanage in Georgia which Mr. Whitefield established.

A Benevolent Society:
Abounding in the Work of the Lord
1 Corinthians 15:58

As the nineteenth century progressed, women's capacity to influence major societal changes increased dramatically, leading some to call it the 'Women's Century.' The frail woman of literature, given to fits of fainting or hysteria, was replaced by a stronger character who initiated moral improvement. At the beginning of the nineteenth century, married women throughout the English-speaking world had no legal rights. They could not hold property, had no legal right to money they earned, could not testify in court, and had no legal guardianship over their own children (In women's organizations, a single woman always held the position of treasurer. If a married woman held such a position, her husband might have a legal hold over the organization's funds!). In 1848, New York became the first state to allow property rights for married women. While work considered acceptable for women had been restricted to dressmaking, elementary education, or writing books, the nineteenth century saw a limited acceptance of women into some professional fields, such as nursing and medicine. Women's opportunity for education expanded as women's colleges were established. Women established numerous religious and social organizations to improve and reform society. The active participation of many women in the movement to abolish slavery seemed naturally to lead them into the movement for more women's rights.

Nineteenth-century women organized a plethora of societies, which historians have divided into three basic categories – benevolence, reform, and feminist. Benevolent groups grew most directly out of the revival movements. Women organized benevolent societies to bring the message of Christ to the urban poor as well as to ameliorate social ills. These groups offered both physical and spiritual aid to the poor and needy. Working in Christian benevolent organizations was an acceptable public activity for Christian women for whom family responsibilities were still paramount. In the 1830s, reform organizations arose to eradicate social evils, such as slavery, alcoholism, or prostitution, rather than minister to individuals suffering from such evils. The reform organizations most often were involved in the political process, seeking laws to stamp out a particular evil. Women became involved in petition drives, public rallies, and public speaking, activities many saw as improper for women. By the middle of the century, organizations were formed specifically devoted to expanding women's rights. Though some historians claimed that the benevolent societies were training grounds for later feminist movements, evidence seems to indicate that those in benevolent societies did not enter the feminist camp. For some, however, working in the reform movements was a stimulus to later feminist activities.

Prison Reform and Nursing

One woman who saw a moral evil which cried out for remedy, and devoted her time, energy and resources to correct that evil, as well as rallying others to remedy the problem, was Elizabeth Gurney Fry (1780-1845). Elizabeth was from the prominent Barclay banking family in England. Her mother was a devout Quaker vigorously engaged in charity work and helping the poor in her neighborhood. Elizabeth's mother died when Elizabeth was twelve, and Elizabeth found herself largely responsible for caring for her younger brothers and sisters. At eighteen, Elizabeth herself became a Quaker and dedicated her life to Christ. She became actively involved in helping the poor, collecting clothes for those in need and visiting the sick. She set up a Sunday School to teach the local children to read, and soon eighty children were attending her school.

When she was twenty, Elizabeth married Joseph Fry, a fellow Quaker and a wealthy tea merchant. The couple eventually had eleven children. Elizabeth combined her care for the poor with her

---

Teenage Inspiration for the British and Foreign Bible Society

Mary Jones (1784-1864) was from a poor but devout family in Wales. When she was eight years old she professed faith in Christ. Welsh Bibles were scarce, and the nearest one to Mary was at a cottage two miles away. Mary greatly desired to have a Bible of her own. She worked and saved money for six years before she thought she had enough money for a Bible. The nearest bookseller was twenty-five miles away. In 1800, when she was sixteen, Mary walked the twenty-five miles to Bala, much of the time barefoot to save her shoes. When she came to Rev. Thomas Charles, Rev. Charles said there was only one Bible left, and it was promised to another. Hearing Mary's story, however, Rev. Charles sold Mary the Bible, knowing the other customer could wait. Rev. Charles was so moved by Mary's desire for a Bible that he proposed to the Council of the Religious Tract Society that it form a society to provide Bibles in Wales. This was the beginning of the British and Foreign Bible Society, established in 1804.

responsibilities as a wife and mother. She became a preacher for the Society of Friends and attended the opening meeting of the British and Foreign Bible Society. In 1813, a friend of the Fry family visited Newgate Prison and was shocked by the condition and suffering of the prisoners, especially the women. When he described the scene to the Frys, Elizabeth decided she must visit the prison herself.

In Newgate Prison, Elizabeth found three hundred women and their children in four rooms built for holding half that number. The women were clothed in rags; babies born in prison lived in nakedness and squalor. Bullies ran the prison, and there was no order or discipline. All eating, sleeping, and bodily functions were performed in the same cramped rooms. Women in prison for petty crimes were in the same rooms as women convicted of murder. Appalled, Elizabeth quickly worked to reform prison conditions for females. Using her own funds as well as donations, she gathered clothes and supplies and formed committees. She formed classes in knitting and sewing, encouraging the women to become productive. By selling her handiwork, a prisoner could buy soap and more food for herself. Elizabeth organized instructional classes so that those more educated could teach the less educated prisoners. Daily, Elizabeth came and read from the Bible to the women. She encouraged the appointment of matrons rather than male jailers to oversee the women prisoners and encouraged the prisoners to develop rules for their community, which they themselves then voted on and approved.

In 1816, Elizabeth Fry founded the Association for the Improvement of the Female Prisoners of Newgate, 'to provide for the clothing, instruction, and employment of the women; to introduce them to a knowledge of the Holy Scriptures, and to form in them as much as possible those habits of sobriety, order, and industry, which may render them docile and peaceable while in prison, and respectable when they leave it.'[1] In 1818, she described conditions at Newgate before the House of Commons Committee on London prisons and recommended a series of changes in the prison system. Elizabeth traveled throughout England and Scotland examining the prison conditions with her brother, Joseph Gurney. Gurney published a report of their findings in *Prisons in Scotland and the North of England*. Many of the prison reforms Elizabeth Fry worked for were incorporated into the 1823 Prison Reform Act.

Though prison reform was Elizabeth Fry's primary concern, her interests in helping and improving the life of others extended to other causes as well. At that time in England, the death penalty was applicable for over 200 offenses, including theft and forgery. Elizabeth sought unsuccessfully to have death sentences lessened in a number of individual cases. When ships of convicts were

---

1   Mrs. E.R. Pitman. *Elizabeth Fry*. Boston: Roberts Brothers, 1884. Available as an ebook at www.gutenberg.org/ebooks/16606 (2005-08-27).

deported to Australia or other British colonies, Elizabeth visited the ships before they sailed, making certain the women had cloth and thread so they could make articles on the long voyage which they could sell when they arrived. Elizabeth also established a visitation society in Brighton to regularly visit the poor to determine how best to help them. This society was replicated in numerous villages throughout England. Concerned about the quality of nursing, in 1840 Elizabeth Fry established a training school for nurses in London. Fry nurses were expected to attend to the spiritual as well as the physical needs of their patients.

In all her work in prisons and elsewhere, Elizabeth Fry realized that the amelioration of physical needs was incomplete help to the individual if the spiritual needs were not met as well. Only by providing the prisoners with the truths of the Scripture was a real reformation of prisoners possible, for only the Scriptures could amend and change the human heart. Elizabeth not only brought the truths of the Scripture to the poor, the needy, and to prisoners, but she challenged others to serve Christ in helping the less fortunate. Because of the great love Christ has shown us, we should do much for Him. As Elizabeth exhorted in one address:

> Indeed, it is well for us, my friends, to inquire, 'What owest thou unto thy Lord?' Ah, dear friends, is it not well for us to do this when we reflect on what he hath done for us, even He who was wounded for our transgressions, who was bruised for our iniquities; the chastisement of our peace, we may remember, was on him, and by his stripes we are healed.[2]

Nurses from Elizabeth Fry's training school were among the thirty-eight nurses Florence Nightingale took with her to Turkey in 1854. Florence Nightingale's work there among soldiers wounded during the Crimean War established her reputation in nursing reform, but Florence's dedication to nursing began eighteen years before, in 1836.

Florence Nightingale (1820-1910), the daughter of wealthy English landowners, was named after the city of her birth, Florence, Italy. Her father took personal responsibility for the education of his two daughters, and Florence learned Greek, Latin, French, German, Italian, history, philosophy and mathematics. When she was fifteen or sixteen, Florence was converted to faith in Christ through the reading of *The Cornerstone* by Jacob Abbott, an American Congregational minister and educator who wrote numerous books for children. Central to *The Cornerstone's* theme was that Jesus Himself was the foundation and cornerstone of salvation. Abbott stated that his purpose was to explain the elementary principles of 'the gospel of Christ...for a human soul hungering and thirsting after righteousness.' Florence was particularly moved by Abbott's descriptive

---

2   *Sermons Preached by Members of the Society of Friends.* London: Hamilton, Adams, and Co., 1832, p. 28, available at http://www.qhpress.org/quakerpages/qhoa/fryserm.html.

reflections on Jesus' crucifixion. Abbott showed that all of the characters at the crucifixion, including the Pharisees, Peter, and Judas, had their followers and imitators in Florence's own day. Florence later made a detailed chronology of Jesus' last days and made it available to friends and family who requested it.

Florence also read Abbott's *The Way to Do Good, or the Christian Character Mature,* which developed the practical life built on repentance:[3]

> Upon the cornerstone of faith in Jesus Christ, as the atoning sacrifice for sin, there is reared the superstructure of holy life and action; and a holy life is one which, from the impulse of love to God, is occupied with doing good to man.

Sisters of Charity and St. Elizabeth Ann Seton

In 1617, Vincent de Paul organized an association of women in a small French parish to care for the sick and poor. The organization spread, relocated its headquarters to Paris, and had the rule established by Vincent de Paul confirmed by Pope Clement IX in 1668. By the end of the eighteenth century, the order had 500 houses, primarily in France and Poland. Sisters of Charity did not isolate themselves in convents, but ministered in the homes of the sick and in hospitals. Their vows of poverty, chastity, obedience and service to the poor were taken annually. Under the Sisters of Charity, nursing became a skill, and principles of nursing Florence Nightingale developed were significantly influenced by the Sisters of Charity she met in Egypt.

In 1809, Elizabeth Ann Seton (1774-1821) established an order of the Sisters of Charity in the United States, the first sisterhood native to the United States. From a prominent New York family, Elizabeth had a lifelong concern for the poor and helpless. She worked with Isabella Graham in founding The Society for the Relief of Poor Widows with Small Children (1797) and regularly nursed the sick and dying among her own family, as well as friends and needy neighbors. After a trip to Italy and the death of her husband, Elizabeth converted to Roman Catholicism. Though her husband's death left her with five young children to care for alone, Elizabeth continued her work in educating and caring for the poor, establishing numerous schools and institutions. In 1814, she sent Sisters of Charity to Philadelphia, where they managed Saint Joseph's Asylum, the first Catholic orphanage in the United States. At the time of her death, there were over twenty communities of Sisters of Charity in the United States, overseeing free schools, orphanages, boarding schools, and hospitals. In 1975, Elizabeth Seton became the first American canonized by the Catholic Church.

The first chapter, in this narrative of the boy Alonzo, showed that the Christian has no hope in his own works, but only in the undeserved mercy of Christ. Yet, because of Christ's mercy, the Christian seeks to do good to others. The personal happiness of the Christian consisted in cooperating

---

3   Both Jacob Abbott's *The Cornerstone* (1834) and *The Way to Do Good* (1836) are available at http:// books.google.com.

234 | Feminine Threads

with God in extending a reign of holiness among men, beginning with one's own life. Florence was also influenced by principles of personal piety, working among the poor, Church relationships, and ministering among the sick which Abbott incorporated in his story.

The year after her conversion, on February 7, 1837, Florence perceived a distinct call to serve God. Later, as she cared for the sick in her own family and on her family's estate, Florence felt that her calling was to nursing. Such a call was not at all pleasing to Florence's parents, whose skeptical Unitarian beliefs did not accord with Florence's Christian faith. Nursing was suitable for working-class women but not for women of the Nightingales' social standing. Florence was expected to marry an eligible gentleman and take her proper position in society. Yet, Florence rejected several suitors, including Lord Houghton. She was called to the moral purpose of nursing and could not be satisfied by society and domesticity. Florence's own health suffered as she struggled to maintain her sense of God's calling in the face of her family's opposition.

When family friends planned a trip to Egypt in 1849-50, they invited Florence to accompany them. She hoped the trip would improve her health. She also found her conviction of God's purpose in her life solidifying as she viewed the ancient wonders of Egypt. Florence paid several visits to the schools and hospitals of the Sisters of St. Vincent de Paul in Cairo, where she admired the discipline and organization of the sisters in the work of caring for the young and poor. The Sisters of Charity, founded by Vincent de Paul in France in the seventeenth century, were an example to Florence of both the spiritual and physical care women nurses and teachers could provide.

Kaiserwerth's Influence

The Kaiserwerth training program for nurses was a three-year program. Upon completion, the women took vows of service for five years. Frequently, they continued their service for a lifetime.

In 1849, Theodor Fliedner went to Pennsylvania and brought four deaconesses to work in the Pittsburgh Infirmary, the first Protestant church hospital in the United States. This was the origin of the American Lutheran Deaconesses Foundation, established to 'serve God's people through spiritual care and works of mercy.' The work of the Lutheran deaconesses included nursing, social work, parish ministry, chaplaincy, and counseling.

By the time of Fliedner's death in 1864, 30 mother-houses had been established, and 1600 deaconesses had been trained. One of these was Florence Nightingale.

On the way home from Egypt, Florence visited Kaiserwerth, Germany, where she studied at the Institute of Kaiserwerth Deaconesses. The following year Florence anonymously published her first work, *The Institution of Kaiserwerth on the Rhine, for the Practical Training of Deaconesses.* In many ways, Florence's visit to Kaiserwerth was an important turning point in her life. This hospital and school to train nurses had been established by Theodor Fliedner some fifteen years earlier. Fliedner was a Lutheran pastor who observed the work of deaconesses while visiting Mennonite communities in Holland. Kaiserwerth was affected by the devastation and misery following the Napoleonic wars, and Fliedner thought that an organization of deaconesses could provide spiritual and physical help to the suffering. He raised funds and purchased the largest house in Kaiserwerth to establish a hospital and a school to train nurses. Before this time, nurses were often considered unseemly women and were indeed sometimes prostitutes and alcoholics. Fliedner restored the role of deaconesses to much of what they had been in the early Church. The deaconesses were trained and encouraged in the fourfold tasks of nursing, relief of the poor, care for children, and work among unfortunate women.

Florence's father finally relented in his opposition to his daughter's calling to nursing, resigned himself to her not marrying, and settled an annual stipend of £500 (roughly $50,000 in present dollars) upon her. Florence could then freely pursue her career. In 1853, Florence became resident superintendent of the Institute for the Care of Sick Gentlewomen in Upper Harley Street, London. In the same year, Russia invaded Turkey and the Crimean War began. France and Britain sent soldiers to aid Turkey in the fight. Large numbers of British soldiers at the front soon succumbed to cholera and malaria. Florence volunteered to go to the war zone as a nurse. Though the government at first resisted her offer, it finally gave its permission. Florence organized a group of thirty-eight nurses and went to Turkey. In addition to nurses from the teaching school established earlier by Elizabeth Fry, many of the nurses were from the Sisters of Mercy at Bermondsey, a convent established in 1839 (the first convent established in England since the Reformation).

Florence found the conditions at the hospital in Scutari horrific. During her first winter there, 4,077 soldiers died. With ventilation poor and a defective sewer system, many of the deaths were caused by poor living conditions. Death rates sharply declined when sanitation conditions improved. The editor of *The Times* drew attention to the poor treatment of the soldiers and focused attention on Florence Nightingale's efforts to better the soldiers' treatment. Florence kept careful statistics of diseases and health conditions, providing evidence to the Government for improving Army hospitals. When she returned to England in 1856, she began a campaign to improve nursing in military hospitals. Her published *Notes on Hospitals* and *Notes on Nursing* gained public support for her reforms. In 1860, she founded the Nightingale School & Home for Nurses at St. Thomas' Hospital; many of the school's students established other nursing schools throughout Britain and the world. Florence is often recognized as the founder of the modern nursing profession. She demonstrated that nursing was an honorable profession for women and set an example of thoughtful hospital administration blended with compassionate patient care.

Nursing was a calling Florence received from God, and she saw her work as a service to God. That Christ identified Himself with the poor and weak of society was always an example to her:

> I don't think any words have had a fuller possession of my mind through life than Christ's putting himself in the place of the sick, the infirm, the prisoner – and the extension which the Roman Catholic Church (especially) gave to these words, as it were *God* putting Himself in the place of the leper, the cripple and so forth, telling us that we see Him in them. Because it is so true.

In her Bible Florence commented on 1 John 4:10-11 ('In this is love, not that we have loved God, but that he loved us and sent his Son to be the propitiation for our sins. Beloved, if God so loved us, we also ought to love one another.'):

> We love him, because he first loved us. What we ordinarily want is a belief of God's love to us. We do not realize to ourselves all that Christ's death shows us of God's love; we do not believe that our own single individual soul is and ever has been the direct object of the infinite love of the most high God. It is hard, both because of our own *littleness*, and because of our own *hardness*. But, if this belief once takes possession of our hearts, then are we redeemed indeed.

In responding to God's call, Florence saw herself as God's servant. She once told her father:

> Nay, it strikes me that all truth lies between these two: man saying to God, as Samuel did, Lord, here am I, and God saying to man as Christ did, in the storm, Lo it is I, be not afraid. And neither is complete without the other. God says to man in suffering in misery, in degradation, in anxiety, in imbecility, in loss of the bitterest kind, in sin, most of all in sin, Lo, it is I, be not afraid. This is the eternal passion of God. And man must say to him, Lord here am I to work at all these things. ... The Bible puts into four words of one syllable what whole sermons cannot say so well. The whole of religion is in God's Lo, it is I, and man's Here am I, Lord.[4]

Sunday Schools and Education

One of the earliest organizers of benevolent societies for women was Isabella Marshall Graham (1742-1814). Isabella's early Christian training had been in the Presbyterian congregation in Paisley, Scotland, pastored

---

4   Quotes from Florence Nightingale are taken from Lynn McDonald, 'Florence Nightingale: Faith and Work,' keynote address for the 7th Annual Conference of the Canadian Association for Parish Nursing Ministry, Toronto, May 27, 2005, http://www.uoguelph.ca/~cwfn/spirituality/faith.html.

by John Witherspoon. She married a British Army surgeon and spent some time in America before her husband's death in 1772. At her husband's death, Isabella had three daughters under the age of five and was pregnant with a son, who was born shortly after his father's death. Isabella returned to her native Scotland and supported herself by teaching and administering a large boarding school in Edinburgh. Dr. Witherspoon, who had come to America to become president of the College of New Jersey (Princeton) and was a signer of the Declaration of Independence, encouraged Isabella to move to the United States. She moved to New York City, where she established a school for young women. In the ensuing years, Isabella founded and supported several benevolent societies in New York – the Society for the Relief of Poor Widows with Small Children (1797), the Orphan Asylum Society (1806), the Magdalene Society (1811) for the mentally ill, and the Society for the Promotion of Industry among the Poor (1814).

Isabella's second daughter, Joanna, was born in Fort Niagra, New York, but grew up in Scotland. Joanna Graham (1770-1860) came to America with her mother in 1789 and worked with Isabella on several of her benevolent projects. When Isabella learned of the Edinburgh Gratis Sabbath School, she and Joanna began a class to teach poor adults to read. Joanna married Divie Bethune, a Scottish immigrant with an import-export business in New York City. He liberally supported the Christian benevolent works of Isabella and Joanna. On a business trip to England in 1802, the Bethunes learned more about Sabbath or Sunday Schools.

In their inception, Sunday Schools were principally for children in the lowest elements of society. They provided rudiments of education for children who were not given an education or spiritual instruction in their homes. Often these were children who worked in factories six days a week, and Sunday was the only day the children were able to go to school. Robert Raikes, who began the Sunday School movement in England in the 1780s, began with four women who held weekly Bible classes for children.

After the Bethunes returned to America, Joanna and her mother began a Sunday School in New York and encouraged other women to begin similar schools. The Bethunes shared with acquaintances in New York and Philadelphia what they had learned about Sunday Schools in England. In 1804, a group of women from various denominations formed a society for the education of poor girls in Philadelphia. When they applied to the state for incorporation in 1808, the Superior Court had to decide whether or not women could make such an application. After due deliberation, the Court decreed that women were 'citizens of the commonwealth' and entitled to file such a request! The curriculum for the poor girls included reading, writing, sewing, Scripture memorization, hymns, and the catechism.

The clergy were at first opposed to Sabbath schools for numerous reasons. Many were appalled at the idea of lay people, especially women, teaching the Bible. Some ministers feared the Sunday Schools would undermine their own teaching ministry. Some thought it was breaking the Sabbath to study or teach on Sunday. Others thought Sabbath schools usurped the rights of parents and local churches. Sabbath schools were not a part of the local church and often involved women of various denominations working together. Some held such interdenominational cooperation was dangerous or that church buildings should not be used for the general education of non-members. The very fact that the initiative was undertaken by women caused alarm in some quarters. When Mrs. Ann Rhees wanted to start a school at the First Baptist Church in Philadelphia in 1815, the pastor had little faith in the project but permitted it, saying, 'Well, my sisters, you can but try it; blossoms are sweet and beautiful, even if they produce no fruit.'[5] Deacons in Medway, Massachusetts feared that women would be in the pulpit next.

Though individual Sunday Schools were being established in many cities, Joanna felt the need for an organization to encourage Sunday Schools. Her husband told her, 'My dear wife, there is no use waiting for the men; do you gather a few ladies of different denominations and begin the work yourselves.'[6] Accordingly, on January 24, 1816, Joanna Bethune called a meeting in the lecture room of the Wall Street Church to organize a Female Sunday School Union. The pastor opened the meeting with prayer, then withdrew, leaving the room to the ladies. Joanna spoke of a 'great need of such an institution in a city where a number of one sex were training for the gallows and state prison and of the other for prostitution.' She read articles describing Raikes' Sunday School in England as a pattern to be followed. At the next meeting, a constitution was drawn up, with the purpose of the organization given: 'to stimulate and encourage those engaged in the education and religious instruction of the ignorant; to improve the methods of instruction; to promote the opening of new schools; to unite, in Christian love, persons of various denominations engaged in the same honourable employment.'[7] Board members included members of the Presbyterian, Methodist, Baptist, and Dutch Reformed denominations. By February, members were teaching 1000 people. By July, 250 women were teaching 3000 students. In six

5   Nancy Hardesty. *Great Women of Faith*. Nashville: Abingdon, 1980, p. 73.

6   *Great Women of Faith*, p. 71.

7   Ibid., p. 74.

years, there were 600 teachers in the city with about 7000 students, and 30 graduates were training for the ministry.

In 1817, Joanna Bethune was instrumental in establishing the American Sunday School Union, with an auxiliary female society. The American Sunday School Union, along with other educational, home mission, and Bible and tract societies, became important in evangelizing the nation as it expanded westward. On the frontier, women often organized and taught Sunday Schools even before churches were established. Over the years, Joanna launched programs concentrating on the evangelism of particular regions of the country – the 1830 Valley Campaign was to saturate the Mississippi Valley with the gospel. The 1834 Southern Enterprise focused on Maryland and the other southern states.

Isabella Graham and Joanna Bethune were examples of the tremendous influence women in the nineteenth century could have from their own personal initiative, even without having the right to vote or preach in the pulpits. This same power and influence could be seen in many of the benevolent enterprises in which women engaged, especially in the work of Mary Lyon.

Mary Lyon (1797-1849), a child of Puritan New England, grew up on a remote farm in western Massachusetts. Her father, who had fought in the American Revolution, died when she was five, leaving her mother to raise seven children while managing the 100-acre farm. Mary early learned the domestic skills necessary in that day – making butter and cheese, preserving fruits and vegetables, hearth cooking, making candles, washing clothes, spinning, weaving, and sewing clothes. She also was an eager student who learned quickly at the village schools, which she attended until she was thirteen. At seventeen she began to teach in the village schools, while seeking additional education for herself in various Massachusetts academies. One of the schools she attended was operated by Rev. Joseph Emerson, who 'talked to the ladies as if they had brains,' which apparently was a novel experience for Mary. From Emerson Mary learned that the joy of cultivating the intellect and acquiring knowledge was not enough. Knowledge should be acquired for its usefulness, and attention should be given to the heart as well as the mind. Mary began to see that the Christian faith encompassed and included everything, including history, science, and other categories of learning. Rev. Emerson found Mary Lyon superior to any other student he ever had, and he encouraged her to open a school of higher learning for women.

Mary Lyon was also heavily influenced by the thinking of Jonathan Edwards and his pupil Samuel Hopkins. From reading Edwards' *History of Redemption*, Mary gained an understanding of the broad scope of God's plan of redemption in man's history. That all of history was moving towards the coming Kingdom of God was a great incentive to evangelism. From Hopkins,

Mary absorbed the ideals of impartial benevolence, a habitual selflessness and devotion to the good of others. Hopkins and others claimed that it was in the area of disinterested benevolence that the American republic would succeed and the conversion of the world would be won or lost.

In 1837, Mary Lyon opened Mount Holyoke Female Seminary. The school today remains the oldest college for women in the United States. The school provided the best intellectual education available to young women at the time. In order for the school to be as affordable as possible, Mary planned for the students to do much of the maintenance work of the school – washing, cleaning, cooking. She carefully developed a disciplined way of living which incorporated healthy habits of diet and exercise.

Foundational to Mount Holyoke were the Christian principles which undergirded the school and its curriculum. Mary Lyon used every opportunity to cultivate a reverence for the Bible, demonstrating that history and natural science supported its truths. She used the beauty in the Bible to awaken the consciences of her pupils. Morning and evening Scripture reading was part of the daily routine, and three times a week Mary Lyon addressed the young ladies on important Biblical themes. She said she would not know how to guide the school without the history of God's dealings with His people:

> If we would learn of God let us read that history. If we would know ourselves, we shall find our hearts well portrayed there. More knowledge of human nature is to be derived from its study than from any other source.[8]

An early historian of Mount Holyoke listed some of the subjects of Mary Lyon's Biblically grounded teaching:

> the evangelical doctrines, the ten commandments in their order, the sermon on the mount, the book of Proverbs in course, the connection between the law and the gospel, and such specific topics as Consecration, Responsibility, Doing Good, Economy, Regulation of Desires, Cheerfulness, Health, Use of Time, Forgetfulness, etc.[9]

Mary regularly strove for the conversion of her students and the spiritual growth of those already converted. On Sabbath evenings she met with the unconverted, 'and led each to see from the Bible in her hand that if she should fail of fulfilling the highest end of her being, it would be not because she had broken the law of God, but because having broken it she

---

8   Sarah Stow. *History of Mount Holyoke Seminary, South Hadley, Mass. During its First Half Century, 1837-1887.* Springfield, Springfield Printing Company, 1887, p. 106, available at http://clio.fivecolleges.edu/mhc/stow/.

9   *History*, p. 106.

did not accept offered grace.'[10] With a tender passion she set before the young ladies the claims and invitation of Christ and their responsibility for acceptance or refusal. Once a week she also met with each Christian student, encouraging them in their Christian walk. Mary considered religious instruction the most important part of her work:

> None but God knows how the responsibility of giving religious instruction weighs on my heart. Sometimes in preparation, my soul sinks with trembling solicitude which finds no relief but in God. When I am through I can only pour out my heart in prayer that the Spirit may carry home the truth…Everything I do is such a privilege. It is so blessed, too, to depend hourly for light and strength and for success on our Heavenly Father through Jesus Christ our Redeemer.[11]

Mount Holyoke also was founded with the goal of cultivating benevolence or Christian service in its students. Mary sought to develop a social and domestic character in the students which was distinctively Christian and manifested itself in quiet, consistent service to others. The Christian woman

> may promote the interest of the Sabbath school, or be an angel of mercy to the poor and afflicted – she may seek in various ways to increase the spirit of benevolence, and zeal for the cause of missions, and she may labor for the salvation of souls. But her work is to be done by the whisper of her still and gentle voice, by the silent step of her unwearied feet, and by the power of her uniform and consistent example.

In one graduating address Mary Lyon encouraged her pupils:

> We are said to be crucified with Christ – to be partakers of his sufferings; to weep with him; to rejoice with him; to reign with him. He is not ashamed to call us brethren – brethren in labors – brethren in sufferings – brethren in the rich harvest of immortal souls.
>
> You will find no pleasure like the pleasure of active effort…Never be hasty to decide that you can not do, because you have not physical or mental strength. Never say you have no faith or hope. Always think of God's strength when you feel your weakness, and remember that you can come nearer to him than to any being in the universe. We have desired to educate you to go among the rich or the poor, to live in the country or the village, in New England, the West, or a foreign land. And, wherever you are, remember that God will be with you, if you seek to do good to immortal souls.

Mount Holyoke was established at a time when, with the shift to industrialism, the home was no longer an economic center. Women were less occupied with spinning, and candle and soap making. Mary Lyon recognized these changes,

---

10 *History*, p. 106.

11 Ibid., p. 107.

and thought they were providential. She thought female teachers had a role to play in God's plan. Mount Holyoke was 'another stone in the foundation of our great system of benevolent operations which are destined, in the hand of God, to convert a world.'[12] Many of Mount Holyoke's graduates went out to do just that, becoming missionaries to every part of the globe. No other institution was as closely associated with women missionaries as was Mount Holyoke. In 1859, one-fifth of all missionary women were Mt. Holyoke alumnae. One hundred and seventy-five women missionaries had been sent out to eighteen countries. They were especially active in Persia, India, Ceylon, Hawaii, and Africa. Many went west to become teachers, or to the south after the Civil War to teach southern blacks. Amanda Porterfield, in her study of the Mt. Holyoke missionaries, noted how important these women missionaries were in bringing about cultural change around the globe:

> American influence in the nonwestern world has been shaped more by women and women's issues than many historians have realized... submissiveness was an important aspect of Puritan piety in New England, and underlay the emphasis on disinterested benevolence that developed in the late eighteenth and early nineteenth centuries. A broken will was a basic constituent of Puritan piety, and Puritan writers celebrated self-sacrifice and suffering as characteristics of grace.[13]

From their Puritan heritage the missionaries also had a strong sense that marriage and family life were at the core of society and the model for Church and state. Women were important to the construction of a Christian society.

In later years, students from Mount Holyoke testified to the importance of the school in their lives. A graduate from 1871 wrote, 'My school life has earnestly interested me in the great moral questions of the day, and made me realize that upon the Christian women of the land is laid a responsibility which God alone can enable them to carry.' A graduate from 1849 wrote:

> What has my Holyoke education helped me to be, or do, or bear? I incline to answer 'everything.' My Christian life began in the seminary. There I learned to hold myself responsible for my part of the Christian work in the world, just as for my daily share of the domestic work; I learned to take part in and to conduct meetings, and to try to win others to Christ as I myself was won – by personal appeals in the friendly way which is habitual there. During the three years spent in teaching after graduation I learned that the influences of the seminary are not confined within its walls but may be carried into other schools with gracious results.

---

12   Amanda Porterfield. *Mary Lyon and the Mount Holyoke Missionaries*. New York: Oxford University Press, 1997, p. 45.

13   Ibid., p. 7, 15

Whatever I have been permitted to do as a teacher, a minister's wife, or a mother, I have been taught to do as unto Christ.[14]

The Second Great Awakening

Mary Lyon's establishment of Mount Holyoke was one of the fruits of the Second Great Awakening. After the American Revolution, a time of spiritual malaise seemed to have settled once again upon America. However, at the beginning of the nineteenth century, revival brought renewed vitality to Christians throughout the land. Often called the Second Great Awakening, this revival had both similarities and differences with the colonial revival of the 1730s and 1740s. Geographically, the Second Great Awakening was more widespread, including the southwest, old northwest and frontier, as well as the New England and middle states. Methodist and Baptist circuit riders especially traversed the west and southwest establishing churches. Theologically the two revivals differed as well. The Great Awakening of Edwards and Whitefield was more Calvinistic, emphasizing God's inscrutable, sovereign grace in saving sinners. The Second Great Awakening was more Arminian, emphasizing man's ability to choose or reject salvation.

Timothy Dwight, Jonathan and Sarah Edwards' grandson, was president of Yale College and became concerned about the prevalence of unbelief among the Yale students. He began leading students in personal discussions and debates over the question, 'Is the Bible the Word of God?' Many were converted to Christian faith through his efforts. Lyman Beecher, one of Dwight's students, became convinced of the need for evangelistic efforts and became an important Christian leader in America.

The man, however, who most came to most embody the Second Great Awakening was Charles Finney (1792-1875), sometimes called the 'Father of Modern Revivalism.' Finney did not believe that revival was a miraculous movement of the Spirit of God, but held that the proper application of humanly contrived means could produce revival. He emphasized the importance of human effort to obey divine laws and promote religious awakenings. Finney was convinced it was possible for any man or woman to make a decision for salvation. Revival would occur whenever the proper means were used. He adopted techniques which had been used by the Methodists for several decades. In his meetings, Finney pressed the crowds for an immediate conversion, sometimes exerting public pressure on individuals by name. He was not content to leave the timing of the conversion to God. With his legal background, Finney appealed to the reason of his audience, much as he would appeal to a jury. One of Finney's new methods was the 'anxious bench,' an area just below the preacher

---

14   *History of Mount Holyoke Seminary*, pp. 311-12.

where people went to pray and mourn over their sins. This was the origin of the practice of asking people to come forward at evangelistic meetings.

Female converts outnumbered male converts three to two, according to one minister's estimate, and most of the converts were young people. The decline of domestic spinning and weaving with the growth of textile manufacturing allowed young women to devote more time to religious activities. While American men during this period were generally becoming more secular in orientation, women often found a new identity and support in prayer groups and religious associations.

Finney arranged for 'protracted meetings' for several days in one city. In preparing for a series of meetings in a city, Finney sent out advance teams to pray for and publicize the scheduled event. The advance teams, which participated in door-to-door visitation, were largely made up of women. Finney also encouraged women to pray publicly in his meetings. In 1826, at a conference in New Lebanon, New York, the issue of women participating publicly in meetings arose. Lyman Beecher argued at length that the practice was unscriptural. Asa Nettleton joined Beecher in opposing women's participation in mixed groups. Finney encouraged women's participation in many levels of the revival meetings, from helping in organizing the meetings to testifying and praying in the meetings themselves. He stated that 'the Church that silences the women is shorn of half its power.'[15] Some historians have found the roots of feminism in the nineteenth-century Finney revivals. Yet, Finney did not encourage women to seek positions of leadership over men and discouraged them from speaking if there was opposition to them doing so. He firmly believed the woman's primary sphere continued to be the home.

In 1851, Finney became the second president of Oberlin College, founded in 1833 as a Christian evangelical school. Established particularly to train teachers and preachers, through its graduates Oberlin sought to perpetuate the Second Great Awakening in the west. A theology called Oberlin Perfectionism had its impact on the school's graduates and society. Variously called 'entire sanctification,' 'holiness,' 'Christian perfection,' and later 'the baptism of the Holy Spirit,' or 'second blessing,' this belief emphasized a greater degree of conformity of the human will to the divine will. While Finney believed this ethical transformation came about by a process of spiritual growth, later in the century a more experiential event with 'physical evidence' of the Spirit was sought after.

For Finney, revival should lead not only to individual conversion, but to the creation of a more moral society. Oberlin itself was committed to the abolition of slavery from its beginning, and it supported an expanded role for women, being the first coeducational college in the United States. Other

---

15   Ruth A. Tucker and Walter Liefeld. *Daughters of the Church: Women and Ministry from New Testament Times to the Present*. Grand Rapids, Michigan: Zondervan Publishing House, 1987, p. 252.

reform efforts, such as the peace movement and various kinds of educational reform, were also promoted by Oberlin's faculty and students. Activism in society was seen as a natural expression of the Christian's conformity to the will of God in this world. During the Second Great Awakening, there was a proliferation of voluntary societies to bring Christian help to individuals and to reform American society (see chart). Women were at the forefront of supporting and working within many of these organizations, including those already examined above in the subjects of nursing and education.

American Voluntary Societies	
American Board of Commissioners for Foreign Missions	1810
American Bible Society	1816
Colonization Society for liberated slaves	1817
American Sunday School Union	1824
American Tract Society	1825
American Education Society	1826
American Society for the Promotion of Temperance	1826
American Home Missionary Society	1826
American Anti-Slavery Society	1834

Foreign Missions

The early English settlements in America in part began as missionary enterprises. In 1613, Jamestown's Alexander Whitaker reminded the people that they were planting the Kingdom of God in the New World. The Puritans hoped to transform the wilderness into a Paradise. The royal charters of Massachusetts, Virginia, Plymouth, and Connecticut cited as a main objective the imparting of the gospel to the heathen. The Great Seal of Massachusetts depicted a Native American uttering the Macedonian call, 'Come over and help us.'[16] John Elliott became an early leader in evangelism among the Native Americans. Jonathan Edwards later had a mission to the Stockbridge Indians, and David Brainerd also had an important Indian ministry. Revivals brought about a realization of the importance of home missions. There were many 'heathen' in the churches who were in need of conversion, and churches needed to be planted as the country expanded westward. Foreign missions, however, did not become a focus in most American minds until the early nineteenth century.

William Carey in England had encouraged the organization of the Baptist Missionary Society and sailed for India in 1792. His courage and example spurred some in America to consider more strongly the importance of missions. The birth of the foreign missions movement in

---

16   Acts 16:9.

the United States is often traced to the 'Haystack Prayer Meeting' held by a group of students at Williams College in 1806. The young men met in a meadow to pray for foreign missions, were caught in a rain storm, and found cover in a haystack. Their prayers and vision for establishing an American foreign missionary enterprise led to the establishment in 1810 of the American Board of Commissioners for Foreign Missions (ABCFM), the first overseas mission agency in the United States. The first American missionaries, Samuel and Harriet Newell and Adoniram and Ann Hasseltine Judson, set sail for India in 1812. Both wives were the first American women commissioned for missionary work and became heroines to many Americans, challenging other women to follow them in their missionary calling.

Ann Hasseltine (1789-1826) was born the year of the U.S. Constitutional Convention into a Massachusetts family with strong Puritan roots. For a time as a young person, she was drawn to the fun and society of youth, but in 1806 she was awakened to a sense of her own sinfulness and lostness. Gradually she came to take comfort in the redemption which was through Christ. The things of the world lost their attraction, and she thirsted for the Scripture and truth. Ann's conversion in part came through the reading of Hannah More's *Strictures on the Modern System of Female Education*. Miss More wrote that education for women should not merely make them ornamental to catch a husband, but useful in service for others. As Ann read, she was struck by the futility and sinfulness of a life devoted to herself and began to desire a life of usefulness to others. She set herself upon a course of reading and study comparable to what students were studying in Andover Seminary, studying the Scriptures with the commentaries of Orton and Scott and reading the works of Jonathan Edwards, Phillip Doddridge, and Samuel Hopkins. A friend of Ann's wrote:

> With Edwards on Redemption, she was instructed, quickened, strengthened. Well do I remember the elevated smile which beamed on her countenance, when she first spoke to me of its precious contents. She had transcribed, with her own hand, Edwards' leading and most striking remarks on this subject. When reading Scripture, sermons, or other works, if she met with any sentiment or doctrine, which seemed dark and intricate, she would mark it, and beg the first clergyman who called at her father's to elucidate and explain it.[17]

When Adoniram Judson proposed marriage to Ann, he knew his proposal was a radical one. Adoniram had dedicated his life to missions. He could

---

17   Arabella M. Stuart Wilson. *The Lives of Mrs. Ann H. Judson and Mrs. Sarah B. Judson with a biographical sketch of Mrs. Emily C. Judson, missionaries to Burmah*. Auburn: Derby and Miller, 1852, pp. 17-18, available at http://www.archive.org/details/livesofmrsannhju00will.

only imagine the difficulties such a life would entail and the hardships he was asking Ann to endure if she joined him in this undertaking. She would be leaving behind a life of comfort and protection with the likelihood of never returning and seeing her family and loved ones again. Ann struggled with whether marrying Judson and becoming a missionary was God's will for her life:

> An opportunity has been presented to me, of spending my days among the heathen, attempting to persuade them to receive the Gospel. Were I convinced of its being a call from God, and that it would be more pleasing to him, for me to spend my life in this way than in any other, I think I should be willing to relinquish every earthly object, and, in full view of dangers and hardships, give myself up to the great work.

In spite of much opposition from friends, Ann concluded this was God's will:

> Yes, I think I would rather go to India, among the heathen, notwithstanding the almost insurmountable difficulties in the way, than to stay at home and enjoy the comforts and luxuries of life...O, if [God] will condescend to make me useful in promoting his kingdom, I care not where I perform his work, nor how hard it be. '*Behold, the handmaid of the Lord: be it unto me according to thy word.*'[18]

When Ann told her friend Harriet Atwood (1793-1812) about her decision to spend her days in India among the heathen, Harriet was deeply affected:

> Is she willing to do all this for God; and shall I refuse to lend my little aid, in a land where divine revelation has shed its clearest rays? I have *felt* more for the salvation of the heathen this day, than I recollect to have felt through my whole past life. How dreadful their situation! What heart but would bleed at the idea of the sufferings they endure to obtain the joys of paradise! What can *I* do, that the light of the Gospel may shine upon them? They are perishing for lack of knowledge, while I enjoy the glorious privileges of a Christian land! Great God, direct me! O make me in *some way* beneficial to immortal souls.[19]

Harriet's concern for the heathen led her to marry Samuel Newell, one of the founders of the ABCFM, who was to go to India with Adoniram Judson. Harriet was only eighteen. At the consecration of the missionaries before their departure, William Goodell, a farmer's son and student, was especially moved as he looked at Harriet's young face:

18 James D. Knowles. *Memoir of Ann H. Judson, missionary to Burmah*. Boston: Gould, Kendall and Lincoln, 1846, pp. 46, 48, available at http://books.google.com/books?id=bb4u5bmWDGU C&vid=ISBN0837013887&dq=annhjudson&jtp=1/#m-judson.

19 *Memoir of Ann H. Judson*, p. 43.

> I could not restrain my tears while looking on her likeness. It brought
> to my mind her piety, devotedness to God, and ardent love for the
> millions of Asia. When I consider her activity, self-denial, and readiness
> to forsake all for Christ, I feel as if I had no religion. Oh that a flame of
> that divine love which warmed her breast might be kindled in this heart
> of mine![20]

The Newells and Judsons headed for India, where William Carey had
first gone as a missionary the year before Harriet was born. When the
Americans landed in Calcutta, they were met by William Carey, who
brought them to his home in Serampore. In Serampore they met the
other British missionaries and their families and learned something
of the missionary work being done there. They admired the gardens as
well as the schools established for the Indian children and the Christian
instruction provided the Indians. Ann and Harriet were able to visit with
Hannah Marshman (1767-1847), the first woman to leave England for
missionary work. She and her husband, along with William Carey, were
the pioneers in the Serampore mission. The Marshmans established the
first schools for children in North India, with Hannah as the teacher. She
worked to establish schools for girls as well, the first to do so in India.
In the mission house still in use today, a memorial plaque describes
Hannah's pioneering work in founding girls' schools in northern India and
concludes by quoting Revelation 14:13, 'Blessed are the dead which die
in the Lord from henceforth: Yea, saith the Spirit, that they may rest from
their labours, and their works do follow them.'

The Serampore mission produced the first editions of the New
Testament in more than thirty Oriental languages and dialects and printed
the first books in Bengali. The Serampore missionaries insisted that the
caste system be excluded from the Christian community and the Church.
William Carey and the mission also worked assiduously to eliminate the
practice of *suttee*, the burning of the widow on the funeral pyre of her
husband. The Americans could learn much from their more seasoned
laborers in the mission field.

However, the British East India Company, then a controlling force
in India, was unfriendly to missionaries and especially to American
missionaries, since Britain and America were then at war. The Americans
were ordered to leave India and return to their country immediately. The
Judsons and Newells ultimately planned to go to Burma, but conditions
there seemed unfavorable at the moment. A ship bound for the Isle of
France (off the coast of Africa and currently known as the Republic of

---

20   From Goodell's journal, quoted in Dana L. Robert, 'The Influence of American Missionary
     Women on the World Back Home,' *Religion and American Culture*, Winter 2002; 12:1, p. 61.
     Goodell did become a missionary and served forty years in Turkey with only one furlough.

Mauritius) could take two of the missionaries on board, and it was decided the Newells would take that vessel. Harriet was not well and was pregnant. Once en route, she lost her baby in a premature birth at sea. She died at Port Louis, barely nineteen years old. Samuel Newell, Harriet's husband, sent a message to Harriet's mother that, 'her dear Harriet never repented of any sacrifice she had made for Christ; that on her dying bed she was comforted with the thought of having had it in her heart to do something for the heathen, though God had seen fit to take her away before we entered on our work.'[21]

Harriet Newell was the first American missionary to die on a foreign field and became something of a martyr. A memorial sermon and her memoirs went through several editions and perhaps had more influence than if she had lived a long life on the mission field. Many later traced their missionary call to her example. At Harriet's memorial service, Leonard Woods of the ABCFM noted that, 'The *wife of a Missionary* when influenced by the Spirit of Christ gives still more remarkable evidence of self-denial and devotion' than her husband because 'the tie which binds her to her relatives and home is stronger.' The woman who 'forsakes all for the name of Christ…makes a higher effort and thus furnishes a more conspicuous proof, that her love of Christ transcends all earthly affection.'[22]

Ann Judson deeply missed her dear friend, but continued to Burma with her husband. The couple established their home in Rangoon. Learning the language and becoming familiar with the customs and ways of an alien culture and society occupied the first months in the new land. Ann became fluent in Burmese and Siamese and was able to help Adoniram in his translation work. She translated the catechism into Burmese and, aided by a native teacher, the Gospel of Matthew into Siamese. Having seen the importance of the school established by Hannah Marshman near Calcutta, at the earliest opportunity Ann set up a mission school for girls in Burma.

When war broke out between England and Burma, the Judsons were suspected of being English spies, and Adoniram was imprisoned. Ann, with a baby in arms, followed Adoniram from prison to prison as he was moved about, bringing him and other prisoners food and needed medicine. She was able to have some influence with the governor and regularly petitioned the government for Adoniram's release. It was undoubtedly because of Ann's persistence that, though Adoniram was several times condemned to death with others, he was never executed. When peace was declared

---

21   Harriet Newell. *Memoirs of Mrs. Harriet Newell, wife of the Rev. S. Newell, American missionary to India, who died at the Isle of France, Nov. 30, 1812, aged nineteen years.* Edinburgh: Ogle, Allardice, & Thomson, 1817, available at http://www.archive.org/details/memoirsofmrsharr00newerich.

22   *Memoirs of Harriet Newell*, p. 215.

The Other Two Mrs. Judsons

Eight years after Ann died, Adoniram Judson married the widow of another missionary to Burma, Sarah Hall Boardman (1803-1845). The Boardmans had followed the Judsons to Burma in 1825. They established a mission among the wild Karen tribe, where Sarah established a school. When her husband died in 1831, Adoniram wrote her, 'You are now drinking the bitter cup whose dregs I am somewhat acquainted with. And though, for some time, you have been aware of its approach, I venture to say that it is far bitterer than you expected.'*Three years later, Adoniram and Sarah were married. Sarah made translations of Christian works into Burmese and was translating *Pilgrim's Progress* at the time of her death. Adoniram and Sarah had eight children before Sarah passed on in 1845.

After Sarah's death, Adoniram read a book written by Emily Chubbuck (1817-1854), and he soon enlisted her to write a biography of Sarah. As the two collaborated on the work, a romance developed, and they were married. Emily's memoir of Sarah Judson sold 28,000 copies when published in 1848. Describing life in Burma soon after her arrival there, Emily wrote, 'Frogs hop from my sleeves when I put them on, and lizards drop from the ceiling to the table when we are eating; and the floors are black with ants.'** Adoniram died at sea four years after they were married. Emily returned to America to raise her daughter and three children of Sarah and Adoniram.

**Great Women of the Christian Faith*, p. 373.
**Ibid., p. 375.

---

between the two countries, Adoniram was released. Ann, however, was so weakened by the ordeal, that she died two months later.

Ann had written a history of the Burmese mission which gave insight and inspiration to Americans who had little knowledge or commitment of overseas missions. Her vivid descriptions of the condition of Burmese women increased the concern about the plight of women in heathen lands.

Another pioneer ABCFM missionary, Lucy Goodale Thurston (1795-1876), was among the first missionaries to the Sandwich Islands (Hawaii). American missionaries went to the Sandwich Islands in 1819 in response to appeals by Hawaiian converts to Christianity, who saw idol worship, drunkenness, and foreign sailors bringing disorder to the islands. Lucy Goodale's father arranged a meeting between his pious 24-year-old daughter and recent seminary graduate Asa Thurston. Within a month the two were married, and on October 23, 1819, they sailed for Hawaii. It was a good match. Lucy recorded in her journal:

> When I gave my hand to Mr. Thurston and came out from my father's house to go far away to a land of unknown, I felt assured of the care and friendship of one precious friend, but my expectations have been more than realized. To be connected with such a husband and engaged in such

an object, in the present state of the world, is of all situations in life, what I choose.[23]

Lucy believed that a woman missionary could best serve not as a translator, evangelist, or teacher (though she might be involved in all of these activities) but as a servant of her family. She developed the concept that the Christian home should be established in pagan lands as an example that natives could see and follow. The missionary wife could be an example of how to rear and train children. Missionary H.G.O. Dwight later wrote of this importance of a Christian home in missionary work:

> The heathen want not only ministers of the word, but *pious, well-educated, families*, in all the various departments of life, to be the living, bright examples of the doctrines of Christianity ... Then would the dwelling of domestic love, the altar of morning and evening sacrifice, the school-room of public worship, preach more powerfully than volumes of abstract teaching.[24]

William Goodell, Lucy Thurston's cousin, wrote:

> In these countries, where so much more can be done by living than by preaching, a missionary family is, or ought to be, the very nursery of heaven ... Should not his [this missionary's] family be such that it may be referred to by the whole community as a specimen of what a Christian and well-regulated family ought to be? But whether such a beautiful example be exhibited in the family of the missionary, or not, turns chiefly on the point whether 'she [the missionary's wife] looketh well to the ways of her household.'[25]

Lucy Thurston especially reached out to the Hawaiian women, teaching them the Scriptures, hygiene, and how to care for their children. Lucy led the female Friday meetings with fellow missionary wife Elisabeth Bishop, which had an attendance of 2,600 women by 1830.[26]

The earliest missionary societies only sent out married couples. The husband was often listed as the missionary, with his wife listed in a secondary role. Mission boards did not accept unmarried missionaries.

Women had been involved in the support of missions from the beginning of the century. Numerous local mission aid societies were formed through

---

23 As quoted in 'Lucy Thurston Missionary Wife,' *Coffee Times*, www.coffeetimes.com/thurston. htm, accessed July 5, 2008.

24 H.G.O. Dwight, *Memoirs of Mrs. Elizabeth B. Dwight*, 1840, p. 170.

25 E.D.G. Prime. *Forty Years in the Turkish Empire: a Memoir of Rev. William Goodell*. New York: Robert Carter & Brothers, 1876, pp. 189-190.

26 Lucy Goodale Thurston. *The Missionary's Daughter or Memoir of Lucy Goodale Thurston of the Sandwich Islands*. New York: Dayton and Newman, 1842, available at http://books.google. com/books?hl=en&id=OzA4AAAAMAAJ&dq=lucy+goodale+thurston&printsec=frontco ver&source=web&ots=BVv5rGI0gd&sig=XOxlPo-UFiGbKqk7IX2zgcccneU&sa=X&oi=bo ok_result&resnum=2&ct=result.

which women raised support for missions. Women brought their egg money or butter money to contribute to the numerous Female Cent or Mite Societies organized for mission aid. In sewing and Dorcas Societies women produced needlework which they could sell, sending the proceeds to missions.

Countless stories could be told of women in prayer for missions or saving from meager funds to produce a potent gift for the gospel in foreign lands. The first legacy received by a foreign missionary society was given by a domestic servant, Sally Thomas. From her earnings of 50¢ a week, over a lifetime Miss Thomas saved $345.88, which she bequeathed at her death to the ABCFM. In Brookline, Massachusetts, a small group of women met and prayed for missions. In the home of their hostess was a little bamboo basket, the gift of a sea captain. The little basket sparked an interest in Japan among the ladies, and they began praying for the Christianization of Japan – 25 years before Perry had sailed to Japan, 30 years before the first pioneer missionaries went to Japan, and 40 years before the ABCFM had a mission there! Yet, the women prayed and regularly donated funds to the ABCFM for a Japanese mission. They contributed $600 over the years, which the ABCFM set aside. Forty years after the group had begun to pray, the money had grown to $4,104.26.

Early Women's Mission Aid Societies*
*Helen Barrett Montgomery. *Western Women in Eastern Lands*. N.Y.: Macmillan Co., 1911, p. 19.

1800   Boston Female Society for Missionary Purposes (Baptist and Congregational)

1801   Boston Female Society for the Promotion and Diffusion of Christian Knowledge (Congregational)

1803   Female Missionary Society of Southampton, MA. (Congregational)

1808   Female Mite Society of Beverly, MA. (Baptist)

1811   Salem Female Cent Society, MA. (Baptist)

1812   Female Foreign Missionary Society of New Haven, CT. (Congregational)

1814   Fayette Street Church Women's Missionary Society. (Baptist)

1816   Female Charitable Society of Tallmadge, OH (Congregational) (Sent first contribution received from west of the Alleghanies by the American Board)

1819   Female Missionary Society Auxiliary to the Missionary and Bible Society (Methodist)

1828   Society for the Support of Heathen Youth, New York, NY. (Presbyterian)

1835   Society for the Evangelization of the World, Newark, NJ. (Presbyterian)

1847   Free Baptist Female Missionary Society, Sutton, VT, Never disbanded.

1848   Ladies' China Missionary Society, Baltimore, MD (Methodist)

Sarah Doremus (1802-1877) became a leader in supporting unmarried women missionaries. Married to Thomas Doremus, a wealthy businessman, Sarah had eight daughters and one son, and adopted several other children. She was involved in numerous philanthropic interests, which her husband encouraged. She taught Sunday School, aided the Greeks against the Turkish persecution, did prison work in New York, formed the Women's Prison Association to work with discharged prisoners, managed the City and Tract Society to help the poor, helped the Bible Society distribute Scripture, and organized a Presbyterian home for Aged Women as well as a Child's Hospital. Sarah was most interested in the work of missions. Her house was almost a hotel for returning and departing missionaries. In 1861, she formed the Women's Union Missionary Society of America, especially to send out unmarried women missionaries.

Denominational groups generally did not trust women's boards, but the upheaval of the Civil War seemed to provide greater latitude for women's work. Helen B. Montgomery wrote:

> In its educative force on the women of the nation the Civil War overtops all other agencies. During the awful struggle the women both North and South received a baptism of power. They were driven to organize, forced to cooperate by their passion of pity and patriotism, and in the management of the great commission for raising and distributing aid to the soldiers they discovered powers of which they themselves and the nation had been quite unconscious. It is no accident that it was the decade following the close of the Civil War that saw the launchng of scores of organizations, among them the Missionary Societies.[27]

By the war's end, with fewer men available, there were more single women available for service. The Women's Missionary Society emphasized 'Women's Work for Women.' Women were able to go into homes and places in foreign countries and minister to women in ways that men could not do. Christianity had elevated women from the abject position they often held in other cultures, and Christian women sought to reach out to other women with the liberating truth of the gospel. By 1900, sixty per cent of American missionaries were women.

In the foreign lands, native women also were important in evangelism and Christian work. 'Bible women' distributed Bibles and Biblical literature to many areas where a missionary might not be allowed. They taught the native women how to read as well as the good news of the gospel itself. Many often suffered persecution for their witness.

Women became important cultural bridges between America and the foreign lands. Mission magazines for the various women's organizations were important educational tools on a variety of levels. They provided information

---

27   *Western Women in Eastern Lands,* 10, quoted in R. Pierce Beaver, *American Protestant Women in World Mission,* (Grand Rapids, Michigan: William B. Eerdmans, 1968), p. 89.

on the history and culture of different parts of the world, included testimonies by native Christians, supplied Bible studies about missions, and often had children's activities with a mission theme. Whether on the mission field itself or as part of the numerous women's missionary organizations, women involved in mission work increased in Biblical understanding and global awareness while also developing greater organizational skills.

FIVE UNMARRIED WOMEN MISSIONARIES –
A small sample of the hundreds of women who devoted their lives to the cause of Christ in foreign lands.

Missionary	Dates of Missionary Service	Place of Missionary Service	Noted Contributions
Lottie Moon (1840-1912) from a prosperous family in Albemarle County, Virginia	1873-1912	China – first in Dengzhou and then in the areas of P'ingtu and Hwangshien	• Urged that women on the mission field have freedom to minister and have equal voice in missionary affairs • Wore Chinese clothes and adopted Chinese customs, being sensitive to Chinese culture • Worked as an evangelist and church planter • Wrote letters pleading for mission support and encouraged Southern Baptists to organize missionary societies • Established week before Christmas as time of giving to foreign missions. The Lottie Moon Christmas Offering today finances half of Southern Baptist missions budget annually
Mary Slessor (1847-1915) from a poor family in Scotland	1876-1915	Calabar, on the slave coast of Africa	• Ministered in a land of witch doctors, lions, killer elephants and cannibals • Went fearlessly alone into the interior to bring the love of Christ to warlike and cannibalistic tribes of the Okoyong and Azo • Hundreds came to Christ. Brought schools and trade to the interior

Lilias Trotter (1853-1928) from a wealthy London family	1888-1928	Algeria	• Gave up a career as an artist so she could serve God • Went to Algeria with her own funding • Created booklets about Jesus and the gospel with Arabic script and Arabic designs • Founded the Algiers Mission Band • Visited interior regions for personal witnessing, especially to the women • Wrote books illustrated with her art and especially for Moslem audiences
Amy Carmichael (1867-1951) from Millisle, Ireland	1893-1951	Dohnavur, India	• Suffered severely from neuralgia, often putting her in bed for weeks • Dressed in native costume and even colored her skin to blend in with the natives • Rescued young ladies dedicated to temples and forced into prostitution to earn money for the temple • Founded Dohnavur Fellowship as a sanctuary for children • Prolific writer on her mission as well as devotional literature and poetry
Gladys Aylward (1902-1970) from a working-class family in London	1930-1947 1958-1970	• Yangchen, China, in Sansi Province • Sian in Szechewan Province • Taiwan	• Little scholarly ability, but a passion for service • Office of foot inspector allowed her to bring gospel to villages of region • Dressed as the locals and adopted local customs • Adopted orphans and established an orphanage • Mandarin (public official) became a Christian through her witness • Became influential with government in province because of her principles and strength of character • During Sino-Japanese War, led 100 orphans to safety, traveling for twelve days through difficult terrain • Established orphanages in Siam and Taiwan after the War

Victorian Christian Women:
Keepers at Home

Titus 2:5

Queen Victoria was the longest reigning British monarch, reigning from 1837-1901, the greater part of the nineteenth century. Her name became descriptive of the era, not only in Britain, but in America as well. It was a time of tremendous prosperity for Britain and America, with the British Empire at its zenith and industrialization spawning a growing middle class. Photography, electric lights, and numerous other inventions transformed how life was lived and how it was perceived. As more and more people moved to the cities, the poverty and vice of urban areas became growing social evils. Women often became leaders in the reform movements to eradicate these social ills.

Victoria and her husband Albert became models of domesticity during this period, and the couple consciously strove to set an example of morality that all within the kingdom might emulate. Even though Queen, Victoria was convinced that 'we women, if we are to be good women, feminine and amiable and domestic, are not fitted to reign.'[1] Without ever relinquishing her queenly authority, Victoria delegated much of the actual work of her position to 'prince consort' Albert. Though providence had placed her on the throne, Victoria did not believe the woman's natural place was in politics or the public, and she strongly opposed the 'women's rights' movement. She urged everyone 'who can speak or write to join in checking this mad, wicked folly of "Women's Rights", with all its attendant horrors, on which her poor, feeble sex is bent, forgetting every sense of womanly feeling and propriety.' She thought feminists should 'get a good whipping' for claiming equality with men and unsexing themselves. They certainly would not be able to survive without male protection and would become 'the most hateful, heathen and disgusting of beings.'[2]

---

1   Carolly Erickson. *Her Little Majesty:The Life of QueenVictoria*. NewYork: Simon & Schuster, 1997, p. 147.

2   *Her Little Majesty*, pp. 198-9.

During the Victorian era, Biblical Christianity was interwoven in the very fabric of society, and the evangelical faith molded middle-class Victorian family life. Sunday worship and regular family Bible reading were standard features of life for many. Yet, it was also a period of increasing doubt and skepticism. Biblical higher criticism and developments in the natural sciences, such as the publication of Darwin's *Origin of Species*, raised questions about the validity of the Christian faith, with which many struggled.

True Womanhood and Domesticity

The nineteenth century saw the development of what some have called the cult of True Womanhood or Domesticity. This was an almost sacred idea found in many women's writings of the day, including numerous women's novels and *Godey's Lady's Book*, the most popular ladies' magazine in nineteenth-century America. At a time of increasing industrialization, the family was no longer the main economic unit, as it had been when the family farm was the backbone of the economy. As men increasingly worked in industry or businesses away from the family farm, many believed the proper place of the woman was in the home, not in the world of business or politics. The woman was to manage the home and create there a place of stability and calm, a refuge from the world. Woman's place was complementary, not inferior to the man's. The woman was to be a nurturer and supporter, providing comfort and cheer to her husband, raising her children and caring for the sick and needy. Any extra time could be spent in needlework, flower arranging, letter writing, and reading inspiring literature. Women were thought suited to such activities because they were considered to be more affectionate and emotional beings, as well as less rational, than men. They were also thought to be more prone to both physical and mental illnesses. Yet, women were seen as morally superior to men (a reverse of the moral inferiority of women found in much medieval writing).

Religion became particularly a part of the domestic sphere. It was the woman's task to guard the social order. She was to tame the wild natures of her husband and children both by a quiet persuasion and by diligent example. She worked in church and reform agencies and exercised her influence behind the scenes, always deferring to the authority of her husband. Motherhood was glorified in the nineteenth century, and mothers were deemed most responsible for passing on religion and morality to future generations.

There was a growing consideration of the role of women throughout the nineteenth century. In 1853, Sarah Josepha Hale, editor of the popular *Godey's Lady's Book*, sponsor of the movement to make Thanksgiving a national holiday, and author of 'Mary Had a Little Lamb,' published *Woman's Record: Sketches of all distinguished women from the creation to A.D. 1850*. The work was indeed as comprehensive as the title indicated. Hale's introduction to the mammoth work summarized woman's role as seen by many during this period. She asserted that a woman's function and position was set forth in the Bible:

> The Bible is the only guarantee of women's rights, and the only expositor of her duties. Under its teachings men learn to honour her. Wherever its doctrines are observed, her influence gains power…If the Gospel is the supreme good revealed to the world, and if the Gospel harmonizes best with the feminine nature, and is best exemplified in its purity by the feminine life, giving to the mother's instinctive love a scope, a hope, a support, which no religion of human device ever conferred or conceived, then surely God has…a great work for the sex to do. 'Christ was born of a woman;' woman must train her children for Christ. Is this an inferior office?[3]

Mrs. Hale claimed that where the Bible was read, female talents were cultivated. God's Word was woman's shield, His power her protection, and His gifts her encouragement to fully develop, cultivate, and use her talents.

In her comprehensive work, Hale referenced at least 2500 women, about 2300 of them from Christian nations. She saw many of these women as virtuous guides, who often won their fame through suffering:

> As the stars of heaven guide the mariner safely over the night-enveloped waters, so these stars of humanity are required to show the true progress of moral virtue through the waves of temptation and sin that roll over the earth. The greater the number, and the more light they diffuse, the greater will be the safety of society.[4]

Hale saw women as God's appointed agents of morality and virtue. The permanent improvement of the human race depended on how this mission of women was treated by men. Woman was not created to satisfy man's sensual desires, 'but to refine his human affections, and elevate his moral feelings.' She was to help him, especially in his spiritual nature. Even in paradise, man needed help and was not to stand alone. Woman was 'intended as the teacher and inspirer of man, morally speaking, of "whatsoever things are lovely, and pure, and of good report."'[5] The Bible's clear statement in 1 Corinthians 11:9 that the woman was created for the man revealed woman's superior moral nature. She was needed to make man perfect and complete.

Hale noted three ways male and female were different in creation: their mode of creation was different; the materials from which each was formed were different; and the functions for which each was designed

3   Sarah Josepha Hale. *Woman's Record: Sketches of all distinguished women from the creation to A.D. 1854.* NewYork: Harper and Brothers, 1855, 2nd edition, viii-ix, available at http://books.google.com.

4   *Woman's Record*, x.

5   Ibid., xxxvii.

were dissimilar. Yet in spite of these differences, Hale visualized an ideal unity between a maried man and woman:

> They were never equal; they were <u>one</u>; one in flesh and bones; one in the harmony of their wills; one in the unison of their souls; one in their hope of earthly happiness; one in the favour of God.[6]

In saying that male and female were not equal, Hale was pointing out what she deemed important differences between the male and female natures. Women were not mechanical or inventive. Not one of the women in *Woman's Record* gained fame through great discoveries in science or for a mechanical invention. This had nothing to do with a woman's learning, for many unlearned men had made such discoveries or inventions. Rather, Hale believed there was an organic difference in the operation of the male and female mind. The woman was more intuitive; the man was more logical. The image and glory of God in man was his creative ability. But man's greatest glory was not his creativity but his worship of God in spirit and in truth. It was in this worship, in her moral goodness, that women excelled. In her beauty of moral goodness, the woman became the glory of the man. The woman's holy vocation was to work

> ... in the elements of human nature; her orders of architecture are formed in the soul; - Obedience, Temperance, Truth, Love, Piety, - these she must build up in the character of her children; often, too, she is called to repair the ravages and beautify the waste places which sin, care and the desolating storms of life, leave in the mind and heart of the husband she reverences and obeys. This task she should perform faithfully, but with humility; remembering that it was for woman's sake Eden was forfeited, because Adam loved his wife more than his Creator; and that man's nature has to contend with a degree of depravity into which the female, by the grace of God, has never descended.[7]

Christianity elevated women, but they were degraded by the influence 'of false religion, of bad governments, and of wicked men.' Constitutional liberty always improved woman's position, because this liberty ultimately came from the Bible and the reading of the Bible. Where the Bible was read, women's lot always improved.

The moral influence women were to wield raised both female education and the position of mother to the highest importance: 'If the mind which stamps the first and most indelible impression on the child is in a state of mental darkness, how can the true light be communicated? A mother will teach the best she knows to her son; but if she does not

6 *Woman's Record*, xxxvii.

7 Ibid., xlvi.

understand the true, she will, of necessity, imbue his mind with the false.'[8] The office of mother

> is the highest a human being can hold. On its faithful and intelligent performance hangs the hope of the world. Next to the sacred office of the mother in her family, who takes the children God has given her and trains them for His service on earth and His Kingdom in heaven, comes that of … the faithful female Missionary, who gathers under her loving care the lost lambs of Christ's flock.[9]

Interestingly, Sarah Hale's description of women's valued and unique position in nineteenth-century America was shared by visiting foreigners. When writing his perceptive description and analysis of the American democracy, the Frenchman Alexis de Tocqueville spent several chapters on the American female – her sense of equality, her rapid maturity, strong reasonableness, and her distinctive position in society. He noted that those in Europe who contended that the sexes were alike and should have the same duties, rights, occupations, and businesses, actually degraded both sexes. Such a forced sameness could result in nothing but 'weak men and disorderly women.' In America, however, there was a democratic equality, but also an admission that there were wide differences between the physical and moral natures of man and woman:

> The Americans have applied to the sexes the great principle of political economy which governs the manufacturers of our age, by carefully dividing the duties of man from those of woman in order that the great work of society may be the better carried on. In no country has such constant care been taken as in America to trace two clearly distinct lines of action for the two sexes and to make them keep pace one with the other, but in two pathways that are always different.[10]

The woman recognized the man as the natural authority in the family and willingly seemed to submit to the husband's rule: 'Such, at least, is the feeling expressed by the most virtuous of their sex…' The Americans

> do not think that man and woman have either the duty or the right to perform the same offices, but they show an equal regard for both their respective parts; and though their lot is different, they consider both of them as beings of equal value.

Morally and intellectually, women were the equal of men. De Tocqueville concluded:

---

8   Ibid., xlvii.

9   *Woman's Record*, p. 899.

10   Alexis de Tocqueville (trans. Henry Reeve). *Democracy in America.* 1899, III.xii. Available at http://xroads.virginia.edu/~HYPER/DETOC/ch3_12.htm.

As for myself, I do not hesitate to avow that although the women of the United States are confined within the narrow circle of domestic life, and their situation is in some respects one of extreme dependence, I have nowhere seen woman occupying a loftier position; and if I were asked, now that I am drawing to the close of this work, in which I have spoken of so many important things done by the Americans, to what the singular prosperity and growing strength of that people ought mainly to be attributed, I should reply: To the superiority of their women.

Women Writers

Many women of the 19th century who thoroughly believed in 'true womanhood' and feminine domesticity found an influential voice and a Christian ministry in writing. Many of the women wrote fiction for both adults and children, most often with a moral message woven throughout. Others wrote more devotional works to help other women or encourage others in their Christian faith. Teaching was one vocation women could honorably pursue. The training of children, whether inside or outside the home, was part of a woman's noble calling. Some of the female teachers wrote educational works and school books. Most of the women's writing was within the woman's sphere of moral improvement and could be composed while the woman remained at home in her domestic sphere.

Elizabeth Prentiss (1818-1878), for example, was both a daughter and wife of prominent Presbyterian ministers. She was active in caring for the sick in body and soul in her husband's church, as well as with the numerous responsibilities of her own family. Beginning with her father's death when she was nine years old, Elizabeth learned the lessons which could be learned through suffering. Often in ill health, when she was twenty-two she commented that 'I never knew what it was to feel well.' Throughout her life she suffered from insomnia, leading to restless nights and weary days. Yet, she learned that suffering could often be a way of God's preparing His children for further service, and joy came to characterize her life.

In 1852, her four-year-old son Eddy died; within three months Elizabeth bore a little girl who died shortly after birth. Later, found among her manuscripts was a scrap of paper entitled 'My Nursery, 1852':

> I thought that prattling boys and girls
> Would fill this empty room;
> That my rich heart would gather flowers
> From childhood's opening bloom.
> One child and two green graves are mine,
> That is God's gift to me:
> A bleeding, fainting, broken heart —
> That is *my* gift to Thee.[11]

---

11 George Lewis Prentiss. *More Love to Thee: The Life and Letters of Elizabeth Prentiss*. New York: A.D. F. Randolph & Co., 1882, p. 138.

In the years that followed, Elizabeth did indeed give her heart to God by authoring children's books that taught moral truths of Christianity. In 1853, she wrote *Little Susy's Six Birthdays*, which became a children's classic. For the next several years she wrote a book a year, including *Only a Dandelion, and other Stories*; *The Flower of the Family: A Book for Girls;* and *The Little Preacher*. In her children's stories, Elizabeth used examples and allegories to teach simple moral principles. Many of the works were translated and published into French and German as well. All of her books were born in prayer; Elizabeth never sat down to write anything without first praying, 'that I might not be suffered [allowed] to write anything that would do harm, and that, on the contrary I might be taught to say what would do good.'

More Love to Thee
by Elizabeth Prentiss

More love to Thee, O Christ, more love to Thee!
Hear Thou the prayer I make on bended knee.
This is my earnest plea: More love, O Christ, to Thee;
More love to Thee, more love to Thee!

Once earthly joy I craved, sought peace and rest;
Now Thee alone I seek, give what is best.
This all my prayer shall be: More love, O Christ, to Thee;
More love to Thee, more love to Thee!

Let sorrow do its work, come grief or pain;
Sweet are Thy messengers, sweet their refrain,
When they can sing with me: More love, O Christ, to Thee;
More love to Thee, more love to Thee!

Then shall my latest breath whisper Thy praise;
This be the parting cry my heart shall raise;
This still its prayer shall be: More love, O Christ to Thee;
More love to Thee, more love to Thee!

Elizabeth's most famous work, *Stepping Heavenward*, first published in serial form in *The Chicago Advance*, was published as a book in 1869. It went through six London editions, numerous German printings, and editions in Australia, Switzerland, and France, as well as several American printings. The story of the heroine Katy's loves, mistakes, despairs, successes and gradual, steady progress in Christian devotion and service continues to encourage women today. In the preface to *Stepping Heavenward*, Elizabeth explained the purpose of her writings:

> The aim of [my] writings, whether designed for young or old, is to incite patience, fidelity, hope and all goodness by showing how trust in God and loving obedience to his blessed will brighten the darkest paths and make a heaven upon earth.

Even with growing acclaim for her writings, Elizabeth's family and her remaining children were, after Christ, the central focus of her life. In 1864, she wrote her sister-in-law:

> It seems to me that the sound of my six little feet is the very pleasantest sound in the world. Often when I lie in bed racked with pain and exhausted from want of food – for my digestive organs seem paralysed when I have neuralgia – hearing these little darlings about the house compensates for everything, and I am inexpressibly happy in the mere sense of possession.[12]

Elizabeth did not seek worldly fame or position. She repeatedly prayed that God would 'crowd the self out of me by taking up all the room himself.' It is fitting that she is perhaps best known today as the author of the hymn 'More Love to Thee.' In a loving tribute to his wife, after Elizabeth's death, her husband collected many of her letters and published her biography.

Numerous other women wrote hymns which continue to touch the minds and heartstrings of Christians around the globe. In 1853, Catherine Winkworth (1827-1878) published *Lyra Germanica*, a collection of translations of German hymns into English. She later published *The Chorale Book for England* and *Christian Singers of Germany*, bringing the German chorale tradition of earlier centuries into English worship. Her work was greatly influenced by Charles and John Wesley, and many of her hymn translations were incorporated in later Methodist hymnals.

In America, Fanny Crosby (1824-1915) wrote over 8,000 hymns and religious poems. Fanny became permanently blinded as a baby through a quack doctor's treatment of an eye infection. A few months later, her father died. Fanny's mother, a widow at 21, went to work as a maid while Grandmother Crosby took care of Fanny. Grandmother became the eyes for the little girl, describing the physical world for her and developing Fanny's descriptive abilities. Grandmother also explained and read the Bible to Fanny and emphasized to her the importance of prayer. With the help of the family's landlady, Fanny memorized large portions of Scripture. She knew the Pentateuch, the Gospels, Proverbs and many of the Psalms by heart. Fanny never looked upon her blindness as a terrible thing, but came to regard her blindness as probably the best thing that could have happened to her. When she was eight years old she wrote:

> Oh what a happy child I am
> Although I cannot see!
> I am resolved that in this world
> Contented I will be!
> How many blessings I enjoy
> That other people don't!
> So weep or sigh because I'm blind,
> I cannot – nor I won't.[13]

---

12   *More Love to Thee*, p. 217.

13   Bernard Ruffin. *Fanny Crosby*. Westwood, N.J.: Barbour and Co., Inc., 1976.

Jesus Loves Me

Anna Bartlett Warner (1820-1915) and her sister Susan were the daughters of a prominent New York lawyer who bought Constitution Island on the Hudson River, across from West Point. The two women taught a Sunday School class in their home for West Point cadets and were both buried with military honors for their spiritual help to the military officers. Both women wrote to supplement the family income when a financial depression came. Susan wrote several novels, *Wide, Wide, World* being the most popular. For Susan's 1860 novel *Say and Seal*, Anna wrote 'Jesus Loves Me.' It was a poem spoken to comfort a dying child in the story. The song has become one of the first ones missionaries around the world have taught to new converts.

When she was twelve, Fanny went to the New York Institute for the Blind. After completing her studies there, she continued at the school as a teacher for twenty-three years. She left the Institute after marrying a former pupil at the school, Alexander van Alistine, and devoted more time to the writing of hymns. Under contract with her publishers to write three hymns a week, she sometimes wrote six or seven hymns a day. The evangelistic team of Dwight L. Moody and Ira D. Sankey brought Fanny's songs to the people, and they were used to draw many to the Savior – songs such as 'Blessed Assurance,' 'All the Way My Savior Leads Me,' 'To God be the Glory,' 'Safe in the Arms of Jesus,' 'Rescue the Perishing, 'Jesus Keep Me Near the Cross,' 'I am Thine O Lord,' and many more.

Fanny had a heart for the poor and lowly and chose to live in the tenement buildings of New York to be able to better minister to them. Once a week she opened her home for hymn singing and Bible reading. Often she spoke at nearby home missions meetings. Fanny also enjoyed the friendship of wealthier people, including Phoebe Palmer Knapp, whose husband was a founder of Metropolitan Life Insurance Company. Knapp wrote the melodies for many hymns, including Fanny's 'Blessed Assurance.' At Phoebe's home Fanny met numerous American leaders, including Presidents Grant, Hayes, Garfield, McKinley, and Teddy Roosevelt, as well as Harriet Beecher Stowe.

Well into her eighties, Fanny continued a hectic speaking schedule. Her schedule in the early 1900s, when she was in her eighties, was especially daunting:

> Sunday evening Fanny spoke at the Rescue Mission in Syracuse; Monday she visited the State Fair and delivered a lecture at the Women's Pavilion; Tuesday she spoke at a nearby reservation of Onondaga Indians; Wednesday she recited a poem, written expressly for the occasion, at the Elmwood Grange; Thursday, she had no commitments, save to the Round Table, at which she recited daily anyway; Friday afternoon, she spoke at the Old Ladies home at Syracuse; and Sunday she spoke at noon to the Chevaliers of the Goodwill Congregational Church and the same day delivered the sermon at the evening service there.[14]

14   *Fanny Crosby*, p. 184.

From *The Christian Recorder*

The Christian Recorder was a weekly newspaper published in Philadelphia by the African Methodist Episcopal Church from 1854 to 1902. Many black women writers published poems and articles in the *Recorder*. Julia C. Collins' *The Curse of Caste*, the first novel written by a black woman, was serialized in the paper. Following is a poetic prayer written by Belle Goode in the middle of the Civil War:

'The Anxious Young Pious Mother'
Belle Goode (30 May 1863)

If I loved thee, oh! my Saviour,
The vain heart of mine would be
Free from every carnal pleasure,
And content to follow thee.

If I loved thee, oh! my Saviour,
I would strive to please thee here,
Then my soul would find acceptance,
In a higher, brighter sphere.

If I loved thee, oh! my Saviour,
Earth would be a pleasant place,
But alas! 'tis sad and dreary,
With no smile from thy dear face.

If I loved thee, oh! my Saviour,
I would delight in all that's good,
Ever willing to obey thee,
Then I'd love thee as I should.

Thou hast said, exalted Master,
They who love thy law will keep,
Help me Lord, incarnate Saviour,
To learn of thee, low at thy feet.

Wilt thou let thy Holy Spirit,
Change this sinful heart of mine,
Then my weary burdened soul,
Will be renewed by divine grace.

Then, dear Saviour, wilt thou guide me?
O'er the rugged path of life,
Make me humble, make me prayerful,
Cleanse my heart from every vice.

Fanny's personal life as well as her hymns brought many people to the Savior. It was always her delight that the first person she would ever see when she crossed into eternity would be her Savior.

Frances Ridley Havergal (1836-79) was Fanny Crosby's English contemporary. Though the two never met, they did correspond with each other, and there was a special bond between them. Frances inherited her musical talent from her father, Rev. William Havergal, who composed cathedral music and hundreds of sacred songs. Like Fanny Crosby, Frances began writing verses from a very young age, and poetry flowed from her pen with ease. Like Fanny too, Frances was energetically engaged in Christian philanthropic work. She published numerous collections of poems and children's works, and many of her poems were published as individual pamphlets. Her most famous hymns are 'I Gave My Life for Thee,' 'Lord, Speak to Me, that I May Speak,' and 'Take My Life, and Let it Be.' The last has been translated into French, German, Swedish, Russian, and other

European languages, as well as into several African and Asian tongues. It is sung to *Patmos,* a tune composed by Frances' father. In poor health since childhood, Frances died at the age of forty-three. In her memory, a fund was raised to support native Bible women in India and to circulate her works.

Two of the most important poets in nineteenth-century England were the Christian poets Elizabeth Barrett Browning and Christina Rossetti. Elizabeth Barrett (1806-1861) was the oldest of twelve children. She was educated at home, sharing her brother's tutor, and read the Greek and Latin classics as well as Dante in their original languages. She also learned Hebrew and read the Bible in its original Hebrew and Greek. The Barretts were dissenting Congregationalists, and the family regularly attended services at the Dissenting Chapel. Throughout her life, Elizabeth regularly read seven chapters of the Bible daily.

Elizabeth began writing poetry as a child. Her father encouraged her, publishing the epic she wrote as a teenager. By the time she was twenty, Elizabeth began struggling with lifelong pulmonary problems which left her weak and frail. She learned, however, that suffering and pain were tools God often used for spiritual growth. In suffering she learned to find delight in submitting to God's will:

> For us, - whatever's undergone,
> Thou knowest, willest what is done.
> Grief may be joy misunderstood;
> Only the Good discerns the good.
> I trust Thee while my days go on.
>
> Whatever's lost, it first was won;
> We will not struggle nor impugn.
> Perhaps the cup was broken here,
> That Heaven's new wine might show more clear.
> I praise Thee while my days go on.
>
> I praise Thee while my days go on;
> I love Thee while my days go on;
> Through dark and dearth, through fire and frost,
> With emptied arms and treasure lost,
> I thank Thee while my days go on:[15]

Elizabeth's illness caused her to become a virtual recluse, confined to her bedroom; but there she wrote poetry for various periodicals. In 1838, *The Seraphim and Other Poems,* the first volume of her mature poetry, was published. References to God and her Christian faith were frequent in these poems. One editor asked Elizabeth to mention God and Jesus Christ a little less since this did not accord with his secular publication. Elizabeth, however, would not restrict her Christian expressions:

---

15   Elizabeth Barrett Browning, 'De Profundis,' XXI-XXIII.

> The Christian religion is true or it is not, and if it is true it offers the highest and purest objects of contemplation. And the poetical faculty, which expresses the highest moods of the mind, passes naturally to the highest objects. Who can separate these things? Did Dante? Did Chaucer? Did the poets of our best British days? Did anyone shrink from speaking out Divine names when the occasion came?[16]

In her writing, Elizabeth wanted, 'the sense of the saturation of Christ's blood upon the souls of our poets, that it may cry *through* them in answer to the ceaseless wail of the Sphinx of our humanity.'[17]

After reading a collection of Elizabeth's poems in 1844, poet Robert Browning wrote her to tell her how much he admired her poems. A friend arranged a meeting between the two, and a courtship followed. Elizabeth, an invalid and six years older than Robert, at first could not believe he loved her; but in 1846, the two were married and went to live in Italy, where Elizabeth's health improved somewhat. Elizabeth's most famous works, *Sonnets from the Portuguese* and her verse-novel *Aurora Leigh*, were written after her marriage. Her fame was so great that she was seriously considered for poet laureate after the death of Wordsworth; however, Tennyson was chosen instead.

The poetry of Elizabeth's younger contemporary, Christina Rossetti (1830-94), is marked by a deep Christian devotion. Christina was born into an Italian immigrant family; her mother was a strong evangelical Christian. The four Rossetti children were all artistic and talented: Maria published a commentary on Dante; Dante Gabriel was a prominent Pre-Raphaelite painter; and William Michael was a literary critic and editor. All of the siblings remained close throughout their lives.

Much like Elizabeth Barrett, Christina became ill as a teenager; the family feared she would die. She did not die then, but continued to suffer from heart problems, anemia, and a kind of nervous exhaustion. Themes of death and the vanity of life naturally found their way into many of her poems, though heavenly joys surpassed any temporary, earthly pain or pleasures. Twice Christina was asked her hand in marriage, but each time she refused, since the proposer did not share her evangelical Christian faith.

Christina's poetry is rich with Biblical references and allusions as well as meditations on the person of Christ. Besides poetry, Christina also wrote a book of short stories for children and a series of prose works for the SPCK (Society for Promoting Christian Knowledge). Two years before her death she published *The Face of the Deep*, a commentary on Revelation. 'None Other Lamb,' one of Christina's numerous hymns, was in that work:

> None other Lamb, none other Name,
> None other Hope in heaven or earth or sea.

16   Martha Foote Crow. *Modern Poets and Christian Teaching: Elizabeth Barrett Browning*. New York: Eaton and Maine, 1907, p. 25.

17   Elizabeth Barrett Browning. *The Complete Poetical Works of Mrs. Browning*. Boston: Houghton Mifflin Company, 1900, p. 515.

None other Hiding-place from guilt and shame,
None beside Thee.

My faith burns low, my hope burns low,
Only my heart's desire cries out in me
By the deep thunder of its want and woe.
Cries out to Thee.

Lord, Thou art Life tho' I be dead,
Love's Fire Thou art however cold I be;
Nor heaven have I, nor place to lay my head,
Nor home, but Thee.

Undoubtedly the most famous Christian woman writer of the period was Harriet Beecher Stowe (1811-1896). Harriet was one of eleven children born to Lyman Beecher, a nationally prominent Presbyterian minister and leader in the Second Great Awakening. In 1832, Harriet moved with her family to Cincinnati, Ohio, where her father became head of Lane Theological Seminary, a center of abolitionism. While there she visited a plantation in nearby Kentucky, observing firsthand the condition of the slaves. The experience affected her deeply. In 1836, Harriet married Calvin Stowe, a professor of theology at Lane Seminary. The couple had seven children, and Harriet was a devoted wife and mother.

Early in their marriage, Calvin recognized Harriet's writing abilities and encouraged her to be a 'literary woman.' Harriet made time for writing while raising seven children and managing the household. In a period of 51 years, she published 30 books and numerous shorter works. The most influential was *Uncle Tom's Cabin*, written when she was 40 years old.

When the Fugitive Slave Law, requiring runaway slaves to be returned to their masters, was passed in 1850, Harriet's sister-in-law encouraged Harriet to write something which would 'make this whole nation feel what an accursed thing slavery is.'[18] Harriet proclaimed she would write something, if she lived. The resulting novel was a gripping story which showed the effects of slavery not only on the slaves but on the owners as well. *Uncle Tom's Cabin* was the first important American novel to publicly address the slavery issue. In the novel, the domestic values of the Christian home were to replace the evils of slavery. As historian Glenna Matthews noted:

> The novel is a stunning achievement because it combines moral and religious passion with the realistic detail of a genre painting. Stowe wanted to replace the sordid, unchristian, money-grubbing values of the marketplace and the accommodationist politics of those who voted for the Fugitive Slave Act with a new set of values based on true Christianity and love. But rather than a utopian approach to what could replace the status quo, she had a very

---

18 'Uncle Tom's Cabin,' *Harriet Beecher Stowe Center*, http://www.harrietbeecherstowecenter.org/utc/.

practical vision, which was the set of values and behavior to be found in a loving Christian home presided over by a large-hearted woman.[19]

Over seventy Scripture references were woven into the story, for Harriet could not but view the world from a Biblical perspective. The last words of the novel were a call to the nation:

> A day of grace is held out to us. Both North and South have been guilty before God; and the Christian church has a heavy account to answer. Not by combining together, to protect injustice and cruelty, and making a common capital of sin, is this Union to be saved, - but by repentance, justice, and mercy; for, not surer is the eternal law by which the millstone sinks in the ocean, than that strange law, by which injustice and cruelty shall bring on nations the wrath of Almighty God!

Uncle Tom's Cabin was serialized in the *National Era* and published in book form in 1852. Within a year, over 300,000 copies were sold, and the book was later translated into every major language. The power of *Uncle Tom's Cabin* came from the intense feeling Harriet wrote into the novel, and the strong Christian message throughout. Harriet said the story was

> ... to show how Jesus Christ, who liveth and was dead, and now is alive and forevermore, has still a mother's love for the poor and lowly, and that no man can sink so low but that Jesus Christ will stoop to take his hand. Who so low, who so poor, who so despised as the American Slave? ... Yet even to the slave Jesus Christ stoops, from where he sits at the right hand of the Father, and says, 'Fear not, for I have redeemed thee, I have called thee by thy name, thou art mine.'[20]

In the preface to the European edition of the novel, Harriet wrote:

> The great mystery which all Christian nations hold in common, the union of God with men through the humanity of Jesus Christ, invests human existence with an awful sacredness; and in the eye of the true believer in Jesus, he who tramples on the rights of his meanest fellowman is not only inhuman but sacrilegious, and the worst form of sacrilege is the institution of slavery.[21]

Harriet Stowe's novel deeply aroused passions in both North and South. Many for the first time came to realize the personal evil brought by slavery. So great was the effect of the novel, that when Abraham Lincoln was introduced to Harriet Stowe during the Civil War, he said, 'So, you're the little lady who started this

---

19   Glenna Matthews. *'Just a Housewife':The Rise and Fall of Domesticity in America.* New York: Oxford University Press, 1987, pp. 50-1.

20   Charles E. Stowe. *The Life of Harriet Beecher Stowe.* Boston & New York: Houghton Mifflin & Co., 1891, p. 149.

21   *Life of Harriet Beecher Stowe*, p. 193.

big war.'[22] Within ten years of *Uncle Tom's Cabin*'s publication, Abraham Lincoln issued the Emancipation Proclamation, and three years later the Union victory in the Civil War assured the freedom of the slaves.

Harriet had received her education and training at Hartford Female Seminary, the school founded by her older sister Catherine Beecher (1800-1878). Catherine never had the radical conversion experience which had become central to her father's and the Second Great Awakening's teachings. She had been courted by a professor of mathematics at Yale who died when his ship sank in a voyage to England. Catherine knew he too had not had a conversion experience either and struggled with his fate. She wrestled with the Puritan faith of her ancestors, yet found the Bible which was foundational to that faith ever true and reasonable. For three years Catherine's father pressured her to have a conversion experience, but this was something Catherine could not produce. She studied the truth of Scriptures and came to believe conversion was not an excitement of the feelings but a question of obedience to truth. Catherine's father consented to her joining the church based on her confession of faith rather than a particular experience of conversion.

In 1836 Catherine published *Letters on the Difficulty of Religion* and dedicated it to her 'honored and beloved father'. The twenty-three letters written to skeptics and atheists were a winsome apologetics for the truth of the Bible and the Christian faith. The letters undoubtedly reflect Catherine's own earlier struggles with Christian truth and the particular features of American Christianity during the Second Great Awakening. Catherine's arguments were from common sense and the Bible. She avoided sectarian or denominational differences, but clearly presented reasons to believe truths accepted by all known as Evangelicals, regardless of other denominational or sectarian distinctives:

> All these Evangelical sects are united in believing and teaching the Divinity of our Lord Jesus Christ, and the efficacy of his atoning sacrifice, to save from future punishment, all who devote to Him the love of the heart, and the service of the life. They unite in believing that the sanction of the law and gospel, is eternal ruin, to all who die without this indispensable preparation for a future state. They all acknowledge their entire dependence on the Holy Spirit for all holy desires, right purposes, and acceptable service, and they all believe that it is by the Word of truth, or the motives and sanctions of the gospel, that the Spirit acts to regenerate and purify. They all acknowledge it to be their duty, to aid in spreading the knowledge of the gospel through all lands, and are united in efforts to promote this great object.[23]

---

22   Charles E. Stowe, *Harriet Beecher Stowe. The Story of Her Life*. Houghton Mifflin, 1911, p. 203

23   Catherine A. Beecher. *Letters on the Difficulties of Religion*. Hartford: Belknap & Hamersley, 1836, p. 333, available through Google Books (http://books.google.com).

In the *Letters* Catherine discussed issues such as the nature of free will, the need for revelation, the divine authority of the Bible, the importance of the future state in men's moral decisions, the relation of the law of God to the gospel, and Christian morality contrasted with Unitarian morality. Many ministers and church members were shocked that a woman could plunge into such deep doctrinal areas with such competence.

Catherine did not support the growing cry of feminists for women to assume a more public role and be allowed to vote. She was against women speaking in public gatherings, believing men should have the superior position in the political and public spheres. However, she believed the woman's role was morally superior to the man's and that women should be the dominant molders of morality within the home and schools. She believed the home and educational institutions were the real agents of moral change. Though men should have a superior position in the political and public spheres, women were the dominant molders of morality within the home and schools. Catherine held that women had more influence in their domestic roles than if they held positions of power and authority in government or business.

With this framework of beliefs, Catherine found her calling in the education of women. When she established the Hartford Female Seminary in 1823, she developed a course in moral philosophy to train young women to be the moral guardians of society, starting at home and in the schools. In 1831, she published her ideas in *Elements of Mental and Moral Philosophy,* founded upon experience, reason and the Bible as a foundation for her educational theory. The work was an analysis of the mind, what its purpose was, how it worked, why the mind of man is disordered and how this is to be rectified. Combining the best of human philosophy and wisdom with lessons learned from man's history and the foundational truths of the Scripture, Catherine masterfully developed a philosophy, principles, and methods for the instruction of children. Catherine ended the work with an almost millennial prayer for the "Prince of all the kings of the earth" to bring renewal to His people. In 1841, Catherine wrote *Treatise on Domestic Economy for the Use of Young Ladies at Home*, one of the earliest and most influential books on organizing the woman's domestic sphere. Catherine attempted to apply scientific principles to cooking, housekeeping, and child-rearing, an approach used in the later development of 'home economics.' Later she expanded the work in collaboration with her sister Harriet, publishing *The American Woman's Home* in 1869. The subtitle was 'Principles of Domestic Science; being a guide to the formation and maintenance of economical, healthful, beautiful, and Christian homes.' The work was dedicated 'To the Women of America, in whose hands rest the real destinies of the Republic, as moulded by the early training and preserved amid the mature influences of home.' Catherine and Harriet believed that the woman's highest position could best be achieved by serving in the domestic sphere, not by organizing for rights and special privileges. The introduction to *The American Woman's Home* concluded:

> ...to intelligent, reflecting, and benevolent women – whose faith rests on the character and teachings of Jesus Christ – there are great principles revealed by Him, which in the end will secure the grand result which He taught and suffered to achieve. It is hoped that in the following pages these principles will be so exhibited and illustrated as to aid in securing those rights and advantages which Christ's religion aims to provide for all, and especially for the most weak and defenseless of His children.[24]

Beginning with a chapter on the Christian Family, the work included chapters discussing the importance of discipline, the self-sacrificing example of Christ, and the importance of self-denial in mutual relations, as well as the different roles of the woman and man in the family. Later chapters covered the topics of the wisdom in building a Christian house and its arrangement, ventilation, stoves and chimneys, home decoration, personal health, domestic exercise, healthful food, cleanliness, clothing, economy of time and expenses, care of infants, health of mind, care of the sick and aged, propagation of plants, accidents and mending, domestic animals, care of the homeless, and the Christian neighborhood!

Any woman reading through such a vast collection of advice and guidelines would undoubtedly become discouraged at her past failures and inability to measure up to such standards. Fittingly, the Beecher sisters concluded their compendium with the following Biblical encouragement:

> In this painful review, the good old Bible comes as the abundant comforter. The Epistle to the Romans was written especially to meet such regrets and fears. It teaches that all men are sinners, in many cases from ignorance of what is right, and in many from stress of temptation, so that neither Greek nor Jew can boast of his own righteousness. For it is not 'by works of righteousness' that we are to be considered and treated as righteous persons, but through a 'faith that *works by love;*' that *faith* or *belief* which is not a mere intellectual conviction, but a *controlling purpose* or spiritual principle which *habitually controls* the feelings and conduct. And so long as there is this constant aim and purpose to obey Christ in all things, mistakes in judgment as to what is right and wrong are pitied, 'even as a father pitieth his children,' when from ignorance they run into harm. And even the most guilty transgressors are freely forgiven when truly repentant and faithfully striving to forsake the error of their ways.[25]

The Beechers also looked hopefully to the 'dawning day to which we are approaching, when a voice shall be heard under the whole heavens, saying,

---

24   Catherine E. Beecher and Harriet Beecher Stowe. *The American Woman's Home*. Hartford, Conn.: reprint of 1869 edition by the Stowe-Day Foundation, 1991, p. 16, available at www.gutenberg.org/etext/6598.

25   *American Woman's Home*, p. 460.

"Alleluia" – "the kingdoms of this world are become the kingdoms of our Lord and of his Christ, and he shall reign forever and ever."[26]

Holiness and Spiritual Reform

Women became important encouragers of the Holiness movement which developed from the Wesleyan revivals and the work of Charles Finney and Asa Mahan at Oberlin College. Phoebe Palmer (1807-1874), from a cultured, educated background, was among the earliest Holiness leaders. She was married to Walter C. Palmer, a New York physician, and the two jointly participated in Methodist gatherings. After the death of one of her children, Phoebe became greatly depressed. After a time, however, she experienced a 'second blessing.' Phoebe believed that the first blessing was received at conversion, but when the Christian gave his entire life to God, he received a second blessing. In 1845, Phoebe published *The Way of Holiness*, explaining its underlying principles. She defined gospel holiness as

> ... that *state* which is attained by the believer when through *faith* in the infinite merit of the Saviour, body and soul, with every ransomed faculty, are ceaselessly presented, a living sacrifice, to God, the purpose of the soul being steadily bent to know nothing among men, save Christ and Him crucified, and the eye of faith fixed on 'the Lamb of God which taketh away the sin of the world.' In obedience to the requirement of God, the sacrifice is presented *through* Christ, and the soul at once proves that 'He is able to save them to the *uttermost* that come unto God by Him.'
>
> Holiness implies salvation from sin, a redemption from *all* iniquity. The soul through faith, being laid upon the *altar* that *sanctifieth* the gift, experiences, *constantly* the all-cleansing efficacy of the blood of Jesus.[27]

Phoebe wrote that it was important to see that holiness or complete sanctification was *for the present*, not something in the future:

> It is of great importance that you look at this great Salvation as a *present* Salvation, received momentarily from above. The blood of Jesus *cleanseth*, not that it can or will cleanse at some *future* period, but it *cleanseth* now, while you lay your all upon that 'altar that sanctifieth the gift.' ... Holiness is a state of soul in which all the powers of the body and mind are consciously given up to God; and the witness of holiness is that testimony which the Holy Spirit bears with our spirit that the offering is accepted through Christ. The work is accomplished the moment we lay our all upon the altar.[28]

Phoebe's 'laying all on the altar' was a phrase she repeatedly used to describe the living sacrifice which Paul had written about in Romans 12:1,

---

26 Ibid., p. 461.

27 *In Her Words*, p. 285. *The Way of Holiness* is available online at http://utc.iath.virginia.edu/christn/palmerhp.html.

28 Ibid., pp. 289-90.

the total consecration of oneself to God and trust that He would sanctify what had been consecrated. This 'altar theology' was adopted by many Methodists, as well as later by the Church of the Nazarene, the Keswick movement, and the Salvation Army. For thirty years, Phoebe led the Tuesday Meeting for the Promotion of Holiness in New York, shaping the views of many ministers as well as laypeople. Sometimes several hundred people attended on a Tuesday morning. Phoebe also ministered to camp meetings and revivals in the United States, Canada, and Britain.

Among those influenced by Phoebe's teaching was Amanda Berry Smith (1837-1915), a woman born into slavery in Maryland. After her father purchased his own freedom and that of his family, Amanda went to work as a domestic servant. She attended Phoebe's Tuesday meetings, and in 1868 received a second blessing while listening to a Methodist minister. The death of her husband and youngest child the following year freed Amanda from family responsibilities, and she began teaching in African American churches in New York and New Jersey. Soon she was a full-time evangelist, frequently speaking in holiness meetings. In 1878, she went to England as an itinerant preacher, and for the next fourteen years ministered as a preacher or missionary in India, Burma, Africa, England, Scotland, and Ireland.[29]

At the same time, Hannah Whitehall Smith (1832-1911) and her husband Robert Pearsall Smith were preaching the Higher Christian Life in England, Germany, France, and Switzerland. The Smiths both were Quakers from Philadelphia whose ancestors held deeply to the Quaker faith. During the 1858 prayer revivals, Hannah and Robert committed themselves completely to God. They held holiness meetings in America, but were especially popular in England. In 1875, Hannah published *The Christian's Secret of a Happy Life*, which continues to be a popular devotional today.[30] Hannah wrote that the Christian should totally abandon himself as a lump of clay in the Potter's hands.

Catherine Booth (1829-1890) and her husband William were also working in England at this time. Catherine was the only daughter of five children whose father was a lay preacher. Remarkably precocious, she could read by the age of three, and by the age of twelve had read the Bible through eight times. She read voraciously, especially works of theology and Church history. Catherine was converted and joined the Wesleyan Church when she was sixteen.

One Sunday Catherine heard the itinerant evangelist William Booth preach and was impressed. A friend of Booth's told him of Catherine's regard, and a correspondence developed between the two young people. Catherine had definite ideas of what she wanted in a husband. He had to be a true Christian and a man of common sense. She knew she could never respect a fool or someone weaker mentally than she was. Her husband should totally abstain from liquor.

---

29   *An Autobiography: The Story of the Lord's Dealings with Mrs. Amanda Smith, the Colored Evangelist*, 1893 can be found at Google Books http://books.google.com.

30   Available online at http://www.ccel.org/s/smith_hw/secret/secret.html.

R.L. Dabney on 'The Public Preaching of Women'

In the last quarter of the 19th century, the growing number of women preachers became the subject of public discussion and criticism. Addressing the issue from a theologian's perspective, R.L. Dabney (1820-1898), began with the major premise: The Bible clearly forbade a woman assuming authority over men in the Church. Though certain women, such as Elizabeth Fry, might be particularly gifted, the Holy Spirit, who had inspired the Bible, would not contradict Himself and call someone to do what the inspired Scriptures had forbidden. Their gifts could be used in ways which did not violate the Bible's injunctions. Women who violated the Scripture in this area were presumptuous and following their human wisdom or feelings rather than the Scripture. Dabney said they were like King Uzziah, who thought he was helping God when he presumed to touch the ark to keep it from falling though in doing so he violated God's Word, since he was not a Levite (2 Chron. 26). That spiritual fruit could be produced from the ministry of women who preached in violation of God's commands was a testimony to God's mercy and grace. It is 'one of God's clearest and most blessed prerogatives to bring good out of evil,' as Paul recognized when he rejoiced the gospel was preached, though some preached Christ out of envy and strife (Phil. 1:15).

For Dabney, at issue was the obedience to the Bible. When women ignored the Bible in attempting to establish their own rights, they were undermining the very foundation of the greater respect and honor they had achieved in Christian countries:

> If they [women aspiring to preach] read history they find that the condition of woman in Christendom, and especially in America, is most enviable as compared with her state in all other ages and nations. Let them ponder candidly how much they possess here which their sisters have enjoyed in no other age. What bestowed those peculiar privileges on the Christian women of America? The Bible. Let them beware then how they do anything to undermine the reverence of mankind for the authority of the Bible. It is undermining their own bulwark. If they understand how universally in all but the Bible lands the 'weaker vessel' has been made the slave of man's strength and selfishness, they will gladly 'let well enough alone,' lest in grasping at some impossible prize beyond, they lose the privileges they now have, and fall back to the gulf of oppression from which these doctrines of Christ and Paul have lifted them.*

---

*'The Public Preaching of Women,' *Southern Presbyterian Review*, October 1879, p. 713.

Catherine also believed that a husband and wife should have 'a oneness of views and tastes, any idea of lordship or ownership being lost in love.'[31]

In May 1852, Catherine and William were engaged. Women's rights became an issue in their courtship, however. At one point William wrote that he felt woman had 'a fibre more in her heart and a cell less in her brain.' Catherine said she would not marry a man who did not totally consider her an equal. She believed the woman's subjection to the man was part of the curse which was cancelled by Christ's death and resurrection.

---

31   Quoted in Nancy Hardesty. *Great Women of Faith*, p. 104.

She wished ministers would truly search the Scriptures, for she believed their interpretations were wrong about women's ministry. She held that women should not be made to bury the gifts God had given them.

Catherine's first published writing was an 1854 letter to the Methodist *New Connection* magazine on how to care for newborn souls. She ended the article with a plea for women to use their gifts:

> There seems in many societies a growing disinclination among the female members to engage in prayer, speak in love feasts, band meetings, or in any manner bear testimony for their Lord ... And this false God-dishonouring timidity is but too fatally pandered to by the church. [32]

Shortly before her marriage to William in 1855, Catherine wrote William that she was convinced of the rightness of women preaching:

> I have searched the Word of God through and through, I have tried to deal honestly with every passage on the subject, not forgetting to pray for light to perceive and grace to submit to the truth, however humiliating to my nature, but I solemnly assert that the more I think and read on the subject, the more satisfied I become of the true and scriptural character of my own views.

William replied,

> I would not stop a woman preaching on any account, I would not encourage one to begin. You should preach if you felt moved thereto: felt equal to the task. I would not stay you if I had power to do so. *Altho', I should not like it.* I am for the world's salvation; I will quarrel with no means that promises help. [33]

In 1859, Catherine published *Female Ministry, or Woman's Right to Preach the Gospel*, a rebuttal to attacks on the ministry of Phoebe Palmer. Catherine contended that women in the early Church had preached and prophesied and that the prophet Joel had predicted that women prophesying was a distinguishing mark of preaching the gospel. If the Holy Spirit was leading a woman to preach, Catherine believed it was wrong to prevent her doing so. Accordingly, when William became ill from exhaustion in 1860, Catherine stepped in and took over his teaching responsibilities for a time, and eventually his entire circuit.

When the Methodists refused to license Catherine and William as evangelists, they left that denomination and began to work among the prostitutes and slums in southeast London. They worked together as a team in ministering to the spiritual and physical needs of the poor in the area, trusting the Lord for their support while they were doing His work. By 1878, this mission had been transformed into the Salvation Army, an army of Christian soldiers battling the forces of evil and wickedness in, and soon

---

32   *Great Women of Faith*, p. 105.

33   Ibid.

278 | FEMININE THREADS

throughout, the world. While always making Jesus Christ and His redeeming work central to their preaching and social work, the Booths developed a disciplined regimen and doctrine for the Salvation Army, to effectively wage spiritual battle against the unbelief and social evils found especially in the cities. Military metaphors were woven throughout the organization. Prayers were called 'knee drills'; Bible reading was 'taking one's rations.' Revivals were 'battles,' and every convert was a 'prisoner of war.' Catherine designed a distinctive women's uniform, including a bonnet which came to be known as the 'Hallelujah Bonnet.' Catherine believed that the Christians' appearance should announce to the world that they were no longer a part of the world.

As leaders of the Salvation Army, the Booths traveled widely, yet they always cared for the Christian welfare of their eight children. All of the eight children, except one daughter who was handicapped, continued as leaders in the Salvation Army in its worldwide ministries. Seeing her children carrying out their Christian responsibilities, Catherine declared, '"My soul doth magnify the Lord," for His grace and truth shown to my children. He hath given me the desire of my heart.'[34]

When Catherine died in 1890, she lay in state in London's Congress Hall for five days while fifty thousand people filed by. At the end of her funeral service, her husband William spoke of her as a flower in his garden of years and a shadow from the burning sun. She was a servant who cared in love for his health and comfort and a friend who understood his feelings, thoughts, and the purpose for his life. He praised her as a mother who trained her children in service for her God and as a wife who 'had stood by his side, ever willing to interpose herself between him and the enemy, and ever strongest when the battle was fiercest.' He was deeply grateful that God had lent him such a treasure, a real warrior for Christ, for so long a time.[35] In 2008, the Salvation Army that Catherine and William Booth had established was operating in 115 countries, with numerous social programs, Christian educational programs, and relief missions to reach the neediest with the truth of Christ and with material help.[36]

34   *Great Women of the Christian Faith*, p. 225.

35   Ibid., p. 226. Many of Catherine Booth's writings can be found at 'Victorian Women Writers,' http://www.indiana.edu/~letrs/vwwp/vwwplib.pl?#booth.

36   Salvation Army, International Headquarters statistics, http://www.salvationarmy.org/ihq/www_sa.nsf/vw-dynamic-arrays/D46980EA862CD1FD80256D4F00411840?openDocument.

At the End of Two Millennia:
Professing Godliness

1 Timothy 2:10

Even as the Victorian era's cult of domesticity elevated the home and woman's moral influence, the growing force of the Industrial Revolution was diminishing the centrality of the home in American and British society. For centuries the home had been the major economic unit. In rural areas, the family farm was the norm. In towns, workshops and stores were located in the front room or the first floor of the family dwelling. In either case, families worked together in one common area. Mothers and fathers might have different tasks, but they were an economic team with a common enterprise. With industrialization, the public and domestic spheres were bifurcated as men went away from the home to work in offices or factories.

In America, the home was recognized as crucial to the success of the new experiment in republican government. If the new nation were to succeed, children must become citizens with civic virtues and character, a task seen in great part as falling to women as they educated their children. Ironically, as women came to be seen as the protectors and guardians of morality, the spiritual and moral leadership of men was diminished. Unfortunately, the Church did not speak against the nineteenth-century notions of the moral superiority of women, notions which lacked a Scriptural basis. Several scholars have noted the resulting 'feminization' of the Church or society during this period.[1] During the closing decades of the second millennium, various movements for greater rights and changing roles for women made the question of women's nature and position in society a major political and social issue.

Clamoring for Women's Rights

The Women's Rights movement had its beginnings in the reform movements of the Second Great Awakening. However, the movement was

---

1   Leon J. Podles, *The Church Impotent: The Feminization of Christianity*. Spence Publishing Company, 1999; David Murrow, *Why Men Hate Going to Church*. Nelson Books, 2004; Nancy Pearcey, *Total Truth: Liberating Christianity From Its Cultural Captivity*. Crossway Books, 2004.

largely overshadowed by the abolitionist movement until after the Civil War. Some women thought that their sex was being oppressed and rights denied in a manner similar to the way the slaves had been oppressed. Abolitionist Sarah Grimke thought there were links between the misuse of Scripture to endorse slavery and the demands for female submission. Others, such as Lucretia Mott, thought that social justice for women was more important than anything the Scriptures might say.

Lucretia Mott (1793-1880) was a Quaker minister, a social reformer, and mother of six. She and her husband were among the founders of the American Anti-Slavery Society. In 1833, Lucretia established the Philadelphia Female Anti-Slavery Society, and from 1866 to 1868 she was president of the American Equal Rights Association. Lucretia preached that many in the Church were following Christian traditions and creeds rather than truly following Christ. Lucretia believed the Holy Spirit might inspire modern preachers so that their words were authoritative for their day as the Scriptures for an earlier people:

> How much does this society lose by this undue veneration to ancient authorities, a want of equal respect to the living inspired testimonies of latter time? Christianity requires that we bring into view the apostles of succeeding generations, that we acknowledge their apostleship and give the right hand of fellowship to those who have been and who are sent forth of God with great truths to declare before the people …

Though Lucretia identified herself with the Christian faith, she was unorthodox in her beliefs, questioning inerrancy of Scripture and the supremacy of its authority as the Word of God:

> … the great error in Christendom is, in regarding these scriptures taken as a whole as the plenary inspiration of God and their authority as supreme. I consider this…one of the greatest drawbacks, one of the greatest barriers to human progress that there is in the religious world …[2]

Lucretia, along with Elizabeth Cady Stanton (1815-1902), was a leader at the famous Seneca Falls women's rights convention in 1848. Stanton and her husband were also active in anti-slavery conventions, but Elizabeth soon realized that women were not equal in the anti-slavery organizations. Stanton became a strong advocate of women's access to all of the professions, women's right to vote, and divorce reform allowing women to escape from intolerable marriages. In July 1848, Stanton and Mott, along with three other women (all but Stanton were Quakers) called for a convention in Seneca Falls, New York, 'to discuss the social,

---

2   From 'Likeness to Christ,' a sermon delivered in Philadelphia, September 30, 1849, quoted in *In Her Words*, pp. 293-8.

civil, and religious condition and rights of woman.'[3] Stanton drew up the draft 'Declaration of Sentiments' to be discussed. She used the U.S. Declaration of Independence as a pattern, substituting the tyranny of 'man' for the tyranny of King George III. The 'Declaration of Sentiments' stated that, 'The history of mankind is a history of repeated injuries and usurpations on the part of man toward woman, having in direct object the establishment of an absolute tyranny over her. To prove this, let facts be submitted to a candid world.' There followed a list of grievances – women lacked the right to vote and had to obey laws they had no voice in making; marriage laws gave the husband power over his wife; married women could not own property; men monopolized all profitable employments so that a woman could not even teach theology, medicine, or law; women were denied a college education. Man, 'allows her in Church, as well as State, but a subordinate position, claiming Apostolic authority for her exclusion from the ministry, and, with some exceptions, from any public participation in the affairs of the Church.' Lucretia Mott added a final resolve that 'the speedy success of our cause depends upon the zealous and untiring efforts of both men and women, for the overthrow of the monopoly of the pulpit.'[4] One hundred men and women signed the Seneca Falls Declaration, though some later had their names removed.

Elizabeth Stanton had even more antipathy towards Christian teaching than Lucretia. Raised a Presbyterian, she rejected special revelation and providence and asserted that organized religion was the chief cause and root of woman's oppression. Believing that the Bible had been twisted and distorted by men to oppress women, she put together *The Woman's Bible*, in which a group of educated women commented on the Biblical text from a female perspective. In the introduction to *The Woman's Bible*, Stanton summarized how she thought the Bible denigrated women:

> The Bible teaches that woman brought sin and death into the world, that she precipitated the fall of the race, that she was arraigned before the judgment seat of Heaven, tried, condemned, and sentenced. Marriage for her was to be a condition of bondage, maternity a period of suffering and anguish, and in silence and subjection, she was to play the role of a dependent on man's bounty for all her material wants, and for all the information she might desire on the vital questions of the hour, she was commanded to ask her husband at home. Here is the Bible position of woman briefly summed up.

---

3   'Seneca Falls Convention Began Women's Rights Movement,' *America.gov – engaging the world*, http://www.america.gov/st/diversity-english/2005/June/20080229183432liameru oy0.6444055.html.

4   'Seneca Falls Declaration of Sentiments and Resolutions,' July 19, 1848, available at http:// www.fordham.edu/halsall/mod/Senecafalls.html, accessed June 2, 2011.

Stanton said the world was changing. If the common law of England could be changed, why not change the Law of Moses? If the Bible said women are equal, why couldn't they be ordained? Women who still believed in the plenary inspiration of the Scriptures should take the higher criticism of the Scriptures into account. The Old and New Testaments were filled with contradictions; miracles were opposed to scientific laws; and the Bible was filled with degrading customs. Stanton did not believe any man ever saw or talked with God or that the Mosaic code was inspired:

> The canon law, the Scriptures, the creeds and codes and church discipline of the leading religions bear the impress of fallible man, and not of our ideal great first cause, 'the Spirit of all Good,' that set the universe of matter and mind in motion, and by immutable law holds the land, the sea, the planets, revolving round the great centre of light and heat, each in its own elliptic, with millions of stars in harmony all singing together, the glory of creation forever and ever.[5]

Because of Stanton's negative treatment of Scriptures, in 1896 the National American Woman Suffrage Association renounced any connection with the first volume of *The Woman's Bible*.

The unorthodox and blatantly anti-Christian views of Mott and Stanton revealed the unbiblical foundations of a leading section of the women's rights movement. Yet, not all those who were part of the women's rights movement were as eager to completely jettison the Christian Scriptures as was Stanton. Probably the most well-known and influential of the women organizers of the period was Frances Willard (1839-1898), who distanced herself from those who claimed Christian patriarchy was the cause of woman's woes. Frances was reared a Congregationalist but converted to Methodism in 1859. Frances came from a family which valued education; her mother had been educated at Oberlin and was responsible for much of Frances' early schooling. As soon as she completed her own education, Frances began teaching, first in one-room schools in Illinois, then in secondary schools in Pennsylvania and New York. She was well thought of as a speaker and for a time assisted Dwight L. Moody in evangelistic work. However, when it became evident that Moody considered her the speaker for women's groups only and would not allow her to speak to mixed audiences, she separated from his ministry.

Frances was one of the organizers of the Woman's Christian Temperance Union (WCTU) in 1874 and was its president from 1879-1898. Under her leadership the organization grew to one of the largest worldwide organizations for women. At a time when alcohol abuse was rampant, the WCTU became an organization for moral reform of society. There were

---

5   Introduction to *The Woman's Bible* found in *In Her Words*, pp. 315-20 and at http://www.sacred-texts.com/wmn/wb/index.htm.

no legal limits on the alcohol content of whiskey, nor was there a legal drinking age. A husband could use all of his paycheck on drink, and the wife had no legal recourse. Nor were there any laws protecting a wife from physical abuse. Women in the WCTU disseminated information, organized petition drives, and sought legislative changes to promote temperance. They were in a very real sense participating in the political process before they had the right to vote.

Frances herself enjoyed drinking wine and did not believe that alcohol was an absolute evil, yet because of the disastrous effects of alcohol on society and women, she encouraged the complete renunciation of alcohol. 'Signing the pledge' of total abstinence became a ceremony encouraged in all types of social gatherings, from churches to state fairs. Family Bibles were even printed with an elaborately decorated temperance page for family members to sign. The primary purpose of these efforts was, as Frances Willard often said, the 'protection of the home.' The slogan of the WCTU was 'For God and Home and Native Land.'

Though best known for alcoholic temperance, the WCTU under Frances became a voice on many other issues touching women's welfare. Frances campaigned for changes in prostitution laws, making men and women equally guilty for the crime. In all sexual cases, she believed men should be held to the same level of sexual purity as women. The WCTU raised international awareness of the evils of narcotics, urging governments to stop the legal sale of opium. Frances also put the WCTU behind the issue of women's right to vote. She argued that legislation for prohibition would more easily pass if women were part of the electorate, and her efforts led the way to the adoption of the Eighteenth and Nineteenth Amendments to the United States Constitution.[6]

Frances also urged fashion designers to avoid the spider-thin waists which were a health hazard to women and design clothes in accord with normal health conditions. She promoted sports for women and encouraged bicycle riding as good exercise. It was while on a bicycle tour of Europe that she learned about Armenian refugees who had escaped massacre in Turkey. She then worked with the Salvation Army to bring 300 of the Armenians to the United States under sponsorship by WCTU families. The WCTU under Willard had a wide-ranging social vision which went far beyond the issues of temperance or even women's right to vote.

---

6   The Eighteenth Amendment prohibited the manufacture, importation or exportation of intoxicating liquors in the United States. The Nineteenth Amendment stated that the rights of citizens should not be denied or abridged on account of sex.

The Changing American Church and the Blackwells

The Congregational Church grew from the early Puritan churches of New England, holding a firm belief in the Bible as the guiding truth for life. When the churches first began to lose their convictions in the 1700s, the religious revival known as the Great Awakening helped buttress their Biblical faith. In the early 1800s, some of the early Puritan churches became Unitarian; others resisted the Unitarian impulse and preserved their Biblical faith. During the late nineteenth century and early twentieth centuries, however, many of the Congregational churches became more liberal in their theology. They no longer interpreted the Bible literally, and they became leaders in social activism. The churches' active support of abolition and women's rights easily led the churches to embrace the Social Gospel. The Church's replacement of the Gospel of Christ with the Social Gospel can be seen in the feminist leaders connected with the Blackwell family.

The Blackwell family moved to the United States in 1832. Active in social reform in England, the father soon joined in the abolitionist cause. His daughter Elizabeth (1821-1910) was the world's first woman to graduate from medical school and receive a medical degree. Elizabeth's sister Emily followed, also receiving a medical degree. Elizabeth practiced medicine and lectured widely in the United States and England. In 1852, she authored *The Laws of Life: with special Reference to the Physical Education of Girls*. In 1857, she helped incorporate the New York Infirmary for Women and Children. During the Civil War, Elizabeth and her sister Emily organized the Women's Central Association of Relief, which developed into the United States Sanitary Commission. After the war, Elizabeth opened the Women's Medical College at the New York Infirmary. Elizabeth was an Episcopalian, then a Unitarian, then returned to the Episcopal Church and associated with Christian socialism.

Elizabeth's brother Samuel married Antoinette Brown in 1856. Antoinette (1825-1921) was accepted in the Congregational Church at nine and soon decided God wanted her to be a minister. She graduated from Oberlin College in 1847 and studied in Oberlin Seminary until 1850, but was refused a degree because of her sex. Antoinette wrote and spoke frequently on social issues of abolition, temperance and women's rights. The Congregational Church of South Butler, New York, ordained Antoinette in 1853, making her the first ordained woman minister in the United States. She later left the church over discontent with its doctrines and focused on women's rights issues. Unlike other women's rights leaders of the day, Antoinette thought the general improvement of women's opportunities and status was more important than women's suffrage. She also opposed divorce as a solution to the restrictions of women in marriage. Though Antoinette thought she had more freedom as a single woman, Samuel Blackwell persuaded her to marry him in 1856. The couple had seven children. Antoinette took her family responsibilities seriously and discontinued her lecturing. While holding that the woman's primary role was the care of the home and family, she continued to write on women's issues and theology, and encouraged women to seek professional positions traditionally filled by men. She held that women and men were equal while still maintaining important differences between them.

Lucy Stone, a friend of Antoinette's from Oberlin, married Elizabeth and Samuel Blackwell's brother Henry in 1856. A Cincinnati merchant, Henry Blackwell was also a staunch abolitionist and supporter of women's rights. Henry supported Lucy when she chose not to take his Blackwell surname after their marriage. Lucy was a prominent speaker and organizer in many women's rights organizations and was editor of the *Woman's Journal* she and her husband established in 1867. Lucy broke with Elizabeth Cady Stanton and Susan B. Anthony when they refused to support the 14th amendment and any constitutional changes which did not also enfranchise women. Lucy supported advances in civil rights of former slaves while continuing to work for increased women's rights.

Frances was greatly influenced by the holiness teachings of Phoebe Palmer, and in all of the social activities of the WCTU, a spiritual message was always present. WCTU women organized Bible readings and charitable work everywhere – among seamen, police stations, prisons, railroad workers, and soldiers. Frances wrote that these women 'make an aggregate of several thousands of women who are regularly studying and expounding God's word to the multitude, to say nothing of the army in home and foreign missions, who are engaged in church evangelism.'[7]

Lemonade Lucy

Lucy Webb Hayes (1831-1889), wife of President Rutherford B. Hayes, was a devout Christian and the first college-educated First Lady of the United States. Both she and her husband had taken the temperance pledge and saw no reason to go against their convictions by serving wine in the White House. Lucy became known as 'Lemonade Lucy' for her stand.

While in the White House (1877-1881), the Hayes continued their practice of daily family prayers and held Sunday evening hymn sings which inspired all who attended. The Woman's Home Missionary Society of the Methodist Episcopal Church was organized while Lucy was First Lady, and she became the organization's first president, serving for nine years.

Lucy Hayes always recognized that the Christian home was the foundation of society and the strength of the country, believing that 'America is the cradle of the future for all the world. Elevate woman, and you lift up the home; exalt the home and you lift up the nation.'*

Quoted in *Great Women of the Christian Faith*, 229.

Frances had wanted to be ordained as a young woman, but the Methodist Episcopal Church at the time did not ordain women. In 1880, she wanted to bring greetings from the WCTU to the Methodist Church's General Conference but was prevented from doing so because she was a woman. The motion to allow her to speak for ten minutes led to a two-hour debate. She finally left the conference a note for them to read which included a quote from Charles Finney, 'The church that silences

---

7   *Daughters of the Church*, p. 273.

the women is shorn of half its power.' In 1888, she published *Woman in the Pulpit* in favor of ordaining women evangelists and preachers. Though Frances never repudiated the Scriptures to the degree done by Elizabeth Stanton, she increasingly came to favor Christian socialism, an early form of what became known in the twentieth century as the Social Gospel.

By the end of the nineteenth century, then, a variety of positions on women's role had developed. As seen from earlier times, the different perspectives on women's roles were in part determined by one's attitude towards Scripture. Was the Bible the authority for life? Was the Bible the inspired Word of God to be followed literally, or was there an inner light from God which should be the guiding light? Should the Bible be recognized as an ancient book with some truths in it, but not totally applicable to the changing world? Were creeds and beliefs important, or were beliefs irrelevant to how life was lived in the world? Was there any difference between men's and women's roles in society? These were all questions women of the nineteenth century began to consider, and with which their daughters in the twentieth century grappled.

Expanding the Globe

The American Civil War had affected the activities of women in several ways. First, with so many young men killed in the war, many women who might otherwise have married lived lives of singleness. Some of these spent their lives as missionaries in foreign lands. Second, with the men away at war, women taking care of the home front developed organizational and administrative skills which

---

Helen Montgomery's Firsts

Helen Barrett Montgomery was a leader whose businessman-husband encouraged her to use her talents to the fullest in Christian service. Together the Montgomerys were able to substantially contribute to Christian causes, and Helen was able to use her numerous abilities in volunteer work, especially in the field of missions. A lady of scholarship and integrity, she accepted leadership positions as places of further service. Helen was the first female member of the Rochester School Board. In 1914, she became president of the Women's American Baptist Foreign Mission Society, a position she held for ten years. She became a licensed Baptist minister, and in 1921 was the president of the Northern Baptist Convention, becoming the first woman president of a religious denomination.

Helen is often noted as the first woman to translate the New Testament into English, but that accomplishment rightly goes to Julia Smith, whose complete Bible translation was published in 1876. However, Helen Montgomery's *Centenary New Testament*, first published in 1924 for the centennial of the American Baptist Publication Society, was a clear translation still in print today. A capable Greek scholar, Montgomery's English translation tried to make the Scriptures intelligible to young people, Sunday-School teachers, and foreigners.

they continued to expand in other ways after the war's end. From 1861 to 1894, women in thirty-three denominations established foreign missionary societies. Home mission societies, focusing on missions to the Native Americans, freed slaves, and the expanding population in the west, were established in seventeen denominations. These were organizations totally operated and funded by women within the denominational structure.

In 1888, American, Canadian, and British women missionary leaders created the World's Missionary Committee of Christian Women, the first ecumenical missionary agency which was universal in scope. In conjunction with the Chicago World's Fair of 1893, the group organized a meeting of women's missionary societies at the Woman's Congress of Missions. They also organized a woman's work program at the 1900 Ecumenical Missionary Conference in New York. At this conference the World's Committee created a united study program to produce study material about missions. Annually the committee published a textbook

---

Agnes Smith Lewis & Margaret Smith Gibson
(1843-1926)(1843-1920)

Two weeks after Agnes and Margaret Smith were born on January 11, 1843, their mother died. The twins were raised by their father, who brought the girls up in the Presbyterian Church and made certain they had a good education. Noticing his daughters' gift for languages, John Smith promised them that when they learned a language, he would take them to visit the country where the language was spoken. At a very young age the girls mastered French, German, Spanish, and Italian, and they traveled with their father throughout Europe.

John Smith inherited a very large sum of money from a distant relative and legal client — something like $10.5 million in today's values. He died when the twins were 23, leaving them with a vast fortune. Agnes and Margaret sought to use these funds and live their lives with purpose and to God's glory. They taught Sunday School and reached out to help others in numerous ways. They also continued to travel and to develop linguistic skills — learning modern and ancient Greek, Arabic, and Syriac. They became special friends with the monks at the famed St. Catherine's Monastery in the Sinai, making major discoveries among the ancient manuscripts in the monastery and cataloguing the monastery's rare manuscript library.

Though both sisters were happily married, their marriages were brief, each ending with the death of her husband after three years. When many thought academic pursuits not fitting for women, Agnes and Margaret became Biblical scholars and authors respected throughout Europe. Both were awarded honorary doctorates by universities in Scotland, Germany, and Ireland.

Agnes and Margaret continue to be an inspiration to Westminster College, a Presbyterian College which located in Cambridge in 1899, largely through the twins' benefaction.

Janet Soskice. *The Sisters of Sinai: How Two Lady Adventurers Discovered the Hidden Gospels*. New York: Alfred A. Knopf, 2009.

for women to use in mission study groups in local churches. Helen Barrett Montgomery (1861-1934) was a primary author of the study books, which included *Christus Redemptor,* a study of the Islamic world; *The King's Highway*; *The Bible and Missions*; *Prayer and Missions*; and *From Jerusalem to Jerusalem.* Many women in cities, on farms, and on the frontier met together once a month to read together the missionary magazines about the Church's activities in foreign lands. In 1904, a summer school to study missions was established.

Montgomery's *Western Women in Eastern Lands*, issued in 1910, summarized the fifty-year history of the women's missionary movement. She particularly endorsed the importance of reaching women in heathen lands to transform the pagan home with the truth of Christ. Improving the condition of women in pagan lands contributed to evangelization. Montgomery looked forward to the establishment of the Kingdom of God on earth through the work of missions:

> To seek first to bring Christ's Kingdom on the earth, to respond to the need that is sorest, to go out into the desert for that loved and bewildered sheep that the shepherd has missed from the fold, to share all of privilege with the unprivileged and happiness with the unhappy, to lay down life, if need be, in the way of the Christ, to see the possibility of one redeemed earth, undivided, unvexed, unperplexed, resting in the light of the glorious Gospel of the blessed God, this is the mission of the women's missionary movement.[8]

Western Women in Eastern Lands led to a Jubilee celebrating the women's missionary movement. A traveling team of speakers spoke at teas and luncheons in forty-eight major cities as part of the Jubilee. The very organization of the celebration affirmed the grassroots character of women's missionary involvement. Over a million dollars was collected during the Jubilee, to be spent for women's colleges in Asia.

In 1913, Montgomery and her dear friend Lucy Peabody, a former missionary in India and editor for the Women's American Baptist Foreign Missionary Society, toured missionary fields in India, China, and Japan. Not only did they produce additional study materials on missions and collect funds for women's colleges in Asia, they proposed a World Day of Prayer. The World Day of Prayer continues as a worldwide ecumenical movement today in over 170 countries.

By the 1920s, there were three million women in missionary societies, more than in any other type of women's organization. The women's missionary organizations had experience in fundraising and distributing information. They even taught the general missionary boards the value

---

8   *Western Women,* 68, quoted in Dana L. Robert, *American Women in Mission: A Social History of Their Thought and Practice,* (Macon, Georgia: Mercer University Press), 1996.

of publicity. They organized missionary exhibits and jubilees to focus the public's attention on the needs and fruits in foreign lands. The women were the first to organize missionary training schools, which were forerunners of the Bible College. In 1881, the Woman's Baptist Missionary Training School in Chicago was established by the Woman's American Baptist Home Mission Society. By 1916, there were sixty religious training schools, mostly for women. The course of study was usually for one or two years and very practical. Students were taught the Bible, the history of missions, and the practical aspects of city work. Prayer meetings were an important part of the training, as were visits by missionaries from the field.

After World War I, many of the women's missionary boards were absorbed by the denominational boards. Since the denominational boards had begun accepting single women into the mission field, the original purpose for which the women's boards were established had been accomplished. Some of the denominational boards included women in the combined boards, but the women's missionary movement generally declined. Yet, through the work of the women's missionary organizations, the gospel had reached women in many portions of the world who never would have otherwise heard the gospel. Helen Montgomery noted there were six thousand Bible women and native helpers, as well as 800 teachers, 140 physicians, 79 nurses, and 380 evangelists on the mission field in 1909, all sent out by the women's boards.

The impact of a Christian woman in foreign lands can be seen by the example of Pandita Ramabai of India. Pandita Ramabai (1858-1922) has been recognized as one of India's greatest women. Ramabai's father, Anant Shastri Dongre, was a Brahmin priest and widower who married the daughter of a Brahmin pilgrim when she was nine years old. A reformer, Dongre resolved to educate his young wife himself, but his people were horrified that he would disregard tradition and educate a woman. Dongre built a small house for his young bride in the forest, where he continued to educate his wife. Ramabai was born in the forest of Gangamula in the Western Ghats of India in 1858, and named after the goddess Rama. Her father educated his daughter as well, teaching her the Sanskrit puranas, as well as the Indian languages of Marathi, Kanarese, Hindustani, and Bengalese. The little family went on pilgrimage visiting shrines and sacred temples. Poverty overtook the family, and Ramabai's parents and older sister died. Ramabai's faith in her father's idols was shaken. She and her brother continued on pilgrimage throughout India. In Calcutta she first learned of Christ, who loved all and did not discriminate based on caste. She saw that Christianity might offer help to the widows and children neglected in India. Ramabai married a lawyer in Calcutta, but he died of cholera eighteen months after their marriage, leaving Ramabai a widow with an infant daughter. With her excellent education, Ramabai became a teacher and writer, speaking out about the plight of India's women. She traveled to England and America, where her book, *The High Caste Hindu Woman*, opened the hearts of many to the plight of India's women. In Boston in 1887, a group of Christians of several different denominations formed the Ramabai Association to support Ramabai in establishing a school to educate child widows in India. As she worked to establish the school, Ramabai came to realize fully that she did not just need the Christian religion, but she needed Christ: 'I had at last come to an end of myself, and unconditionally surrendered myself to the Saviour; and asked Him to be merciful to me, and to become my righteousness and redemption, and to take away all my sin.'[9]

Ramabai purchased land and expanded her school, calling it the Mukti (meaning Salvation) Mission. The Mission is still in operation today, with the purpose of providing a 'Christ centred home where destitute women and children irrespective of their background are accepted, cared for, transformed, and empowered to be salt and light in the society.'[10]

In the last fifteen years of her life, with all the responsibilities of the hundreds of people under her care at the Mission, Ramabai taught herself Greek and Hebrew, and translated the Bible into Marathi. She used simple wording that the unlearned and common people could understand. Thousands of copies of the Gospels in Marathi were printed and distributed.

Waves of Feminism

The last century of the second Christian millennium was a time of global conflict and intellectual upheaval. World War I (the 'war to end all wars'), crushed mankind's hope and optimism for an improving world order. With the advent of the Great Depression, man and his world did not seem to be getting better and better. World War II embroiled the major nations and their peoples in brutal conflict. Fascist or communist totalitarian governments extinguished liberty and belief in human dignity. As society became more secular, Darwinian evolution, Freudian psychology, and Marxist economics replaced the Christian teachings of God as Creator, man made in God's image (though fallen in sin), and God's Providence in history. It was in this period of political and intellectual upheaval, that feminism increased its cultural influence. The unchristian and often anti-Christian guiding principles behind the movement in time became accepted by many in the Church.

Historians of the feminist movement have noted three 'waves' of feminist activity, each with distinctive goals and methodoligies. Though there are wide variations in goals and activities within each of the movements, some general

---

9   'Pandita Ramabai Mukti Mission', www.indiagateway.net/prmm/.

10   Ibid.

characteristics for each of the three 'waves' are clearly discernible. The first wave is dated from Mary Wollstonecraft's *A Vindication of the Rights of Women* in 1792, includes the Seneca Falls Declaration and early efforts for women's rights, and ends with women gaining universal suffrage in the United States in 1920 and England in 1928 (women's suffrage came later elsewhere – 1944 in France and the 1960s in Switzerland). The focus of the first wave was securing the legal rights of women as citizens under the law and opposing the hus-

Christabel Pankhurst (1880-1958)

Christabel Pankhurst, along with her mother Emmeline and her sisters Sylvia and Adela, was a leader of the militant suffrage movement in Britain. Raised in a family with socialist leanings, Christabel and her mother founded the Women's Social and Political Union in 1903. Christabel became known as the 'Queen of the Mob' and was arrested frequently for her protests in favor of women's rights.

Though women gained the right to vote in England after World War I, Christabel was disillusioned by the inability of politics to bring about true reform. Picking up a book on prophecy by F.B. Meyer in a bookshop, she was awakened to her need of a Savior and the reality of Christ's return. She realized that in campaigning for suffrage, she was trying to build a human-made Utopia, an impossible achievement. She came to faith in Christ and joined the Plymouth Brethren.

Living in both Britain and America, Christabel became an evangelist with the Plymouth Brethren, lecturing and writing books on the Second Coming of Christ. Her lectures were widely attended, as she spoke of her disillusionment with politics and her expectation of the return of Jesus Christ.

Though Christabel is still remembered today as a leader of the suffragette movement, the greater part of her life was spent as a student and lecturer on Christ's Second Coming. Her lectures were filled with examinations of current events for clues to the soon return of Christ. Since Christabel rarely spoke of her conversion or expressed any sense of repentance or forgiveness in Christ, historians debate to what extent Christabel's conversion was simply exchanging one form of political activity for another.

band's virtual ownership over the wife in marriage. Throughout this period, women (and supportive men) argued that women were rational beings, the moral and intellectual equals of men, and capable of being thinking citizens. As such, they worked to share in the equal rights of citizenship with men, including the right to vote, equal protection under the law, the right to own property, and (for some) the right to divorce. Through public demonstrations, pamphlets, organized speeches, and petition drives, these issues were brought before the public and government officials, resulting in important changes in governmental policies and practices. Not only did women obtain the right to vote, but by the middle of the twentieth century all states had adopted legislation which protected married women's property, while also giving women more legal protection and educational opportunities.

As seen above, Christian women were often supportive of this initial phase of the women's rights movement. However, some feminists in the first wave, as well as later waves, had agendas which went far beyond legal equality and were decidedly anti-Christian in their goals. Margaret Sanger, founder of a group which became Planned Parenthood, believed woman's emancipation must include the woman's right to control her own body and reproduction. While she publicly supported birth control as a way to alleviate poverty and crime, privately she also encouraged eugenics and the elimination of certain races. Numerous laws classified birth control information as obscene, but Sanger worked so birth control information and measures could be transported through the mail and across state lines. In 1936, a Supreme Court decision held that birth control information was not obscene, opening a path for dissemination of birth control information. Gradually state laws were changed so that by 1965, married couples in all states could legally obtain contraceptives. The sexual revolution had arrived, challenging traditional restrictions of sexual activity to marriage.

The beginning of the second wave of feminism, which includes the sexual revolution, has been dated to begin with the publication of *The Second Sex* by Simone de Beauvoir, published in France in 1949 and in the United States in 1953. De Beauvoir argued that women were second-class citizens because they were defined by men in every area of society – economics, industry, politics, education and language. She held that men had named and defined the world and all things in it, robbing women of their autonomy. She called for women to identify themselves as a group and collectively wage war on their status as a subordinate sex. Women needed to take control of their own lives, name themselves and set their own destiny. Patriarchy was at the root of all women's problems. Women's equality and superiority could be achieved by destroying the male's superiority and by women refusing to be imprisoned in traditional roles. A socialist who expected women to seek liberation and follow the pattern of a bourgeoisie revolt, de Beauvoir claimed the roles of wife and mother should be replaced by economic and professional independence.

Numerous events during the 1960s brought feminist ideas into the popular culture. In 1963, Betty Friedan, in her best-selling book *The Feminine Mystique,* took Simone de Beauvoir's ideas and made them understandable to a popular readership. Friedan argued that middle-class, educated women were experiencing emotional and intellectual oppression because of their limited life options. Being a mother and homemaker was an unattractive profession. The following year, the World Council of Churches called upon churches to re-examine tradition and canon law to consider the ordination of women. Many were arguing that the Church had adopted patriarchal attitudes of the surrounding culture since its inception. Feminists contended that true equality meant there should be no differentiation in male and female roles, and women should be free to define their own roles.

In 1964, the same year as the World Council of Churches' call, the Civil Rights Act was passed. Title VII of the act prohibited discrimination on the basis of sex. The Equal Employment Opportunity Commission (EEOC) was formed to enforce the Civil Rights Act, but feminists were dismayed when the EEOC decided that sex segregation in job advertisement was permissible. In 1966, the *National Organization for Women* (NOW) was organized, with Betty Friedan as president, to lobby the EEOC for stricter enforcement of the Civil Rights Act. This became the major political arm of the second-wave feminist cause. Birth control rights were an important part of NOW's agenda from its inception.

Mary Daly (1928-2010), Catholic theologian and philosopher, charged the Catholic Church with oppression of women in her 1968 book *The Church and the Second Sex*. Daly asserted that the Church actually caused women's legal oppression and deceived women into an enforced passivity. She contended that Catholic doctrine taught women were inferior and the Church harmed women through its moral teachings and exclusion of women from leadership roles.

Daly believed that experience was more important than theology, which she said was patriarchal. Her 1973 work, *Beyond God the Father*, held that the whole idea of God's being masculine was misleading and harmful to women. She rejected that God was omnipotent, immutable, or providential, because she thought such characteristics would discourage women from seeking change. For Daly, and for a growing number, revelation was open to change and development, based on contemporary experience. Women themselves rather than Scripture could be the source of authority and truth. Though Daly and others might still call themselves Christians, their feminist agenda corrupted their theology, anthrolopogy, and understanding. They sought to conform society and the Church to their own imaginations. 'It's all about me' replaced seeking the glory of God. Christian truth evaporated, and claims for Christian exclusivity were seen as imperialistic.

In 1972, the U.S. Congress sent the Equal Rights Amendment to the states for their approval. The amendment stated that, 'Equality of rights under the law shall not be denied or abridged by the United States or by any State on account of sex.' While the amendment was swifly approved by thirty states within the first year, a 'Stop ERA' campaign began, largely organized by Phyllis Schlafly (b. 1924). Phyllis Schlafly, a Catholic wife, mother of six, lawyer, and popular speaker, thoroughly researched the legal effects of the amendment and showed how it could be used to actually hurt rather than help women:

> The amendment would require women to be drafted into military combat any time men were conscripted, abolish the presumption that the husband should support his wife and take away Social Security benefits for wives and widows. It would also give federal courts and the federal government enormous new powers to reinterpret every law that makes a distinction based on gender, such as those related to marriage, divorce and alimony.[11]

The time limit for approval of the amendment was to expire in 1979. However, of the 38 states required to adopt the amendment, only 35 had approved it. ERA advocates raised five million dollars to stage a conference in Houston, Texas, to build up support for their cause. The International Women's Year Conference received massive media coverage and featured every major feminist leader. However, when the conference delegates voted for taxpayer-funded abortions and for a gay and lesbian rights agenda, it became obvious to most Americans that there was much more to the feminist movement and the ERA than equal pay for equal work. Though an extension was given until 1982 for the amendment's approval, it never received enough votes to become part of the U.S. Constitution.

The feminist agenda was furthered in 1973 with the landmark Supreme Court decision of *Roe vs. Wade*, which asserted a woman's 'right to privacy' as the basis overturning all state and federal laws restricting abortions.[12] The decision sparked a political and religious debate which continues today. The 'right' to an abortion euphemistically became the 'woman's right to choose.' The feminist agenda held that for women to overcome their biological differences and become equal with men, in order for women to properly define themselves, women needed to have control over their own reproductive functions.

The reorganization of the moral world was reflected in the sexual revolution, the ERA and *Roe vs. Wade*. This decline was made possible by the erosion of Christian influence in society and government, and the weakening of a Biblically grounded faith in the Church itself. The growing acceptance of the radical feminist agenda in the populace at large was evidence of the increased secularization of society and its drift from Christian moorings. Some Christians organized in opposition to these events and to the radical feminist agenda. In 1979, in opposition to the Equal Rights Amendment, *Concerned Women for America* was organized by Beverly LaHaye, wife of Pastor Tim LaHaye. LaHaye and her supporters believed they were engaged in a spiritual struggle to bring Biblical principles into areas of public policy. *Concerned Women for America* focused on six main issues:

---

11 Phyllis Schlafly, '"Equal rights" for women: wrong then, wrong now,' *Los Angeles Times*, April 8, 2007. www.latimes.com/news/opinion/la-op-schafly8apr08,0,06143259.story.

12 The 'right to privacy' does not appear in the U.S. Constitution, but is a 'right' developed by the courts, especially since the 1920s.

1. Defining the Biblically designed family as between one man and one woman;
2. Protecting all human life from conception until natural death;
3. Reforming public education by returning authority to parents;
4. Fighting pornography and obscenity;
5. Supporting religious liberty;
6. Protecting national sovereignty, denying the United Nations and any other international organization from having authority over the United States.[13]

Focus on the Family, an organization begun by Dr. James Dobson in 1977, similarly aimed to 'cooperate with the Holy Spirit in sharing the Gospel of Jesus Christ with as many people as possible by nurturing and defending the God-ordained institution of the family and promoting biblical truths worldwide.'[14] *Focus on the Family* was guided by firm beliefs in the pre-eminence of evangelism, the permanence of marriage, the value of children, the sanctity of human life, the importance of social responsibility, and the value of both male and female before God.

The 1970s and 1980s also saw the beginning of women's studies courses on university campuses. Believing that men had imposed their views on society and scholarship, feminists contended a women-centered analysis was a necessary adjustment. Literature, psychology, medicine, sociology, sexual relations,[15] economics, and anthropology were all restructured from a feminist perspective. Women-centered analysis not only restructured all areas of learning, but provided guidelines for restructuring society in the future. More than scholarly studies, feminist courses were tools to indoctrinate students into feminism as a social, political, and religious mindset.

Feminist theology went far beyond the question of women in the pulpit to refashioning the very nature of God. This became evident at the Reimagining 93 Conference held in Minneapolis in 1993, an outgrowth of the 'Ecumenical Decade of the Churches in Solidarity with Women' launched by the World Council of Churches in 1988.[16] Two thousand leaders, mostly women, attended the conference. National leaders from mainline churches associated with the World Council of Churches went well beyond women's equality at the conference to deny the orthodox Christian faith. God's revelation of Himself in Christ and through His Word was denied. Sin was redefined not as disobedience to a Holy God, but the oppression of a patriarchal society.

---

13   www.cwfa.org/coreissues-short.asp.

14   www.focusonthefamily.com.

15   It was argued that lesbians could have important relations with other women without having men define who they were.

16   *Hidden Gospels*, pp.174-7.

From The Council on Biblical Manhood and Womanhood Board

'Biblical feminists seek to retain an evangelical base while at the same time modifying Biblical interpretation to be sympathetic to the concerns of the women's movement. However, in order to embrace both, Biblical feminists need to compromise the Bible. Biblical feminism therefore has become a theological crossing point between conservative evangelical theology and liberalism... Feminism and Christianity are like thick oil and water: their very natures dictate that they cannot be mixed.'

Mary Kassian

'The arguments used in support of the ordination of women require the dismissal or "reinterpretation" of specific biblical texts which disallow women in the teaching office. The same is true of arguments for the ordination of ... homosexuals. I am not accusing all proponents of women's ordination of supporting the ordination of homosexuals. But I am insisting that the basic hermeneutical approach behind these arguments has a common core – a relativizing of prohibitive biblical texts in the name of "liberation", whether of women, or... homosexuals.'

R. Albert Mohler, Jr.

'The meaning of marriage is bigger than anyone had dreamed – it is Christ and the church... If the roles of husband and wife do not portray the different ways that Christ and the church serve each other, then marriage ceases to be a model of Christ and the church.'

John Piper

'So in the end, this whole controversy is really about God and how His character is reflected in the beauty and excellence of manhood and womanhood as He created it. Will we glorify God through manhood and womanhood lived according to His Word? Or will we deny His Word and give in to the pressures of modern culture? That is the choice we have to make.'

Wayne Grudem

A woman should not submit to anyone greater than herself, but should look within for power. Liberation from oppression, not salvation from sin, was what women needed. At the conference, Delores Williams, professor at Union Theological Seminary, said, 'I don't think we need a theory of atonement at all...atonement has to do so much with death...I don't think we need folks hanging on crosses, and blood dripping, and weird stuff...we just need to listen to the god within.' [17] A former evangelical, Virginia Mollenkott, who was on the National Council of Churches commission to prepare an inclusive

---

17 *Hidden Gospels*, p. 176.

language lectionary, said the death of Jesus was child abuse; though Jesus was an obedient child, God was an abusive parent. By embracing a pantheistic, New Age religion, the conference adopted a decidedly un-Christian morality. Sexual pleasure became a human right among friends; the family was to be re-imagined. Sophia was worshipped and considered another name for God. Sophia was the Mother, Creator and Nourisher of all. The esoteric metaphysics of feminist theologians asserted that women had a particular divine connectedness with Nature, entangling feminism with ecological awareness, animal rights, and preservation of rain forests.

Feminism was restructuring God and the universe according to its own imaginings. Part of this restructuring was directed toward changing language. Feminists believed that language discriminated against women and favored males. 'Man' had been a word which could mean male or a human being; feminists believed that such language was simply a way men held power over women. The generic pronoun 'he,' which for centuries could refer to a specific male or a person, whether male or female, was similarly considered a power-wielding pronoun. Feminists also considered words such as 'chairman,' 'postman,' and 'serviceman,' which were used to speak of a human being, whether male or female, as discriminatory. By the 1980s, such words were replaced by 'chairperson,' 'postperson,' and 'serviceperson.' 'She' often replaced 'he' as the generic pronoun. Having renamed themselves, feminists renamed God as well.

God was renamed as He/She or frequently called 'Mother,' so as not to offend those who felt God as Father was misogynistic. In order to avoid any masculine references to God, 'God Himself' was replaced with 'God Godself,' never mind that God Himself had revealed otherwise.[18]

At the same time as the development of inclusive language, 'gender' became a new construct for understanding and replaced the previously held determinants of physical biology. While 'female' and 'male' had previously been seen as determined by the biological sex of a person, 'gender' came to be considered sociologically or culturally determined. Some have called the period since 1995 in which 'gender' ideas were changing previous dogmas the 'third wave' of feminism.

Christians have entered into the debate over the feminist agenda with differing responses. As seen earlier, those with a Wesleyan or Holiness background who emphasized personal experience and an inner light readily accepted women preachers and leaders in the Church. Most often they explained away Paul's words against a woman teaching or having authority over a man as temporary, provisional instructions with no relevance for later

---

18   Some of the theological implications in changing gender language in Scripture translations and liturgy are found in David L. Jeffrey, 'Scripture, Gender, and Our Language of Worship,' *Houses of the Interpreter: Reading Scripture, Reading Culture*, (Baylor University Press, 2003), pp. 195-211.

generations. As many of the mainline denominations fell to liberalism in the first part of the twentieth century, their commitment to the literalness of the Scripture waned. Since these denominations no longer considered the Bible as the authoritative Word of God, feminism easily became a powerful influence in the major denominational seminaries during the 1960s and 1970s. Those who adopted feminist perspectives, but still accepted the Bible as God's Word, had to reinterpret the Bible. Most frequently, these 'Biblical feminists' stated that Paul's teachings about women's roles were simply for his own day and not authoritative for ensuing centuries.

In 1973, a group of Christian feminists organized the *Evangelical Women's Caucus* (EWC) to work for feminist causes within Christianity.[19] They endorsed the Equal Rights Amendment, supported inclusive language in Bible translations, and favored the ordination of women. Letha Scanzoni and Nancy Hardesty's *All We're Meant to Be* and Fuller Professor Paul Jewett's *Man as Male and Female* both tried to reinterpret the Bible to support feminism, accepting the fallibility of the Bible in order to embrace a contemporary opinion.

In 1986, the EWC passed a resolution supporting the rights of homosexuals and the 'lesbian minority' in the group. Some of the feminists could not support this stance and separated to form *Christians for Biblical Equality* (CBE) in 1987. CBE advocated 'a biblical basis for gift-based, rather than gender-based ministry of Christians of all ages, ethnicities and socio-economic classes.' An overarching principle of Bible hermeneutics for CBE was that men and women are created equal in God's image: 'CBE holds that any interpretation of scripture that prohibits women from using their spiritual gifts and abilities in ministry constitutes injustice. CBE defines injustice as an abuse of power, taking from others freedom, dignity, resources, and even life itself.'[20]

The Council on Biblical Manhood and Womanhood (CBMW) also was organized in 1987.[21] With the goal of addressing the growing impact of feminist ideas on the Church and the larger society, CBMW held to what some call the *complementarian*, as opposed to the *egalitarian* view, of women's position: 'men and women are of equal worth and are both equally created in the image of God, but have distinct roles in Church, home and society as a whole.' The rationale and affirmations of the CBMW were set forth in *The Danvers Statement on Biblical Manhood and Womanhood*.[22] In this foundational document, CBMW

---

19   In 1990, the EWC added 'ecumenical' to its name, becoming the Evangelical and Ecumenical Women's Caucus. http://www.eewc.com/.

20   Christians for Biblical Equality website at http://www.cbeinternational.org/.

21   The Council on Biblical Manhood and Womanhood, http://www.cbmw.org/.

22   *The Danvers Statement on Biblical Manhood and Womanhood*, http://www.cbmw.org/Danvers.

summarized the Scriptures, from Genesis through the New Testament, which addressed the nature and role of women and their relationship with men. One of the strongest criticisms CBMW had for the Christian feminists was that they were abandoning the teaching of Scriptures, conforming to the surrounding culture rather than being transformed by the Word of God. Only by abandoning the Scriptural teaching could the feminist perspective be fully embraced. Abandoning the teaching of Scripture on the issue of male-female relationships seemed the beginning of a slippery slope which could only lead to the jettisoning of all Scriptures. The path the EWC had taken towards embracing homosexuality exhibited the danger involved in neglecting the standards of the Scriptures as the guide for faith and practice.

While the positions of the CBMW and CBE are irreconcilable, both groups have recognized that the gender issue should not prevent them from cooperative ministry. Unlike the radical feminists, Christian egalitarians in CBE maintained belief in the foundational Christian truths. In important ways, both groups shared

> a passion to magnify Christ – crucified, risen, and reigning – to a perishing society; and a passion to mobilize the whole church – men and women – to complete the Great Commission, penetrate all the unreached peoples of the world, and hasten the day of God...We long for a common mind for the cause of Christ...[23]

In 1988, a Vatican paper, 'On the Dignity and Vocation of Women' (*Mulieris Dignitatem*), addressed the growing feminist movement within the Catholic Church.[24] The document, an extensive pastoral letter on the nature of women and their place in Church and society, opened with a quote from the closing message of the 1965 Second Vatican Council:

> The hour is coming, in fact has come, when the vocation of women is being acknowledged in its fullness, the hour in which women acquire in the world an influence, an effect and a power never hitherto achieved. That is why, at this moment when the human race is undergoing so deep a transformation, women imbued with a spirit of the Gospel can do so much to aid humanity in not falling.

Beginning with an analysis of the nature of Mary, Jesus' mother, and her service to God, *Mulieris Dignitatem* then looked at the woman's beginning in Genesis 1–2. These opening Scriptures clearly said that both the man and

---

23   John Piper and Wayne Grudem, eds. *Recovering Biblical Manhood and Womanhood: A Response to Evangelical Feminism*. Wheaton, Ill.: Crossway, 1991, p. 406. The book's full text can be found at www.cbmw.org.

24   John Paul II, 'On the Dignity and Vocation of Women,' August 15, 1988, www.vatican.va/holy_ father/john_paul_ii/apost_letters/documents/hf_jp-ii_apl_15081988_mulieris-dignitatem_ en.html.

the woman were made in the image of God. Unlike the other living beings in the world around them, the man and woman were equally persons.

The Persons of the Triune Godhead are interrelational. It follows that both man and woman, being in the image of God, were created as relational beings. Together they were a 'unity of the two.'[25] The man and woman were created to exist side by side, together, and to exist mutually one for the other. In this interpersonal communion there is a distinction between what is masculine and feminine.

In 2004, the Vatican issued a further letter on 'the Collaboration of Men and Women in the Church and in the World.'[26] Written by Cardinal Joseph Ratzinger, the future Pope Benedict XVI, the letter specifically addressed the new approaches to women's issues. One emerging tendency noted was for women to make themselves the adversaries of men, to seek power for themselves and superiority over men. The Vatican saw this as not only harmful to individuals, but as having a lethal effect on the structure of the family. A second tendency was to deny any essential differences between man and woman, viewing all differences as merely culturally conditioned:

> In this perspective, physical difference, termed *sex*, is minimized, while the purely cultural element, termed *gender*, is emphasized in the maximum and held to be primary. The obscuring of the difference or duality of the sexes has enormous consequences on a variety of levels. This theory of the human person, intended to promote prospects for the equality of women through liberation from biological determinism, has in reality inspired ideologies which, for example, call into question the family, in its natural two-parent structure of mother and father, and make homosexuality and heterosexuality virtually equivalent, in a new model of polymorphous sexuality.

Attempting to be freed from biological conditioning, this viewpoint assumes there is no such thing as human nature and all persons can determine their own nature. To take such a position requires that women must liberate themselves from the teachings of Scripture as well as consider unimportant and irrelevant 'the fact that the Son of God assumed human nature in its male form.'[27] The Church, however, saw a relationship of *collaboration* between the sexes and recognized the difference between man and woman. In its analysis of the Scriptures' teachings on the nature of man and woman, the Vatican especially noted that differences between

---

25   'On the Dignity and Vocation of Women', p. 7.

26   'Letter to the Bishops of the Catholic Church on the Collaboration of Men and Women in the Church and in the World,' May 31, 2004, http://www.vatican.va/roman_curia/congregations/cfaith/documents/rc_con_cfaith_doc_20040731_collaboration_en.html.

27   Letter to the Bishops of the Catholic Church on the Collaboration of Men and Women in the Church and in the World,' p. 1.

man and woman are not merely biological, but are psychological and spiritual. The whole mystery of marriage and the spousal relationship between Christ and the Church is a theme shown throughout Scripture:

> From the first moment of their creation, man and woman are distinct, and will remain so for all eternity. Placed within Christ's Paschal mystery, they no longer see their difference as a source of discord to be overcome by denial or eradication, but rather as the possibility for collaboration, to be cultivated with mutual respect for their difference. From here, new perspectives open up for a deeper understanding of the dignity of women and their role in human society and in the Church.

Women's capacity to give life structures their personality profoundly:

> It is women, in the end, who even in very desperate situations, as attested by history past and present, possess a singular capacity to persevere in adversity, to keep life going even in extreme situations, to hold tenaciously to the future, and finally to remember with tears the value of every human life.

This is not merely biological, but part of the feminine nature seen even in those remaining virgins.

Many within the Catholic Church have protested these two Vatican letters addressing the issues raised by the feminists. A vocal group within the Church continues to speak in favor of women as priests and a dismissal of all male and female differences as culturally engendered.

Last Decades of the Second Millennium

As the second Christian millennium came to a close, women continued to be integral to the life and growth of the Church. In the wars, genocides, and upheavals of the 20th century, many women faced martyrdom; others suffered hardship in the mission field; some led quiet lives of service and devotion to Christ; others organized ministries to children, other women, and to those who were suffering and hurting – and some became celebrities who attracted widespread public attention.

Surely one of the most flamboyant Christians of the twentieth century was Aimee Semple McPherson (1890-1944). Aimee grew up as a farm girl in Canada. Her mother was active in the Salvation Army, and as a child Aimee was taken to its meetings. Evangeline Booth, daughter of founders Catherine and William, was the Army's Commissioner for Canada, and Aimee seems to have gravitated to the pageantry and drama of the Army's services. Yet, as a teenager, she began to lose interest in God and questioned the truth of the Bible. An evangelistic sermon by young Robert Semple pierced her heart with conviction, and Aimee prayed for God's mercy with deep repentance. At the revival services Aimee later said she received the baptism of the Spirit and began speaking in tongues. Aimee and the evangelist Robert Semple were married, and later went to

China as missionaries. Aimee's first child was born in China two months after they arrived; her husband died two months later. Aimee returned home and soon married businessman Harold McPherson, with whom she had one son. She found a settled, married life unsatisfying, however, and believed God called her to a public ministry. While remaining fiercely devoted to her two children, Aimee left her husband and began traveling around holding evangelistic meetings and tent revivals. McPherson later divorced Aimee on the basis of her desertion.

In 1918, Aimee moved to Los Angeles and established her base of ministry there. Aimee's charismatic personality drew people to her, and her sermons were always entertaining. With pageantry as her specialty, Aimee produced 'illustrated sermons,' which were complete with stage sets and costumes, attracting many from Hollywood. Aimee knew how to use the media; she regularly was in the newspapers – whether it was for winning the grand prize for a float in the Tournament of Roses or providing meals for people during the Great Depression. In 1922, she bought a radio station, becoming the first woman to possess a radio license and operate a station; of course Aimee became the first woman to preach a sermon over the radio as well. In 1923, she dedicated the newly built Angelus Temple, which could seat 5,300 people. The Pentecostal services at the Angelus Temple included speaking in tongues and healing.

In 1921, Aimee said she saw a vision of the four-faced beings from Ezekiel 1. She interpreted the faces of a man, a lion, an ox, and an eagle as the fourfold gospel of salvation, baptism in the Holy Spirit, divine healing and the Second Coming of Christ. Based on this vision, and with the Angelus Temple as a base, Aimee founded the Foursquare Gospel denomination. A Bible school to train ministers and missionaries helped the denomination expand.

There were also rumors of scandal surrounding Aimee. In 1926, she was swimming in the Pacific when she disappeared; it was presumed she drowned. A month later, however, she surfaced in Mexico saying she had been kidnapped. Her recording engineer seems to have disappeared at the same time. The whole situation was in keeping with the Hollywood/celebrity persona Aimee had created for herself. In 1944, Aimee died from an overdose of sedatives.

In spite of Aimee's publicity-seeking antics and questionable morals, the Foursquare Gospel Church she founded grew into a global evangelical Pentecostal denomination with 64,000 churches in 140 countries.[28] Aimee's blending of feminism, drama, Hollywood, Pentecostalism, mass appeal, contemporary music, the latest technology and superstar status at the expense of faithfulness to the Scriptures presaged the era of the televangelist and the direction many churches at the end of the twentieth century would take. However, another Christian woman in Hollywood had a strong global impact of a different kind.

---

28   http://www.foursquare.org/ .

What Henrietta Mears' students said about her:

'She is certainly one of the greatest Christians I have ever known.'
— Billy Graham

'She established Gospel Light Press, Forest Home Christian Conference, Gospel Literature International and was largely instrumental in founding Campus Crusade.'
— Bill Bright, founder of Campus Crusade

'The times of prayer with her through the years, in many places and for many purposes, are among the fondest memories because they brought me so close to our Lord.'
— Jim Rayburn, founder of Young Life Campaign

'In my mind, Henrietta Mears was the giant of Christian education — not only in her generation, but in this century. She was an extraordinary combination of intellect, devotion, and spirituality; and administrative genius, a motivator, an encourager and a leader.

'I thought of Henrietta Mears as a female Apostle Paul; in fact, I often referred to her as the "Epistle Paul". There is simply no way to exaggerate her effectiveness as a teacher, communicator and inspirer.'
— Dr. Richard C. Halverson, Chaplain, United States Senate

'She never yielded to the fashion of the day in toning down the atoning work of Christ or the peril of those who live without the gospel. Her zeal for missions at home and abroad probably enlisted more men and women for Christ's service than has any other woman's voice in the history of the church.'
— Pastor Dr. Don Moomaw

Henrietta Mears (1890-1963) was reared by devout Christian parents in Minnesota. Early in life she developed extreme myopia and always wore thick glasses, an impairment she later believed kept her absolutely dependent upon God. When her mother died during Henrietta's freshman year in college, her pastor told her he was praying that her mother's Christian mantle would fall upon her. Henrietta couldn't imagine how she could measure up to such high expectations. However, one evening, alone in her room, she totally surrendered everything she held dear to the Lord and dedicated herself to living a life of dependence on Him. She later described the evening:

> I [had] felt absolutely powerless from the thought that I could possibly live up to what my mother had been and had done, and I prayed that if God had anything for me to do that He would supply the power. I read my Bible for every reference to the Holy Spirit and His power. The greatest realization came to me when I saw that there was nothing I had to do to receive His power but to submit to Christ, to allow Him to control

me. I had been trying to do everything myself; now I let Christ take me completely. I said to Christ that if He wanted anything from me He would have to do it Himself. My life was changed from that moment on.[29]

After graduating from college, Henrietta taught chemistry and served as the principal in a small town. She then taught high school in Minnesota for several years, before being invited to become director of Christian Education at Hollywood Presbyterian Church. From 1922 to 1963, she served as both director of Christian Education and teacher of the College Department at Hollywood Presbyterian.

When Henrietta arrived, Sunday School attendance was 450. After two and a half years, attendance grew to more than 4,000. When she began reviewing a shipment of Sunday School literature at the church, Henrietta discovered that much of the routinely ordered literature did not clearly teach the Bible. One lesson even said that 'Paul survived shipwreck because he had eaten carrots and was strong.' Henrietta rewrapped the books and returned them. She realized she would just have to write the lessons herself. Henrietta sat down with her staff, set goals for each grade level, and began handwriting the lessons. Four lessons were prepared at a time. Her secretary typed, mimeographed, and stapled the lessons together for use; pictures from out-of-date calendars were pasted on the front for decoration. Even so, the Sunday School books were ahead of anything else available at the time. In the 1930s, some parents began driving fifty miles to Sunday School so their children could study from these materials. In 1933, at the trough of the Great Depression, Henrietta found a Christian printer in Glendale to print the materials; this was the beginning of Gospel Light Press. Henrietta's goal was to teach the Bible to children from two years old through high school, progressing through the Bible four times, so the Bible became 'a powerful magnet drawing children and youth to Christ.'[30] Gospel Light Press became the first publisher of closely graded Bible lessons. By the end of 1933, 13,366 copies were sold to 131 Sunday Schools in 35 states. In 1934, sales tripled to 2,126 churches across the United States, and by 1937, more than quarter of a million books were sold.[31] With the spread of these published materials, Henrietta was soon in demand as a lecturer on Christian education across America and became co-founder of the National Sunday School Association. At a Sunday School convention in 1950, she challenged the audience: 'It is my business as a Sunday School teacher to instill a divine discontent for the ordinary. Only the best

---

29   Earl O. Roe. *Dream Big: The Henrietta Mears Story*. Ventura, California: Regal Books, 1990, p. 74.

30   Ibid., p. 141.

31   Ibid., pp. 142-5.

possible is good enough for God. Can you say, "God, I have done all that I can?'" She often told Sunday School workers that the goal of the Sunday School was not just to lead children to Christ:

> That, of course, is part of it – and you know the emphasis I place on evangelism – but if your task stops there, you will never be successful. Our job is to train men and women, boys and girls, to serve the Master. They must feel that there is a task for them to do, that there is a place marked *X* for every person in God's Kingdom. Here is my *X*; no one can stand on this place but me. Now I must help others to find their places.[32]

Henrietta Mears created a College Department at Hollywood Presbyterian which challenged all to reach others for Christ and serve the Lord in some way. She organized deputation teams of her college students to witness in jails, hospitals, and on the college campuses. Her passion for evangelism, missions, and serving Christ was transferred to many of the young people. Over 400 young people in Henrietta's college class went into some area of Christian ministry.

Henrietta's Bible study discussions always were interesting. Not only did her fabulous hats and coordinated dress capture the attention of the young people, her techniques were simple but effective:

- Have someone read the passage and give a summary of it.
- Have someone else give a brief outline of the passage.
- Ask what the passage teaches about God, Christ, the Holy Spirit, man, and his responsibility.
- Find the key verse.
- Read another passage that sheds light on this one.
- Have specific questions read on the passage itself.[33]

Henrietta's Bible study handbook, *What the Bible Is All About*, followed a similar pattern of Bible analysis. The book has sold over three million copies and remains in print today. Though Henrietta was a superb Bible teacher, she never spoke in the pulpit, following Paul's admonition to take authority over men.

In 1938, Henrietta established Forest Home Christian Conference Grounds for young people to learn the Scriptures surrounded by the beauty of God's creation. Seminars were given on Christian fundamentals of Bible study, prayer, ministry of the Holy Spirit, and doctrine. When requests for the materials came from around the globe, she established GLINT – Gospel Literature in National Tongues, which distributed literature in more than 85 languages. When Billy Graham had doubts about his Christian faith after his first Crusade, he came to Forest Home and resolved his spiritual quandaries

---

32   *Dream Big: The Henrietta Mears Story,* p. 191.

33   *Dream Big,* p. 160.

with the help of Henrietta Mears. Numerous other Christian leaders found healing and direction at Forest Home, including Campus Crusade founder Bill Bright and Chaplain of the United States Senate Richard Halverson.

Henrietta Mears had saturated herself with the Scriptures since a child, and she could quote long passages of Scripture from memory. Her deep commitment to God's Word bore much fruit throughout her life. She died quietly in her sleep in 1963. Someone remarked, 'It was nothing new for her to meet her Lord alone, for she had often done so. This time she just went with Him.'[34]

Leaders in Inductive Bible Studies

Women have often been leaders in inductive Bible studies. Many concur that this pupil-oriented method of Bible teaching prevents women from exercising an undue authority over others. Jane Hollingsworth learned the principles of inductive Bible study at Biblical Seminary in New York. Jane became one of the first members of the InterVarsity staff in America, joining in 1942. She stressed inductive Bible study in her extensive training of both InterVarsity staff and students and wrote the first Bible study guides for InterVarsity Press. Through her teaching, inductive Bible study became a hallmark of InterVarsity.

Barbara Boyd developed her passion for Bible study from a summer camp taught by Jane. Barbara, who also went to Biblical Seminary, joined InterVarsity with the responsibility of developing training in inductive Bible study for students. She developed the *Bible & Life* conference to train students in the basics of Christian discipleship.

Jack and Kay Arthur were missionaries in Mexico when poor health forced them to return home. They began a ministry of in-depth inductive Bible studies which grew into Precept Ministries International. Focusing on establishing people in God's Word, Precept Ministries has Bible studies in nearly 150 countries and nearly 70 languages.

The teaching of Audrey Wetherell Johnson (1907-1984), a younger contemporary of Henrietta Mears, has also continued to have an important influence in the lives of many to the present day. Although born into a devout Christian family in Leicester, England, as a young woman Audrey came under the influence of secular philosophers and intellectuals during her studies in France. Her agnosticism only led her to despair. In the midst of her hopeless dejection, Audrey recalled Jesus' words, 'And whosoever liveth and believeth in me shall never die. Believest thou this?' (John 11:26). She cried out to God in prayer and, as she wrote later:

> Suddenly God's mysterious revelation was given to me. I can only say with Paul, 'It pleased God to reveal His Son in me.' I could not reason out the mystery of the Incarnation, but God caused me to know that this was a fact. I knelt down in tears of joy and worshiped him as Saviour and Lord, with a divine conviction of this truth which could never be broken.[35]

---

34   Ibid., p. 334.

35   Quoted in 'Miss J: A. Wetherell Johnson and the Bible Study Fellowship,' John Woodbridge, ed. *More Than Conquerors*. Chicago: Moody Press, 1992.

The importance of Scripture in her conversion taught Audrey the importance of the authority of Scripture, a truth which was reinforced throughout her life and became a foundation of her Christian life.

In 1936, Audrey went to China as a missionary with China Inland Mission. During World War II, she became a prisoner of war of the Japanese when they invaded China. By the time the war

---

Streams in the Desert

One of the most popular devotional books of all time is *Streams in the Desert*, written by Lettie Cowman. Lettie and her husband Charles were founders of the Oriental Missionary Society (now OMS International) and pioneer missionaries to Japan and China from 1901 to 1917. Poor health forced the couple to return to the United States. Until her husband's death six years later, Lettie cared for her invalid husband. *Streams in the Desert*, first published in 1925, grew out of her sufferings and sorrow. The collection of Scripture, sermons, poems, and spiritual meditations became daily reading for millions. The book continues in print today and can be readily read from numerous Internet sites.

Lettie Cowman published eight other books and encouraged Scripture distribution. She died at the age of ninety on Easter Sunday, 1960.

---

ended, Audrey had spent thirty months as a prisoner, sharing a stable with almost ninety other prisoners. After a time of recuperation in England, Audrey returned to China in 1947 to teach at the China Bible Seminary in Shanghai. The following year, the Communists placed her under house arrest, and she was forced to flee the country in 1950.

In the United States and under a doctor's care, Audrey was uncertain where the Lord would lead her. Her heart was in China, but a group of five women asked her to lead them in a Bible class. Audrey was not enthusiastic, but she agreed to do so if the women would agree to study the Bible beforehand and share their studies with each other. As they read the Bible passage, the women were to answer three simple questions: What does the passage say? What did it mean when it was written? What does it mean to me? Audrey closed the women's discussion with a summary lesson on the passage. The study grew. In 1958, Audrey was asked to organize a follow-up Bible study for those who were expected to come to Christ during a Billy Graham Crusade in California's Bay area. The results were so encouraging that Audrey incorporated Bible Study Fellowship in 1959. The goal always was for people to study the Bible for themselves. Audrey developed a series of five studies which covered nearly the entire Bible. Each series was thirty weeks or lessons, corresponding to the school year. Audrey's notes focused on Jesus and the practical application of Bible truths.

In her own life, Audrey recognized that at different times God used particular circumstances and reflection on Scripture to open her eyes to a previously unrecognized aspect of God's glory. She described 'God's Path of Life' as teaching her five key lessons:

1. The authority of the Scripture.
2. The power at the cross of death to self [dying with Christ on the cross and living a new life in Him].
3. The fulness of the Holy Spirit.
4. The sufficiency of God's love.
5. The abundance of God's grace.[36]

Throughout her life she was re-educated in these lessons again and again on deeper levels. Audrey believed that through Bible study people would come to know the Lord and live a life of obedience to Him.

After several struggles with cancer, Audrey went to be with her Lord on December 22, 1984. The nurse heard her say, 'The Lord is coming for me today. He's at the foot of my bed now.' At the end of her earthly life, she did not see death but the face of her Lord Jesus Christ.[37]

At the same time as Audrey was a prisoner of the Japanese during World War II, Corrie ten Boom (1892-1983) was a prisoner of the Nazis in Europe. Corrie grew up in Haarlem, the Netherlands, in the family quarters above the watchshop her grandfather Willem had built in 1837. The watchshop and home had been passed down to Willem's son Casper, who in turn passed it to his daughter Corrie. In 1922, after two years of training, Corrie became the first woman licensed watchmaker in the Netherlands. Corrie's brother Willem and her sister Nollie each married and had children, but Corrie and her sister Betsie continued to live with their father in their home above the watchshop.

The ten Booms were Christians who were always helping others and were active in social work in Haarlem. Corrie began a club to teach neighborhood children and reach out to help those in need. When the Nazis began promoting anti-Semitic propaganda and threatening Dutch independence, the ten Booms joined the Dutch underground resistance. Both their home and watchshop became a safe haven for refugees fleeing from Nazi oppression. Many were hidden in the attic recesses of the ten Boom home until a safe passage to freedom could be found for them. Estimates are that the ten Booms saved the lives of 800 Jews and protected many in the Dutch resistance. However, an informer turned the ten Booms in to the Nazi authorities, and on February 28, 1944, the Gestapo raided the home. The Gestapo set a trap and arrested everyone who came into the house throughout the day – about thirty people in all. Corrie, Betsie, and their eighty-four-year-old father Casper were taken to Scheveningen

36   Audrey W. Johnson. *Created for Commitment*. Tyndale House Publishers, 1989, pp. 45-6.

37   'Miss J: Audrey Wetherell Johnson,' *More Than Conquerors* (John Woodbridge, ed.), Chicago: Moody Press, 1992, p. 83.

Prison, where Casper died ten days later. The sisters spent ten months in different prisons; the last was Ravensbruck concentration camp near Berlin. Though conditions in the camps were indescribably horrible, the sisters always tried to show Jesus' love to their fellow prisoners. At night they read their Bible and prayed for release. Betsy was released when she died on Christmas Day, 1944. Corrie was released soon afterwards through a clerical error, in which Corrie saw God's miraculous hand. The next week all the women in her age group at the camp were exterminated.

In the years after the war, Corrie traveled to over sixty countries, inspiring millions with the love of Christ she had experienced in prison. In Ravensbruck she and Betsy had learned that 'There is no pit so deep that God's love is not deeper still.'[38] Corrie also believed that 'God will give us the love to be able to forgive our enemies.'[39] She learned this herself in 1947 when she returned to Ravensbruck to share the gospel of Christ with the German people. After speaking to the large audience about God's love and forgiveness, a man came up to her and extended his hand for forgiveness. He was one of the cruelest of the guards at Ravensbruck who had caused her and her sister much suffering. Extending her hand to this man in Christian forgiveness was the most difficult thing Corrie ever did. Yet, Jesus died for this undeserving sinner as for her, and she had no choice but to forgive. Corrie later wrote, 'For a long moment we grasped each other's hands, the former guard and the former prisoner. I had never known God's love so intensely as I did then.'[40] *The Hiding Place*, Corrie's book about her family and her experiences during World War II, was a best-seller which was made into a motion picture in 1975.

Forgiveness and the love of Christ were also two important lessons Elisabeth Elliot (b. 1926) learned and shared with others. The daughter of missionary parents, Elisabeth studied classical Greek at Wheaton, where she met her husband Jim Elliot. The couple became missionaries to the Quichua Indians in Ecuador. Jim wanted to reach the Auca Indians, a fierce people who had killed any outsider who previously tried to meet them. Once the whereabouts of the Auca were discovered, Jim and four other missionaries prepared to meet them, bringing presents and the Good News of Christ. The five missionaries, including Jim Elliot, were speared to death on the beach near the Auca village. Elisabeth was left a widow with a ten-month-old daughter, Valerie. For two years after Jim's death, Elisabeth continued to work with the Quichua Indians. During that time two Auca Indian women who were living among the Quichua taught Elisabeth the Auca langauge. Learning to speak the native tongue was the opening Elisabeth needed to reach the Auca people. Elisabeth

---

38   'History', *Corrie ten Boom Museum*, http://www.corrietenboom.com/history.htm.

39   Ibid.

40   Corrie ten Boom. *Tramp for the Lord*. New York: Jove Books, 1976, p. 55.

and her three-year-old daughter went to live with the Auca, bringing the forgiveness of Christ to those who had killed her husband and the four other missionaries. Elisabeth wrote of her husband and her experiences in Ecuador in two best-selling books: *Shadow of the Almighty: The Life and Testament of Jim Elliot* and *Through Gates of Splendor*. When she and Valerie returned to the United States in 1963, Elisabeth became a noted speaker and writer, especially encouraging women in Biblical, godly living.

The writings of numerous Christian women, many of them pastor's wives, encouraged and strengthened others in their Christian walk. Catherine Marshall (1914-1983) was the wife of Peter Marshall, the charismaticv Presbyterian preacher from Scotland whose ministry flourished in America. When Catherine first heard Peter preach, she wrote her parents, 'it's as if when he opens his mouth there is a direct line between you and God.'[41] She had never heard such spirited, spiritual prayers. Peter pastored the historic New York Avenue Presbyterian Chruch in Washington, D.C. and was chaplain of the U.S. Senate from 1947 until his sudden death by a heart attack in 1949. At 35, Catherine was left a widow with a six-year-old son to raise. The year Peter died, Catherine collected twelve of his sermons and thirteen of his prayers and published them as *Mr. Jones, Meet the Master. A Man Called Peter*, Catherine's biography of her husband, published in 1951, remained on the bestseller list for over three years and was later made into a successful film. Catherine continued to publish inspirational books, including the novel *Christy*, based upon her mother's experiences as a young lady teaching in rural Appalachia. Catherine wove into the story numerous lessons on prayer and faith in God.

Two daughters of missionaries to China, Ruth Bell (1920-2007) and Edith Seville (1914 -), became wives of ministers with global ministries. Ruth lived in China until she was seventeen, when she moved to the United States and attended Wheaton College, where she met fellow student Billy Graham. The two married shortly after Ruth's graduation. While Billy went on to have a world-wide ministry as an evangelist, preaching to millions of people across the globe, Ruth was his constant spiritual suppprt. When asked once where he went for spiritual guidance, Graham answered, 'my wife, Ruth. She is a great student of the Bible. Her life is ruled by the Bible more than any person I've ever known.'[42]

While Billy Graham preached across the country and the world, Ruth maintained a stable home for the couple's five children, all of whom are in some Christian work today. In raising her children, Ruth recognized, 'I must faithfully,

---

41 'Catherine Marshall,' Biographicval Dictionary of Evangelicals (ed. Timothy Larsen). Intervarsity Press, 2003, p. 410.

42 Meghan Kleppinger, 'Ruth Bell Graham: A Legacy of faith,', June 18, 2007, http://www.crosswalk.com/news/religiontoday/11544172/. All quotes about and by Ruth Graham are taken from this article.

patiently, lovingly, and happily do my part – then quietly wait for God to do His.'
Daughter Ann Graham Lotz testified to her mother's sterling Christian life:

> I believe that our heavenly Father, our Savior, saved my mother from
> loneliness [while Dad was away from home so often] because of her
> daily walk with the Lord Jesus – He was the love of her life. I saw that in
> her life. It was her love for the Lord Jesus, with whom she walks every
> day, that made me want to love Him and walk with Him like that.

Ruth loved to work behind the scenes, helping her famous husband with
his books and writing fourteen of her own. She told her own life story in
Footprints of a Pilgrim, a scrapbook of old photos, journal entries and poetry.
The day before Ruth died, Billy said, 'Ruth is my soul mate and best friend,
and I cannot imagine living a single day without her by my side. I am more
in love with her today than when we first met over 65 years ago.'

Edith Seville was also born in China of missionary parents and met her
husband, Francis Schaeffer, in college – Beaver College in Pennsylvania. The
couple married, and in 1948 were sent to Switzerland by the Independent
Board for Presbyterian Foreign Missions. In 1955, the Schaeffers stepped out in
faith and established a mission in Huemoz, Switzerland, naming their mission
L'Abri, the French word for 'shelter.' L'Abri became a shelter for thousands of
students and seekers wrestling with the growing secularism of the 20th century.
While Francis provided answers to spiritual and intellectual questions, Edith
provided a home of warmth, beauty, and caring, not only for the Schaeffers'
four children but for a stream of visitors and students. Together the Schaeffers
were beacons to Biblical truth and a life warmly living out that truth.

Christianity was a way of living (or *A Way of Seeing*, as the title of one of Edith's
books notes) not only doctrinal promulgations. Edith ws a constant support
to Francis through her intense prayer life as well as her ability to bring creative
beauty into the mundane and commonplace, which she wrote about in her book
Hidden Art. After Francis' death from cancer in 1984, Edith wrote extensively
about L'Abri, the family, marriage, parenting, prayer, and art. In her hospitality,
teaching the younger women, and creativity, Edith reflected her love of Christ.

Joni Eareckson Tada (1947-) has also written numerous inspirational books
based upon her Christian reflections on her unusual life of suffering. Injured by
diving into shallow water when she was 17, Joni became a quadriplegic, unable
to use her legs or hands. Joni uses her platform of pain, suffering and immobility
to demonstrate the sufficiency of Christ to others, providing both an example and
ministry to others with diasabilities. In 1979 she established Joni and Friends,
a Christian ministry to those with disabilities throughout the world. Through
Wheels for the World, the organization provides refurbished wheel chairs for
those in developing nations. Through family retreats, radio and TV programs,
conference speaking and writing, Joni has reached thousands with the love of
Christ in a way she never would have if not a quadriplegic. Her devotion to Christ

is reflected in her love of singing the hymns of the faith, which she has been known to do at any moment, even in crowded airports. When she was diagnosed with breast cancer, she continued to find strength and courage from the Scriptures, such as I Peter 2:21, 'To these hardships you were called because Christ suffered for you, leaving you an example that you should follow in his steps.' Suffering brings one closer to Christ, and Joni noticed that 'In a way, I've been drawn closer to the Savior, even with this breast cancer. There are things about his character that I wasn't seeing a year ago or even six months ago. This tells me that I'm still growing and being transformed. First Peter 2:21 is a good rule of thumb for any Christian struggling to understand God's purposes in hardship.'[43]

The author of Hebrews 11, after describing the actions of several people of faith, wrote, 'And what more shall I say? For time would fail me to tell of Gideon, Barak, and Samson....' Similarly, after studying two millennia of Christian women, there is not enough time to adequately survey the thousands of Christian women and their works.

Many of these women are of course totally unknown, yet they are all feminine threads in the tapestry of Christian history. Reflecting back on her own life, the author of this history remembers many of these unknown godly women important to her Christian growth:

Annie Allen, the grandmotherly babysitter who first read to the little nine year old girl from the Bible and explained this book was written by God; Evelyn Palmer, the Christian schoolteacher who encouraged the fifteen year old adolescent in her study and writing of history; Grandmother Antonia Kucera who lived a life of prayer and made her granddaughter promise she would pray for her children and grandchildren when she was gone; Doris Wright, the dear friend in England, who opened her home to a young people's Bible study and saw many of them in Christian ministry; and most notably mother Dorothy Walzel, who came to faith in Christ at 30, then immersed herself in Scripture and became a woman full of discernment, wise counsel, love, and godly beauty.

Millions of women in following Christ have followed the New Testament pattern of Christian women – lifting up the needs of others in prayer, mentoring other Christians, supporting church leaders, showing hospitality, fellow-laboring as missionaries, supporting their husbands in Christian work, instructing other women, evangelizing and sharing the Word with others, teaching children, and helping those in need and distress. These Christian women were from the poor and rich, from every class of society, and from every continent on the globe. They were not perfect, but they have obtained a good testimony through faith in the One who gave His life a ransom to redeem them for God. They are the feminine threads in the rich tapestry of Christian history.

---

43 Sarah Pullam Bailey, 'Joni Eareckson Tada on Something Greater than Healing,' Christianity Today, October 8, 2010, www.christianitytoday.com/ct/2010/october/12.30.html.

General Bibliography

American Women's History: A Research Guide, http://www.mtsu.edu/~kmiddlet/history/women.html.

Black, Rev. W.C. *Christian Womanhood*. Nashville, Tenn.: Publishing House of the Methodist Episcopal Church South, 1892.

Blevins, Carolyn DeArmond, ed. *Women in Christian History, a Bibliography*. Mercer University Press, 1995.

Branda, Ann. *Women and Religion in America*. Oxford University Press, 2000.

Cochrane, Charles Norris. *Christianity and Classical Culture*. Oxford University Press, 1944.

Curtis, A. Kenneth and Daniel Graves. *Great Women in Christian History: 37 Women Who Changed Their World*. Worcester, PA: Christian History Institute, 2004.

Disse, Dorothy. *Other Women's Voices*, http://home.infionline.net/~ddisse/index.html . A very useful website which links to over 125 women writers before 1700, many of whom were Christians.

Deen, Edith. *Great Women of the Christian Faith*. New York: Christian Herald Books, 1959.

Drummond, Lewis and Betty. *Women of Awakenings: The Historic Contribution of Women to Revival Movements*. Grand Rapids, MI: Kregel Publications, 1997.

Greaves, Richard L., ed. *Triumph Over Silence: Women in Protestant History*. Westport, Conn.: Greenwood Press, 1985.

Hale, Sarah Josepha. *Woman's Record: Sketches of all distinguished women from the creation to A.D. 1850*. New York: Harper and Brothers, 1855, 2nd edition.

Hammack, Mary L. *A Dictionary of Women in Church History*. Chicago: Moody Press, 1984.

Hardesty, Nancy A. *Great Women of Faith*. Nashville: Abingdon, 1980.

James, Janet Wilson, ed. *Women in American Religion*. University of Pennsylvania Press, 1980.

Lord, John. *Beacon Lights of History, Vol. 4: Great Women and Great Rulers*. Wm. H. Wise & Co., 1921.

MacHaffie, Barbara J. *Her Story: Women in Christian Tradition*. Philadelphia: Fortress Press, 1986.
  ---. *Readings in Her Story: Women in Christian Tradition*. Minneapolis: Fortress Press, 1992.

Malone, Mary T. *Women and Christianity*, vols 1-3. Maryknoll, New York: Orbis Books, 2001.

The New Schaff-Herzog Encyclopedia of Religious Knowledge (ed. Samuel MacCauly), Grand Rapids, Michigan: Baker Book House, 1952.

Oden, Amy. *In Her Words*. Abingdon Press: Nashville, TN, 1994.

Petersen, Willim J. *25 Surprising Marriages: Faith-Building Stories from the Lives of Famous Christians*. Grand Rapids, Michigan: Baker Books, 1997.

Petrou, Ioannis. 'The Question of Women in Church Tradition,' *Anglican Theological Review*, Summer 2002, Vol. 84, Iss. 3, 654-61.

Piper, Noël. *Faithful Women and Their Extraordinary God*. Wheaton, Ill.: Crossway Books, 2005.

Schaff, Philip. *History of the Christian Church*. Grand Rapids, Michigan: Wm. B. Eerdmans Publishing Co., 1989 reprint of 1910 edition.
   ---. Ed., 'Women's Work in the Church,' *New Schaff-Herzog Encyclopedia of Religious Knowledge*, Vol. 12, 413-419, from Christian Classics Ethereal Library, www.ccel.org.

Tucker, Ruth A. and Walter Liefeld. *Daughters of the Church: Women and ministry from New Testament times to the present*. Grand Rapids, MI: Zondervan Publishing House, 1987.

Wilson, Janet James, ed. *Women in American Religion*. University of Pennsylvania Press, 1980.

Chapter 1 – The New Testament Era: *One in Christ Jesus*

Carroll, James, 'Who Was Mary Magdalene?', http://www.smithsonianmag.com/history-archaeology/magdalene.html .

Duncan, Ligon, 'Phoebe: The Ministry of Women in the Early Church,' http://www.fpcjackson.org/resources/sermons/romans/romansvol5to6/46bRomans.htm .

Gombis, Timothy G., 'A Radically New Humanity: the Function of the Haustafel in Ephesians,' *Journal of the Evangelical Theological Society*, June 2005, Vol. 48, Iss. 2, 317-30.

Hughes, Sarah S. and Brady Hughes. *Women in Ancient Civilizations*. Washington, D.C., 1998.

Hunwicke, John, 'Junia Among the Apostles: The Story Behind a New Testament Saint and the Egalitarian Agenda,' *Touchstone*, October 2008, 22-7.

Just, Felix, 'Household Codes in the New Testament,' http://catholicresources.org/Bible/Epistles-HouseholdCodes.htm .

Keener, Craig S. *Paul, Women, and Wives: Marriage and Women's Minsitry in the Letters of Paul*. Hendrickson Publishers, 1992.

Kleinig, John W., 'Ordered community: order and subordination in the New Testament,' *Lutheran Theological Journal*. Aug.-Dec. 2005, Vol. 39, Iss.2/3, 196-210.

Köstenberger, Andreas J., Thomas R. Schreiner, and H. Scott Baldwin. *Women in the Church: A Fresh Analysis of I Timothy 2: 9-15*. Grand Rapids, Michigan: Baker Books, 1995.

The Journal for Biblical Manhood and Womanhood, Spring 2005 (JBMW responds to *Discovering Biblical Equality*) IVP, 2004.

Moo, Douglas. 'What Does it Mean Not to Teach or Have Authority Over Men, 1 Timothy 2:11-15', http://www.bible.org/page.php?page_id=2829 .

Ryrie, Charles. *The Role of Women in the Church*. Chicago: Moody Press, 1970.

Schreiner, Thomas R. 'The Valuable Ministries of Women in the Context of Male Leadership: A Survey of Old and New Testament Examples and Teaching,' http://www.bible.org/page.php?page_id=2843 .

Wallace, Daniel B., 'Bible Gynecology' Part 1, www.bible.org/page.asp?page_id=2487 ; Part 2, www.bible.org/page.asp?page_id=1477, accessed 2-9-05 . 'Did Priscilla "Teach" Apollos? An Examination of the Meaning of ejktivqhmi in Acts 18:26,' www.bible.org/page.asp?page_id=1476, accessed 2-9-05.

'Junia Among the Apostles: The Double Identification Problem in Romans 16:7,' http://www.bible.org/page.php?page_id=1163 .

Winter, Bruce W. *Roman Wives, Roman Widows: The Appearance of New Women and the Pauline Communities*. Grand Rapids, Michigan: William B. Eerdmans, 2003.

Witherington, Ben III. *Women in the Earliest Churches*. Cambridge University Press, 1988.

Women in the Early Church, *Christian History*, Vol. VII, No. 1, Issue 17, 1988.

Women of the Bible: Provocative New Insights, U.S. News and World Report Special Collector's Edition, February 21, 2006.

Chapter 2 – Women in the Early Church: *A Good Testimony through Faith*

Balch, David L. and Carolyn Osek. *Early Christian Families in Context*. Eerdmans, 2003.

Brittain, Rev. Alfred and Mitchell Carroll. *Women of Early Christianity* vol. 3 from the *Woman in all Ages and in all countries* series. New York: Gordon Press, 1976 reprint of 1907 edition.

Burrus, Virginia, 'Blurring the Boundaries: A Response to Howard C. Kee,' *Theology Today*, Vol. XLIX, No. 2, July 1992, 239-42.

Butler, Rex D. *The New Prophecy and 'New Visions': Evidence of Montanism in the Passion of Perpetua and Felicitas (Patristic Monograph Series)*. Catholic University of America Press, 2006.
   ---. 'Perpetua's Use of Sacred Writings,' 1-35, presented at the National Evangelical Theological Society Conference, Valley Forge, Pennsylvania, November 17, 2005.

Castelli, Elizabeth, 'Gender, Theory, and *The Rise of Christianity*: A Response to Rodney Stark,' *Journal of Early Christian Studies*, Vol. 6, No. 2, summer 1998, 227-57.

Clark, Elizabeth. *Women in the Early Church: Message of the Fathers of the Church Series (v.13)*. Liturgucal Press, 1984.
---. 'Woman in Late Christianity,' *Journal of Early Christian Studies*, vol. 2, 1994, 166-84.

Clark, Gillian. *Women in Late Antiquity: Pagans and Christian Lifestyles*. Oxford: Clarendon Press, 1993.

Cohick, Lynn H. *Women in the world of the Earliest Christians: Illuminating Ancient Ways of Life*. Baker Academics, 2009.

Coon, Lynda L., Katherine J. Haldane, and Elisabeth W. Sommer, eds. *That Gentle Strength: Historical Perspectives on Women in Christianity*, Charlottesville and London: University Press of Virginia, 1990.

Cooper, Kate. 'The Voice of the Victim: Gender, Representation and Early Christian Martyrdom,' *Bulletin John Rylands University Library Manchester*. Vol. 80, No.3, Autumn 1998, 147-57.

Cullen Murphy. *The Word According to Eve – Women in the Bible in Ancient Times and Our Own*. Boston & New York: Houghton Mifflin Company, 1999.

Davidson, Ivor J. *The Birth of the Church*. Baker Books, 2004.

Davis, Stephen J. *The Cult of St. Thecla: A Tradition of Women's Piety in Late Antiquity*. Oxford University Press, 2001.

Eisen, Ute E. *Women Officeholders in Early Christianity: Epigraphical and Literary Studies*. Collegeville, Minnesota: The Liturgical Press, 2000.

Ferguson, Everett. *Early Christians Speak: Faith and Life in the First Three Centuries*. Abilene Christian University Press, 1999.
---. *Encyclopedia of Early Christianity*. Routledge, 1990.
---. 'Women in the Post-Apostolic Church,' *Essays on Women in Earliest Christianity* (ed. Carroll D. Osburn). Joplin, MO: College Press Pub. Co., 1993, 493-513.

Fiorenza, Elizabeth Schüssler. *In Memory of Her: A Feminist Theological Reconstruction of Christian Origins*. New York: Crossroad Press, 1983.

Fox, Robin Lane. *Pagans and Christians*. New York: Alfred A. Knopf, Inc., 1986.

Frend, W.H.C., 'The Failure of the Persecutions in the Roman Empire,' *Past and Present*, No. 16, Nov. 1959, 10-30.

Heine, Susan. *Christianity and the Goddess: Systematic Criticism of a Feminist Theology*. London: SCM, 1988.
---. *Women and Early Christianity: Are the Feminist Scholars Right?* London: SCM.1988.

Hoffman, Daniel L. *The Status of Women and Gnosticism in Irenaeus and Tertullian*. Lewiston, NY: Edwin Mellen Press, Ltd., 1995.

Kee, Howard Clark, 'The Changing Role of Women in Early Christianity,' *Theology Today*, Vol. XLIX, No.2, 225-38.

Kraemer, Ross Shepard and Mary Rose D'Angelo, eds. *Women and Christian Origins*. New York: Oxford University Press, 1999.

LaPorte, Jean. *The Role of Women in Early Christianity*. Vol. 7: Studies in Women and Religion. New York & Toronto: The Edwin Mellen Press, 1982.

MacDonald, *Early Christian Women and Pagan Opinion: The Power of the Hysterical Woman*. New York: Cambridge University Press, 1996.

MacKechnie, Paul. 'Women and Christianity' in *The First Christian Centuries*. InverVarsity Press, 191-216.

Macy, Gary. *The Hidden History of Women's Ordination*. Oxford University Press, 2008.

Madigan, Kevin and Carolyn Osiek. *Ordained Women in the Early Church*. Baltimore and London: Johns Hopkins University Press, 2005.

McVey, Kathleen, 'Gnosticism, Feminism, and Elaine Pagels,' *Theology Today*, Vol. XXXVII, No. 4, January, 1981, 498-501.

Miller, Monica Migliorino. 'The Authority of Women,' *This Rock*. July/August 1996, 11-17.

Ng, Esther You L. *Reconstructing Christian Origins?* Paternoster Press, 2002.

Osiek, Carolyn, 'Perpetua's Husband,' *Journal of Early Christian Studies*, Vol. 10, Number 2, Summer 2002, 287-90.

Osiek, Carolyn, and Margaret Y. MacDonald, with Janet Tullock. *A Woman's Place: House Churches in Early Christianity*. Minneapolis: Fortress Press, 2006.

Pagels, Elaine. *The Gnostic Gospels*. Vintage, 1989.

Pursiful, Darrell, 'Ordained Women of the Patristic Era,' *Priscilla Papers*, Summer 2001, 7-13.

Ryrie, Charles. *The Role of Women in the Church*. Chicago: Moody Press, 1970.

Salisbury, Joyce. *Perpetua's Passion*. Routledge, 1997.

Scholer, David M. *Women in Early Christianity*. New York and London: Garland Publishing Co., 1993.

Sebastian, J. Jayakiran. 'Martyrs and Heretics: Aspects of the Contribution of Women to Early Christian Tradition,' in Prasanna Kumari, ed., *Feminist Theology: Perspectives and Praxis*. Chennai: Gurukul Lutheran Theological College and Research Institute, 1999, 135-53.

Spencer, Rev. J.A. *TheWomen of Early Christianity*. NewYork: D.Appleton & Co., 1852.

Stark, Rodney. *The Rise of Christianity: How the Obscure, Marginal, Jesus Movement Became the Dominant Religious Force*. HarperSanFrancisco, 1997.

Thurston, Bonnie Bowman. *The Widows: A Woman's Ministry in the Early Church*. Minneapolis: Fortress Press, 1989.

Torjesen, Karen Jo. *When WomenWere Priests:Women's Leadership in the Early Church and the Scandal of Their subordination in the Rise of Christianity*. New York: HarperSanFrancisco, 1993.

Wace, Henry andWilliam C. Piercy, eds. *A Dictionary of Christian Biography*. Peabody, Massachusetts: Hendrickson Publishers, 1994 reprint of 1961 edition.

Wiesner-Hanks, Merry E., 'Women, gender, and church history,' *Church History*, Vol.71, Iss. 3, September 2002, 600-21.

Wilson-Kastner, Patricia, G. Ronald Kastner, Ann Millin, Rosemary Rader, Jeremiah Reedy, *A Lost Tradition: Women Writers of the Early Church*. University Press of America, 1981.

Witherington III, Ben. *Women in the Earliest Churches*. Cambridge University Press, 1988.

Chapter 3 – Christian Women in Late Antiquity: *Reverent in Behavior*

Augustine, trans. Edmund Hill. *Sermons*. III/8-11. Hyde Park, New York: New City Press, 1990.

Brown, Peter. *Augustine of Hippo*. University of California Press, 2000.

Clark, Elizabeth. *Jerome, Chrysostom and Friends*, vol. 1 in Studies of Women and Religion. NewYork andToronto:The Edwin Mellen Press, 1979.

Clark, Gillian. *Women in Late Antiquity: Pagan and Christian Lifestyles*. Oxford: Clarendon Press, 1993.

Coon, Lynda L. *Sacred Fictions: Holy Women and Hagiography in Late Antiquity*. Philadelphia: University of Pennsylvania Press, 1997.

Ford, David C. *Women and Men in the Early Church:The FullViews of St. John Chrysostom*. South Canaan, Pennsylvania: St. Tikhon's Seminary Press, 1996.

Gould, Graham, 'Women in the Writings of the Fathers: Language, Belief, and Reality,' in *Women in the Church*, eds. W.J. Sheils and Diana Wood. Published for the Ecclesiastical History Society by Basil Blackwell, 1990.

Hill, Edmund. 'St. Augustine – a male chauvinist?' Talk given to the Robert Hugh Benson Graduate Society at Fisher House, Cambridge, Nov. 22, 1994. online at http://www.its.caltech.edu/~nmcenter/women-cp/augustin.html, accessed on 11-30-05.

Jacobs, Andrew S. 'Writing Demetrias: Ascetic Logic in Ancient Christianity', *Church History*, Vol. 69, No. 4 (Dec. 2000), pp.719-48.

Jerome, *Letters and Select Works* in *Nicene and Post-Nicene Fathers of the Christian Church*, Second Series, ed. by Philip Schaff and Henry Wace, Vol. 6, Grand Rapids: Wm. B. Eerdmans, 1983 reprint.

Perry, Tim. *Mary for Evangelicals*. Downers Grove, Illinois: InterVarsity Press Academic, 2006.

Power, Kim. *Veiled Desire: Augustine on Women*. New York: Continuum, 1996.

Rousseau, Philip, '"Learned Women" and the Development of a Christian Culture in Late Antiquity,' *Symbolae Osloenses* Vol. 70, 1995, 116-47.

Yarbrough, Anne, 'Christianization in the Fourth Century: The Example of Roman Women,' *Church History,* Vol. 45. No. 2, June 1976, 149-65.

Chapter 4 – Christian Women in the Early Middle Ages: *Vessels of Gold and Silver*

Atkinson, Clarissa. *The Oldest Vocation: Christian Motherhood in the Middle Ages*. Ithaca, NY: Cornell University Press, 1991.

Barstow, Anne Llewellyn. *Married Priests and the Reforming Papacy: The Eleventh Century Debates*. The Edwin Mellen Press, 1982.

Beach, Maxine Clarke. 'Women Interpreting Scripture in the Middle Ages,' *The Bible: The Book that Bridges the Millennia*, 1998, excerpt at http://gbgm-umc.org/umw/bible/mawomen.stm.

Cherewatuk, Karen. 'Speculum Matris: Duoda's Manual,' *Florilegium,* 10, 1988-91, 49-64.
---. 'Double Monasteries,' *Catholic Encyclopedia* at www.newadvent.org/cathen/10452a.htm, accessed 5/22/2003.

Duvall, Onnie. 'Radegund of Poitiers,' *ORB Encyclopedia: Online Essays*, 1996, http://www.the-orb.net/essays/text01.html.

Fletcher, Richard. *Barbarian Conversion from Paganism to Christianity*. New York: Henry Holt & Co., 1997.

Griesinger, Emily, 'A Hermeneutic of Faith,' *Books and Culture*, July/August 1999,

Head, Thomas. 'Women and Hagiography in Medieval Christianity,' *The ORB: On-Line Reference Book for Medieval Studies,* available at http://www.the-orb.net/encyclop/religion/hagiography/women1.htm.
---. 'Herrad of Hohenbourg,' *OtherWomen'sVoices*, http://home.infionline.net/~ddisse/herrad.html, accessed on 2/7/07.
---. 'Herrad von Landsberg,' *The Grove Dictionary of Art,* at http://www.artnet.com/library/03/0378/T037828.asp , accessed on 2/7/07.

---. 'Hagiography of Saint Kassiani', http://www.antiochian.org/sites/antiochian.org/files/sacred_music/MGF_0192a.HolyWeek.Kassiani.pdf .

Johnson, Brenda A. 'Hrotsvit of Gandersheim: Tenth Century Poet and Playwright,' Mount Saint Agnes Theological Center for Women,' 2001 at http://msawomen.org/works/hrotsvit.html, accessed 5/23/2003.

King, Margot H. 'The Desert Mothers: A Survey of the Feminine Anchorite Tradition in Western Europe,' Peregrina Publishing Co., http://www.peregrina.com/matrologia_latina/DesertMothers1.html.

Labarge, Margaret Wade. *Small Sound of the Trumpet*. Boston: Beacon Press, 1986.

Nichols, John A. and Lillian Thomas Shank. *Distant Echoes*, vol. 1 of *Medieval Religious Women*. Cistercian Publications, Inc., 1984.

Other Women's Voices: Translations of women's writing before 1700, available at http://home.infionline.net/~ddisse/index.html.

Power, Eileen. (M.M. Posten, ed.) *Medieval Women*. Cambridge University Press, 1975.

Rudolf of Fulda. 'Life of Leoba (c. 836).' *Internet Medieval Sourcebook*. http://www.fordham.edu/halsall/basis/leoba.html.
'St. Walburga,' *Catholic Encyclopedia,* at http://www.newadvent.org/cathen/15526b.htm, accessed 1/27/07.

Smith, Lesley and Jane H.M. Taylor, eds. *Women, the Book, and the Godly*. Selected Proceedings of the St. Hilda Conference 1993, vol. 1.

Touliatos-Miliotis, Diane. 'Women Composers in Byzantium,' available at http://www.hellenicnest.com/dianeII.html accessed on 6/02/11.

Wemple, Suzanne Fonay. *Women in Frankish Society: Marriage and the Cloister, 500-900*. Philadelphia: University of Pennsylvania Press, 1981.

'Women in the Middle Ages', *Christian History*, Issue 30 (Vol. x, No.2) [complete issue devoted to subject].

Wood, Ian. 'The Mission of Augustine of Canterbury to the English,' *Speculum*, vol. 69, no. 1, January 1994, 1-17.

Chapter 5 – Christian Women in the Late Middle Ages: *Well Reported for Good Works*

Agrippa of Nettesheim, Heinrich Cornelius. *Female Pre-eminence: or the Dignity and Excellence of that Sex , above the Male*. London: T.R. and M.D., 1670, as at http://www.esotericarchives.com/agrippa/preem.htm, accessed 6/02/11.

Babinsky, Ellen L. 'Christological transformation in *The Mirror of Souls*, by Marguerite Porete,' *Theology Today*, April 2003, vol. 60, Iss. 1, 34-48

Baker, Derek, ed. *Medieval Women*. Oxford: Basil Blackwell, 1978, published for The Ecclesiastical History Society, 1978.

Barton, Richard, trans. 'The Trial of Marguerite Porete,' http://www.uncg.edu/~rebarton/margporete.htm.

Bynum, Caroline Walker. *Holy Feast and Holy Fast: The Religious Significance of Food to Medieval Women*. University of California Press, 1987.

Byrne, Lavinia. *Margaret of Scotland*. New York: Alba House, 1998.

Cahill, Thomas. *Mysteries of the Middle Ages*. New York: Nan A. Talese, 2006.

Dronke, Peter. *Women Writers of the Middle Ages: A Critical Study of Texts from Perpetua to Marguerite Porete*. Cambridge University Press, 1984.

Fox, Matthew. 'Hildegard of Bingen: Cosmic Christ, Religion of Experience, God the Mother,' commentary in *Illuminations of Hildegard of Bingen*. Santa Fe: New Mexico: Bear & Co., 1985 reprinted in *Knowledge of Reality Magazine*, www.sol.com.au/kor/5_02.htm, accessed on 5/17/2003.

Galea, Kate P. Crawford. 'Unhappy Choices: Factors that Contributed to the Decline and Condemnation of the Beguines,' *Vox Benedictina: A Journal of Translations from Monastic Sources*. Saskatoon: Peregrina Publishers, vol.10.1, 1993, 57-73.

George, Marie I. 'What Aquinas Really Said About Women,' *First Things*, December 1999, 11-13.

Goodich, Michael, 'The Contours of Female Piety in Later Medieval Hagiography,' *Church History*, vol. 50, no.1 (March 1981), 20-32.

'Impact of *Malleus Maleficarum* on persecution of witches in England,' *Medieval World*, http://medieval.etrusia.co.uk/malleus/, accessed 1/27/07.

Kiefer, James E. 'Hildegard of Bingen, Visionary,' *Biographical Sketches of Memorable Christians of the Past*, http://www.missionstclare.com/english/people/sep17.html, accessed on 6/02/2003.

Knuth, Elizabeth T. 'The Beguines,' http://www.users.csbsju.edu/~eknuth/xpxx/beguines.html , December 1992.

LaBarge, Margaret Wade. *A Small Sound of the Trumpet: Women in Medieval Life*. Boston: Beacon Press, 1986.

McGinn, 'The Changing Shape of Late Medieval Mysticism,' *Church History*, vol. 65, No.2 (June 1996), 197-219.

Newman, Barbara. *From Virile Woman to WomanChrist* Studies in Medieval Religion and Literature. University of Pennsylvania Press, 1995.

---. 'Visions and Validation,' *Church History*, Vol. 54, No.2 (June 1985), 163-75.

---, ed., *Voice of the Living Light: Hildegard of Bingen and Her World*. Berkeley: University of California Press, 1998.

Noffke, Suzanne, 'Catherine of Siena, justly doctor of the church?' *Theology Today* 60 (2003), 49-62.

Pernoud, Régine. *Women in the Days of the Cathedrals*. San Francisco: Ignatius Press, 1998.

Peters, Marygrace, O.P. 'The Beguines: Feminine Piety Derailed,' *Spirituality Today*, Spring 1991, Vol. 43 No.1, pp. 36-52.

Scott, Karen, 'Catherine of Siena, "Apostola",' *Church History*, Vol. 61, No.1 (March 1992), 34-46.

Thompson, Augustine, 'Hildegard of Bingen on gender and the priesthood,' *Church History*, September 1994, Vol. 63, Issue 3, 349-

Upjohn, Sheila. *Why Julian Now?: A Voyage of Discovery*. Grand Rapids, MI & Cambridge, U.K.: William B. Eerdmans Publishing Co., 1997.

Winston-Allen, Anne. *Convent Chronicles: Women Writing About Women and Reform in the Late Middle Ages*. University Park, PA: The Pennsylvania State University Press, 2004.

Chapter 6 - Women in the Early Protestant Reformation: *Loving their Husbands and Children*

Bainton, Roland, 'Changing Ideas and Ideals in the Sixteenth Century,' *The Journal of Modern History*, Vol. 8, No. 4 (Dec. 1936), 417-43.

---. *Women of the Reformation from Spain to Scandinavia*. Minneapolis, Minnesota: Augsburg Publishing House, 1977.

---. *Women of the Reformation in France and England*. Boston: Beacon Press, 1975.

---. *Women of the Reformation in Germany and Italy*. Minneapolis, Minnesota: Augsburg Publishing House, 1971.

Blaisdell, Charmarie Jenkins. 'Calvin's Letters to Women: The Courting of Ladies in High Places,' *Sixteenth Century Journal*, Vol. 13, No.3 (Autumn, 1982), 67-84.

Classen Albrecht and Tanya Amber Settle, 'Women in Martin Luther's Life and Theology,' *German Studies Review*, Vol. 14, No. 2 (May, 1991), 231-60.

Cohn, Henry J. 'Case Study 9: The Impact of the Reformation on Women in Germany.' University of Warwick, 2000., www.warwick.ac.uk/fac/arts/History/teaching/protref/women/WRcore.htm, accessed June 9, 2007.

DeBoer, Willis P. 'Calvin on the Role of Women,' in *Exploring the Heritage of John Calvin* (David E. Holwerda, ed.) Grand Rapids, Michigan: Baker Book House, 1976.

Dentière, Marie, 'A Very Useful Letter written and composed by a Christian woman from Tournai, sent to the Queen of Navarre, sister of the King of France, Against the Turks, Jews, Infidels, False Christians, Anabaptists, and Lutherans', Geneva, 1539 (trans. Elisabeth Wengler), http://web.archive.org/web/20060912134252/employees.csbsju.edu/ewengler/dentiere.htm, accessed 6/02/11.

> ---. *Epistle to Marguerite de Navarre and Preface to a Sermon by John Calvin* (Mary B. McKinley, trans.). (University of Chicago Press, 2004).

Douglass, Jane Dempsey, 'Christian Freedom: What Calvin Learned at the School of Women,' *Church History*, Vol. 53, No. 2 (June, 1984) 155-73.
> ---. 'Glimpses of Reformed women leaders from our history,' *Semper Reformanda*, World Alliance of Reformed Churches, www.warc.ch/dp/walk/03.html, accessed June 15, 2007.
> ---. *Women, Freedom and Calvin*. Philadelphia: Westminster Press, 1985.

Furey, Constance, 'Intellects Inflamed in Christ: Women and Spiritualized Scholarship in Renaissance Christianity,' *The Journal of Religion*, January 2004, Vol. 84, Iss. 1, 1-23.

Graesslé, Rev. Dr. Isabelle, 'Reformation Sunday,' *Reformed World*, Vol. 53 number 1 (March 2003), http://warc.ch/24gc/rw031/14.html , accessed June 2007.

Good, Rev. James I. *Famous Women of the Reformed Church*. Sunday School Board of the Reformed Church in the United States, 1901.

Greaves, Richard L., ed. *Triumph Over Silence: Women in Protestant History*. Westport, Conn.: Greenwood Press, 1985.

Green, Lowell, 'The Education of Women in the Reformation,' *History of Education Quarterly*, Vol. 19, No. 1, (Spring 1979), 93-116.

Harrison, Wes. 'The Role of Women in Anabaptist Thought and Practice: The Hutterite Experience of the Sixteenth and Seventeenth Centuries,' *Sixteenth Century Journal*, Vol. 23, No. 1 (Spring, 1992), 49-69.

Healey, Robert. 'Knox's Curious Attitude Toward Women,' *Christian History*, Issue 46 (Vol. XIV, No. 2), 36-8.

Irwin, Joyce L. *Womanhood in Radical Protestantism*. Lewiston, NY: Edwin Mellon Press, 1979.

Karant-Nunn, Susan C. and Merry E. Wiesner-Hanks. *Luther on Women: A Sourcebook*. Cambridge University Press, 2003.

Matheson, Peter. 'Breaking the Silence: Women, Censorship, and the Reformation,' *Sixteenth Century Journal*, Vol. 27, No. 1 (Spring, 1996), 97-109.

MacCuish, Dolina. *Luther and his Katie: The Influence of Luther's wife on his ministry*. Ross-shire, UK: Christian Focus Publications, 1999.

Markwald, Rudolf K. and Marilynn Morris Markwald. *Katharina von Bora*. St. Louis, MO: Concordia Publishing House, 2002.

'Memoirs of Madame Du Plessis-Mornay,' from the *Edinburgh Review*, reprinted in *Littel's Living Age*, vol. CIX (4 Series, Vol. XXI), April-June, 1871, 598-606.

Miller, Patrik. 'Bullinger – the Family Man,' *Annex*, 2004, 7.

Petersen, William J. 'Idelette: John Calvin's Search for the Right Wife,' *Christian History*, Vol. V, No. 4, 12-15.

Roper, Lyndel. *The Holy Household: Women and Morals in Reformation Augsburg*. Oxford: Clarendon Press, 1989.

Russell, Paul A. *Lay Theology in the Reformation: Popular Pamphleteers in Southwest Germany, 1521-1525*. Cambridge University Press, 1986.

'Songs of Anabaptist Women,' at www.warwick.ac.uk/fac/arts/History/teaching/protref/RR0834.htm.

Smith, Jeanette C. 'Katharina von Bora Through Five Centuries: A Historiography,' *Sixteenth Century Journal*, Vol. 30, No. 3 (Autumn, 1999), 745-74.

Thompson, John Lee. *John Calvin and the Daughters of Sarah: Women in Regular and Exceptional Roles in the Exegesis of Calvin, His Predecesors, and his Contemporaries.*. Geneva: Librairie Droz S.A., 1992.

Wiesner, Merry. 'Luther and women: The death of two Marys,' in *Disciplines of Faith: Studies in Religion, Politics and Patriarchy* (Jim Obelkevich, Lyndal Roper, and Raphael Samuel, eds.). London: Routledge & Kegan Paul Inc., 1987.
 ---. 'Women's Response to the Reformation,' in *The German People and the Reformation* (R. Po-Chia Hsia, ed.). Ithaca, NY: Cornell University Press, 1988.

Wilson, Katharina M. *Women Writers of the Renaissance-Reformation*. Athens, Georgia and London: University of Georgia Press, 1987.

'Women,' *Global Anabaptist Mennonite Encyclopedia Online*, www.gameo.org/encyclopedia/W645ME.html, accessed June 16, 2007.

Zophy, Jonathan W. 'We Must Have the Dear Ladies: Martin Luther and Women,' in *Pietas et Societas: New Trends in Reformation Social History, Essays in Memory of Harold J. Grimm* (Kyle C. Sessions and Phillip N. Bebb, eds.). Kirksville, MO: Sixteenth Century Journal Pubs., Inc., 1985.

Chapter 7 – Women in the Catholic Reformation and the English Reformation: *The Household of Faith*

Elaine V. Beilin. *Redeeming Eve:Women Writers of the English Renaissance*. Princeton University Press, 1987.

Bernard, G.W. 'The Fall of Anne Boleyn,' *The English Historical Review*, vol. 106, No. 420 July 1991), 584-610.

Dill, Elizabeth. 'Reformation Women: The Case of Ann Askew,' *Sites of Cultural Stress from Reformation to Revolution*. Folger Institute, http://www.folger. edu/html/folger_institute/cultural_stress/church_reformation.html.

Elizabeth I. *CollectedWorks* (eds. Leah S. Marcus, Janel Mueller, Mary Beth Rose). Chicago & London:The University of Chicago Press, 2000.

Freeman,Thomas S. 'Research, Rumour and propaganda:Anne Boleyn in Foxe's "Book of Martyrs,"' *The Historical Journal*,Vol. 38, No. 4 (Dec. 1995), 797-819.

Green, Lowell. 'The Education ofWomen in the Reformation,' *History of Education Quarterly*,Vol. 19, No. 1 (Spring 1979), 93-116.

Ives, Eric W. 'Anne Boleyn and the Early Reformation in England: the Contemporary Evidence,' *The Historical Journal,* Vol. 37, No. 2 (June 1994), 389-400.
   ---. 'The Fall of Anne Boleyn Reconsidered,' *The English Historical Review*, Vo. 107, No. 424 (July 1992), 651-64.
   ---. *Lady Jane Grey:A Tudor Mystery*.Wiley-Blackwell, 2009.
   ---. *The Life and Death of Anne Boleyn*. Blackwell Publishing Ltd., 2005.

'Lady Jane Grey: Nine Days a Queen, a Martyr Forever,' *Leben*, April-June 2005, 3-15.
   ---. 'Reformation Women:The Case of Ann Askew,' *Sites of Cultural Stress from Reformation to Revolution*, Folger Institute, 2003, www.folger. edu/html/folger_institute/cultural_stress/church_reformation. html.

Todd, Margo. 'Humanists, Puritans and the Spiritualized Household,' *Church History*,Vol. 49, No. 1(March 1980), 18-24.

Walker, Greg, 'Rethinking the Fall of Anne Boleyn,' *The Historical Journal*, vol. 45, Issue 1 (March 1, 2002), 1-29.

Warnicke, Retha M. 'The Fall of Anne Boleyn Revisited,' *The English Historical Review*, vol. 108, No. 429 (July 1993), 653-65.

Withrow, Brandon G. *Katherine Parr: A Guided Tour of the Life and Thought of a Reformation Queen*. P & R Publisher, 2009.

Zahl, Paul F.M. *FiveWomen of the English Reformation*. Grand Rapids, Michigan, and Cambridge, U.K.:William B. Eerdmans Publishing Co., 2001.

Chapter 8 – Heiresses of the Reformation: *Joint Heirs with Christ*

Anderson, James. *Memorable Women of the Puritan Times*, 2 volumes. Soli Deo GloriaPublications, 2001 reprint of 1862 London edition.

Anselment, Raymond A., 'Katherine Paston and Brilliana Harley: Maternal Letters and the Genre of Mother's Advice,' *Studies in Philology*, Vol. 101, No. 4 (Fall 2004), 431-53.

Beilin, Elaine V. *Redeeming Eve: Women Writers of the English Renaissance*. Princeton University Press, 1987.

Brown, Sylvia, ed. *Women's Writing in Stuart England: The Mother's Legacies of Dorothy Leigh, Elizabeth Joscelin, and Elizabeth Richardson*. Sutton Publishing, 1999.

Collinson, Patrick. 'The Role of Women in the English Reformation, Illustrated by the Life and Friendship of Anne Locke,' in *Godly People – Essays on English Protestantism and Puritanism*. The Hambledon Press, 1983.

Como, David R. 'Women, Prophecy, and Authority in Early Stuart Puritanism,' *The Huntington Library Quarterly*, Vol. 61, No. 2 (1998), 203-22.

Dinan, Susan E. and Debra Meyers, ed. *Women and Religion in Old and New Worlds*. New York and London: Routledge, 2001.

Dodds, Elisabeth. *Marriage to a Difficult Man*. Philadelphia: Westminster Press, 1971.

Dunn, Mary Maples, 'Saints and Sisters: Congregational and Quaker Women in the Early Colonial Period,' *American Quarterly*, Vol. 30, No. 5, Special Issue: Women and Religion. (Winter, 1978), 582-601.

Freeman, Thomas, '"The Good Ministrye of Godlye and Vertuouse Women": The Elizabethan Martyrologists and the Female Supporters of the Marian Martyrs,' *The Journal of British Studies*, Vol. 39, No. 1 (Jan., 2000), 8-33.

Greaves, Richard L., 'The Role of Women in Early English Nonconformity,' *Church History*, Vol. 52, No. 3 (Sep. 1983), 299-311.

Heyrman, Christine Leigh, 'Religion, Women, and the Family in Early America,' *The Seventeenth and Eighteenth Centuries*. National Humanities Center, http://nationalhumanitiescenter.org/tserve/eighteen/ekeyinfo/erelwom.htm, accessed 6/02/11.

Irwin, Joyce L. *Woman in Radical Protestantism, 1525-1675*. Lewiston: E. Mellen Press, 1979.

Kistler, Don. *A Spectacle unto God: The Life and Death of Christopher Love*. Soli Deo Gloria Publications, 1994.

Koehler, Lyle, 'The Case of the American Jezebels: Anne Hutchinson and Female Agitation during the Years of Antinomian Turmoil, 1636-1640'. *William and Mary Quarterly*, 3rd Ser., Vol. 31, No. 1 (Jan., 1974), 55-78.

---. *A Search for Power: The 'Weaker Sex' in Seventeenth-Century New England.* Urbana: University of Illinois Press, 1980.

Kunze, Bonnelyn Young. *Margaret Fell and the Rise of Quakerism.* Stanford: Stanford University Press, 1994.
    ---. 'Religious Authority and Social Status in Seventeenth-Century England: The Friendship of Margaret Fell, George Fox, and William Penn,' *Church History*, Vol. 57, no. 2 (June, 1988), 170-86.

Larsen, Anne R. 'Legitimizing the Daughter's Writing: Catherine des Roches' Proverbial Good Wife,' *Sixteenth Century Journal*, Vol. 21, No. 4 (Winter 1990), 559-74.

Larson, Rebecca. *Daughters of Light: Quaker Women Preaching and Prophesying in the Colonies and Abroad, 1700-1775.* New York: Alfred A. Knopf, 1999.

Lell, Erica M., 'Mother's Legacy,' *Renaissance Motherhood*, www.users.muohio.edu/mandellc/projects/lellem/legacy.htm, accessed 9/13/2007.

Macek, Ellen, 'The Emergence of a Feminine Spirituality in the Book of Martyrs,' *Sixteenth Century Journal,* Vol. 19, No. 1 (Spring, 1988), 62-80.

Malmsheimer, Lonna M., 'Daughters of Zion: New England Roots of American Feminism,' *The New England Quarterly*, Vol. 50, No. 3 (September 1977), 484-504.

Mather, Cotton. *Ornaments for the Daughters of Zion, or The Character and happiness of a vertuous woman: in a discourse which directs the female sex how to express the fear of God in every age and state of their life and obtain both temporal and external blessedness.* Cambridge, Massachusetts: S.G. & B.G., 1692.

Morgan, Edmund S. *The Puritan Family: Relations in Seventeenth Century New England.* New York: Harper and Row, 1966.

Nicholas, Heidi L. *Anne Bradstreet: A Guided Tour of the Life and Thought of a Puritan Poet.* P & R Publisher, 2006.

Porterfield, Amanda. *Female Piety in New England: The Emergence of Religious Humanism.* New York: Oxford University Press, 1992.
    ---. 'Women's Attraction to Puritanism,' *Church History*, Vol. 60, No. 2 (June, 1991), 196-209.

Ruether, Rosemary Radford and Rosemary Skinner Keller, eds. *Women and Religion in America.* Volume 2, *The Colonial and Revolutionary Periods: A Documentary History.* San Francisco: Harper and Row, 1983.

Ryken, Leland. *Worldly Saints: the Puritans as They Really Were.* Grand Rapids, MI: Zondervan Acadamie Books, 1986.

Sizemore, Christine W., 'Early Seventeenth-Century Advice Books: The Female Viewpoint,' *South Atlantic Bulletin,* Vol. 41, No. 1 (Jan. 1976), 41-8.

Travitsky, Betty, 'The New Mother of the English Renaissance: Her Writings on Motherhood,' in Cathy N. Davidson and E.M. Broner, eds. *The Lost Tradition: Mothers and Daughters in Literature.* New York: Frederick Ungar Publishing Co., 1980, 33-43.

Thomas, Keith V., 'Women and the Civil War Sects,' *Past and Present*, No. 13 (April, 1958), 42-62.

Todd, Margo. 'Humanists, Puritans and the Spiritualized Household,' *Church History,* Vol. 49, No.1 (March 1980), 18-34.

Ulrich, Laurel Thatcher. *Good Wives: Image and Reality in the Lives of Women in Northern New England, 1650-1750.* New York: Alfred A. Knopf, 1982.
      ---. 'Vertuous Women Found: New England Ministerial Literature, 1668-1735,' *American Quarterly,* Vol. 28, No.1 (Spring, 1976), 20-40.

Warnicke, Retha. 'Lady Mildmay's Journal: A study in Autobiography and Meditation in Reformation England,' *Sixteenth Century Journal*, Vol. 20, No. 1 (Spring 1989), 55-68.

Westerkamp, Marilyn J. *Women and Religion in Early America, 1600-1850: The Puritan and Evangelical Traditions.* New York: Routledge, 1999.

'William Penn's Letter to His Wife, Gulielma,' in Maria Webb's *The Penns and Peningtons of the Seventeenth Century.* London: F. Bowyer Kitto, 1867, 340-343, from www.qhpress.org/quakerpages/qwhp/pp340.htm, accessed 6/4/2003.

Chapter 9 - Reform and Revival: *Renewed Day by Day*

Cook, Faith. *Selina, Countess of Huntingdon: Her Pivotal Role in the 18th Century Evangelical Awakening* Banner of Truth, 2001.

Dallimore, Arnold A. *Susanna Wesley: The Mother of John & Charles Wesley.* Grand Rapids, Michigan: Baker Book House, 1993.

Dodds, Elisabeth D. *Marriage to a Difficult Man: The Uncommon Union of Jonathan & Sarah Edwards.* Laurel, MS: Audobon Press, 2003.

Faull, Katharine. *Moravian Women's Memoirs: Their Related Lives, 1750-1820.* Syracuse: Syracuse University Press, 1997.

Irwin, Joyce, 'Anna Maria van Schurman: From Feminism to Pietism,' *Church History,* Vol. 46, No. 1, (March 1977), 48-62.

Knight, Helen C. *Lady Huntingdon and her Friends.* New York: American Tract Society, 1853.

Marsden, George M. *Jonathan Edwards*. New Haven and London: Yale University Press, 2003.

Rogal, Samuel J., 'The Epworth Women: Susanna Wesley and Her Daughters,' *Wesleyan Theological Journal*, Volume 18, Number 2, Fall, 1983, http://wesley.nnu.edu/fileadmin/imported_site/wesleyjournal/1983-wtj-18-2.pdf. accessed 6/02/11

Sensbach, Jon. *Rebecca's Revival: Creating Black Christianity in the Atlantic World*. Harvard University Press, 2005.

Tyson, John R. 'Lady Huntingdon's Reformation,' *Church History*, Vol. 64, No. 4 (Dec. 1995), 580-593.

Van Schurman, Anna Maria. *Whether a Christian Woman Should be Educated and other writings from her intellectual circle* (ed. and trans. by Joyce L. Irwin). Chicago and London: The University of Chicago Press, 1998.

Wakely, J.B., 'Susanna Wesley and the Unauthorized Meetings,' *John Wesley: Holiness of Heart and Life*, at http://gbgm-umc.org/umw/Wesley/susannawesley.stm.

Wheatley, Phillis. *Poems of Phillis Wheatley, a native African and a slave*. Bedford, Massachusetts: Applewood Books, 1995 reprint of 1838 edition.

Chapter 10 – A Benevolent Society: *Abounding in the Work of the Lord*

Aylward, Gladys. *Gladys Aylward: The Little Woman*. Moody Publishers, 1980.

Bednarowski, Mary Farrell, 'Outside the Mainstream: Women's Religion and Women Religious Leaders in Nineteenth-Century America,' *Journal of the American Academy of Religion*, Vo. 48, No. 2. (June, 1980), 207-31.

Black, Rev. W.C. *Christian Womanhood*. Nashville, Tenn.: Publishing House of the M.E. Church, South, 1892.

Boylan, Anne M., 'Evangelical Womanhood in the Nineteenth Century: The Role of Women in Sunday Schools,' *Feminist Studies*, Vol. 4, No. 3 (Oct. 1978), 62-80.
    ---. 'Timid Girls, Venerable Widows and Dignified Matrons: Life Cycle Patterns Among Organized Women in New York and Boston, 1797-1840,' *American Quarterly*, Vol. 38, No. 5, (Winter 1986), 779-97.
    ---. 'Women in Groups: An Analysis of Women's Benevolent Organizations in New York and Boston, 1797-1840,' *The Journal of American History*, Vol. 71, No.3 (Dec. 1984), 497-512.

Braude, Ann. *Sisters and Saints: Women and Religion in America*. Oxford University Press, 2007.

Conway, Jill K. *The Female Experience in Eighteenth-and Nineteenth-Century America: A Guide to the History of American Women.* New York and London: Garland Publishing, Inc., 1982.

Cott, Nancy F., 'Young Women in the Second Great Awakening in New England,' *Feminist Studies,* Vol. 3, No. 1/2 (Autumn, 1975), 15-29.

Dabney, Robert Lewis, 'The Public Preaching of Women,' *The Southern Presbyterian Review,* October 1879.

Elliot, Elisabeth. *A Chance to Die: The Life and Legacy of Amy Carmichael.* Revell, 2005.

Epstein, Barbara Leslie. *The Politics of Domesticity:Women, Evangelism, and Temperance in Nineteenth-Century America.* Middletown, Conn: Wesleyan University Press, 1981.

Gage, Matilda Joslyn. *Woman, Church, and State,* from *Classics in Women's Studies Series.* New York: Humanity Books, 2002.

Goodwin, Rev. Prof. H.M., 'Women's Suffrage,' *New Englander and Yale Review,* vol. 43, Issue 179 (March 1884), 193-213.

Greaves, Richard L., ed. *Triumph Over Silence:Women in Protestant History.* Westport, Conn.: Greenwood Press, 1985.

Grimké, Angelina. *Appeal to the Christian Women of the South.* New York: New York Anti-Slavery Society, 1836.

Harper, Keith. *Send the Light: Lottie Moon's Letters and Other Writings.* Mercer University Press, 2002.

James, Janet Wilson. *Women in American Religion.* University of Pennsylvania Press, 1980.

Johnson, Dale A., 'Gender and Models of Christian Activity,' *Church History,* June 2004, 247-71.

Knowles, James D. *Memoir of Ann H. Judson, missionary to Burmah.* Boston: Gould, Kendall and Lincoln, 1846. A Google e-book available at http://books. google.com/books?id=bb4u5bmWDGUC&vid=ISBN0837013887&dq =ann-h-judson&jtp=1/#m-judson.

Lasser, Carol and students, 'How Did Oberlin Women Students Draw On Their College Experience to Participate in Antebellum Social Movements, 1831-1861?,' *Women and Social Movements in the United States, 1600-2000.* Alexander Street Press, http://womhist.alexanderstreet.com/index. html.

Lord, John. 'Hannah More – Education of Woman,' *Beacon Lights of History,* William H. Wise, 1921, vol.5.

McDonald, Lynn. 'Florence Nightingale: Faith and Work,' 7th Annual Conference Canadian Association for Parish Nursing Ministry, Toronto, May 27, 2005, http://www.uoguelph.ca/~cwfn/spirituality/faith.html, accessed 6/02/11
---. 'Florence Nightingale: Her Spiritual Journey,' a presentation in celebration of National Nursing Week, The Cathedral Church of St James, Toronto, ON, May 5, 2002, http://www.uoguelph. ca/~cwfn/spirituality/spiritual-journey.html. accessed 6/02/11

Montgomery, Helen Barrett. *Western Women in Eastern Lands*. New York: Macmillan Co., 1911.

Porterfield, Amanda. *Mary Lyon and the Mount Holyoke Missionaries*. New York: Oxford University Press, 1997.

Portraits of American Women in Religion, Library Company of Philadelphia, http:// www.librarycompany.org/women/portraits_religion/intro.htm.

Phelps, Elizabeth Stuart, 'A Woman's Pulpit,' *Atlantic Monthly*, July 1870, 11-22.

Robert, Dana L. 'The Influence of American Missionary Women on the World Back Home,' *Religion and American Culture*, Winter 2002; 12.1: ProQuest Religion, 59-89.

Rockness, Miriam Huffman. *A Passion for the Impossible*. Discovery House Publishers, 2003.

Stow, Sarah D. *History of Mount Holyoke Seminary, South Hadley, Mass. During its First Half Century, 1837-1887*. Springfield, Springfield Printing Company, 1887.

White, Barbara A. *The Beecher Sisters*. New Haven: Yale University Press, 2003.

Wilson, Arabella M. Stuart. *The Lives of Mrs. Ann H. Judson and Mrs. Sarah B. Judson with a biographical sketch of Mrs. Emily C. Judson, missionaries to Burmah*. Auburn: Derby and Miller, 1852.

Chapter 11 – Victorian Christian Women: *Keepers at Home*

Beecher, Catherine. *The Elements of Mental and Moral Philosophy, founded upon Experience, Reason, and the Bible*. Hartford, Connecticut, 1831.
---*Letters on the Difficulties of Religion*. Hartford: Belknap & Hammersley, 1836.
---and Beecher Stowe, Harriet. *American Woman's Home*. Hartford, Conn.: reprint of 1869 edition by the Stowe-Day Foundation, 1991.

Bednarowski, Mary Farrell. 'Outside the Mainstream: Women's Religion and Women Religious Leaders in Nineteenth-Century America,' *Journal of the American Academy of Religion,* Vo. 48, No. 2 (June, 1980), 207-31.

Choi, Sara, 'Christina Rossetti's Dialogical Devotion,' *Christianity and Literature*, Vol. 53, No. 4 (Summer 2004), 481-94.

Crow, Martha Foote. *Modern Poets and Christian Teaching: Elizabeth Barrett Browning*. New York: Eaton & Maine, 1907.

Dabney, Robert Lewis, 'The Public Preaching of Women,' *The Southern Presbyterian Review*, October 1879, Vol. 3, 689-713.

Epstein, Barbara Leslie. *The Politics of Domesticity: Women, Evangelism, and Temperance in Nineteenth-Century America*. Middletown, Conn.: Wesleyan University Press, 1981.

Gage, Matilda Joslyn. *Woman, Church and State*. Amherst, New York: Humanity Books, 2002 reprint of 1893 edition.

Goodwin, H.M. 'Women's Suffrage,' *New Englander and Yale Review*, volume 43, Issue 179 (March 1884), 193-213.

Hale, Sarah Josepha. *Women's Record: Sketches of all distinguished women from the creation to A.D. 1854*. New York: Harper and Brothers, 1855, 2nd edition. The 1853 edition is available at http://www.archive.org/details/womansrecordorsk00hale.

Lavender, Catherine, 'The Cult of Domesticity and True Womanhood,' http://www.library.csi.cuny.edu/dept/history/lavender/386/truewoman.html.

Matthews, Glenna. *'Just a Housewife': The Rise and Fall of Domesticity in America*. New York: Oxford University Press, 1987.

Phoebe Palmer, Christian History and Biography, issue 81 (Spring 2004).

Prentiss, George Lewis. *More Love to Thee: The Life and Letters of Elizabeth Prentiss*. New York: A.D.F. Randolph & Co., 1882.

Ruffin, Bernard. *Fanny Crosby*. Westwood, N.J.: Barbour and Company, Inc., 1976.

Stowe, Charles E. *The Life of Harriet Beecher Stowe*. Boston and New York: Houghton Mifflin & Co., 1891.

Taylor, Marion Ann and Heather E. Weir, eds. *Let Her Speak for Herself: Nineteenth Century Women Writing on Women in Genesis*. Waco, Texas: Baylor University Press, 2006.

Welter, Barbara, 'The Cult of True Womanhood: 1820-1860,' *American Quarterly*, Vol. 16, No. 2, Part 1, (Summer, 1966), 151-74.

White, Barbara A. *The Beecher Sisters*. New Haven: Yale University Press, 2003.

William and Catherine Booth, Christian History and Biography, issue 26 (Volume IX, No.2).

Chapter 12 – At the End of Two Millennia: *Women Professing Godliness*